ENTHUSIAST'S RESTORATION MANUAL

HOW TO RESTORE
TRIUMPH
TR4 &
TR4A

First published in 2001 by Veloce Publishing Ltd., 33 Trinity Street, Dorchester, DT1 1TT, England. Fax: 01305 268864/e-mail: info@veloce.co.uk/website: www.veloce.co.uk
ISBN: 1-903706-04-1/UPC: 36847-00204-6
British Library Cataloguing in Publication Data - A catalogue record for this book is available from the British Library.
Typesetting (Soutane), design and page make-up all by Veloce on AppleMac. Printed and bound in the EC.

ENTHUSIAST'S RESTORATION MANUAL™

HOW TO RESTORE
TRIUMPH TR4 & TR4A

ROGER WILLIAMS

VELOCE PUBLISHING
THE PUBLISHER OF FINE AUTOMOTIVE BOOKS

Contents

Acknowledgements and about the author

ACKNOWLEDGEMENTS

This book would never have been written without the help of a great number of people. Help in the sense of encouragement, but more particularly practical help by the unstinting provision of information, photographs and diagrams. Whilst I have appreciated every contribution, the full list is too extensive to mention everyone, but I hope all will accept my grateful thanks.

I wish to particularly single out a small number of absolutely crucial contributors, starting with John Sykes of TR Bitz. John suggested the book, got me started with a huge initial contribution, and provided much by way of technical help along the way. Neil Revington and Carl Kiddell of Revington TR provided a great deal of technical support and photographic help, but, in particular, read this manuscript and made many invaluable suggestions. Alex, my wife, has provided moral support and a very practical contribution through hours spent in front of her laptop. (As an aside, I really wonder how authors wrote books before the days of computers, spell checks and auto-correction!) Gary Bates of TRGB and Malcolm Jones of PDI made significant contributions through the provision of technical information and boxes of photographs. Alan Wadley of the TR Workshop and Steve Hall of TR Enterprises were other major sources of information, while Howard Vesey and Adam Bell of Faversham Restorations provided countless photographic opportunities. Books like this would remain stillborn without the collective help of these professionals, for which I am most grateful.

Last but not least, I must record my thanks to Steve Redway (of the TR Register), Jon Korbin (VTR Vehicle Registrar) and Bill Piggott for their invaluable help with my assessment of the numbers of TRs remaining. I also extend my grateful thanks to Bill Piggott for his Foreword.

ABOUT THE AUTHOR

Roger Williams was born in 1940 in Cardiff, brought up in Guildford and attended Guildford Royal Grammar School.

Aircraft became Roger's first love and he joined the de Havilland Aircraft Company in 1957 as a production engineering apprentice, and very quickly added motor cars to his list of prime interests. During the ensuing six years he not only completed his apprenticeship and studies, but built two Ford-based "specials" and started on a career in the manufacturing engineering industry as production engineer. Works managerial and directorial posts followed, and these responsibilities, together with his family commitments, reduced his time for motoring interests to exiting the company car park at the fastest possible speed!

Roger's business interest moved on to company doctoring, which he enjoyed for some ten years, specialising in turning round ailing engineering businesses. In 1986 he started his own consultancy business and renewed his motoring interests. His company specialised in helping improve client profitability by interim management or consulting assignments, whilst his spare time was - and continues to be - devoted to motor cars or writing.

Roger has owned numerous MGBs, all of which he rebuilt over a period of some seven years. He still has two of his all-time favourites - the V8 powered variants - and has two MGB books in print. More recently Roger has become involved with the Triumph marque and has restored a TR6 and, currently, a Stag.

Roger is married and lives in Folkestone, Kent in semi-retirement. He has two married daughters and is a Fellow of the Institution of Mechanical Engineers and a Fellow of the Institution of Production (now Manufacturing) Engineers.

Foreword

I feel honoured to have been asked to write the foreword to this new series of books relating to the much-loved TR sportscars built between 1953 and 1981. As an author of TR subjects myself, I know only too well how difficult is the incorporation of highly technical subject matter within a readable framework, but in this awkward task I feel that Roger Williams has succeeded admirably.

We now have, for the first time, a comprehensive guide to the purchase, maintenance and restoration of the TR sportscar, written in an easily under-standable form which is both accurate and practical. Such a series of books on the various TR models was much needed; we have had books on TR history, books on TR originality, books on TR competition success, but not previously any definitive title on TR restoration and purchase, despite several earlier attempts.

What I should stress is that this new series is an addition to the TR enthusi-ast's library, not a replacement for existing literature such as workshop manuals and parts catalogues. Roger Williams' books are designed to be used in conjunction with official Triumph literature and to disseminate the collec-tive and edited experience and expertise of owners and professional restorers as an overlay to the purely descriptive 'by-the-book' methods of the TR manuals. Many aspects of TR restoration covered by Roger are absent from the manuals, perhaps for no other reason than that those who compiled the factory litera-ture decades ago could not have envisaged that 'restoration' of such cars would ever take place.

Roger's perception - with which I agree - is that the average TR owner is now older, as is indeed the case with most classic car marques. There are several reasons for this, but the principal one must be the cost factor; the cars are quite simply too expensive for a younger person to acquire and restore. These books aim to make home restoration easier for the amateur TR enthusiast, and enable him to save the considerable cost of a professional restoration. If they succeed in that aim, and in my opinion they do, then they will have made TR ownership more affordable to young and old alike, which can only be a good thing.

Roger's style is easy to read, yet informative; he writes from a practical 'hands-on' point of view, encapsulating the opinions and hard-won experience of many TR restorers, both professional and amateur. This series of books will pay for themselves many times over - they have achieved exactly what was intended, and I commend them to you.

Bill Piggott
North Yorkshire, England

Introduction and using this book

INTRODUCTION

This is the second in a series of books written to help would-be and existing owners select, buy and restore a basically standard TR. This book will primarily focus on the later TR models that used the superb four-cylinder engine and the Michelotti body-shape; in other words, the TR4 and the TR4A.

Virtually every reader will already know that the Triumph range of TR2 to TR6 cars are regarded as the 'classic' sportscars from Triumph's extensive model range, and, as such, enjoy a special place in the hearts of all motoring enthusiasts. The TR7 and TR8 are still not regarded in quite the same light for some reason. There again, there are a few who do not consider the Michelotti cars in the same classic tradition as the earlier sidescreened cars. Since there is no logical reason for excluding them, my overview of the range of Triumph Roadsters includes the TR7 and '8 and, in due course, they'll get the same detailed attention as we are giving their predecessors here.

So, looking across the whole TR range, they were produced from 1953 to 1981, and all were exported extensively to the USA (earning many

needed Dollars for the UK economy) and were always at the forefront of popularly priced performance cars.

I must also mention that I plan to focus upon the restoration of a standard, rather than a highly modified TR. That decision was made partly for reasons of available space, but also because I appreciate that a number of readers may not wish to change their TRs from the original factory specification. For those who would like to read about upgrading their TR, this omission will be rectified in due course by a volume that deals solely with 'improvements'.

However, I should tell you that I have had some difficulty deciding what is an improvement and what is not! It's easy when it comes to some issues, like, for example, installing a V8 engine in a TR, which is certainly such a major change that it's excluded from this volume. However, how would you view fitting an overdrive to a TR model for which it was only available as an optional extra, or what about welding additional strengthening gussets to known weak spots in a TR chassis? I *have* included both these last two modifications and a number of other, strictly speaking, non-original details, so this book is not solely about restoring a

completely standard car. However, I have tried to highlight the fact when I'm suggesting a variation from standard and my reasons, which you will find are mostly safety or reliability inspired.

The Triumph TR marque was success story. The Beach Boys sang of 'Fun Fun Fun' roughly in the middle of the TR production run. Their song actually refers to the T-Bird (Ford Thunderbird), of course, but could so easily have been about the TR range - since fun was what these cars were all about and why they have retained their popularity.

However, the cars are all getting older as, sadly, are many of their owners. I would guess that the majority of current owners first saw a TR when they were rather younger, thought how much they'd like one, but couldn't possibly afford it, and only realised this long dormant ambition in later life. Simultaneously, the costs of a professional restoration have inevitably soared as inflation has risen inexorably, whilst the marques numbers has shrunk. This combination of circumstances could mean that a younger generation of potential owners rarely sees the remaining TRs in use, so are neither fired with the same ambition to own a

TR, as us more senile owners once were, or are understandably daunted by the cost of purchasing or restoring a TR. I cannot instil the ambition of ownership by these words, you have to see (and hear) the real thing! So it's up to current owners, the motoring clubs and the spares suppliers to so publicise these superb classics, so that those starting out on their careers learn to love the marque in preference to the growing range of (often Japanese) competition.

The prime objective of this book is to help owners and would-be owners carry out as much of the repair and restoration work as possible. Indeed, I believe that many can contemplate participating in the TR experience only if they can carry out much of the work themselves, and know when and why to subcontract certain key tasks. This book will help, encourage and guide them, for only by encouraging a constant flow of new, and hopefully younger, enthusiasts to know, love and afford these classics will we ensure the long-term health of the TR marque. I sincerely hope the information in these pages will help many new and existing owners to select, restore and enjoy any Triumph Roadster, but particularly, the pivotal Michelotti TR4s and '4As.

USING THIS BOOK

The author, editors, publisher and retailer cannot accept any responsibility for personal injury, mechanical damage or financial loss, which results from errors or omission in the information given. If this disclaimer is not acceptable to you, please immediately return your unused pristine book and receipt to your retailer who will refund the purchase price paid.

Safety!

During work of *any type* on your car, **your personal safety MUST always be your prime consideration**. You must not undertake any of the work described in this book yourself unless you have sufficient experience, aptitude and a good enough workshop facilities and equipment to ensure your personal safety **at ALL times**.

As stated in the Introduction, the primary purpose of this book is to guide the reader through the selection, purchase, repair and home restoration of a classic TR sports car. The book is *not* intended to be a workshop, operations or spares manual, but is meant to supplement and complement these invaluable sources of information.

Consequently, you would be well advised to purchase the manual(s) relevant to your particular model before embarking upon a significant repair, and certainly before starting a complete restoration.

All of the component/service (approximate) prices given in the text were those prevailing in the UK at the time of publication. These prices will be subject to normal market forces and will, of course, tend to rise with inflation. You would be well advised to allow for these factors when calculating your budget. Bear in mind that it's possible that the goods and services mentioned will become unavailable or altered with the passage of time.

Note that dimensions given in the illustrations are in millimetres (unless otherwise stated) and that line illustrations are not to scale.

References to 'right side' and 'left side' are from the point of view of standing behind the car looking forward.

You may find references to non-TR4/4A models in some text and some pictures. This is because some material within this book is common to other TR restoration books within the series. Use the information relevant to your model.

Chapter 1
Selecting your first TR and buying tips

WHICH TR TO CHOOSE?

In all probability you have already decided which TR is your heart's desire. A decision probably made quite subconsciously on the basis of a very brief glimpse of some lucky so-and-so flashing past you, a drop-dead-gorgeous blonde's hair streaming behind, or some equally illogical reason. Me, well I LOVED the sound of the six-cylinder engine and lines of the TR6. Anyway I am (almost) past noticing blondes; on the very rare occasion I might spot one it takes all my concentration to focus on the lady in question, consequently, I rarely notice the car she is in!

However, if you have not quite made up your mind, there are some very logical and unemotional points we should discuss as part of your TR selection process. Sadly, the first consideration must be money, so before deciding anything decide where you think you fit into the various price bands for each model: clearly, it is pointless looking at £10K cars with £5K available. Take care, however, for you need to cross-check prices carefully.

Along with the basic price issue is the related question of whether you are buying from a dealer or privately. What is your Safety Net Position? Put another way, how much redress do you want? Only you can decide this; many will be happy to pay, perhaps, £1000 more to a reputable dealer, comfortable in the knowledge that if anything goes wrong - even, say, on the M25 on a Bank Holiday Monday - they can pick the up 'phone and get help. Buying privately may save some money but there's little comeback, so you are best advised to take this route only if you have good technical knowledge or the close support of someone who "knows his onions."

Furthermore, buying privately does not guarantee the lowest price. There are occasions when buyers take their privately purchased car to a dealer for work or restoration only to hear that they could have bought a similar car for less from that dealer! Bear in mind, too, that it is very difficult to value a classic car. The magazine *Classic Cars* carries a monthly valuation review under the headings of Mint, Average and Rough, whilst *Practical Classics* also offers valuation information under Excellent, Regularly-Used and Rebuild-Required categories. While you would be wise to take into account these valuations, the price guide in *Classic and Sports Cars* magazine is probably your best cost reference. All price guides need to be used very carefully, however, for, at best, they give an average figure for each category of car. You may note that a particular model's 'show' (or, as I interpret the heading, 'mint') price is quoted as £10,000 when, in fact, several cars have an asking price of £15,000 - and may well be good value for money even at that price. At the other end of the scales you could find a restoration project price of £4500 but could buy from several dealers for £2500! Nothing, therefore, beats seeing the car, asking questions and getting the feel of the market.

It is essential that you view a number of cars that fall into your target of model, price and condition before actually getting your money out of the bank! If you really have not made up your mind which TR to shortlist, it will resolve several uncertainties at once if we go through the range of TRs open to you. Not only will this give you a feel for each car's appearance (via a photograph, of course), but I will try and outline each car's major features, too. We should also evaluate its scarcity and value at the time we went to press by recording the price spread for each car as shown in a recent issue of *Classic and Sports Cars* magazine. I hope you will accept in a spirit of fun the personal views I record for each model, even if

1-1. No, there's no 'hidden' TR, but this seemed so in keeping with the early days of TR motoring - at least in the UK - that I felt it set the scene for times past. Not that I expect all readers to remember these days, but this was how things were when the first TRs hit the road.

1-2. Interested in classic TRs but can't tell one from the other? This picture could help you, from left to right: TR2, TR3A, TR4, TR6 and TR7.

they do not completely align with your own opinion. Lastly, I hope you find it interesting and relevant if I sketch in the major technical developments of the TR range and the main competitors in the popular sports car market, for you will notice a definite correlation between each company's technical improvements and what their competitor does next!

A REVIEW OF THE TR RANGE

Origins

Spurred on by MG's success, particularly in the USA, Triumph set about its own two-seater sports car design early in the 1950s. The contemporary MG that Triumph must have used as an initial benchmark was the highly successful MG TD model. This had a 57bhp, 1250cc engine and "traditional" upright body styling comprising "humped" scuttle, flat-folding windscreen and cut-away doors.

The TR prototype for what turned out to be an extensive range of Triumph TRs, was an amalgam of a Standard Nine chassis and Triumph Mayflower suspension. It had a re-linered (to 1991cc) version of a 2088cc (85mm bore), wet-linered, ex-Standard Vanguard/Triumph Roadster engine, a Triumph Roadster 2000 gearbox and 3.7:1 ex-Mayflower rear axle. The front suspension for all TRs up to 1976 was almost the same throughout the whole period, and was, in fact, based on the Triumph Mayflower Saloon of the early 1950s! The car was shown at the 1952 Motor Show as "20TS", and visitors to the show must have thought the TR's smooth aerodynamic body shape both a revelation and really far-sighted, compared to the traditional MG TD.

However, the TR was subsequently tested by Ken Richardson and the chassis in particular declared a death trap! With Ken Richardson's close supervision the car was redesigned. The characteristic TR2 faired headlamps and flat windscreen were retained, but the rear body shape was squared-up slightly from the original prototype. It was the chassis that received the most radical change in order to do away with the original's flexing.

The prototypes that followed were called TR (for Triumph Roadster)1 but there were no TR1 production units made, and, to the best of my knowledge, all prototypes were scrapped. They were a vital step in realising the Triumph Company's ambition to offer a choice to those seeking a low cost, fun sports car who, to date, had had to look no further than the nearest MG showroom. The next link in the TR chain occurred in 1953 with the introduction of the TR2.

Sidescreen TRs

My personal opinion is that the TR2, TR3 and TR3A offer the appeal of rarity, and will turn heads wherever they go. I think few would argue, however, that they are not best suited as daily transportation except in the most pleasant of climates. The space available within the cockpit is limited, as is luggage capacity. They leak, the steering is heavy, and, in standard form, there's a couple of inches (roughly 50mm) of "play" at the steering wheel. They are best bought as a second or third car for occasional use, and the price needs to be seen in that context.

You should be aware that these cars do not have wind-up side windows. The TR2 and TR3 have (removable) sidescreens. Obviously, if you enjoy a Californian-like climate this is, as they say, no problem. If you are resident in less balmy climes, you need to decide whether this is acceptable. It depends upon the use you expect to put the car to and your own fortitude. If it's your first and only mode of transport, well, I would not recommend a sidescreened TR in anything but the warmest of climates! There again, many TR owners would totally disagree. I can still remember the admiration I felt when we saw off a lovely couple I'd just met in their 2, top-down, from a hotel "do". Nothing remarkable about that, I hear you mutter, but it was a very frosty, mid-January night with a temperature of about -10C (about 20F). Mind you, they did don leather helmets, and, I guess, sneaked the heater on just a little after they had left the hotel grounds! As a general rule-of-thumb, though, I think it prudent to steer you towards the wind-up windows of the TR4 (and onwards) if you envisage the car providing long-distance, all-weather transportation. That said, there is a major focus these days on the sidescreened cars and they are generally selling well, with good examples finding new homes quite quickly. Lets look at each of the sidescreen cars in a little more detail.

TR2 (1953- 1955)
(Photograph 1-3)
By the time production of the TR2 commenced, the chassis had been dramatically stiffened, but the ex-Vanguard, wet-linered, four-cylinder engine was retained in 1991cc/83mm bore format. The original gearbox and rear axle were also retained. The formula proved a success, for 8636 cars were built, of which 5182 were exported.

The MG of the day was now the "TF" model with its 1250cc engine and identical performance to the preceding MG model. MG was forced to uprate the engine to 1466cc but, not surprisingly, this did little to stimulate sales and the TR2's streamlined body shape must have appeared a significant improvement to the buying public and motor manufacturers alike. Furthermore, the TR's 90bhp gave it a top speed of 108mph. This was faster than the TF and no doubt contributed to the TR2 breaking into a sports car market long dominated by MG.

1-3. The TR2, first of the TR range of sports cars. Introduced in the early 1950s, the TR2 retains its classic style today.

This first TR used drum brakes on all four wheels. The front suspension was by unequal length wishbones and telescopic shock absorbers, whilst steering was by worm and peg. The rear suspension was totally conventional for the era, using a pair of leaf springs to provide the suspension and locate the rigid rear axle. Rear shocks were lever-arm type. Overdrive was available as an optional extra on top gear, which was an innovative development.

One development took place during the production run - the original doors stopped at the bottom of the sill, effectively hiding the sill, and cars with these deeper doors subsequently became known as 'long door' TR2s. Some found the original doors struck the kerb, which made exiting the car difficult, so a shallower door with a visible sill was introduced in 1954. The later cars became known as 'short door' TR2s.

It is estimated that a total of only some 2500 TR2s remain in existence today worldwide, the majority of which - nearly 1800 - in the USA. I estimate that nearly 600 remain in the UK, however. *Classic Car* valuations range from £7500, and £9000 to £12000 at the time of going to press.

TR3 (1955 to 1957)
(Photograph 1-4-1)

10,032 of the 13,377 TR3s produced were exported, maintaining Triumph's steady penetration into this (to Triumph) new market. This was in spite of the fact that the competition was not standing still, and the improved handling (due to a lower centre of gravity) streamlined MGA was launched in 1955 with rack and pinion steering, and a new 1489cc, 72bhp engine.

TR innovation continued too, with the introduction of 11 inch front disc brakes, several years ahead of Triumph's arch rivals! These were initially an optional extra but were standardised in 1956. The TR3 retained the 1991cc, wet-liner Vanguard engine, which, as an aside, was a development of a Ferguson Tractor engine, although power was increased to 95bhp. The TR3 used the more robust Vanguard Girling rear axle, but otherwise had few significant differences.

Approximately 1700 TR3s are thought to remain throughout the world, with close to 900 in the US and approaching 600 in the UK.

Classic Cars' values are £7000, and £8500 right up to £12,500.

TR3A (1957 to 1962) and TR3B (1962) (photograph 1-4-2)
MG upgraded the MGA in 1958 with a 1588cc engine and disc brakes, and again in 1961 with a 1622cc/93bhp

engine, and the car did much to revive MG's image.

Triumph introduced the "3A" with its optional 2138cc 100bhp engine. The 3A's appearance was revised slightly by a new front (panel and grill), and exterior door handles that were lockable! The Triumph had yet to match the MG's handling, however, and weatherproofing was still by sidescreens. Nevertheless, the 3A was an outstanding success, as illustrated by the 58,309 cars produced - of which 52,478 were exported - or an average of over 10,000 cars per year. This production rate is something in the order of three times the average annual output of the previous model.

TR development continued and, in 1962, the TR3s standardised on the 2138cc engine and front disc brakes. To Triumph this was just a continuation of the 3A's production run, but, to the majority of Triumph enthusiasts, this amounted to the introduction of the "TR3B". This model still does not officially exist but 3334 were manufactured - solely for export markets! Whatever the model was called, this production run was the last of the sidescreened TRs since the TR4 design showed the way forward by introducing TR drivers to the comfort of wind-up windows.

There are thought to be a total of about 9500 surviving TR3As but only perhaps 250/300 TR3Bs are available for us to enjoy. Of the sidescreened TRs, the 3A is not only the most numerous, but probably the best loved. This is probably why the *Classic and Sports Car* values for the 'A' are £7000, and £8500 to a high of £12,500, whilst the 'B' has the slightly lower but still impressive price profile of £7500, £9000 and £12,000.

Non-sidescreen TRs

The TR4, TR4A, TR5 (and TR250) and the TR6 provide much more in the way of creature comforts in almost every respect. To be fair, I do not believe there are many TRs made before the TR7 which are in true daily use. Many are available for daily use but when snow, ice or salt are around their owners mostly take the bus. Not, mind you, because they're concerned about their car's performance or reliability, but are understandably anxious to keep it in pristine order.

1-4-1. The second of what became known as the 'sidescreen' TRs, this is the TR3. A relatively small proportion of TRs left the factory fitted with wire wheels, but this car is non-standard by virtue of its retro-fitted, heavy duty wire wheels and broader section tyres. It still looks very attractive, though.

1-4-2. The TR3A model which was built in greater numbers than the 3. It would be difficult to tell the two apart at this distance were it not for the wide pressed aluminium radiator grille, although the 3A's door handles are just visible. The 3A has a huge and committed following still.

These later TRs were made in (increasingly) larger numbers than the earlier models, which means two things: there were more to survive (and more did survive); and more spares are more readily available to help keep the survivors on the road. Furthermore, the numerous common parts within the TR4A, 5, 250 and 6 range of models means that, generally, the volume of spares used is higher and the cost is consequently more affordable.

1-5. The TR4 is quite different in appearance with its very pretty Michelotti-designed body. Underneath, it was not so different, however, and took advantage of the best features of the sidescreen model's engine and running gear. The TR4 offered greater comfort in the form of higher door lines and wind-up windows, and provided the basics for two subsequent models.

TR4 (1961 to 1965)

(photograph 1-5).

For the TR4 Triumph revealed its clever "one major change at a time" development policy retaining an almost unchanged chassis, suspension and engine design, but introducing an Italian redesigned body style - the Michelotti shape, that was, in fact, retained for the subsequent TR4A and TR5. There were some other improvements - notably rack and pinion steering and a wider track (no doubt intended to improve handling), and synchromesh on all four forward gears. Manufacturing volume was retained at the 10,000 units per annum level with a total of 40,253 cars produced, of which a very creditable 36,803 (over 90%) were exported.

However, the competition leapt ahead by introducing the MGB in 1963. This was significant by virtue of its unitary construction that integrated a now redundant chassis into a stress-carrying bodyshell with significant weight and rigidity benefits.

There are thought to be about 4000 TR4s worldwide, with the majority (2250) Stateside. The model has a UK valuation spread of £4000, £7000 and, in show condition, £13,000.

The TR4A (1964 to 1967)

(photograph 1-6)

Whilst the competition fundamentally took a development "time-out",

Triumph TRs took their own leap forward with the introduction of the TR4A, with its new chassis and IRS (Independent Rear Suspension). Critics of the day complained that the engine had not been updated, and that the car was under-powered. They may have been right, but it is my view that Triumph probably got its development program about right, and the introduction of a new chassis and IRS was enough to swallow in one step.

Besides, the TR4A was more different than it appeared at first sight as the body had numerous under-the-surface changes, although the outer panels remained the same. I wonder if the critics of the day realised or cared about such detail?

However, that is hardly material to our current day review of the offerings available to you, the prospective TR'er, so let us conclude with the current numerical assessment. Of the 28,465 TR4As produced, 22,826 were exported and about 4000 remain worldwide. Some 1400 to 1500 can be found in the UK, but the US can boast something approaching 2500. Valuations range from a low of £4500, excellent examples are valued at £7000, and up to £12,500 is asked for show standard examples.

The TR5/TR250 (1967 to 1968)

In 1967, MG made what appeared to be, and should have been, a significant development, with the introduction of the 150bhp, straight-6, 2912cc MGC. This MG appeared initially to have the major advantage of a unitary constructed bodyshell.

Fortunately, Triumph TRs also developed - at least in the engine department, and at least in some markets - with the introduction of the TR5 (photograph 1-7) and its US version, the TR250 (photograph 1-8). Both variants were fitted with a 2498cc,

1-6. The TR4A had the same beautiful Michelotti body and basically the same four cylinder engine as earlier TRs. Underneath, however, Triumph introduced the exciting concept of Independent Rear Suspension, and a number of detailed changes, too. I doubt you will need me to tell you that the 4A is on the left, and we get another chance to enjoy the TR2 shown in photo 1-3.

straight 6-cylinder engine developed from Triumph's saloons, but the induction systems, compression ratios and rear axle ratios were dramatically different, depending on the destination of the finished car. Vehicles bound for the USA had twin Stromberg carburettors, low compression (and correspondingly low performance), and were designated TR250. Some 8480 were built but only 600 or so survive.

The UK and many other export markets did rather better in that not only was the TR5's engine petrol injected (hence the PI), but the compression ratio, camshaft and performance of the car were rather more compatible with a sports car. In fact, the 2947 TR5s produced were quite brisk as a result of their reputed (but probably optimistic) 150bhp. Top speed was in excess of 115mph, but more importantly, acceleration was very satisfying.

Why such a short production run? Retention of the basic TR4/4A Michelotti shape was only an interim "bridge" until the restyled TR6 shape was ready. The 5 acted as the perfect development stepping stone for the petrol injected, 6-cylinder engine, and was completely compatible with Triumph's development policy.

It is very satisfying to report that about 800 TR5s are thought to remain, which is a very high number, considering the small initial production run and the years that have passed. For once the UK can claim the lion's share, but I did initially establish, to my surprise, that at least nine examples reside in the US. Josh Mazer of VTR recently updated that information with another four 'finds'.

TR5 valuations reflect its desirability, spreading from £5800 through £10,000 to £14,000. The TR250 comes, of course, solely with left-hand-drive with about 1500 remaining, mostly in the USA. I guess the *Classic and Sports Car* valuations of £3500, £5000 and £8000 in the UK reflects these facts.

While many TR owners, and many non-owners, for that matter, would not agree, it is my belief that the TR5 is the most desirable of the TR range; its performance, rarity, spares availability and superb lines make it the best. There must be those who do agree, however, as it is currently amongst the most expensive TR available.

1-7. Arguably the best TR of the lot - the TR5, which is certainly one of the rarest of the marque. The Michelotti body styling augments this technically superb vehicle, with its fuel injected, six-cylinder engine and Independent Rear Suspension.

1-8. The USA had a carburettor inducted version of the TR5 called the TR250. The carburettors are the give-away under the bonnet whilst, outside, it is easily distinguished by the bonnet cross stripes.

The TR6 (1969 to 1976)

The TR6 enjoyed a 7 year life - the longest production run of all the TRs - but not the highest sales volume, as we will see shortly.

Like the earlier 5, the 6 was also produced in two versions - the de-tuned US model and the sportier UK/rest-of-the-world offering. The situation is slightly complicated by the fact that the tune of both versions was adjusted in 1972: basically, further de-tuning both versions and (on US models) introducing the first of an ever-escalating amount of de-tox, anti-pollution equipment. The chassis of these cars was fundamentally the same as the TR5 (some variations will be explored in the appropriate chapters), and, as we have already established, the engine from the 5 was put to further use.

What was different - but, cleverly, not as different as it at first appeared - was the TR6 body. The Karmann Company redesigned it to utilise many of the existing TR4A/TR5 body pressings. The external boot/trunk and bonnet shapes were changed significantly, and I cannot but point out that Triumph TR6s still used a separate chassis and body construction, which does not bear comparison with the 6 to 13 year headstart MG enjoyed with the far superior unitary construction roadster bodyshell. I suppose it makes little difference to our perception and valuation today of how up-to-date a car's design was at the time of manufacture. To prove the point, I confess to owning the pictured (photograph 1-9) TR6, and loving it! Just imagine, however, what a car the TR6 would have been with a unitary bodyshell, it would have knocked spots off the competition ...

In fact, perhaps fortunately for Triumph, it did not have to, for MG was being knocked about by the press and the buying public. All hated the MGC's poor handling, and as a consequence the MGC was withdrawn in 1969, leaving the TR6 with no competition in the popular 6-cylinder sports car market. Sales responded and production volumes were respectively 77,938 (carburettor US) and 13,912 (UK), with average units sold reaching 13,000 per annum.

The numbers of TR6s remaining today are also encouraging: there are nearly 6500 examples of the US carburettor model still around, and it is thought that some 4500 petrol injection cars are still in existence worldwide. The *Classic Car* values span £4800, £7800 with £12,000 for show quality examples of the latter model. You can probably think in terms of a 10% reduction for the carburettor version in the UK.

The 'Wedgies'
These TRs had a surprisingly shallow (front to back) boot/trunk area which is considerably smaller than it's predecessor's - the TR6. The 6, however, was unusually well equipped as far as luggage capacity was concerned. Not worried about luggage you cry. Fair enough, but do note the 7 and 8 are slightly more difficult to enter by virtue of the very deep sills (*a la* E-type Jaguars).

Once seated, however, two major 7/8 advantages became clear: the cockpit width is wider than its non-sidescreened predecessors, and the top of the TR's windscreen seems higher

1-9. The TR6 was a very clever updating exercise by Karmann (of Karmann-Ghia fame), using all but the front and rear skin panels of the TR5. This 1972 car has a particular place in my affections and is shown beside my 1970 3500cc MGB. This might not be the right place to say which is the quicker of the two, but the TR does have a rather nicer registration plate ...

than the earlier TRs - which not only helps forward visibility but makes driving the TR7 quite comfortable, even with the hood raised.

The TR7 is known in the USA as the "flying doorstop", I suspect not always affectionately, but even if you are not entirely sold on its wedge shape, do note that it definitely reduces wind noise at high speed, doubtless aided by the lower frontal area and sharply swept screen.

The TR7 and TR8 (1975 to 1981)
(photograph 1-10).
I mentioned earlier that the TR6 had not

achieved the distinction of being the highest number model TR produced. In fact, the TR7 achieved 112,368 units and the 8 a further 2095, making a grand total of 114,463 in 6 years of production. Exports were a creditable 88,000 units, while the average annual sales figure was now slightly over 19,000.

The car did finally enjoy a unitary-constructed bodyshell, and Triumph took the opportunity to make other changes, too. In fact, Triumph swept aside its previously conservative "one major change at a time" approach and changed ... everything ... radically! The

1-10. The TR7 was a radical change of shape and technology, and is none the worse for that. The model attracted more buyers than any other TR. The same aerodynamic shape was also used for the 3500cc TR8 variant.

buying public of the day clearly liked the "clean sheet of paper" approach, as sales figures show.

I believe sales could have been higher still had build quality and continuity of production allowed the car's full potential to be realised. The sleek, wedge-shaped bodyshell was wider than the previous TRs, wind noise was much reduced, and the rear suspension reverted to a well-located live axle with a consequentially improved ride. All factors that I applaud. However, do not go looking for a Roadster (open-topped) version of the TR7 before 1979; there were only Coupes up to this date.

This oversight may have something to do with the fact that the number of cars thought to remain in existence today (Roadsters and Coupes) is in the order of just 3500 to 4000. What is even more of a surprise is that I could find only some 1000 remaining in the US, and that the majority of 7s remain in the UK. I find these numbers sad, considering this was the most recently produced model, yet it appears to have suffered almost the highest attrition rate of all the TRs.

The company may not have engendered long-term love for the model either by reverting to a 105bhp, four-cylinder, 1998cc engine for the TR7 and, at least initially, a 4-speed, no-overdrive gearbox. The gearbox decision was corrected with a good 5-speed 'box but the V8 engine the car needed was only fitted late in the model's life, creating the superb TR8. Too late, though, to undo the suicidal policies, actions and quality of previous years.

So, after a basically sad story, is this a TR you should contemplate? Yes, I believe the 7 has many fine qualities and the 8 (or a well-converted TR7-V8) is a great car. The attrition rate I spoke of earlier has the benefit of ensuring there are lots of spares available, which could work to your advantage. Indeed, the coupe versions are so available that their price almost enables Roadster owners to have one in the back yard just for spares! Even more important is the fact that the unitary bodyshell build allows for the car to be used as everyday transport, and the coupe versions should allow even those without garaging to consider a TR7 as everyday use. It is still a TR, after all ...

These TRs offer a more comfortable ride than earlier cars, yet with probably slightly superior cornering capability. Track is approximately 10% wider than the non-sidescreened cars. If I had to drive 500 miles in a day and could choose any of the TRs, it would be the TR7 (V8, of course!) Roadster.

This leads me to conclude on a cheerful note. There seem to be about 1250 TR8s remaining; about 50 to 75 in the UK and the rest in the US. A very low attrition rate, from which, I conclude (as the advertisement says), size really does matter!

Conclusion

So you think you're narrowing down the field by virtue of the price you are prepared to pay; that's not the end of it, however. The useful life of the car is an equally important factor.

Obviously, we all want our classic to last indefinitely, but even a well restored classic has a finite life span. You should reckon that an average, well restored car will probably require further major attention in about 8-12 years. Therefore, do you want a car that requires further restoration in 1 or 10 years? If it's the former, then clearly you are looking for a car in the bottom half of the "Excellent" range, or possibly top of the "Good" range. If you're not into restoration, and want years of (hopefully) trouble-free enjoyment, then you are into the "Show" range of cars on offer, so make your shortlist of TR models accordingly.

If you are buying a donor car for its components then you'll be more interested in the parts than the price. The completeness or availability of parts, rather than, say, condition of the chassis, will be most important, as you could have decided, even before seeing the car, that you will fit a new chassis. If you are buying a CP 150bhp fuel injected 6, is the correct distributor and fuel injection equipment in place, or at least supplied loose with the car. If loose, why? The distributor is rare in that it has a mechanical tachometer drive, which you must ensure is there.

If you are after a car to bring up to concours standard, then you are looking for a host of ORIGINAL detail - far better to have an original part in any condition than a brand new, shiny, non-original replacement.

Hopefully, by now you've settled

on a shortlist of models. Let's hope it's a model you can afford, in which case it's time to refine your options still further by spending a few seconds on the matter of colour. If you are buying a donor vehicle for immediate restoration, then colour is not too important. If, on the other hand, you are buying a car to drive and enjoy for the next 10 years, then getting it in a colour you like moves up the priority list somewhat! There's no point in even looking at a car, particularly one at the top of your price bracket, if you hate the colour. Further, although it sounds obvious, do establish what colours you do wish to pass over; some colours enjoy an impressive official name that we may not initially recognise for what it is. I will upset too many if I actually mention the official colour by name, but I recall travelling many miles to view a Triumph that I thought would be a very acceptable shade of blue, but which turned out to be (to me) a quite unacceptable colour. So, before you leave home, establish what the base colour really is!

I have taken you through the practical steps, which I hope has helped. At the end of the day, you will have to go and see for yourself, in which case be prepared for the heart taking over! Everyone has a view and/or opinion of which is the best model, what colours are beautiful and what body shape is the most pleasing. It might be as well to look at some of the problems and pitfalls that await the first-time TR buyer, starting with a few more golden rules ...

BUYING - SOME GOLDEN RULES

Take particular note of the first rule: Do NOT buy the first car you see - shop around.

Strangely enough, the second rule applies to personal chemistry and requires you ignore the car for starters! Talk to the man who is selling the car and establish whether he is the sort of guy you would want to buy a car from. Are you comfortable with what he is saying, how he says it and the general interaction between you? Of course, many vendors - particularly professional car salesmen - have a natural ability to sell anything; nevertheless, this is an excellent starting point.

Thirdly, establish that the vendor has the right to sell this car. Is it his car, does he have the log book? If so, ask to see it. Is he the registered owner, and if not, why not? Do all numbers in the log book tally with the car? Is the engine number (in particular) right for the car: a 150bhp CP engine in a 125bhp CR series TR6 may be no bad thing, but the reverse would devalue the car. TR2 engines appear in TR3s. Some six-cylinder cars have an engine with an MG prefix. This could be an ex-Triumph Saloon engine with 135bhp power output, but it could also be a factory replacement engine, in which case you should see the original receipt. Remember, if you do not check this detail you can be sure that your buyer will be sure to note the discrepancy when you come to sell the car! Do all of this before you agree a price.

Throughout the review, resist the temptation to pick fault with the car. Try and establish a mutual rapport with the vendor so that he will find it harder to reject your offer. Do not go into the reasons why you cannot pay his asking price; they are not his problem. You can say that the car is basically what you are looking for, and that it is sound apart from a couple of remediable items. However, you've set your heart on a car

with, say, overdrive, an unleaded engine conversion and chrome wire wheels, and if you were to pay his asking price and fix the problems, then you wouldn't be able to afford to bring the car up to the desired specification. NEVER offer what you think the car is worth. For example, if the asking price is £7500, but you believe it will cost around £1100 to bring up to condition and with the facilities you require, you may be tempted to offer the vendor £6400. DON'T! Offer £5300, by all means, which, of course, will be refused, but hopefully this will start the haggling that will result in an amicable mid-point handshake.

If you simply cannot reach agreement be prepared to walk away. This will give the seller time to think again about your offer and you the opportunity to check out the cost of rectifying the faults found. Don't make the mistake here of presuming that if a rebuilt differential is priced at £250, then this is the total cost. Add on the necessary mounting rubbers, and perhaps some new brackets, and the total cost is likely to rise to £400. So take notes, go away and find out what the total costs are in each case. Armed

with this irrefutable information you are in a better position to argue your case.

It's also a good idea during this time to do some more homework, particularly if the seller is a dealer. Phone the area secretary of your local TR Register and ask if anyone knows the car, dealer or owner. Most area secretaries will be pleased to give you all the advice you need if you explain that you are seriously considering buying the car. Be on your guard against non-specialist dealers, especially those that do not have workshops; anyone that sells from home and does not have his own repair facilities should be treated with caution. Even if you get a warranty from this type of trader it may be very difficult trying to enforce it should you ever need to. If you buy your car from a one-make specialist who has his own workshop you will get more detailed and expert attention, and if things should go wrong, the cost to the dealer wth his own workshop of putting things right will not be as high as it would be to a non-workshop concern (which would have to pay another company the full workshop rate).

Chapter 2
What to check

Much of the inspection will require your crawling underneath an elevated car. Dress accordingly, of course, but above all ensure the car is SAFELY elevated and securely positioned on axle stands. If in doubt take your own axle stands, trolley jack and a powerful torch.

BODY, PAINTWORK AND TRIM

Bodywork

Unquestionably, this is the most time consuming and expensive part of a TR to repair, and, consequently, warrants your very careful attention. An overall impression of the car's bodywork is best obtained from the rear of the body. All TRs are longitudinally fish-shaped - by which I mean that there is a gradual but steady side curve from front to back. So go to one rear corner and kneel down to

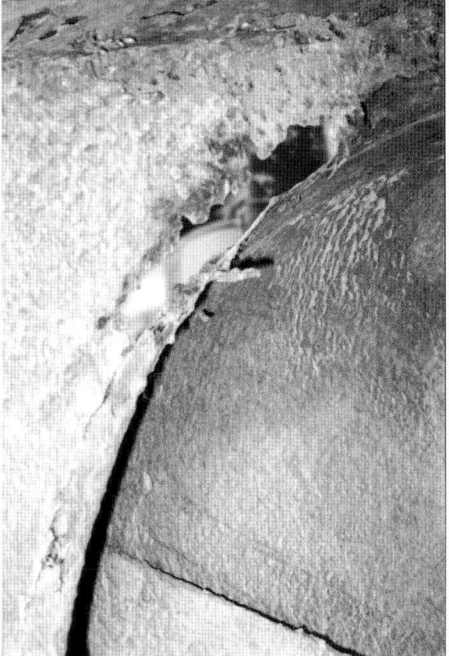

2-1. Rear inner wing problems like this signal that this is a car to be particularly cautious about buying. Although the wheelarch itself looks sound enough in this picture, and it's the inner wing panel that shows most corrosion, if you were to poke the wheelarch with a small screwdriver you would certainly find a similar amount of corrosion there too. It is repairable, but even an experienced body repair specialist will find it tricky and time consuming, and you'll find it expensive. In fact, the back half of this TR4A was replaced completely.

sight your eye down the coach line. The car should have a steady curve, like a fish! Go to the other side of the car and look for its steady curve. What you should particularly look out for is one very curvaceous side and one straight or flat side. This signals a knock, poor rebuild or even a front half/rear half marriage from two different cars! The latter problem doesn't mean that a car should be rejected out of hand, but it does need to be carefully and, therefore, invisibly repaired.

Sadly, it is an inescapable fact that all TR's have a number of corrosion weak spots. Some of the illustrations shown are certainly on the dire side of what you may be offered, but they nevertheless serve to show you the sort of rust holes that can occur and should alert you to watch for fillered cover-ups in the areas listed below. Most vulnerable spots are common to all models. All but the last one listed (the door-gaps) apply to both the cars we are focused upon and, consequently, each should be examined carefully and a magnet used to test for body-filler when in doubt:

● Rear inner wing repairs are possible, but involve a great deal of skilled work, so cars with rear inner wing rot are best avoided. Establish this from inside the boot with the boot trim panels removed and by looking and feeling each side of the fuel tank (photograph 2-1).
● Any external bubbling on the rear deck panel and forward deck section will signal trouble in the near future. Note that top repairs can be *effected* quite professionally, as photograph 2-2

2-2. The rear deck on this car will not have looked too bad at first glance since the body filler (seen here sideways on) will have covered much corrosion. In fact the true extent of the problem will only have been revealed by looking at these panels from the inside of the boot/trunk or when the wing/ fender was removed.

2-5.

2-3. Although this is, of course, a TR6, it does demonstrate the care with which one needs to examine any potential purchase. This TR6 looked great from the outside but, a peak at the bonnet hinge area from within the engine compartment revealed the impending expense!

2-4 and 2-5 (top). Not as smart looking, this TR4 had a rusting door, but you would never have thought that the rear baffle behind the front wheel would be completely rusted away. This would have been obvious, though, from a look from within the engine compartment. This is not untypical of what you must expect when you remove the front wings. Devoid of a worthwhile amount of original paint, the splash plate has rotted away at the top, allowing corrosion to attack and hole the top inner wing. Note, too, the bottom inner wing is also corroded and holed.
This car has still got its original sills as you can see the indentation (arrowed) pressed in the sill to allow water to escape from the original plenum chamber's drain hose, also arrowed. Less obvious, this picture also demonstrates the typical upturn that occurs with years of use at both rear corners of the bonnet. It is a good idea to reinforce the inner lip of the bonnet for about 12in (300mm) in front of both rear corners to stop it kinking in future. A special repair panel is available.

shows, and hide, for a short while, the true seriousness of the situation - which is why an examination from inside the boot is particularly valuable. Feel where the rear wing is bolted to deck sections alongside the fuel tank. There will be cars where you will see daylight here because the panel has completely rusted away.
• Above and around the headlamps - the corrosion works back to the inner wings where the bonnet hinges mount, so look there too (from inside the engine bay). You will see an example of what to look for in photograph 2-3.
• Baffles behind front wheels. The corrosion often manifests itself by the fuse-box on the inner wing and can be seen from inside the engine-bay,

although the real problem may be obvious from a very quick look under the front wings. The baffle can almost

completely rot away, as photographs 2-4 and 2-5 show.
• As photographs 2-6, 2-7 and 2-8 illustrate, the TR4 and 4A wing-to-body joints generate corrosion all along their length, partly due to an electrolysis reaction of dissimilar metals. The stainless steel strips react with the body's mild-steel material and the problem is exacerbated by the sad fact that no paint or sealer were applied at the factory to these joints. Do view the vulnerable area from inside the boot/trunk and apply both paint and sealer to all joints upon re-assembly. In fact, in the case of cars with a stainless strip, ensure the sealer is also applied to both sides of the stainless strip.
• Bottoms of doors - run your hand (carefully) along the bottom where the

2-6. This picture demonstrates the extra vulnerability of the pre-TR6 cars. The stainless strip looks very attractive, but the reaction between dissimilar metals undoubtedly accelerates corrosion.

2-7.

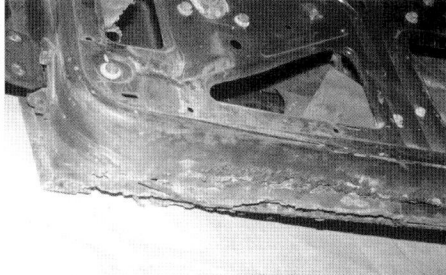

2-9. The doors seem somewhat vulnerable in the TRs we are exploring; here, the door bottom and the edge of the door skin need adding to the 'to do' list. The door-skin certainly looks beyond help but, although corroded along the bottom, the rest of frame looks sound enough to warrant repair.

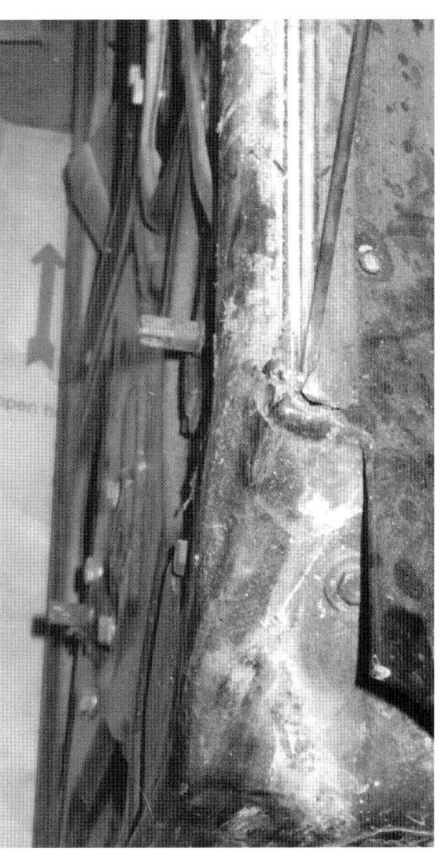

2-11. For some reason, the window channels can cause cracking around the front top of the door frame.

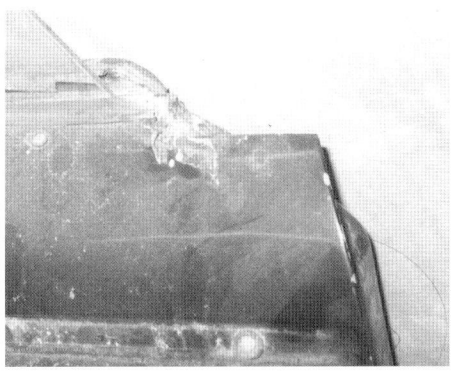

2-10. The top of this door has clearly been filled and then has cracked again. A not uncommon problem which has the merit of making it clear to potential buyers that a replacement door skin will be essential. What you will need to watch for is the appearance of the door(s) in this area, for they could have been skilfully filled and painted making the underlying fault much more difficult to detect.

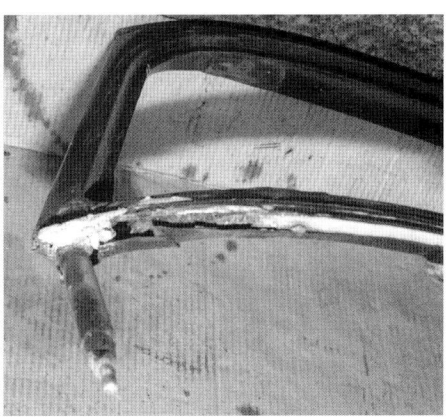

2-12. A rather worse than average windscreen frame. This one is actually in such bad shape (and has been filled) that you will have spotted it without much difficulty. Although it can be repaired, the availability of good ex-USA frames makes repairing most examples like this not worth the time and trouble, not to mention the high level of skill needed!

2-7 and 2-8 (above). The first photograph might seem to be a duplication of 2-6, but in fact serves to emphasise the 'body-filler' problem. Although this looks bad, picture 2-8 shows the full extent of the corrosion with a lump of filler removed. You could not have failed to see the extent of this corrosion had you looked from the boot/trunk side of these panels.

door shell joins the outer skin. As can be seen in photograph 2-9, the rust can sometimes be obvious without the need to feel along the underside of the door!
● Front top of doors (where they sit adjacent to the windscreen panel) is, for some reason, prone to the sort of corrosion shown in photograph 2-10.
● Door glass movement can also crack the tops of the doors, particularly if they

are weakened by corrosion, as picture 2-11 demonstrates.
● The windscreen frame is a bolt-on affair. It is a lightweight pressing and can rust from the inside or from cracks (due to loads imposed by the hood). The early stages of corrosion can only be seen when the screen is off the car, but take a close look anyway, bearing in mind what you see in photograph 2-12.
● There is a weakness where the rear wing attaches to the "B" post. This usually rots from the bottom up, as photograph 2-13 illustrates perhaps a little too vividly!
● The rear valance is particularly vulnerable where it joins with the rear wings, but run your hand (carefully) along the whole bottom edge of the rear valance (particularly where the exhaust

pipe exits) to check for corrosion. Photograph 2-14 does not look too bad at first sight but the valance is, in fact, full

2-13. You are unlikely to come across as blatant an example as this but, nevertheless, be on your guard for corrosion problems at the base of the rear-inner wing where it attaches to the 'B' post. The damage will be worse than you can see but should stop short of this example!

2-14. The condition of the boot/trunk floor would have put you on your guard were you looking at this car, but, again, the severe corrosion in this rear valance is masked by body-filler. It would be more obvious when viewed from the underside of the car.

2-15. From the outside this bottom lip corrosion does not look too serious, and you might be pleasantly surprised when you look inside. However, it is important that you open the boot and look closely at the bottom edge and lip of the boot lid, for they are susceptible to corrosion, as photograph 2-16 shows.

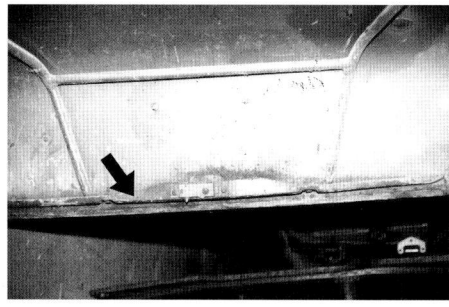

2-16. The bottom edge of this Michelotti boot/trunk lid appears only slightly corroded along the susceptible bottom 2in. No doubt, were you to gently shot-blast (only) this edge, you would be surprised at the extent of the rust. However, you can still see the turned-in lip of the skin (arrowed) which shows that there have been no previous attempts to fill this area of the car - which is very good news.

2-17. One needs to watch out for the sort of accident or corrosion damage shown here in any prospective purchase, but particularly when a TR4 or 4A is involved in view of the potential remedial cost of a wing/fender.

2-18. This Michelotti rear wing, actually from a TR5, is almost as good as can be found on a car that is 30-plus years old. Nevertheless, hours of work will still be necessary to remove and replace the rusted rear lip/light surround (nearest the camera).

of body-filler. You would get a hint of this from the condition of the adjacent boot/trunk floor, which should make you look closely at the rear valance from underneath and at the adjacent panels.

• The boot lids on Michelotti bodyshells are susceptible to rust along the bottom 2in (50mm). Photograph 2-15 shows some corrosion from an external perspective but, however good or bad the corrosion is on the outside you must look inside too - where the panel is doubled skinned and is shown in picture 2-16. If corrosion is not evident, do check that the (internal) seam is visible, for often corrosion has been filled and the seam disappears - whereupon you really do need to be on your guard!

• Corrosion or damage to any Michelotti wing (photographs 2-17 and

2-18) is a worry. New wings are expensive at £300 apiece but then a skilled and experienced panel beater can take two days to get each to fit, and, consequently, you could be looking at a cost of £500/600 per wing - before painting! Fortunately, some repair panels are available and, overall, it is more cost-effective to have a skilled and experienced specialist repair a damaged or corroded wing.

• TR sills go in two places - the outside below the doors is usually pretty obvious, normally visible, and replacement is straightforward. However, photograph 2-19 shows where the outer sill is disintegrating behind the front wing, and this is not so easily spotted. However, corrosion to this degree will have worked through to the inner sill, which forms part of the

floor panel, and outer sill corrosion of this severity is likely to manifest itself in at least the inner front corner, as shown in photographs 2-20 and 2-21. From photograph 2-20 you will note the inner sill has been holed right in line with that part of the outer sill (arrowed) that hides behind the front wing! If you find the sill is suspect also check the floor at the four corners nearest each of the wheels since, if the sill is gone, then it is likely the floor is corroding in several of these four corners. Separate inner-sill repair panels are available but if corrosion has spread to the floor then you should budget for replacing the complete floor/inner sill

2-19. This hole was covered by the bottom of the car's front wing, but a good look at the four corners of the inner sills should have given some clue, although not perhaps quite to the extent of the problem shown in 2-20 and 2-21.

2-20.

2-20 and 2-21 (above). No one could miss the advanced corrosion in this TR4A's floor, nor fail to appreciate that new floors are an essential. However, note the advanced corrosion in the inner sills too. The photograph of the right side of the car shows the plenum chamber running right across the car, with its small stub-tube drain (arrowed). This is an area that corrodes when both left and right corners of the plenum get blocked and the water has no escape. A pair of rubber drain tubes exit the cockpit via one hole each side, one of which is visible, situated about 3in (75mm) below the bottom of the plenum chamber. A modification is recommended and explained in chapter 4.

2-22. The sill needs to be checked for corrosion and for filler in the gaps between the sills and wings/fenders ... front and rear. The presence of filler here should alert you to think about the condition that the sill/ wings were in to warrant such an obvious and completely non-original modification.

2-23.

2-23 and 2-24 (above). Bonnets are vulnerable too.

panels - whereupon the body becomes a candidate for the kind of two-piece rebuild outlined in Chapter 4.

• There used to be a tendency to fill the gaps between all four wings and the sills in an effort to make the car appear smoother than it really is. If you are offered a car where there is no clear and obvious gap between each wing and its mating sill, view that area with some suspicion since it may have started out looking like photo 2-22 just a few weeks before.

• Photograph 2-23 shows that the bonnet tends to corrode at the front (a very typical scenario). It is double skinned in the "nose" area where corrosion sets in. The other area to look at is both rear corners, where owners have forgotten about the safety catch, lifted the bonnet too enthusiastically, and, over the years, slightly raised the rear corner of the bonnet. You will find other less dramatic examples as we progress though the detail but, in the case of the TR4 and 4A you can even find a split of about 12in in front of the bonnet's rear edge, as illustrated by photograph 2-24. In this case, the corners need to be bent back down, welded, and, of course, repainted. The problem is so prevalent that Revington TR has even produced a strengthening insert which is pictured later in the book!

• The plenum chamber is a double-skinned cavity that goes across the full width of the car under the scuttle/ windscreen. It catches water entering the scuttle's air vent and dissipates it through two outboard pipes down into each (front) inner-wing area. You can see the

hole for the drain tube in photograph 2-21. I have arrowed the original drain pipe in photograph 2-25 too. If the pipes become blocked, or the car stands outside for a prolonged period, water can gather in the plenum chamber and rot it away, as is shown all too clearly in photograph 2-25. There is a modification to duct the pipes away from the inner wing area, which we will explore in due course. To detect problems look first for signs of water

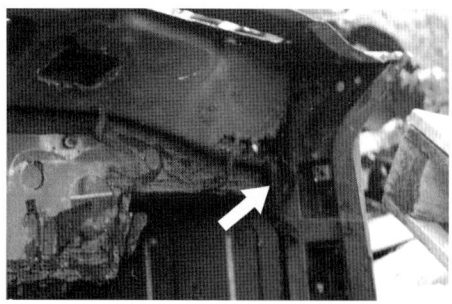

2-25. A view upwards onto the back of the right-side plenum. The oblong hole allows access to the wiper wheel-box and is intended to be there, but the corrosion in the right corner is not shown on any Triumph drawing! Can you spot the drain tube that was intended to take water from the plenum down the outside of the passenger compartment? I doubt it had any work to do for many years, and I suspect that the floor on this car will be very badly corroded ...

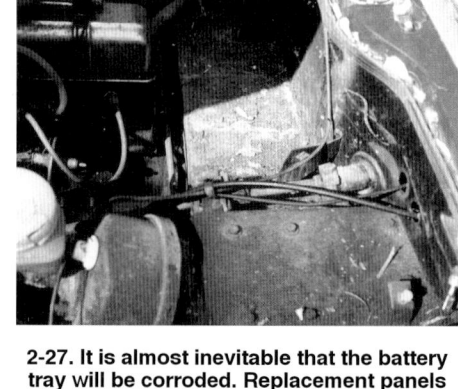

2-27. It is almost inevitable that the battery tray will be corroded. Replacement panels are available, and once the shell has been repainted you can, today, buy a plastic moulding (highly recommended) that at least contains the acid until you can mop it up.

2-29 and 2-30 (right). The door gaps on the IRS TRs open as the chassis weakens. Beware of any car where you see this. The excessive gap could be due to the chassis rotting, or inexpert repairs resulting in 'hogging'. 2-30 shows the sort of gap you want. As a matter of interest, note the door locking arrangements on the TR4A, compared to those on the TR5 shown in photograph 2-29.

2-26. ... Yes, I thought so!

2-28. Clearly not a happy picture of the boot/ trunk of this TR4A, looking forwards into the passenger compartment with the fuel tank removed. This photograph shows that more than the boot/trunk floor needs to be repaired, for there should be two triangular strengthening gussets at the base of each inner wing, just in front of where the fuel tank normally sits. These dramatically increase the sideways strength of the rear of all TRs, and must be left in place. Some owners weld a whole sheet of steel across the rear of their cars at this point to further increase the structural rigidity of the rear of their car, as well as providing a firewall between them and the fuel tank. However, in this example a previous owner has hacked most of both gussets away, which, though may have enabled him to install a couple of speakers for his hi-fi, did absolutely nothing for the back-end strength of his bodyshell! Not all bad news - the wheelarches look fine!

ingress across the car under the windscreen. Wet carpets, rust on the floor panels (photograph 2-26) will give clues, but, you will also need to look up under the dashboard (with a good torch). Start by looking for the pipes in each corner (right under the windscreen corner) and work your way towards the centre of the car. This is a difficult repair and is expensive in that it involves removal of the steering column, dashboard and heater, so look carefully for it's better to find such problems sooner rather than later.

• Battery trays go when battery acid corrodes them, as is illustrated by photograph 2-27. The replacement panel is available and is not too difficult or time consuming to change. Nevertheless, if corrosion is present, add it to your (growing) list of faults.

• As photograph 2-28 demonstrates,

the boot/trunk floor is vulnerable, although, in this example, the rear inner wings look good, making this a restorable proposition.

• I mentioned earlier that there was only one detail that was of particular importance to the TR4A/IRS cars.

Contrary to most sports cars, including the TR4, the door gaps expand on the IRS cars when the chassis structure weakens. Unsatisfactory and excellent examples can be seen in photographs 2-29 and 30.

Paintwork

You must assess the car's paintwork and decide whether it is right for you. Like bodywork repairs, paintwork can be very expensive to properly correct. It takes time to remove all chrome work, wings and fittings, and carry out the chemical pickling necessary to bring the car back to bare metal. And note, this work is required before the pre-paint preparation and actual painting can take place. It takes time to do the complete job properly and you are, therefore, looking at £2000 to £4500 to have the car fully prepared, the paintwork applied, and the car re-assembled. Do not be tempted to shortcut this aspect of the restoration, or to try to get it done 'on the cheap'. Even new Heritage or rust free Californian shells need to be stripped (i.e. wings-off) before painting in order to ensure the paint is applied to the mating surfaces and then reassembled with sealer if you are to enjoy a lasting and impressive finish. Not to do the job correctly repeats the errors of Triumph back in the '50s, '60s and '70s, and eventually wastes much of the remedial bodywork repairs you may have carried out. Certainly, you can help the situation by doing the stripping prior to painting yourself, and even some of the painting at home, and we will discuss that in some detail in a later chapter. Remember that good paintwork, though expensive, will pay for itself in due course.

Interior and external trim

You should not buy or reject a car on the basis of its hood, carpets and internal lining panels. A poor car beautifully trimmed is not a good buy while conversely, a sound car with tatty trim is worth purchasing at the right price. Unless you have a potential concours car in mind, the condition of the external bright work and badges should not take up too much of your time and attention either. If the originality of the car to concours standard is important to you, note that most cars need to include their original steering wheel, as genuine replacements are becoming progressively harder to find and expensive. If the original wheel is not in place, ask if it is available, or add another item to your list.

Potential purchasers of concours-standard cars may need to look at the bright work with a more critical and concerned eye. Replacement front bumpers, in particular, are not up to the standard of the original item and, consequently, a good original bumper will be important to potential concours entrants. Indeed, all bright work needs to be quite carefully viewed, for some badges, although available new, are not quite true replacements of the originals. In normal circumstances the variation will go unnoticed, but sharp-eyed concours judges will mark your car down for such a discrepancy. As an example, the original TR5 badge was in a buttermilk/cream colour, while replacements are white. Most of us would not notice, nor would we be able to detect a non-original jack, wheel brace, *etc.*, but concours judges would!

INSPECTING THE CHASSIS

Although logic might suggest reviewing the features of each chassis

2-31. This is an IRS chassis - a beautifully restored one. Note that, without the clutter of the rear suspension, you can see that all the stresses are focused just behind the middle of the chassis - at the narrowest/weakest point of the structure. You need to bear this in mind when examining a prospective purchase!

chronologically, I think there is an opportunity to simplify our discussion by examining the TR4A IRS chassis first, and the earlier TR4 chassis second. Obviously, the chassis are very different from each other, and each will, therefore, have its own problems. However, I think it's fair to say that the 4A's chassis is the much more problematic. This is particularly true of the rear half, and is why I felt it best to tackle the later car's chassis first.

The TR4A chassis

The TR4A had independent rear suspension and it is most important that the condition of the chassis fits in with your game plan, for, if not, it can be expensive to remedy. Even if you have already decided to buy a new chassis, examine the one in front of you with some care. The vendor does not know your plans and a poor chassis may be a bargaining point later in your discussions.

The first thing to check is the chassis 'legs' that connect to the central cruciform and carry the two trailing arms, see photograph 2-31. These chassis members are the first things to rot. Often you can crunch them with

2-32. The dreaded swelling due to corrosion in the crucial central 'T-shirt' pressing signals an expensive repair, probably sooner rather than later. You should proceed with due caution for this area, along with the IRS mounting 'arm' sections, is the most prone to rust and most expensive to repair (*in situ*) since you either have to take the body off the chassis to get at the corrosion, or cut out the rear floors!

your finger, even though they are the major load-bearing part of the chassis!

The second point to check is just as crucial and that is the central cruciform located just in front of the differential into which the aforementioned chassis legs are welded. The junction is 'plated' top and bottom with diamond shaped pressings called in the trade the 'T-shirt' pressings. When rusted metal is present underneath the pressings, the pressing swells, as shown by photograph 2-32. The metal can even de-laminate in some cases - and it's not unknown for a bodged repair to be carried out and the rusted parts of the pressing to be pushed into the internal cavity and the whole mess plated over. So look (closely) for evidence of welding or added material on/in these diamond shaped pressings.

Superficial and frequently unsafe 'bodges' are often carried out to get the car through an MOT. If corrosion is present above the bottom pressing, the only way the chassis can be repaired properly, safely, and with long term security is to remove the bottom plate completely and first replace the otherwise (probably considerable) hidden corroded metal in the junction and chassis members above the plates. Then, a complete new pressed plate should be re-fixed. A properly executed repair is likely to set you back £600-£700 (a little more if the differential mounting is simultaneously strengthened).

A badly repaired TR will show its chassis ends beneath the rear valance as per photograph 2-33. This is the

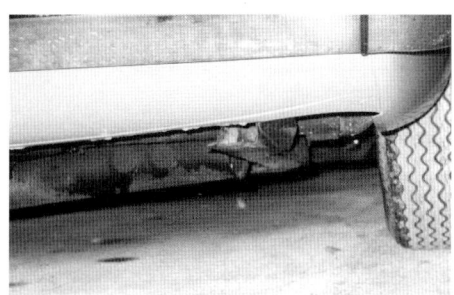

2-33. The tell-tale sign of a 'hogged' IRS TR4A chassis. You will need above-average home restoration skills to correct this yourself. A professional TR restoration company may be able to, depending upon the chassis detail, or you should budget for a replacement chassis that you can at least consider changing at home.

2-34. A creased chassis leg tells you that this car has had a significant thump at some stage in its life. Not necessarily terminal, since the IRS chassis can be shimmed to correct minor defects, but you should be on your guard from the moment you spot this. If you are not inclined to lay down to look for such damage at that stage of the inspection, you can actually feel any creases by running your hand along the outside chassis rail, and taking a closer look only if you think you feel something untoward. Repairing the crease itself may not seem a major problem, but it is a body-off task and may signal other, possibly more serious, accident damage and consequential problems requiring close scrutiny and repair. The presence of a crease need not put an end to your interest in that particular car, as the car may have been well repaired, shimmed, and drive perfectly well. However, it may mean you need to have a more expert second opinion on the car - should everything else prove to be acceptable. In very bad cases the 12in (300mm) or so of supposedly straight chassis in this area can actually be formed into a slight 'Z' shape - which is bad news since it's almost certain that the turret has been moved backwards by the impact. A repair is impossible on an assembled car, and even with a bare chassis, almost impossible for the amateur to properly repair at home without the necessary chassis jig and powerful hydraulic correction ram, not to mention the expertise to know where to 'doze' the problem out. Definitely a 'proceed with caution' car.

2-35.

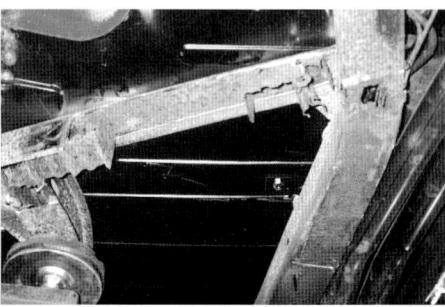

2-35 and 2-36 (above). Corrosion of this (already patched once) severity in one spot, should set you looking elsewhere, since there are likely to be similarly rusted areas of chassis or body, whether the car is a live axle or IRS. Photograph 2-36 may just show what you probably do not want to find ... certainly once you have paid for the car and got it home!

infamous 'hogging' we will talk more about in the chassis restoration chapter. Budget for a body-off replacement chassis type expense or walk away. As you go round the car list the discrepancies you find and then take your list to a competent, experienced TR specialist. There is nothing on a TR that can't be fixed, it just costs money - and you don't want it to be your money, do you?

Next go to the front of the car, lift the bonnet and study closely the rear lower wishbone attachment brackets (visible through the inner wings aperture). It is acceptable and almost normal that these have been welded, but they MUST have been welded competently.

Moving backwards, find where the chassis goes from two side members to one (roughly underneath the 'A' or front door pillar). If the car has had any significant frontal impact it will show at the point where the chassis is down to a single 'leg' each side of the car. If you look down the side of these chassis members they should be perfectly straight. A crease will indicate a significant impact - a typical example is shown in photograph 2-34 - and, if present, should trigger a much closer examination of the front of the chassis, since a replacement chassis could be needed. All is not lost, however, as reconditioned chassis for all independently sprung TRs are available for about £1000, and new replacement chassis can be purchased for about £2000.

If you are forced into seriously contemplating such a task, remember and budget for the absolute fact that the costs and amount of work involved NEVER just stops here. You will at least find that all suspension bushes, fuel and brake lines, and body mountings, *etc.*, will have to be replaced. Bear in mind, too, that a poor chassis is unlikely to carry a super body, and that translates into more remedial time and expense. Replacing the chassis, even under a solid bodyshell, often entails about double the time and treble the expense of your initial estimate!

Furthermore, potential TR-ers from Europe should note that spliced or patched chassis repairs (photograph 2-35) are not acceptable, particularly for the German TUV (MOT) test. All chassis repairs have to be 'invisible', which means if a chassis member is to be repaired and the car is destined for Europe, that chassis member must be replaced in its entirety.

Even if you find no single item of major concern, the chassis needs to be reviewed in the context of how long do you expect the car to last. Is the chassis scaly and original, or is there any sign of the corrosion typified by photograph 2-36, in which case it may mean that your plan to get married in the car in 10 years' time is somewhat ambitious ... If the car has been completely rebuilt and the original chassis was sand blasted, repaired and subsequently properly coated, and there is plenty of evidence to support this, then it could well last the 10 years you may expect of it. Otherwise, consider the implications of having to carry out a body-off restoration in months, or possibly, in only a few years' time. Mark it up on your list accordingly!

If you have looked at several cars in your price bracket and found that all

2-37. The much more straightforward 'ladder-chassis' of a live axled TR4. Compare the simplicity of this structure with the much more complex, but less rigid, IRS chassis shown in 2-31.

2-39. The correct upwards 'cant' of the rear part of an upside-down TR4 chassis.

2-38. The rear suspension is pretty simple too - which you may view as an advantage or as technologically behind the times.

2-40. Whilst inherently more robust and less prone to corrosion than later types, the TR4 chassis does tend to corrode where the body mounting extensions come through the main members. There are kits available to repair this.

would appear to have a relatively short life-span before major restoration work and costs, then it's likely you'll have to rethink your budget! Nevertheless, have fun, take care, and do look at potential purchases with a jaundiced eye!

The TR4 chassis

Even if it's a TR4 you are planning to view, it's still worth your while reading the earlier advice on IRS chassis inspection. However, the 'ladder' chassis of the TR4, as shown in the pictures on this page, is generally less problematic that its IRS successor, and, even though it will be older than any of the IRS variants, the TR4's chassis is likely to be in better overall condition. If in doubt as to which TR you are looking at, the commendably simple rear 'live' axle of the TR4 can be seen in photograph 2-38.

Although the tail of the TR4 chassis might, at first glance, appear to be a problem, such an assessment could, in fact, be premature. The rear few feet of

the chassis was originally welded to the main section just in front of the front spring hanger with about a 5 degrees uplift at the very back of the chassis, as shown by photograph 2-39. If, therefore, you note that the chassis you are examining is not flat (at the rear), and appears to have been welded both at an angle and right around the join, this is likely to be quite original and perfectly satisfactory.

It would, of course, be wrong to say that there are no potential problems with an older chassis, so let's take a look at what to watch for:
- The body mounting feet. These stick outside the chassis rails and essentially comprise a tube (with a flat plate) welded to the main chassis. They can corrode where they join the main chassis (see photograph 2-40) leaving the body unsupported in the middle.
- The cross tube chassis member, shown in picture 2-41, which goes across the rear of the car to support the spare wheel, can corrode. The area is

not often protected by oil but does often gets wet. The problems here are exacerbated by a curl-back of exhaust gases that add to the pace of corrosion. The cross tube carries through on both sides of the chassis members and forms part of the spring hanger. It's essential, therefore, to inspect the whole cross tube for corrosion.
- Check the rear few feet of chassis with particular care, for, like the spare wheel carrier tube, corrosion can occur, as photograph 2-42 shows.
- Check the whole of the rest of the chassis. Any patching, twists, welds or miss-alignments (side to side), are

2-41. The rear of the chassis is not infallible either, probably for the same reasons that the IRS chassis tends to 'go' towards the tail, where water and exhaust gases conspire to accelerate corrosion. This photograph shows the spare wheel support.

2-43. The front of a ladder chassis cannot be forgotten, for, while the chassis is less prone to corrosion here, the front is still vulnerable to accident damage. The ladder chassis is, in fact, at a disadvantage, compared to the IRS chassis, for there are no shims to correct even minor accident damage. Consequently, the straightness of the front suspension turrets is very important for it will require a 'body-off' repair to straighten twisted ones.

2-42. Here we see the very tail-end of a very badly corroded chassis leg. Note, however, how the corrosion has not spread, for, although the spare wheel carrier may not be wonderful, it is not as bad as one might expect.

obviously unsatisfactory, be they on an IRS car or a ladder-chassis TR4. Look at the front end for accident damage, particularly to the front suspension turrets shown in photograph 2-43, and, if necessary, add an entry to your faults list.

ENGINE, GEARBOX AND OVERDRIVE

The TR4 and TR4A present identical initial inspection challenges in respect to their engines, gearboxes, overdrives, so there is no need for me to differentiate between the cars.

Engine condition details
The Triumph four-cylinder engines were

designed initially for Ferguson tractors, and are, consequently, fundamentally tough. They were later developed (still in four-cylinder form) for the Standard Vanguard range of Saloon cars which proved them in a more everyday environment.

Things to check include listening for a few seconds' rattle on start-up. Does it puff blue smoke, thus signifying general wear and tiredness? Do the tappets rattle even when the is engine warm?

Many of Triumph's four-cylinder engines have an oil scroll/seal leak problem at the rear main bearing. A single drop (perhaps two) of oil on the garage floor from an engine with an unmodified crankshaft is unavoidable. More oil than that signals a need to remove the engine and crankshaft, and have the special machining outlined in Chapter 7 carried out. Upon re-assembly, the modified engine uses a modern (lipped) replacement rear crank oil seal which is much more effective.

The gearbox condition/ assessment
When test driving the car, try selecting each gear. It will require a firm, positive and deliberate action to put it into gear and also a full depression of the clutch. However, the gear stick should not fight, refuse to go in, or make complaining

noises as it goes (or does not go) into gear. Second gear, coming down the box, is the weakest aspect of the TR range of boxes. Try the gearbox in every gear on over-run (not in drive) to test for jumping out of gear. Watch the gear stick during the over-runs for clues, as it will inch forward slightly before popping out. If the clutch is stiff or heavy, then it's possible the pin in the clutch fork has gone.

If there's a hissing sound when the clutch is depressed, with the engine running and the gearbox in neutral, the release bearing must be suspect. If the

2-44. Although these creases in the front wheelarches look a problem, they are quite standard. The ones shown here are to be found in every TR.

gearbox hisses, with the engine running and driving slowly forward in first gear, then be warned this is likely to be the sign that the layshaft's needle roller bearings are picking-up on the layshaft's hardened surface - and will require replacement in due course. This hiss will most likely disappear in top gear (*i.e.* direct drive). A broken clutch fork pin may cost pence but the layshaft will be a different matter, and you should budget for fitting a new clutch when the engine is out.

All the foregoing problems will require gearbox-out (and, therefore, at least one seat and some trim) repairs, and will, consequently, be expensive. You would be prudent to seek a professional estimate for your repairs.

Overdrive

Overdrive units were not fitted to every TR. In fact, only 70% of UK cars and 5% of US cars had overdrive fitted. If the car you are viewing has an overdrive fitted it should be an 'A' type to fall in line with originality constraints. Some cars may have been retro-fitted with a later 'J' type overdrive which you may see as an advantage as the later overdrives were stronger, but remember that, should you ever come to sell the car, your purchaser may be more orientated towards originality.

If you are confronted with a potential purchase that is without overdrive, think in terms of at least £500 difference in value compared to an otherwise equal car with the correct overdrive fitted. This is the going rate for a second-hand gearbox with overdrive. It will cost more than this, of course, if you take installation into account, but this difference goes most of the way towards balancing the lack of overdrive. A reconditioned 'A' type box with overdrive will, in fact, set you back about £1000 if you have no compatible trade-in unit to offer, and you would still need to budget for the installation.

Everyone wants to 'move up' to overdrive gearboxes and, consequently, non-overdrive gearboxes have little value as a trade-in. This is because the tailshaft within an overdrive 'box is actually shorter than that of a non-overdrive 'box. A supplier who takes a non-overdrive 'box in part exchange, therefore, will not only be short of the overdrive unit but of the correct tailshaft too.

If the car you are considering has an overdrive unit fitted this is good news, but the overdrive can suffer from the consequence of the worn gearbox layshaft mentioned earlier. If the layshaft surface is breaking up, since gearbox and overdrive share the same oil, the swarf from the failing layshaft will have entered the overdrive unit and will be doing its best (usually successfully) to wear the overdrive pump and eccentric cam. So, not only are you faced with a gearbox rebuild but you MUST budget and arrange for an overdrive strip, clean and inspection. Failure to take this action will result in swarf that has collected in the overdrive getting back into the gearbox and ruining the new layshaft and bearings.

When the overdrive control switch is flicked 'on', overdrive should cut straight in, and with sufficient force to slightly jolt you. An overdrive that is slow to come in could be suffering from one of two faults. The least expensive is a faulty/sluggish solenoid that costs £50 and 10 minutes to fix. However, it is prudent to assume the previous owner has tried this step and, whatever he says, you should presume the problem is due to a worn overdrive pump which is now taking time to build to the requisite 410psi operating pressure. Assume a worst-case scenario and allow £500 to fix this, plus - nine times out of

ten - a new clutch.

All the foregoing problems necessitate removal of the gearbox before remedial work can begin, and should be costed accordingly.

THE DIFFERENTIALS

The TR4's Rear Axle and suspension

The Girling rear axle used in the TR4 was a robust unit, not prone to serious weakness or trouble. Nevertheless, it would, of course, be prudent to check for whine on both drive and over-run.

The hub oil seals can leak and are tricky to replace, so the usual hub bearing check (with the back of the car jacked up), accompanied by a close look for oil leaks is also worthwhile.

The other relatively minor problem to look out for is over-enthusiastic greasing of the rear-hub bearings. This tends to result in contaminated rear brake linings.

If you are looking at a LHD car, be aware that the springs originally fitted were actually different from one side of the car to the other. If they haven't been replaced with a pair of matching rear springs then budget for such a change if you plan to convert to RHD.

The IRS differential on TR4As

Although you will be keen to establish

2-45. It's worth rolling the floor covering back over the rear axle of a TR4A. You may not find a hole like this, but you could find evidence that the floor has been partially removed in order to fix a broken diff mounting-pin. You can actually see the top of the right-front pin (the most vulnerable one) in this shot.

whether the differential whines on drive or over-run, the main issue with an IRS car is: does the diff 'thud' when the clutch is let in or out? If so, this is invariably because the right-hand front mounting pin has pulled out of its chassis mounting. The solution is to remove the differential, re-weld the pin from underneath and box the mountings to prevent re-occurrence. This is a professional job so add at least £250 to your list of costs.

In view of the prevalence of the diff-pin problem, you would be wise to lift the carpet above the diff cross-member and see if someone has tackled the repair unprofessionally (by just cutting a hole in the rear floor and welding the one pin from the top, as shown in photograph 2-45). Not only would this leave a new owner with three un-welded pins to deal with, it means an additional bodyshell repair to budget for too.

A 'click' suggests a worn sliding joint in the rear driveshafts, which can only be resolved by replacement driveshafts at circa £100 apiece. You may also find that, collectively, the 6 U/Js in the propshaft and driveshaft power chain 'chunk'. While the components are not expensive (6 will cost £50) the fitting will take some time and you should get a professional estimate. The main propshaft in particular can only be removed with the differential (or gearbox) removed - so if either of these have to come out it is normally worthwhile replacing at least the two propshaft U/Js as a matter of course.

Chapter 3
Preparing your restoration plan

So, you have taken the plunge and now have your beautiful (or maybe not so beautiful) TR tucked safely in your garage. If you have paid 'top-dollar' and bought a near concours standard car, then the majority of the rest of this book should be of little more than academic interest in the short term. At the other extreme, for those who have bought a 'restoration project', may I strongly recommend rather more thought than action initially, for you need to establish a restoration plan and budget. The positive purpose behind a restoration plan is to ensure things are done in the most effective manner. However, there are some pitfalls to avoid too, and a well thought through restoration plan and associated budget can go a long way to ensure you avoid the three main reasons for those sad 'abandoned-project' advertisments. Restorations are mostly abandoned because the project:
- got beyond the owner's depth of technical experience.
- cost more than was initially envisaged.
- took far longer than was expected.

These three issues are largely trade-offs: the more you can do yourself the less the project should cost but the longer it will take. This book is intended to help would-be restorers appreciate what they are getting into, and hopefully to find a satisfactory trade-off for their particular car, skills, time and budget. There are policies you can adopt which will both minimise the work involved and help you decide what to subcontract. I hope I have covered the vast majority starting in the previous chapter by helping you buy appropriately.

Professionally restored cars price themselves out of the reach of the majority of enthusiasts, particularly the younger enthusiasts. However, there are two things going for a home restored TR. Firstly, everything comes apart, which makes access much easier, and, secondly, if you do the majority of work yourself you can be pretty sure that you will recover most of what you've spent - which is not always the case. So, let's get started with preparing our restoration plan.

STRIPPING THE CAR

Plan for the extra space that a stripped motorcar requires: as a rule of thumb you need three times the space. Secondly, do not throw anything away until the restoration is complete. However rusted, bent or rotten, keep everything for reference, and in case that odd clip, harness connection or bracket may no longer be available. You can certainly categorise and list the parts you strip from the car as 'useless, requiring replacement', or 'good probably reusable' and an intermediate category too. Indeed, the list of missing or useless parts will be very helpful when you get to visit some of the TR specialists. You would be wise to locate all the parts for, say, the trim in one area for use later in the project. Other parts may be required earlier in the rebuild, and these should be stored in another, possibly more accessible, location - perhaps a rack in the main workshop.

I've suggested that some time should be spent thinking and planning, and there's much to be said for checking as many of the larger components as is practical before you remove them from the car. The engine, gearbox, radiator and rear axle are good examples worthy of a moment's consideration.

Let's presume that you have bought a non-running car that is more-or-less in one piece. Now, restoration plans can vary a great deal, but few restorers are keen to spend more than is necessary! For those on a very tight budget it could be particularly advantageous to postpone a major expense like an engine rebuild for a year or so. It would, in any event, be very helpful to learn what the gearbox is like and/or whether the overdrive works. So, before you rush too quickly into taking some parts off the car, consider whether it would not be a good idea to find out in more detail what you have bought.

Do not forget to ensure that the car is safely and securely elevated off the ground, and to check the fluid levels in all the components you are about to test. It may even be prudent to change some of the oils completely before you start. However, if after a few hours' work you can indeed confirm that the engine runs reasonably well without any 'expensive' noises, you may elect to postpone the expense of an engine rebuild. You may find that the overdrive does not work, and establish (perhaps with the help of Chapter 9) that it is not a simple electrical problem.

You may even hear some unpleasant gearbox noises; all of which may lead you to conclude that a rebuilt or replacement gearbox and overdrive are essential prior to reassembly of the car. These early tests may even completely reverse your original engine/ gearbox restoration intentions. Such changes of plan are perfectly acceptable, of course, for restoring these components can be - and, where practical should be - postponed. There's absolutely no point in spending money before you need to!

There are, however, two absolutely vital parts of any TR that need to put right first time round - the chassis and the bodywork: you do not want to postpone or part-restore these.

It's a good idea to empty any petrol/gas from any fuel tank you are not going to use for a while, and replace it with a gallon of diesel fuel before putting it somewhere safe. This does two things - it ensures the integrity of the tank, and acts as a preservative for the period that the tank is in store.

Do not even think about taking the body or the suspension off the chassis until you have established a TR specialist as your 'partner' (discussed in the next section). You can remove the bolt-on panels (wings, doors, bonnet and boot/trunk-lid), exhaust, engine, gearbox, fuel tank, electrics, trim, seats, dashboard, etc., if you want to get a better look at the body and chassis, after which you had better set about establishing your contacts.

DO YOU HAVE THE CONTACTS?

If you have not done this already, I would make a point of joining the TR Register (see Appendix 1) and call your local area secretary before attending the next area meeting. The least you will get from the local area TR group will be a list of local services and recommended suppliers, and you will establish contact with local members, some with very helpful experience, who will be able to offer advice. Most amateurs only do one restoration and, consequently, the experience of others is absolutely indispensable if you are to avoid some (potentially expensive) mistakes.

Time spent planning is never wasted, nor is time spent finding and visiting proven and trusted suppliers and establishing a rapport with all. Again, if you have not met any TR specialists, now would be a very good time to visit one or two. This book chronicles the combined expertise of the five TR restorers whom I consider to be the premier specialists in the UK; (in alphabetical order) Revington TR, TR Bitz, TR Enterprises, TRGB and TR Workshop. However, I must not overlook the significant expertise of Faversham Restorations, which also gave me a great deal of help. Their address details can be found in Appendix 1. It's very important to build-up a rapport at the planning stage with the specialist you are going to buy parts from, probably use for such professional work as is required, and from whom you will seek advice.

Some parts are hard to obtain, and one of the benefits of buying your car, particularly an ex-US LHD TR, from one of the specialist TR businesses listed above is that you can specify that, as part of the overall deal, you must have all the essential components to restore the car (including conversion if applicable). For those who have bought privately, the next best thing is to still approach your preferred specialist with the prospect of a mutually helpful partnership. This time the approach needs to be along the lines that you plan the restoration of a TR and, whilst you have the basic car, you will need at least the following spares (take as comprehensive a list of parts as you can prepare). Your partnership suggestion should be along the lines that you are

prepared to buy all your spares from him and send any specialist work you cannot cope with to him. In return, you ask for help and advice when needed, introductions to suitable contractors (e.g. a shot-blaster) when the time comes, the prospect of a modest discount on purchases and a source for the hard-to-find parts.

Obviously, the specialist most local to your home is going to be the most convenient in many ways, but don't forget that, in these days of next-day delivery parcel post, personal chemistry, co-operation, experience and facilities are actually more important than geographical proximity in most situations. Take some photographs of your car and visit one or two. The three US specialists that come highly recommended are Moss Motors, The Roadster Factory and Victoria British Ltd. Their addresses appear in Appendix 1.

CHASSIS OR BODY FIRST?

This is a really important question that requires some discussion. In fact, there are several important decisions to be made as your restoration plan starts to take shape, but I believe this to be the most crucial. If the chassis seems in good shape, and is to be used again (albeit after refurbishment), it's probably best to carry out body repairs BEFORE separating the bodytub from its chassis. You can then use the chassis, in effect, as the jig to correctly locate those new body panels as are required. This route has the distinct advantage of requiring only one body-off/body-on sequence, and is the recommend route for most non-professional restorers with a suitably good chassis.

The restoration takes on a different sequence if you plan to replace your chassis with a new or exchange/ refurbished unit. The home restorer will not have the facilities, particularly the bespoke jigs, which any good professional TR body restorer enjoys. Consequently, you are well advised to carry out the body repairs with the bodyshell on its permanent chassis. Your restoration plan will require your sending the original chassis away for repairs, or acquiring the replacement before you do the bodyshell repairs. However, there's no point in painting the new chassis and then doing your bodyshell repairs on that chassis. This type of plan, therefore, means two body-off/body-on exercises, for reasons that will become clearer as we explore the various painting options.

Do not overlook the possibility that there could be an easier route to the initial removing/replacing of a bodyshell as part of this 'two-lift' plan. Provided your plan calls for new floors and new sills, then you may just as well take the body off its chassis in two pieces, remove the floor and sills, and then offer the body back up to the (now satisfactory) chassis in two pieces. The refurbished body still has to come off once more for various painting tasks to be carried out, and the second time it must come off in one piece; however, your first off/on will at least be easier.

IRS hogging

If you are uncertain about the true quality of your chassis, how do you decide which way round to effect the body and chassis repairs? This is not a problem that those with ladder-framed TRs need worry about, but the first golden rule for cars with the IRS type of chassis is to establish whether the chassis is 'hogged' at the back. Hogging means that the rear of the chassis (roughly from the rear trailing arm chassis member) cants downwards. It's not uncommon, and we will establish the cause in a moment, but clearly there is no point in using the chassis as a jig to align body panels if the 'jig' is flawed before you start on the body repairs! Hogging can be caused by the obvious - a shunt up the back. In-expert chassis repairs can also bring it about, and probably this is the most common cause. Replacing the chassis members that carry the rear trailing arm would be one potential cause, and replacing the diamond-shaped 'T-shirt' pressing at the centre of the chassis cruciform another. The main problem, however, is often shrinkage brought about by the cooling of the metal after welding. The components may be perfectly aligned before welding, and even properly tacked into position, but too much welding in one place without compensatory stitch welding on the diametrically opposite part of the repair will 'pull' the chassis as the welding cools. Although the shrinkage on or close to the weld will be inconsequential, the cantilevered rear chassis member can droop up to 1in

(25mm) at its tail end!

You do not actually need to look at the chassis itself to become suspicious, since the rear door gaps will probably tell much of the story. All TR door gaps open up as one progressively measures from the rear base of the door upwards. The bottom gap should be about 1/8in (3mm) and the top $1/4$in (5-6mm) - but if the top has opened up to $1/2$in (12-15mm) (photograph 2-29) then you probably have a hogged chassis. Viewing the car from 10 metres behind will also tell you, since you should not be able to see the ends of the chassis members below the rear valance. If you can see part of them (picture 2-33) you certainly have a hogged chassis and repairing it becomes your first priority.

WHAT AND WHERE TO PAINT?

Body and chassis painting are important elements of your plan. With the paintwork on a car being so highly visible, one's first instinct might be to consider subcontracting the work to a professional restorer. Cost, however, comes into play, and I have already said much about the cost of properly painting a car.

However, bear in mind the difference spraying a car regularly can make to your skills. If you last did a paint job three or four years ago, then at least have the outside sprayed professionally. Furthermore, there is considerable environmental pressure to reduce the sales of cellulose paints; the carcinogenic nature of modern 2-pack paints necessitates professional spray and oven facilities. However, there is no reason not to paint the chassis at home. There other options, as we will explore in Chapter 6, but for the sake of this planning review, let us presume you will subcontract at least the external body spraying, and hand-paint the chassis at home.

THE MAIN RESTORATION PLAN

The objective of what follows is to enable you to plan your car's restoration to your best advantage. There is no point, for example, in painting the chassis too early, and then ruining your hard work by building the body on it. There's no point in spending money on an engine rebuild and then leaving the

engine standing in the corner of the garage for several years. Every plan will vary as the particular circumstances of each restoration are taken into account. The premises, tools, time, skills, experience available, distance from the main subcontractors and the target restoration period will all influence your planning, as will the initial condition of the car and the intended standard of the end result. It is impossible, therefore, to give a definitive plan, but, in the broadest outline the following thoughts may serve to prompt you when shaping your own plan.

It is highly likely you will not be completely sure as to whether you will be following the one-piece or two-piece body restoration route until you have assessed what you have bought in some detail. Therefore, the first task (whether it's an IRS or a ladder chassis) is to strip the inside of car completely, including removing electrics, trim (internal and external) and dashboard. Removing the engine, gearbox, front and rear suspension is optional at this stage, and largely depends on the plan and/or whether you need any mobility of the chassis/body.

Photograph 3-1 is of a car that looks like a one-piece body restoration, but if you start to see anything like photograph 3-2 you can be pretty certain you have a two-piece body restoration to plan as the floors and sills are completely corroded. In fact, I have marked photograph 3-2 with a

3-1. This car has been stripped part of the way and already the doors, interior dash, instruments and electrics are completely out. The front and rear wings (fenders) still have to come off, and the engine still needs to be lifted out. It would be prudent to remove the wings before taking the engine out. The floors on this example look to have no more than superficial rust, so this is unlikely to be the sort of car that warrants taking the body off in two parts.

3-2. This Michelotti shell, however, is already looking like a candidate for floor and sill replacement, and, therefore, for cutting and removing the front half separately from the rear; so much so that I have marked the probable cut line to adopt once the car is completely stripped.

3-3. Since the whole bodytub is rebuilt around its doors, the doors are the initial restoration task. Here, the new door skin is being offered for the first time to the already repaired door-frame. A full photographic sequence of a door rebuild will be found in chapter 4.

3-4. Whichever TR you are restoring you will need to brace both door apertures very securely. During the course of this book you will see pictures of several different methods so there is no 'right' way of achieving the objective. Although this idea has merit, you would be prevented from offering-up the doors.

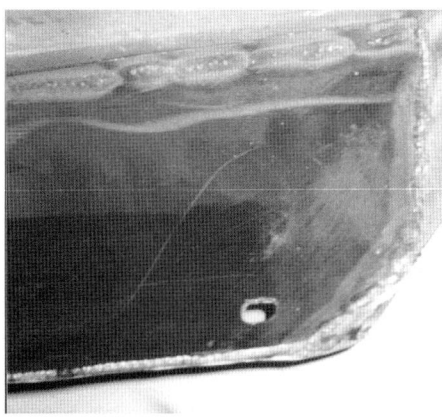

3-5. Here is just one example of the loose panel repairs you will have to carry out after you have finished the main bodytub. As will be explained in more detail in chapter 4, you will probably find there are many such repairs. Here, part of an old outer sill section has been used to provide the material and shape for a lower front wing repair.

proposed 'cut-line'! After this initial and common assessment, the respective plans start to deviate depending upon the car and what you've found. We will look first at the simplest of plans, which, we assume, is a one-piece body repair on a good TR4 ladder chassis.

Example 1 - Ladder chassis TR4/one-piece body repair

- Start by procuring or repairing the doors such that they are primed and ready to use (photograph 3-3).
- Don't forget to brace the door apertures and carry out bodytub repairs on the chassis (photograph 3-4).
- Complete the panel (e.g. wings) repairs. Offer all panels to the bodytub and, when satisfied, remove (photograph 3-5).
- Separate the bodytub from the chassis - although you may chose to transport the tub to the blaster on the chassis (photograph 3-6).
- Sand blast and prime paint the bodytub. Finalise body welding, make good final body details and touch-in primer, as illustrated by photograph 3-7.
- Carry out as much finish bodytub painting as you plan at home (photograph 3-8).
- Send the bodytub and loose panels to the painter, noting the importance of transporting the lot very carefully, and retaining the door bracings (photograph 3-9).
- Repair and paint the chassis at home. Sand blasting the chassis will have to be sub-contracted (photograph 3-10).
- Refurbish the front and rear suspension components and affix to the

3-6. This TR4 chassis has not seen the light of day for many years but looks in good shape. This one was repatriated from California and, therefore, had a less corrosive life than many.

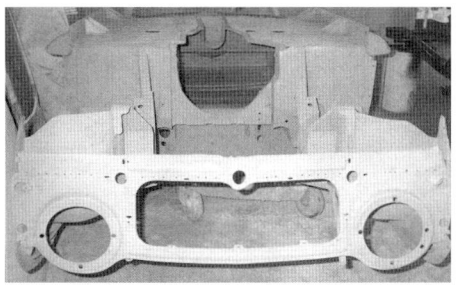

3-7. Remembering to keep the door-braces in place, this TR4 tub has been welded as required and lightly sand blasted. Did you spot the LHD steering column hole?

chassis (photograph 3-11).
- Take the rolling chassis to the painter, as per photograph 3-12, and marry the body to the chassis (using the appropriate body fixing kit) at the painters.
The final phases of the plan are fairly obvious and virtually identical to the conclusion of Plan 2. Consequently, I will summarise both under 'Conclusions' to avoid unnecessary duplication.

Example 2 - IRS TR4A/two-piece body repair
At the other end of the complexity scale I have chosen to plan the IRS car on a worst-case scenario. The following plan

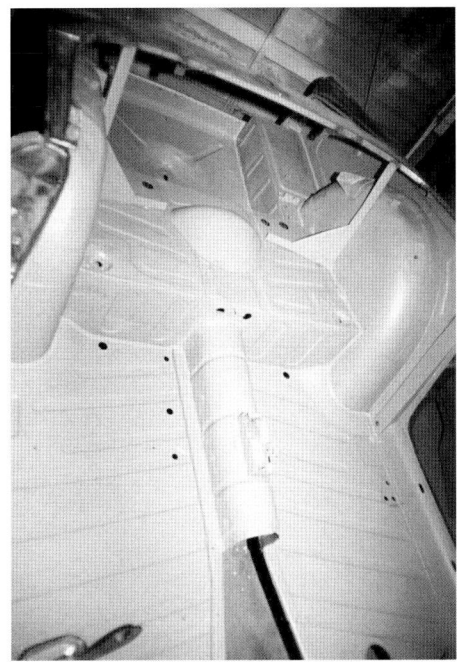

3-8. You can do all the body painting at home, some of it (which I recommend and explain in chapter 6), or none-of it. Only you can decide what's best for your restoration. Here we see a bodytub primered at home and then seam sealed - ready for the next step.

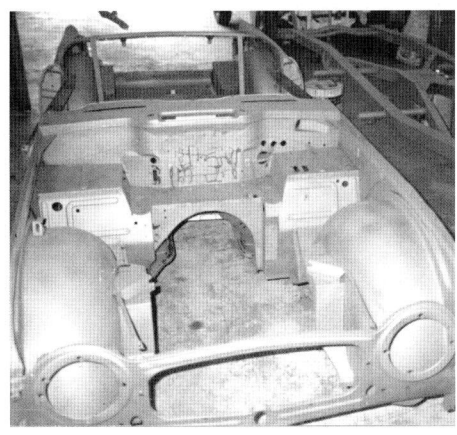

3-9. The tub we saw in picture 3-7 is just about to go back on its chassis for transportation to the paint shop. Can you see the LHD steering column hole now? As mentioned before (several times!), some form of cross bracing is absolutely indispensable and here is another example made from substantial angle-iron section. The braces follow a direct path across the top of, and will be welded to the inside of, the front of the 'A' post, while the rear ends will be securely bolted to the inside of the 'B' post using the hood mounting fastenings. Not only is this door brace very effective, but you can (and will have to) offer the doors up to the bodytub without disturbing the braces.

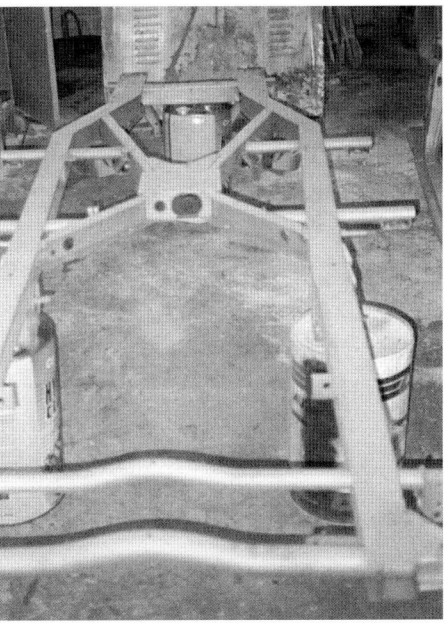

3-10. After shot blasting, there many advantages in repairing and painting your chassis at home.

3-11. A TR4 rolling chassis, complete with all suspension parts beautifully prepared, awaiting the bodytub.

is one route you could follow when the original chassis is unsatisfactory for use as the body-jig, and when the bodytub is so corroded as to warrant a two-piece body refurbishment. Not all IRS cars will be in this state.

- Confirm that the floors and sills are not salvageable, as photograph 3-13

3-12. This photograph of a TR4 obviously shows the engine and gearbox in place on this completed chassis. I prefer the simplicity of taking just a rolling chassis to the painter. Fitting the painted body with exhaust manifolds and/or radiator protrusions can only add to the body-on time, and the engine/gearbox only add to the weight you are required to move.

3-13. I understand that the metal was so thin that the floor would not support the weight of a spanner/wrench!

confirms, and that the chassis is in as poor condition. In such a case, cut the shell across the centre just in front of the propshaft tunnel, as shown in photographs 3-2 and 4-1, and remove the shell in two halves from its chassis.
- Repair, replace or buy a new chassis. An example is shown in photograph 3-14.
- Remove the worst of the oil and dirt and (temporally) replace the original major components and suspensions on the new chassis, noting that no refurbishing of the major components has taken place (photograph 3-15).
- Lift to a slightly more convenient working height and stand the car on its suspension using four 'ramps' or four stands that bolt to the hubs (photographs 3-16-1 to 3-16-3).
- Fit new floors to the chassis, refit the

3-14. The various options for repairing, replacing or procuring a new chassis are explored in chapter 5. While it does not matter which route you choose, it is important that your body is rebuilt on the chassis it will spend the rest of its life married to! Here is a new IRS chassis with some of the front suspension components laid out prior to re-assembly, although the engine, gearbox and diff will also have to be placed temporally in position.

3-16-1.

3-15. This is an IRS chassis - and an excellent example at that, one certainly suited to a body rebuild. The major components have been left in place to provide the weight to stress the chassis as the body is rebuilt. The suspension will have to be supported (as illustrated by the next couple of shots) but the propshaft can be removed if it helps, since it contributes no meaningful weight.

3-16-1 and 3-16-2 (above). This IRS TR4A has been lifted to a more convenient working height by axle-stands positioned under the rear and front suspension hubs. This is ideal for an IRS car since it stresses the chassis in exactly the manner that it will be stressed 'on the road' - provided the weight of the major components are also present or represented by weights.

3-16-3. This is certainly a safe and satisfactory method of lifting the ladder chassised TR4 for body restoration - provided the stands are positioned properly, of course. This, however, is actually a TR250 and, therefore, an IRS car, so, before body restoration is commenced, these axle stands need to repositioned!

3-17. The pair of new floors have been securely mounted to the (new KTM) chassis - which is obviously going to act as both body-assembly jig and permanent base for this Michelotti shell. The front and rear 'halves' of the TR4A bodytub will need to be carefully prepared around their respective mating faces. The old sill and any remnants of the old floors need to be removed before you can contemplate offering either back up to the chassis/new floors.

3-18.

original front and rear halves of the bodyshell onto the new floors and cross-brace the door apertures, as shown in pictures 3-17 to 3-22.
• Carry out bodytub and panel repairs. Photographs 3-23 and 3-24 show a couple of typical examples. Remove all loose panels once their fit is to your satisfaction.
• Remove major components, such as the engine, gearbox and suspension. Either separate the bodytub in one piece from the chassis, as per photograph 3-25, or use the chassis to transport the bodytub to the blaster and separate them there.
• Separate, shot-blast and prime paint the bodytub, as per photograph 3-26. Finalise body welding, make good any

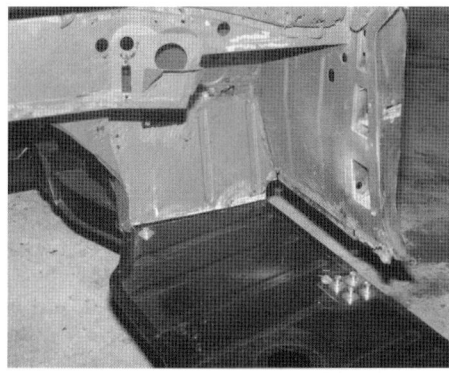

3-18 and 3-19 (above). The front 'half' is offered to the new floors. It sits comfortably in place as the result of the angled turret supports, which have two body-mounting points each. Note how the old floor and sill have been removed. These pictures were 'posed' for my benefit and, in fact, there is some further making-good to carry out at the base of the 'A' posts before the front half will be properly positioned and tacked in place. Then we can try the doors on the 'A' posts and tentatively position the back half-shell.

3-20

3-20 and 3-21 (above). A general shot followed by a close-up of the rear half of this TR4A's body being re-acquainted with its chassis. The floors are new, of course, but there is still some making-good to complete before the floors are welded to the rear-half. Even then, there will undoubtedly be much detailed renovation work to carry out - but this is a major step in any restoration project.

3-22. Cross bracing of the door-aperture is so important that I make no apologies for showing you yet another alternative method.

3-23. There will inevitably be numerous bodytub and panel repairs to carry out on obvious corrosion holes.

3-24. Although this repair has been completed, you'll probably find you have dozens of similar repairs to complete, many of which are studied in more detail in chapter 4.

3-25. Remove the finished body from the chassis, usually accomplished by four strong lifters (six if you leave the loose panels in place). Using a hoist has the added advantage of enabling the finished shell to be stored in the roof-space until shot blasting. Very ingenious!

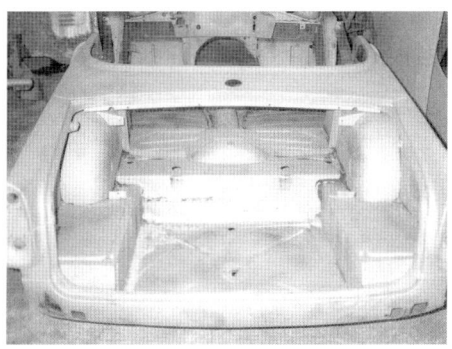

3-26. The blasting operation will usually reveal the odd spot of corrosion. I think I can spot one or two examples in this picture. However, the cross-braces are definitely still in place!

final body details and touch-in primer.
• Finish painting as much of the bodytub as you can at home.
• Send the bodytub and loose panels to the painter, noting the importance of transporting the lot very carefully - possibly on the chassis (photograph 3-27).
• Paint the chassis at home, as shown in picture 3-28, refurbish the front and rear suspension components and affix to chassis.
• Take the rolling chassis to the painter, broadly as per photographs 3-29-1 and 3-29-2. Marry the body to the chassis (using the appropriate body fixing kit) at the painters (photograph 3-30).

Conclusion
Both plans conclude in very similar

3-27. Note that other components await the painter's attention on the back wall, while the bare tub (no panels in place), can be wheeled around the shop with ease.

3-28. You need to prepare the chassis well, and to apply a good protective finish, such as this red-oxide primer. For a variety of reasons discussed in the main text, brush painting is not only the most cost-effective method but also provides the most long-term finish, provided you choose the paint carefully. If you damage the finish during subsequent restoration work it can be touched-in, and any damage later in the car's - hopefully - long life can also be rectified with the minimum of cost and fuss.

3-29-1.

3-29-1 and 3-29-2 (above). Here we see the front and rear suspensions rebuilt and on the chassis; 'ready to go', so to speak! You will find more details in chapters 11 and 13.

3-30. Body reunited to its chassis at the painters. We will explore some of the preparatory steps you can take to ensure this task goes smoothly and causes minimal interruption to the paint-shop's normal routine.

3-31. The four-cylinder engine being rebuilt at home. Some very useful detail is explored in chapter 7 but, as part of your restoration plan you need to decide whether you are going to rebuild the engine yourself or subcontract the whole job (and therefore the responsibility) to a TR specialist. Specialists will be able to buy the parts cheaper than you ever will, their experience enables them to complete the assembly very quickly, and, most importantly, they do offer a warranty!

fashions, summarised as follows:
- Refurbish the engine and gearbox and fit to car, as per photograph 3-31. Fit the exhaust, induction, radiator and brakes, etc., to car.
- Fit the body panels (boot, doors and bonnet), and the external trim, as shown in photograph 3-32.
- Refurbish as required and refit the electrics, dashboard, internal trim and hood, etc. The operations involved are shown in photographs 3-33 to 3-38 but, naturally, are explored in more detail as this book progresses.

SPARE PARTS

It is vital that you order spares that are actually appropriate to your car rather than its registered year of manufacture or commission number. All the cars in question have lived long lives and very few will not have had secondhand (possibly reconditioned, but still used) parts fitted. While most will have been fitted without detriment to the car's operational effectiveness or reliability, not all these parts will have exactly matched the original specification of the car.

It is common practice, for example, for the performance of early cars to be improved by fitting a later (the later the better) cylinder head. Consequently, you should be sure which cylinder head you actually have on your car before you buy related gaskets, etc. Another good example might be the brake

3-32. Here the first of the separate panels is refitted. You will note that the dash/fascia of this TR250 are in fact already in place, which just goes to show there's more than one way to carry out a TR restoration. You may find several tasks inside the cockpit are easier to carry out before the doors are refitted. So, after getting the loose panels lined up, there is a case for temporarily removing the doors yet again!

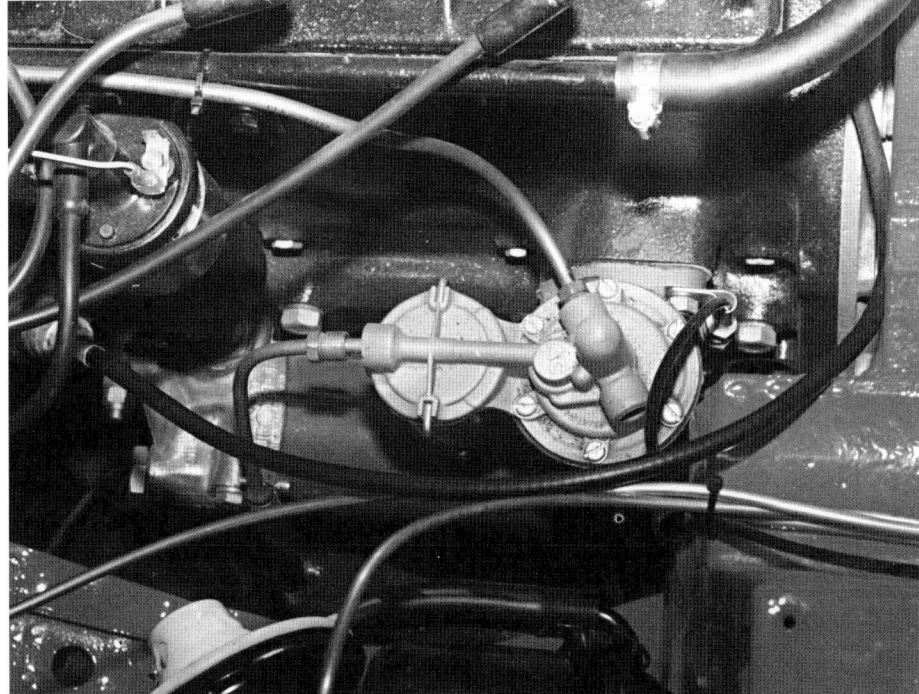

3-35. Hydraulics, fuel pipes and water hoses. At the bottom of the picture you can see the twin hydraulic pipes leading to and from the brake servo that was fitted to this '4. The fuel filter and pump are in the centre of this picture, with the inlet pipe on the left, while the feed to the carburettors exits the picture top left. The heater hose can be seen crossing the top of the picture.

3-33.

3-33 and 3-34 (above). The fascia and electrics in the course of refurbishment and reassembly to the dash/fascia. Although these pictures are of a TR250, I hope they convey the amount of electrical work you must anticipate even when you seem to be near the 'finishing line'.

3-36-1. An early TR4 seat.

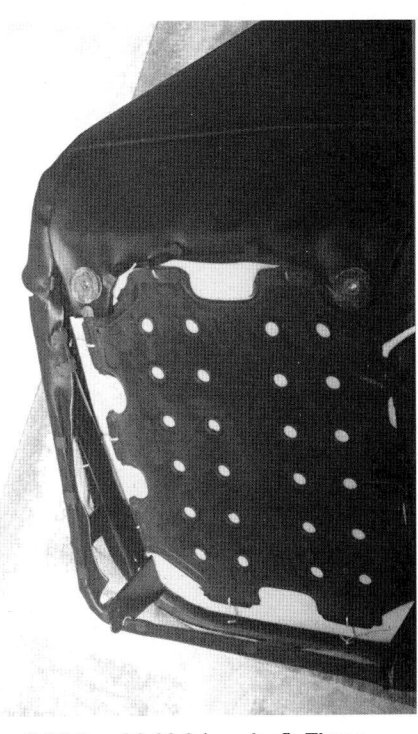

3-36-2 and 3-36-3 (overleaf). These photographs show a late TR4 seat (also used in the TR4A) and reveal the significant difference between the two types of construction.

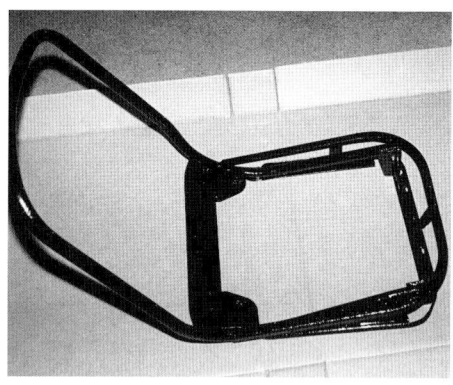

3-36-2.

calipers, which changed, during the course of TR production, from imperial to metric specification. It's not unknown for later calipers to have been fitted to an early car, while, conversely, early components have often been fitted to cars manufactured long after the changeover was concluded. It would be unwise, therefore, to assume that, just because your car is a TR4A, you will necessarily find imperial brake calipers fitted to it.

If you are not alert to such possibilities, you could, for example, find yourself ordering, and even fitting, the wrong brake pipes or manifold gasket. At best, such an eventuality will just be inconvenient, but it could have more serious consequences. Clearly, the year, model and commission number of your car are important factors in identifying precisely what spares you need, but be aware that, at some earlier date, availability or expediency may have changed the basis on which you should be ordering spare parts.

3-37. Trimming the car will take more time and patience than you might initially expect, particularly if you need to refurbish the seats. Chapter 16 will provide the details.

3-38. There are two hoods and hood frames on the cars we are studying. This is a TR4A frame but restoring and fitting both types of frame and hood are explored in chapter 17.

Chapter 4
Body restoration

This chapter may use some component names, for example 'scuttle', that you may not be familiar with. Drawing D4-1 may help to clarify the locations of these parts.

THE TR4 - TR4A DIFFERENCES

Since the TR4, TR4A, TR250 and TR5 are the same shape, it might be assumed that they share a common bodytub. However, as strange as it sounds, this is not quite true. To say we are studying three bodytubs would, on the other hand, be an exaggeration - but

there are more differences between the TR4, TR4A and the TR250/5 tubs than you might realise, certainly at first glance.

Triumph made a number of design changes to the body within the TR4 production run, and there were further alterations between the final '4s and the introduction of the '4A. Although not the focus of this book, for the record there were even more changes between the '4A and the subsequent TR250/5 design, although all the Michelotti cars look identical at first glance.

Many of the design changes during

'4 and '4A production were relatively unimportant, illustrated by the fact that the wings/fenders, boot/trunk, and the whole centre of the bodyshells are the same. This means that the floors, inner and outer sills, front door posts, door skins, etc., are interchangeable and are actually available new, although some hole positions may need to be altered. The new TR4/4A door skins are actually TR5, TR250 and TR6 parts, but need only minor changes to the door handle and lock holes.

TR4 and 4A door frames are also identical (but different to the later Michelotti models) but these are not available new, so, if yours are irrecoverable, you will need to buy secondhand ex-USA replacements.

The teardrop in the bonnet got progressively bigger during the course of production. TR4s up to about CT6430 have a relatively small one. It was then enlarged for the next 31,000 TR4s, and increased again for the final '4s and all the '4As.

The TR4's deck at the rear of the cockpit differs from that of the 4A. This is because the TR4 softtop was stored in the boot, so its frame needed minimal space in the car. The TR4A rear deck is shaped to accommodate the folded frame into the car's bodywork.

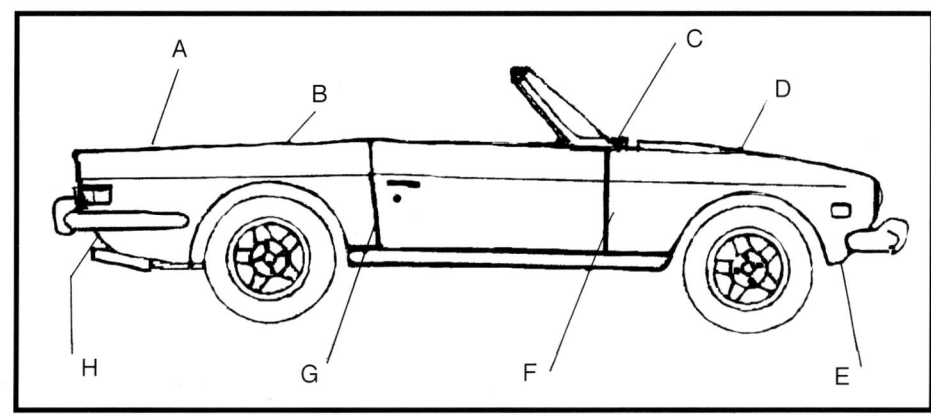

D4-1. Body panel terminology. A. Boot/trunk. B. Rear deck. C. Scuttle. D. Bonnet/hood. E. Front valance. F. 'A' post. G. 'B' post. H. Rear valance.

The other differences between the two cars include the rear wheelarches (more akin to the sidescreened cars than their, apparently, more related Michelotti-designed sisters), and the upper front valances and the respective sill fixings. Many of the Michelotti body panels are produced by original tooling and fit very well, but you should be aware that some crucial ones are made from replica/soft tools (notably the wings) and require considerable skill and patience to get to fit well. It is important, therefore, that those contemplating the purchase of a Michelotti-designed body are aware of this.

MINIMISING BODY REPAIR DIFFICULTIES

Not surprisingly, restoring the bodywork of a TR is not without its difficulties. Identifying those difficulties and the respective solutions is one reason why you purchased this book. I'm not dodging the issue, but, bodywork restoration on all but the TR6 is perhaps best avoided, or at least minimised, particularly if you have never restored a motorcar.

The TR6's replacement panels come largely from original tooling, and the 'fit' is significantly better than with earlier TR panels. This not only makes panel replacement much easier for the amateur/first time restorer, but the subsequent welding does not call for the super skills necessary when panels do not properly abut (fit) one another.

So what are the solutions if you have set your heart on a restoring a Michelotti-bodied TR? You can avoid or at least minimise the body restoration problem by buying a car or bodyshell that has dodged the 'tin-worm'. An ex-Californian car is unquestionably best, but any car that has spent all its first life in a genuinely warm climate has to be an infinitely better restoration prospect for the amateur restorer than a car where the body is little more than a latticework of rust. You will, of course, pay more for a good ex-Californian car, £2000 (possibly even £3000) more than a comparable UK car, but it's certainly worth it., Naturally, the US car must be straight, and it's essential you look closely at the chassis to ensure it has not received the 'cut-and-shut' treatment (two cars into one).

Attracted by a newly rebuilt engine

4-1. This is how you might expect to buy the rear 'half' of a TR body, in this case a TR4A. Note where the body has been cut in two, just in front of the propshaft tunnel. This means that much careful work is required to remove the old sills and floors before this back-end can go for shot blasting and be offered up to the refurbished chassis with its new floors pre-fitted. The same approach is used regardless of which model you are rebuilding.

within a UK 'unfinished restoration project' that has been advertised for sale? Don't be, at least not if the body is very rusty and funds dictate you will have to do the body restoration yourself. Mind you, there are still solutions for you to explore and cost.

Firstly, establish the availability and cost of buying a whole or even half (preferably the rear half) of a compatible ex-Californian body. They are becoming progressively harder to find, which is why you may be forced to seriously consider half a body, like that shown in photograph 4-1! The rear is the more difficult to restore and, if you cannot find a good complete car, the rear half should be your priority as an amateur/first-time restorer. Remembering the differences between the respective cars, do make sure that any ex-Californian shell or back half you contemplate will indeed be compatible with your

restoration project! Don't worry about its reconstruction into a complete car; I will have explained that in some detail before this chapter is finished.

The back-end of all the TRs is constructed from lots of small panels, most of which are available, but the complexity and opportunity for error for the inexperienced restorer is correspondingly large. If you are inspecting a prospective purchase be sure that the panel at the rear of the propshaft tunnel is sound. If this panel is badly rusted, and/or the rear wheelarches appear irreparable, there will, most likely, be nothing left of the rear of the car, and, even with the replacement panels that are available, its repair will challenge even a very skilled and experienced restorer. In this situation you would only be wise to proceed if you can first identify an ex-Californian rear half, or a complete shell. If you buy a complete Californian car or bodyshell you will find Chapter 18 tells you how to change the car to RHD. However, it's now time to address the restoration of the bodytub you have to hand!

BODY RESTORATION - THE 'RULES'

Regardless of which TR you are restoring, there are some golden rules that the amateur restorer really does need to follow:
- ALWAYS complete one side of the body at a time on any car. Perhaps the only exception to this advice is in respect to sorting both the doors out, which we will cover shortly, and aligning both doors with the windscreen. Thereafter it is definitely one side at a time.
- Whatever the car and whatever you do, do NOT strip everything off the car and then try and rebuild it from a giant jigsaw-like pile of parts. We will come to this in more detail later but, if you strip too much off the car you end up with few if any reference points to help you weld the car up in something like the correct shape! Your removals should be restricted to both doors, lights, chrome, trim, seats, door handles, hood-frame, dashboard, heater, wiring, fuel-tank, *etc.* However, do NOT take the windscreen or any body panels, wings, *etc.*, off (whatever their condition) until you know exactly what your restoration plan is.

- Do NOT make the frequently made mistake of sending the body for sandblasting too early in its restoration. I'll tell you when!
- Do NOT, on any account, imagine you can cover rusted base material with body-filler. You will, sooner or later, be very disappointed. Cut out all rusted steel and replace it properly.
- NEVER entertain, even for a moment, patching a steel panel with a fibreglass base. You will totally devalue your car. Personally, I would not want to buy a road-going TR that had been fitted with fibreglass bolt-on panels (bonnet, boot or wings, for example), but those intent on racing/rallying may actually prefer the lighter fibreglass panels. However, if you are restoring a road-going car, do consider the use of fibreglass panels very carefully, you may subsequently be limiting the number of enthusiasts interested in buying your car.
- All cars should ALWAYS be rebuilt around their doors. Always!
- It is very important to use a fixed datum point when measuring the car before disassembly and during re-assembly. Avoid using a corner or edge of a panel where possible. These can easily be bent, moved, and even removed during the restoration. Hopefully datum points such as the windscreen screw holes in the front bulkhead, the door hinge holes (even with a pointed threaded bolt inserted), the hinge holes on the rear deck, and/or the hood mounting holes, offer more consistent reference points. Obviously you are going to take your measurements on both sides of the shell, but be sure to also take the diagonal measurements too, in order to avoid misalignment.

There are some additional body restoration 'rules' that apply solely to the IRS cars. The live-axle/non-IRS/ladder chassis TR4 does not flex to the same degree as that of a TR4A (IRS) chassis. Consequently, you can quite happily rebuild a TR4's body on an empty chassis supported on axle stands. However, this is not so with the IRS cars, in that their bodies must be rebuilt on the chassis, and the chassis itself must be loaded and supported in a very specific manner.

The point is emphasised by the fact that IRS TRs have a major difference to almost any other classic sportscar you can think of. As corrosion sets in and

weakens the structure of most sportscars, including the non-IRS Triumphs, the centre of the shell sags. Hopefully, this occurs very slowly, but, nevertheless, as corrosion advances, most sportscars' door-gaps close-up, and eventually the doors become difficult to open. Unique to the IRS Triumphs (the 4A we are studying and also the 250, 5 and 6), it is the rear of the chassis that sags, opening each door aperture instead of closing it. The actual opening occurs between the rear door edge and the 'B' post, and is the result of the IRS car's rear suspension mounting point being a much further forward than the other sportscars that spring to mind. This all means that, when restoring an IRS car at home:

- It MUST be rebuilt on its final (solid) chassis.
- The chassis must be fitted with its suspension.
- The chassis should have the major (weighty) components fitted, or be represented by corresponding weights; paving stones, for example.
- The laden chassis should sit on its working suspension.
- The loads through the chassis should be in as near the normal places as is possible.

The last 'rule' has several solutions. The wheels could sit on four ramps to ensure the weight distribution is near normal. If you are very careful, from the safety viewpoint, you can use axle stands, positioned under the spring-pans at the front and towards the rear of the trailing arms at the back, to simulate the working suspension. You would then achieve your ends without the use of the wheels and tyres. You may, however, feel that these suggestions leave the chassis/body below a convenient working height. In this case, consider making up four stands that bolt to each of the four wheel-hubs. This will give you maximum and almost unrestricted access to the car, will load the chassis correctly, and position the car at a working height of your choosing. Personally, I would think it ideal if the sills stood a little over 40in (about 1 metre) off the ground, but everyone will have their own preference.

REBUILDING THE DOORS

So, you couldn't find a good ex-Californian body and need to rebuild

your own. We had better therefore face up to what needs to be done then, and, crucially, the best order to tackle the work.

We have already established that TR restorations should always revolve around the doors. The point when you should fit the doors will vary according to whether the body is to come off and whether it will be remarried to the chassis in one or more pieces. To ease us into the concept of rebuilding the body around the doors, we will first explore the ways you can rebuild or procure the doors you plan to use on the finished car - for this is your first priority.

This objective can be achieved, of course, by repairing the doors that came with the car. This solution will inevitably be your first choice and will at least involve reskinning the outside of the door. Unfortunately, it's also highly probable that the base of the door will require repair, or even replacement with a pressed 'repair' section (see photographs 4-2-1 to 4-2-17).

Although amateurs are best using a door-skinning tool, a very satisfactory reskinning job can be achieved with a flat 'dolly'.

4-2-1. Obviously, having taken all necessary safety precautions, the first step to restoring a TR door is to grind around the outside of the original door skin on the front, bottom and rear edges.

4-2-2. You know you are making progress when most of the turned-over lip starts to hang loose from the door frame.

4-2-5. It really is a good idea to keep everything until you are sure it can serve no further useful purpose. Here we see the old bottom pressing being compared to the newly repaired door bottom. It does look a significant improvement, although you may need to drill two water drain holes in the new bottom before skinning and painting the door.

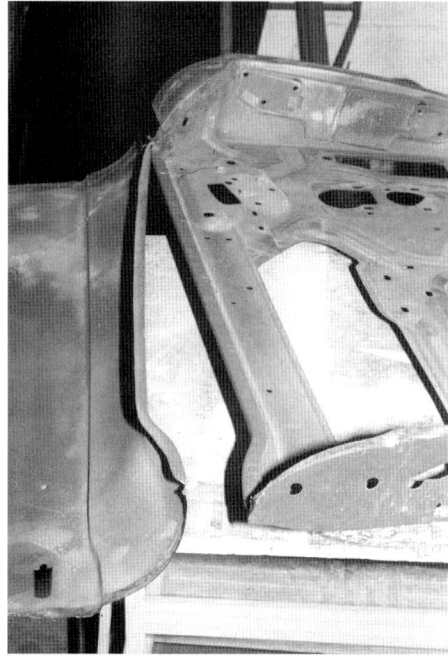

4-2-3. There will always be some local tack welds where things are not quite so easy, and you will need to give each weld some attention with your angle-grinder. In due course, however, you should be able to effortlessly fold the old skin back.

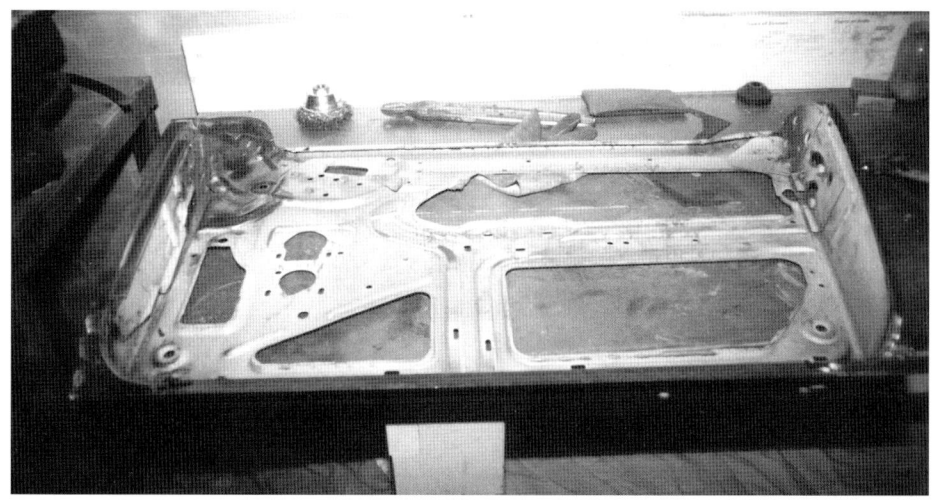

4-2-6. As we discovered in chapter 2, the door frames on our TRs are also prone to corrosion, and cracking at the top, too. Here is an example with both top corners showing signs of rust; the front corner (left of the picture) is in need of replacement.

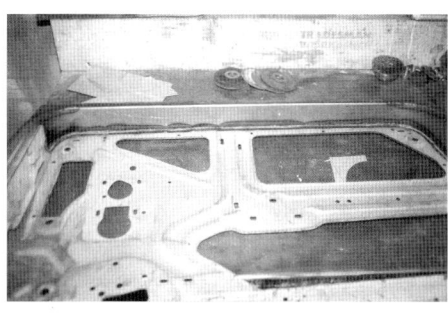

4-2-4. After the door skin, the base of a TR door is the most vulnerable to corrosion. There is little option but to cut out and replace the pressing with a new panel, as shown here.

4-2-7. It always looks worse before it improves. Note how the reference point of the hole almost central to the picture has been retained, along with the great majority of the edge references. A sizeable right-angled piece has been cut away to remove corroded material.

4-2-8. With excellent results, although the resultant repair piece was more complex than you may have first thought when you looked at picture 4-2-6!

It is imperative that you only consider welding the skin to the doorframe when the door has been offered up to the car. Reskinning opens up numerous opportunities for the amateur to twist the door so it's best to reskin the door and offer it to the car with the 'A' and 'B' posts and the sills in place. You will be able to reset the door and avoid the all-too-common TR door problem where the bottom corner sticks out. When fully satisfied, apply about three or four spot tacks across the new door skin to its frame while the door is still in place on the car. Some short, but more substantial, welds will be required but should only take place towards the end of your body restoration with the doors finally back on the car.

There is an alternative to repairing your doors. Most of the premier TR restoration specialists will have good quality rust free TR doors available for about £50-75. The cost varies from model to model, of course, and is bound to increase as the car in question gets older. Given the cost of a replacement, therefore, it is rarely worthwhile trying to repair your own door.

Do be careful, however, for you cannot assume that any component is fine just because the vendor tells you it came off a Californian or other warm-climate car. Firstly, the car may have spent the majority of its time in a more hostile climate and only reached California late in its life. Secondly, the best of the ex-warm climate cars and parts have largely been shipped and sold already. Not everything shipped in today is of poor quality, but you do need to see and carefully examine any replacements you plan to purchase.

With the doors sorted, it's time to look at the best sequence for repairing the bodytub, initially assuming it will be by the less daunting one-piece method. A review of the two-piece approach will, of course, follow.

ONE-PIECE BODY REPAIRS

The following repair sequence should take place with the bodyshell secured in place on its chassis.
1 - Refit the replacement or repaired doors to the body and line up the front door gap/alignment. Don't forget that every door will need space for its door seal to be fitted at a later date. Rest

4-2-9. With the frame repairs complete, it's time to take the first steps towards actually reskinning the door. The new skin will already have the protection of a factory-finished (black) primer, but it is important to provide the frame with as much protection as possible. First, prime the newly-repaired frame, inside and out, with the exception of the inside lips over which you will soon be folding your new door skin. Secondly, make quite sure that the frame's edges are completely free of all corrosion; an angle grinder and abrasive pad are the best method.

4-2-10. The inside edges need protection too, of course, but you will eventually be tack-welding the skin to its frame and, therefore, the paint needs to be of the 'weld-through' type shown here. Apply several coats and allow the primer to dry before offering the skin to the door.

4-2-11. The top of the door is very visible and also has to have enough room for the door glass and inner and outer seals to fit comfortably. The top corners of the skin, therefore, need to be (slightly) trimmed to fit and to provide a parallel gap down the length of the door's top. We were aiming for a gap of about 20mm.

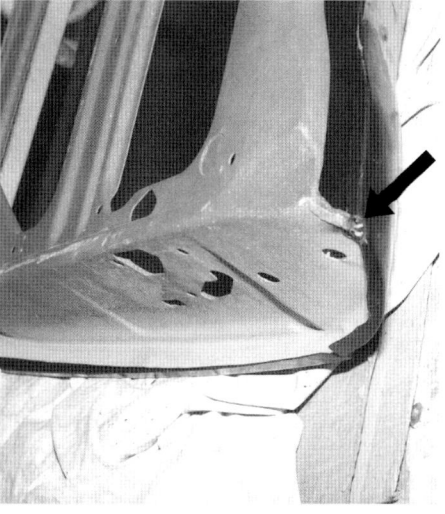

4-2-12. Once the correct height and gap have been achieved the very top corners of the skin are tacked front and rear to the frame. You can still see the skin is separated from the frame; this is most noticeable towards the bottom of the door. Note, too, the soft sheet between the door-skin and the workbench.

4-2-13. The next step is to lightly fold the four corners of the skin onto its frame using, in this case, a hammer and a plenishing dolly. Note that the dolly is held tight to the outer face of the skin to prevent the skin's edge from bulging (slightly) away from the frame as the skin is turned over.

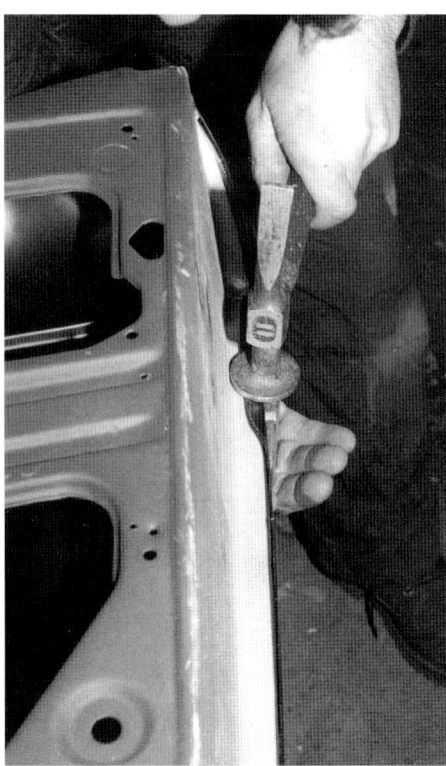

4-2-15. Starting at the top of each side, work town the depth of the door. Run down the full length of the edge you are working on, turning the lip half-way, three-quarterway and then fully.

4-2-17. When all the lips of the skin are turned over, go right round the skin ensuring the 'clinch' of the skin is tight onto the frame, but do not weld anything until you have offered the completed door to the car. The chances are very high that you'll have to twist the door to get it to sit nicely along the original sill and wing panels. Only then should you consider applying a few tack welds (with the door still in place on the car) to hold the new skin to its frame. You should reserve the final door welding until you are fully satisfied with the panel/sill/door alignment on that side of the car.

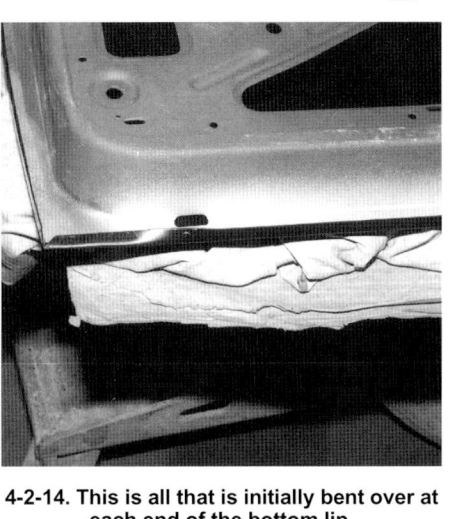

4-2-14. This is all that is initially bent over at each end of the bottom lip.

assured, there are those who get their cars finish-painted and then find they can't close the door with the door-seals in place. Mind you, the situation is not helped by the fact that the door seals you buy today are fractionally larger than the originals. I suggest you use a few short lengths of the latest door seal

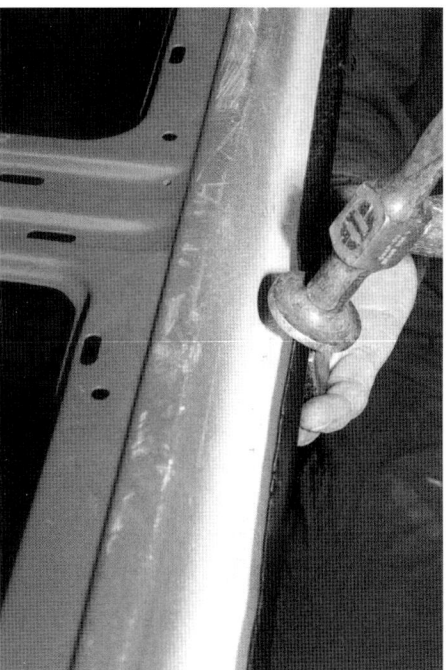

4-2-16. Finally, follow the same procedure along the bottom lip - here we are progressing the half-turned lip into a three-quarter fold.

section as spacers to ensure the doors will close before you progress too far, and certainly well before you even think about painting! As far as is possible, position the door hinges in the centre of their adjustment slots to allow for some subsequent fine-tuning.

2 - Although it sounds premature, you really need to check the reference/relationship of window-glass to the windscreen. If you have followed my earlier advice you will not have removed the windscreen, but, if you inherited a car with its screen in the boot, re-fit the windscreen frame at this point. Refit the widows to both new or rebuilt doors. A small degree of error in the way the door hangs can dramatically affect the way the drop-glass/sidescreen marries up to the screen. Clearly there is some

adjustment in the windscreen's position and this needs to be finalised along with the door position while maintaining your front door gap. Carefully mark the door hinges (perhaps with a light Junior-hacksaw line), so that each time you replace a door on its 'A' post it goes back in the same place. This is important and should be an oft-repeated check you should make as every panel in or around the door (e.g., 'A' posts and/or sections of the bulkhead) is finalised, so do not be in too much of a hurry to remove the windscreen frame.

As an aside, but in the context of welding and grinding in the vicinity of any piece of glass, do ensure the glass is masked over to prevent weld splatter or grinding debris pock-marking it. This happens with amazing speed and, in the case of grinding, from an amazing distance, and can totally ruin a good piece of glass in seconds.

3 - Ensure you are happy with the position of the body on the chassis. For example, if the rear chassis/body spacers need increasing or decreasing, carry out the necessary adjustments. With an IRS car the chassis may have drooped over the years, and if you have not already corrected the fault, you will need to do so before chassis and body are finally reassembled. Now is the moment to adjust the spacers to achieve the door gaps you expect, even if the body has yet to be removed from its chassis. With the door gaps to your satisfaction, securely cross-brace the body across the inside of the door frames ('A' post to 'B' post). The door-brace method you choose will affect on the ease with which you have access to the shell, and how easily the doors can be offered up to the door aperture. Several alternative methods are explored throughout the book, and a very simple one is shown in photograph 4-3.

4 - There are very few details within the restoration of a TR that are 'right' or 'wrong'. Opinions and sequences vary. For example, many one-piece restorations have been carried out on the basis of changing the floors after the sills have been replaced. Indeed, some of the photographs supporting this chapter will confirm this. However, assuming the floors and sills are to be replaced, many would argue that this is the time to cut one floor out and replace it, and then cut out that same side's sill and replace it. Whichever sequence you

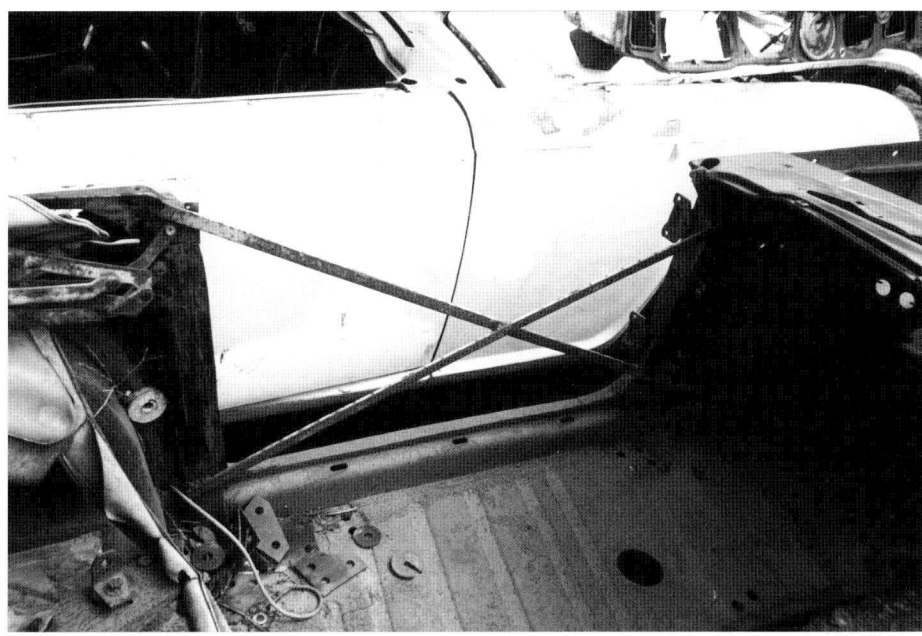

4-3. Crossbracing the door aperture. This is probably the most common way of achieving the essential rigidity of the body before removing it from the chassis. There are several other alternatives illustrated and described in this book, one of which can be seen in photograph 4-4-1.

4-4-1. Time to take a close look at the right side 'B' post on a Michelotti bodytub. This picture is well out of sequence but is included because it gives an overview of the great deal of work required, whilst reminding us of the need to tie everything up with the door braces.

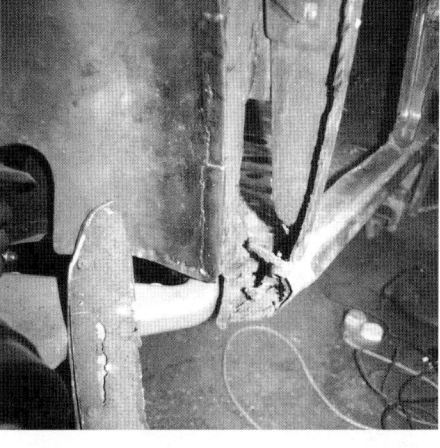

4-4-2. The situation, as is often the case, looks even worse as we strip the corroded metal away searching for solid material from which to start.

decide is best for your restoration project, try hard to leave the doors in place for as long as possible. However, since this is not always practical to do, you should offer the door back up to the car at frequent intervals. Clearly, the point of retaining the door in place is to ensure the sills are tacked in place with a nice parallel gap between the bottom of the door and the sill.

5 - After the floor and sill comes the 'B' post. Again, close reference to the door

gaps and adjacent panels is vital. There is nothing to stop you temporarily tacking the 'B' post to its door, and you can even tack a couple of temporary panel off-cuts (say, about 3in/75mm square) across the door and 'B' post gap. This will hold the various angles in place until the 'B' post's adjacent panels have in turn been affixed. An overview of a typical 'B' post repair will be found in the photographic sequence 4-4-1 to 4-4-10.

4-4-3. This is starting to look like one of those jobs that are best not started in the first place! However, this example has not corroded too far back from the outer edge. Note that the 'B' post reference position is retained by the (rotten) sill and the door brace. Even if the 'B' post were in need of replacement, I suggest it be left in place until other references are established.

4-4-5. Having served as an essential reference, it's now time to take out the completely rotten sill.

4-4-8. This shot gives an excellent overall picture of the nearly completed repair.

4-4-6. Time to concentrate on the 'B' post repairs, after getting the sill in place to give something to build from.

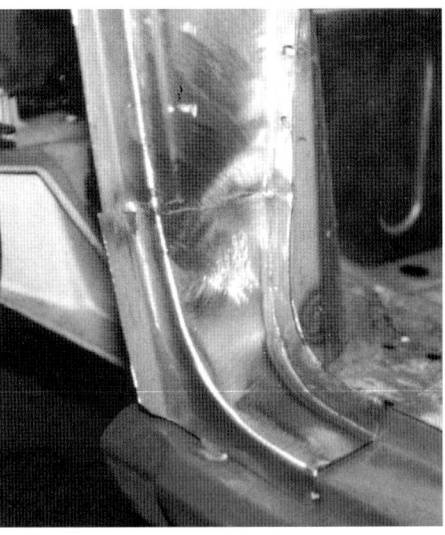

4-4-9. The final pressing is tacked in place. We would, of course, have checked the door gaps long before now, but this is the last opportunity to ensure the door fits its aperture correctly before the final right side 'B' post welding takes place.

4-4-7. Step two inside the 'B' post.

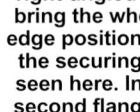
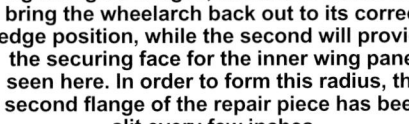

4-4-4. One step at a time: a piece of mild steel has been folded up to provide two right-angled flanges, the first of which will bring the wheelarch back out to its correct edge position, while the second will provide the securing face for the inner wing panel seen here. In order to form this radius, the second flange of the repair piece has been slit every few inches.

6 - Then it's the turn of the 'A' post on the same side of the car. A typical photographic sequence is at 4-5-1 to 4-5-10.

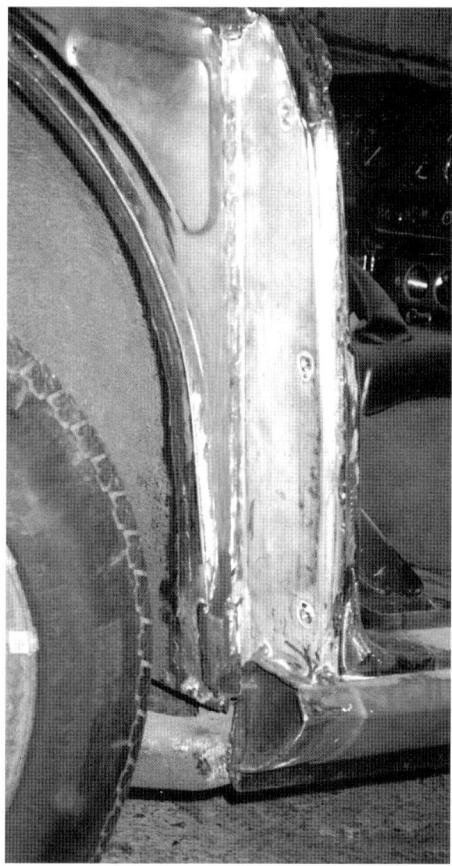

4-4-10. The right side 'B' post fully welded with, you will note, the three wing mounting captive nuts in place.

4-5-1. Staying on the right side of the car, we take a look at the 'A' post. The outer footwell panel does not look too bad in this shot, though, from the liberal application of weld, I would guess it has been repaired before.

4-5-2. A shot from the inside confirms all is far from well!

4-5-3. The first step in the repair is to cut out all rusted metal where our repair will be, whilst leaving as many local reference panels in place as is possible. Note that the floors are still in place to provide references for the sills - although they clearly will have to come right out before this side of the car can be considered restored. However, there was no choice but to remove the sills, the bottom of the 'A' post, and the bottom of the outer footwell panel. In fact, the jury is still out on the top of the outer footwell panel, but it is best left in place for the time being to provide a reference for the 'A' post.

4-5-4. The next step is to fit the sills, and here we see the first reconstructive step for the 'A' post base.

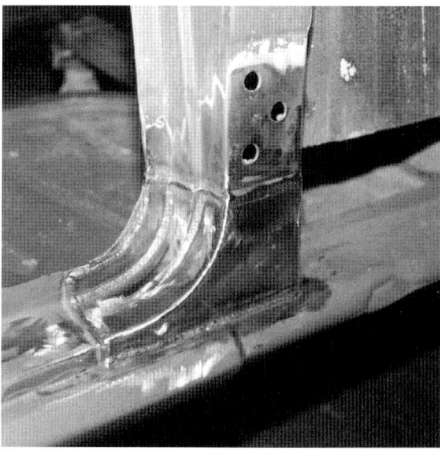

4-5-5. Still following the one-step-at-a-time approach, replace the outer 'A' post base, which securely ties this side 'A' post to its sill.

4-5-6. In fact, the outer footwell panel was thought unacceptable and removed. This picture shows how right the restorer was! I imagine the owner gave a little thought to also replacing the panel that forms the base of the footwell. It can just be seen on the right of this picture. A great deal of work is required to remove this particular panel, with much welding thereafter, so unless the corrosion is dire, edge repairs are usually favourite.

4-5-7. The alternative scenario (picture taken from another car) is that the outer footwell panel can be satisfactorily repaired, in which case the next step would look like this!

4-5-8. By either route, the repaired 'A' post, footwell and sill should look something like this.

4-5-9. The bottom lip (arrowed) on the footwell's front panel has had to be replaced to give the new floor something to weld to. It's far from obvious, but it looks as if the lip and the floor have, in fact, been plug welded already, effecting a very nice repair. I mentioned earlier that this panel is very difficult to repair and that edge repairs, such as we see here, are favourite.

TWO-PIECE BODY SEQUENCE

Note: this sequence is only applicable if you are to replace the floors and sills/ rockers, and/or fit a replacement 'half' body to repair accident damage or a badly corroded half body.

1 - If the bodyshell has not already been cut into two halves, separating the front from the rear should be your first step. The initial cut line is very important. A single straight line right across the tub, just in front of the propshaft tunnel, is the simplest way of establishing your division and getting both body-halves off the chassis. The rear of the body will look something like that shown in

4-5-10. The reasons and details appear in the main text, but this is the recommended revised drain for the plenum chamber that passes an extended tube down through the top of the outer sill and out through the inside of the inner sill. This would be a logical time to effect the changes and to finalise the front right side.

photograph 4-1. Be sure to clear the body mounting bolt positions (photographs 4-6 and 4-7).

2 - Clean up both halves of the shell where the floors and sill join each half. All traces of the old panels need to be zip-cut or drilled off, and the remaining panels ground flat and clean awaiting eventual marriage to new panels.

3 - Bolt the new floors to the chassis, as shown in photograph 3-17, and then hang the front and back halves loosely on the chassis, as illustrated by photographs 3-18 and 3-19 respectively. Remembering our initial purchasing checks, ensure that the general shape of your body is starting to look 'fish-like'.

4 - Fit the doors (not old or scrap ones) to the 'A' pillar and carefully set the front door gaps to the front half of the car and front wings. The next step is to jack the 'A' pillar/doors forward and upward until the bottoms of the doors line up with the

4-6.

4-6 and 4-7 (above). These pictures do not tell us what the full restoration plan is to be, but this IRS car is clearly having some major body restoration carried out. We can see the floor and both parts of the sill have been cut out, revealing in photograph 4-7 the left side trailing arm suspension. From these views the chassis does not look too severely corroded, although the body mounting point, visible just forward of the 'B' post, will not be adequate even to secure the floors for the short while necessary were this a 'body-off after repair' restoration plan. Shortly, we will see this may not be the plan at all!

inner sills, and the door glass lines up with the screen frame. At this point a few light tack-welds might be used to join the front of the body to the floors before you re-check both sides for the fish shape.

5 - It's now the turn of the rear half of the body: move it towards the doors to create the correct equal and parallel door gaps. Some sideways or even twisting movement of the rear half may be required to get things properly aligned. Then it's time for some more light tack welding and more checking.

6 - Offer an outer sill to the car and move it backwards and forwards, up and down, until it is perfect. Tack it in place. Repeat for the other side of the car.

7 - Weld or bolt your door gap cross-braces in place. One of several examples is shown in photograph 4-3. Weld the floors and sills to the front and rear halves of the original body.

8 - You can temporarily weld a couple of panel off-cuts to keep the doors aligned with the 'B' posts, once the 'B' posts are to your satisfaction, of course. Photographs 4-4-1 to 4-4-10 illustrate a typical sequence.

9 - Then it is the turn of the 'A' post on the same side of the car. Photographs 4-5-1 to 4-5-10 show a typical sequence.

10 - Repeat the 'A' and 'B' post repairs on the other side of the car.

PROGRESSING THE RESTORATION

There will still be hours of inner tub repairs to carry out. Photographs 4-8 to 4-16 and their associated text explain how you can expect to progress around the main bodytub. Hopefully, the detailed sequence of pictures and captions numbered 4-17-1 to 4-17-19 will help not only with the considerable work that can be required on some cars, across the bulkhead/firewall, but also how to progress one panel at a time, whilst retaining as many reference points as possible.

Then there are the bolt-on panels to cope with (the wings/fenders, boot/trunk and bonnet/hood). Photographs 4-18-1 to 4-18-5 and their captions have been included to illustrate many of the loose panel repair problems and solutions.

Don't forget to tackle just one side of the car at a time, as far as this is

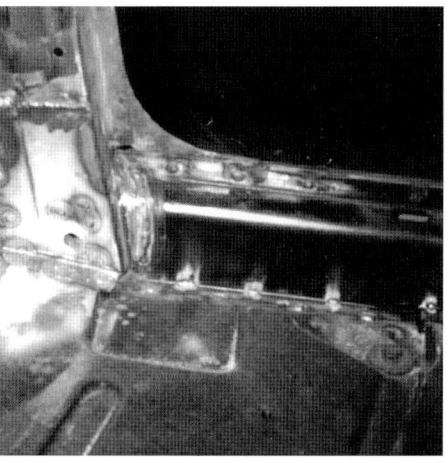

4-8. Here we see the new left-side floor in place. The rear inner-wing has an excellently executed small repair to the bottom of the 'B' post, and the new inner sill shows up well. Note the plug-welds in place along the top lip of the sill and the tack welds along its join with the new floors and the original inner wing. The next step will be to seam weld the wheelarch to the floor, although it may be prudent to carry out this operation as intermittent stitch welds until the weld becomes one long seam. The sill may need spot welding. The bolt head we can see in the lower right of this picture goes down into the chassis mounting bracket that was in need of repair in an earlier shot.

4-9. This is typical of the sort of rear inner wing/fender repair you can expect to have to carry out. A spot welder has been used here but plug welds will be perfectly satisfactory in any home restoration.

4-10. New inner and outer sills, inner wing and floor repairs completed for this side.

4-11. The left side of a TR5/250 showing the sill and some excellent repairs replacing the 'B' post back and inner wing. Primer was applied a short time later and the re-skinned door re-hung. You can't offer up the door(s) too frequently when working in this area, which is why I prefer door braces that permit the re-hanging of the door without their removal. I think I can see a flattening of this sill's convex curvature just under the centre of the door in this picture. If so, this will have been caused by either too localised jacking of the sill to reduce the bow, or over-enthusiastic jacking, even with a length of stout timber in place under the sill.

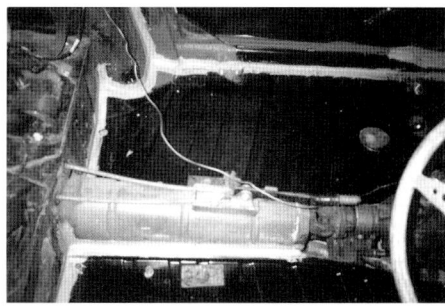

4-12. The new inner and outer sills and the new floor. Once the welding was complete, the raw metal was primed before applying seam sealer. This picture also highlights a couple of interesting points. Firstly, you should prime the inside of both halves of each sill before fitting the outer - see the main text. Secondly, the bracket to the rear of the handbrake can pinch inwards, in which case it requires adjustment, or a strengthening bracket fitted. This one's correct, which means that the pressing has either been readjusted or was never a problem on this car.

4-13. You should prime all surfaces, even those that are to be welded. Faces that are to be welded, however, require a weldable paint, such as that shown here. When painting the inside of your sills, you should generously coat the whole of the inside with this primer, twice. Once the primer is dry, mask off the lips that will be welded and coat the major inside areas with something like Hammerite.

4-15. New left side inner wing, lamp housing and a new rear valance. Watch that you fit the lamp housings inside the inner wing as shown here and in 4-16. They're all too frequently welded to the outside of the inner wing. Such a mistake has a surprisingly bad effect on the subsequent fit of the wing/fender. Note the circular hole for the reverse/back-up lights.

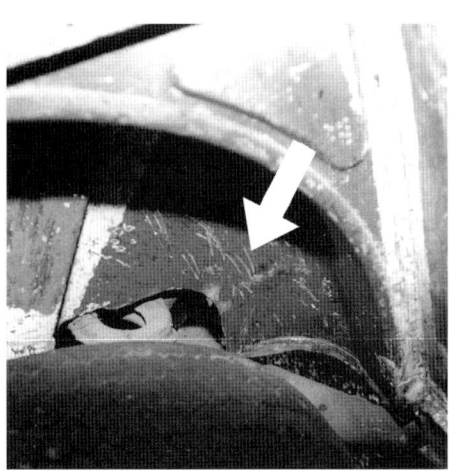

4-14. The good news is that this TR4A has not had a shunt up the rear since there are no creases in the inner wing. The vulnerable area is arrowed. The slight 'cutout' above the rear crossmember is part of the IRS car's design.

practical, and remember to keep offering-up the adjacent opening panels (e.g. boot/trunk lid, doors, etc.), where relevant.

4-16. The new valance will not come with the two rectangular bumper iron holes in place, so you'll need to follow this example and not only cut the holes but cut them smaller than the size you need. You then need to form the strengthening lip you see here right round each hole. Note the rubber boot seal in place (temporarily), to ensure the boot/trunk lid closes properly and retains the line of the car.

In this review we started by establishing the relationship with the door/glass/windscreen, and step by step we have carried that relationship on to each successive panel. This approach is mainly to ensure that the reference points are retained, and that you do not start building in errors.

If you are unfortunate enough to have inherited a giant pile of bits, start by fixing the front bulkhead to the chassis, and, even if the 'A' posts are to be replaced, hang both doors to get some orientation. Tack the bulkhead in place even if you subsequently intend replacing some sections within it, and you may even tack the doors (with the appropriate door/sill gaps) to their respective sills.

However, assuming most readers will avoid the 'pile-of-bits' syndrome, do take lots of little steps. Prior to fitting every new panel, take off the very minimum of old body each time in order to retain the maximum of reference measurements. Your difficulties will be increased by the poor fit of some reproduction panels, which only reinforces the importance of progressing your car one panel at a time.

One solution to the problem of ill fitting panels is to either weld a small extension to the edge (to the rear lip of a

4-17-1. This sequence is intended to illustrate not only how to replace a battery-box, but also to emphasise the importance of tackling one panel at a time when setting out on a bodytub restoration. You will not succeed if you tear every rusted panel in sight off the car, and then try to start from a 'jigsaw'. Therefore, the following sequence ignores the fact that the next panel is corroded and will have to be replaced, after it has been used as a reference point and got the preceding panel accurately in place. This picture shows that we have several related panels to sort in addition to the battery box!

4-17-2. This view from the underside shows we clearly have to replace or repair the plenum chamber too. It runs across and below the front scuttle behind the battery box.

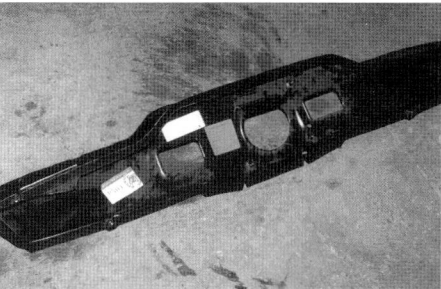

4-17-3. It's possible to buy new plenum pressings, which is definitely the way to go when the corrosion is as extensive as that shown in picture 4-17-2.

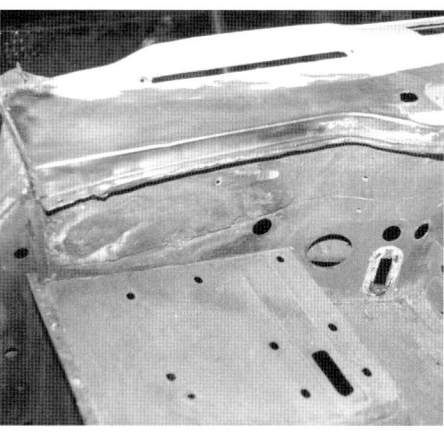

4-17-4. From photograph 4-17-1 it is clear that the right side inner wing has to be replaced. You cannot see from this shot, but the plenum has also been carefully removed. We have also cleaned up the top of the footwell and the bulkhead/firewall and found them corroded.

4-17-5. Note that only a part of the bulkhead/firewall is has been removed. Note, too, that panel distortion has been kept to a minimum by drilling out the spot welds so that even when off the car, the panel (it is parked on top of the scuttle for a while) can be used for reference if required. You can now see that the plenum is missing!

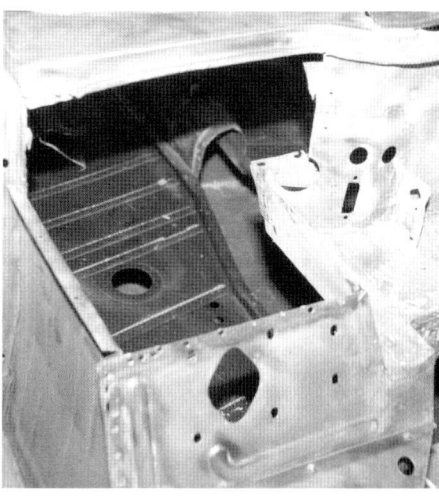

4-17-6. This really is as far as panel removal should go before some 'references' are re-established. Note how the carefully drilled spot welds have eased removal of the corroded footwell top.

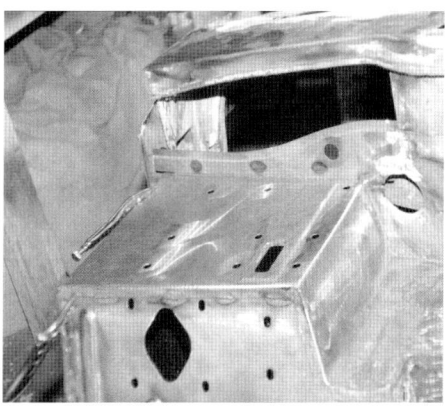

4-17-7. Time to re-establish some references with the top of the footwell and part of the bulkhead/firewall in place, even though we may yet remove the next panel!

4-17-8. Still reconstructing the top of the bulkhead/firewall.

4-17-9. Time to replace the inner wing we removed a few pictures ago, to fix some minor panel edges and remove a corroded corner of the scuttle ...

4-17-12. ... and the rotten panel removed; carefully, so as not to distort the mating panels.

4-17-15. Time to clean-up the plug welds (to get them flush with the panel surfaces - as spot welds would be), panel edges, and any final welding that the wire-brushing and grinding reveals.

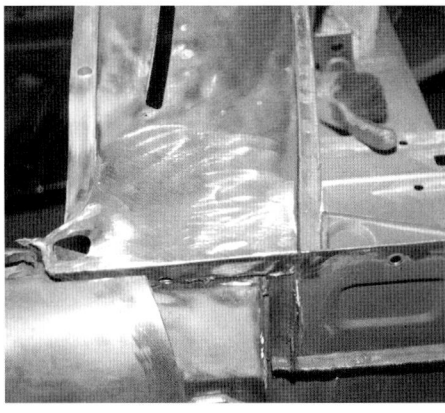

4-17-10. ... and to repair the metal around the windscreen mounts.

4-17-13. Two steps in one picture. We have fitted and welded the battery box (supplied by TR Bitz) and moved on to the next phase of corroded metal removal - the other part of the bulkhead/firewall. It was not absolutely essential as this point, but the left side inner wing has also been removed.

4-17-16. We can just see that the left side inner wing has been fitted, but we still have the left side windscreen mounting to tidy up.

4-17-11. We're getting to the battery box now; note how the spot welds have been drilled out right round the whole panel ...

4-17-14. The replacement bulkhead/firewall looks good. Note that the wiper rack panel looks as if it was transposed from the old panel.

4-17-17. Which, unfortunately, reveals a very corroded part of the scuttle that had to be cut out. However, we can see that the new plenum pressing has been welded in place after being sealed along its bottom joint with Sikoflex and painted.

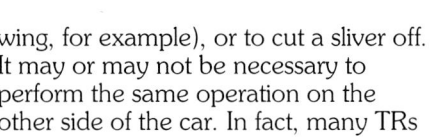

wing, for example), or to cut a sliver off. It may or may not be necessary to perform the same operation on the other side of the car. In fact, many TRs are happily driving round with slight differences from one side of the car to the other. The differences are undetectable to the eye and of no

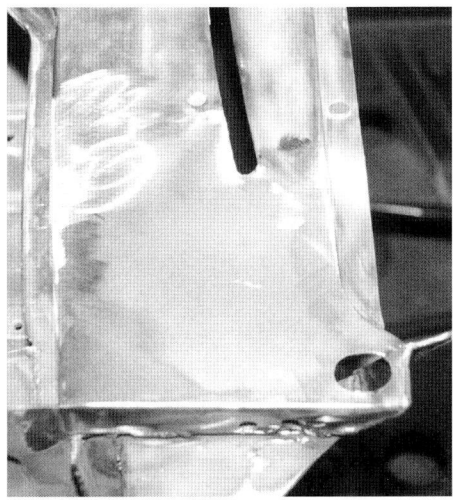

4-17-18. The repair section has front and side lips to fold and weld, as well as rear curves to form, so this was not a five minute job.

when using the chassis as a jig. Most panels on the bulkhead are more or less flat and can be formed up at home. The inner wings can be purchased if need be, although in the majority of cases it's only the edge of the inner wing that is really rotten, and you can make a single curved replacement strip at home without too much difficulty. Most home restorers cope with frontal repairs provided they frequently offer-up the bonnet/hood and make the rear edge of the bonnet and front lip of the bulkhead their datum/reference point. Use the bonnet that you are going to fit as the yardstick for positioning the inner and outer front wings.

If the 'A' posts need repair, then this is the moment to do it, ensuring that you do not distort the existing door hinge positions. Before finally welding your tacked repair (or indeed your

discover a major problem only after painting, often because they lost reference points quite early in the refurbishment of the body.

ADDITIONAL DETAILS

- The removal of each old panel needs to carried out carefully. It may add to the time it takes you but it's better to drill-out each spot weld before trying to force the old panel off the car - particularly if the next-door panel is weakened by corrosion, but, nevertheless, is important from a reference point of view. You can use a 'Zip-cutter' to cut round each spot-weld on the panel nearest to you if you do not want to drill right through a spot-weld. However I must say I have always found a 10mm diameter drill with a flatish cutting angle (say 130 degrees) preferable to a zip-cutter.
- Almost without exception the panels are best initially held in place with a few pop rivets or self-tapping screws, whereupon the panel fit is best checked again. A small amount of tack welding might then be in order, but only after several adjacent panels are definitely fitting well and the most adjacent opening panel, say the boot/trunk lid, have been tried in place. Only then do you get a bit more enthusiastic with the welding torch.
- Remember the old maxim - 'if you can't clean it, don't weld it'. In other words, all panel edges that require welding must be cleaned to bright steel. - both sides. No rust, grease or paint is acceptable. After the initial light tacking and rechecking the fit of the other panels, progress the welding very carefully and evenly around the area you are working on.
- Welding is a gradual process. Do not lay too many welds down too soon. Dodge from left half to right half, front to back, progressively increasing the welding roughly equally all around the panel in order to avoid excessive cooling in one area which can pull your panel fit out of alignment. With the tacking completed to your satisfaction remove the temporary rivets/self-tapers and complete the welding, still remembering to 'dodge-about', to avoid laying too much weld too quickly in one area.
- Slide the floors in from the back if you are having trouble getting the new floor panels into the shell.
- When you remove the old floor the

4-17-19. An overview of the finished inner wings, bulkhead, battery box and plenum area.

consequence. A slight film of body-filler will provide the perfect base for subsequent painting.

The front end is much easier to restore than the rear because there are fewer panels to handle and less potential for error. Basically, the front consists of a pair of inner wings with a pair of triangulated panels at the bottom. Bulkhead repairs are not too difficult either. The floors and doors will help you align bulkhead repairs, particularly

replacement 'A' posts), do (yet again!) offer the doors back up to the car to check that the sill-to-door gap and the glass-to-screen fit remain satisfactory. I know I am repeating myself here, but it is extremely important to keep as many reference points as possible in place while you progress. This will prevent the scenario whereby you get to the end of your rebuild only to find, for example, that you cannot shut the doors with the windows up. Some home restorers even

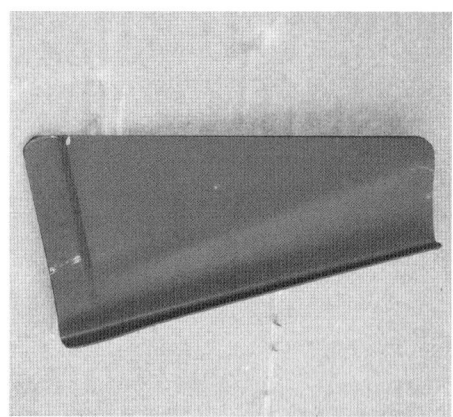

4-18-1. We need to regularly offer up the bonnet as we move towards repairing the front of the car, so it's time to take a look at what might be involved in refurbishing a TR4/4A bonnet/hood. A strengthening edge-piece for the top outside corners of Michelotti bonnets/hoods, is available from Revington TR. This may well be the most frequent repair required as part of a bonnet/hood restoration, but it is far from the only problem you may encounter.

4-18-2. This bonnet is corroded towards the rear edge, to the extent that a repair section is required. The size and shape of the new piece has been carefully marked out ...

4-18-3 ... and cut out. Remember to allow plenty of extra material for the rear lip when cutting the replacement!

4-18-4. In some circumstances you can overlap panels that are to be joined and then plug, seam or spot weld the parts together. However, when both sides of the joint is frequently seen (as would be the case with a bonnet), these methods of joining panels become unacceptable. In such cases it is vital that the repair 'patch' is restrained absolutely flush with the original panel and butt welded. These 'Intergrip' clamps are available from Frost Auto Restoration Techniques. They pass a thin piece of material through the two parts requiring butt-welding. A small piece of rod holds both panels flush with each other on this side of the joint, while the clever arrangement for exerting the clamping pressure from the other side can be seen in picture 4-20-2. Obviously, the clamps should be removed once about 50% of the joint has been welded.

not find perfect examples. Even the best have a slight droop in the centre which must be corrected upon assembly to the car. Fortunately, the task is not too difficult, but necessitates having a long straight piece of stout timber handy. Before you actually start to fit either sill/rocker you should rust-proof the inside of both inner and outer sill by degreasing the inside faces and lips and applying a weldable zinc rich paint. Anything that provides a 99% zinc film will probably be great, but 'Metaflex Zink' or 'U-Pol Weld No. 2' (photograph 4-13) will certainly protect the inside of the sills. You will, obviously, help the long-term preservation of the sills if you apply several coats, in line with the

major component holding the 'A' post up in the correct position is gone, and the 'A' post will drop, and it will drop substantially. It may also move out slightly if unrestrained. You should place a piece of wood under the bottom of the door and jack it up to re-establish the correct position of the 'A' post. A trolley-jack might seem ideal for this job, but don't forget that a hydraulic jack has a tendency to sink over several hours so if you need to retain the position for a while then a screw-jack may be best. The 'A' posts do seem to have a mind of

their own, however, for, regardless how hard you try to avoid it, they will drop. I suggest you weld them, say $1/8$in higher than you think you need, and certainly never on the low side.

● Unfortunately, all sills/rockers come with a slight bow in them. Ask your preferred TR specialist about the quality of their sills, remembering that you will

manufacturer's instructions. The subsequent welding operations to the lip will, of course, burn much of that paint off, but you will be left with at least 50% of the lip protected.

You should then apply a rust inhibiting gloss paint to just the inner faces (omit the lips) of the sills. The longer this is left to dry the better! Jack

4-18-5. The patch can still be seen, but a thin skim of filler will make this repair quite invisible once sprayed.

4-19. We need the back of the car pretty much complete before we can carry out the process of fitting, adjusting and refitting required to get a boot/trunk lid to fit. This picture is included for two additional interesting reasons: firstly, to demonstrate that great care is needed when replacing the rear deck, for the new panel is not as comprehensive a replacement as it might appear. The strengthening panel beneath the rear lip (arrowed) is not included in any new panel you buy, so you'll need to carefully zip-cut the spot welds away to salvage the strengthening panel. Mind you, I don't believe you would be the first to elect to leave the whole of a good rear 'U' channel in place and to shave a little off the back of the new rear deck to compensate! The second unusual feature is the 'rivnuts' along the underside of the front raised lip of this rear deck. Normal 'Surrey top' cars have plain holes in these locations, but it is common practice to fit rivnuts for cars that are converting to softtop. If the car was going from softtop to 'Surrey', one would drill the rivnuts out, so, it's a good bet that this car left the factory with a Surrey top!

the wood/sill upwards until the bottom of the sill is in line with the door - but not to the extent that the sill's outer shape starts to dish inwards - and clamp with mole or panel grips. Photograph 4-11 shows the dishing that can occur with over-enthusiastic jacking. Weld, check, remove the timber, check and weld some more.

Your sill ends may be too big, and you should have no hesitation in grinding off any excess. Remember that you will subsequently have to get your wings over the sill ends so any oversized or 'fat' sills will make fitting the wing very difficult.

- If you have screwed-up the door-glass to screen alignment, you can get your local motor-glass/windscreen company to cut (to your pattern) a pair of laminated window glasses. The original glass is flat, so a laminated replacement is feasible, but expensive. However, this solution is for use only in desperate circumstances, since you will lose the facility to smash the glass in order to make an emergency exit from the car.

- Underneath the rear body mounts there are aluminium spacers. With the IRS cars, you can vary the number to suit the door gaps, and up to three shims is fine. If you find you need more shims, say five or six, your chassis is hogged as was described earlier, and, while your door gaps may be exemplary, you will have great difficulty in fitting the rear bumper when the time comes!

This need not concern you if the body has to come off the chassis for painting. If, however, that step is not part of your restoration plan, the solution is difficult, but worthwhile in the long run. You must support the body while you do the following. Remove all the spacers (but not the rubber pads). Cut all but the top flange of both rear chassis legs about 50in (1259mm) in front of the rear of the car. With the chassis more easily moved, jack the chassis until it is again supporting the body and the door gaps are correct. Reweld the chassis and, just when you feel sure you have everything aligned perfectly, watch everything drop when you remove the support! Now you understand why all the spacers were removed, for now you need to re-jack the body until the door gaps are once again to your satisfaction, insert the

4-20-1. The bottom lip of the Michelotti boot/trunk lid is a well known corrosion spot and usually necessitates cutting the rotten section away. This lid is not too bad for we can still see the bottom return lip; many are rusted away or have been replaced by body-filler! New Michelotti boot-lids are available, but it's probably best to replace the bottom lip on your panel if that's all that is wrong. If you need to go to the lengths shown in this sequence of pictures to correct your boot lid, you may be wise to at least try a new lid in situ before deciding to embark on this exercise.

4-20-2. Here we can see that the lower 2in of skin has been removed, along, of course, with the return lip. A replacement piece has been prepared (note the regular curvature and lock hole) allowing sufficient material for the return lip to be turned over in due course. The replacement bottom has been butt clamped (as explained in photograph 4-18-4). The first welding stage is to butt weld about 50% of the new repair section to the original skin, taking care not to concentrate the heat, then remove the clamps, finish off the welding and dress both sides of the weld.

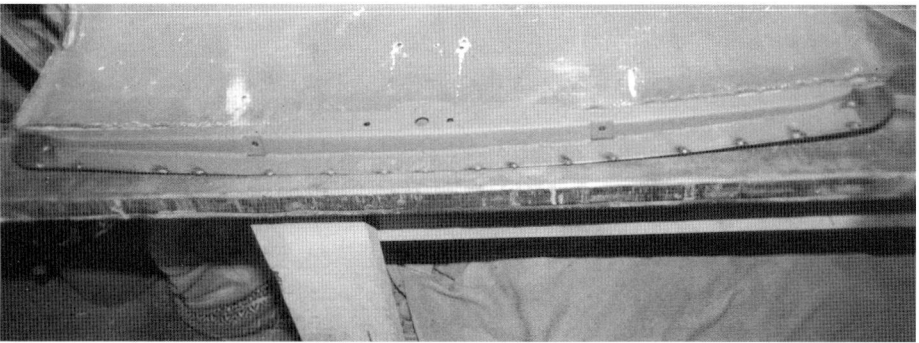

4-20-3. Next, we need to tack the bottom pressing in place. Obviously, it's essential to align the inner and skin lock/handle holes. As mentioned in the main text, it's possible to open the Michelotti boot lids without a key. You should put a (non-original, of course), packer/spacer between the skin and the frame at this point to improve the security of your boot.

appropriate spacers (probably one or two), and re-mate body and chassis. By this route you stand a chance of getting your door-gaps right and mounting your rear bumper at a later date without too much trouble.

• The front of the TR4 and 4A inner wing has two 90 degree bends. Unfortunately, on the reproduction parts, these are not sharp enough and often do not form full 90 degree bends, with the result that the wing appears too long. You need to re-dress these 90 degree bends, correcting what appears to be a problem regarding the length of the wings.

• Tolerances are tight in the area of the TR4/4A rear lights, and great care should be exercised at every step of the body reconstruction. Keep offering-up the rear lamp housings, rear wings and boot-lid. Note the position of the lamp housings shown in photograph 4-15, and check the fit at every step. You have been warned!

• Rust first forms along the top edge of where the outer wing bolts to the inner wing, and where the inner wing joins the wheelarch. The top deck joint to the inner and outer wing forms a rust trap - three layers of (unpainted) material, just waiting to rust! Etch prime all faces and cover in a two-pack primer before seam sealing the joint on final assembly.

• Cars are obviously susceptible to accident damage at the front. All TRs carry the bonnet hinges on the inside of the front inner wings. TR4s/4As, in particular, have a tendency to open-out in this area, due to accident damage, the passage of time, or when you rebuild the car. The problem is easily recognised due to the excessive gap between the front wings and the bonnet. Rectification requires that the wings/fenders be pulled together, aligning both with the bonnet. Fix a suitable fastening to the inside of each inner wing and attach a strong twin loop of rope around both. Twist the rope 'turnbuckle' style until the wings/fenders are once more properly and evenly spaced. Get a helper to secure the twisted rope so that it does not unwind until you want it to. It is vital you ensure that each time you offer-up the bonnet, it is the back-edge that you position (with the desired gap), abutting the front edge of the scuttle to provide your reference. Believe it or not, the inner wings will bend inwards under the turnbuckle's pressure, although you may

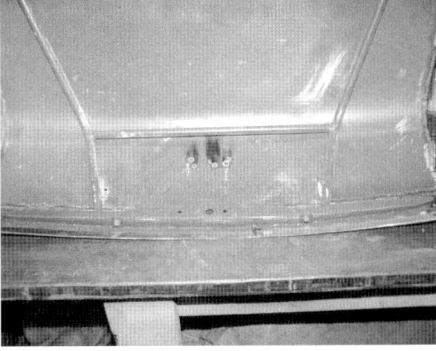

4-20-7. Step-by-step work (with frequent checks as to whether the panel still fits) is slow. Here is the finished boot/trunk lid with the edges/lips replaced completely round three sides.

4-20-4. Take care when tightening the boot/trunk hinges to the frame, you can distort the panel you are so carefully trying to restore. Here, although some spacers may have been necessary, the boot frame has been replaced to give the panel as much rigidity as possible, and the lid offered to the car to ensure we are moving in the right direction and have not created any unacceptable panel gaps. This close-up shows all must have been satisfactory, for the bottom lip has now been turned over and tacked in a few spots. No doubt the panel will have been offered up once again before the bottom part of the corroded right side lip was removed.

4-20-5. The next stage is to remove and replace the top part of the right side lip, and offer the lid to the car to ensure all the shapes and gaps are okay.

4-20-6. Then it's the left side's turn. Note that the old lip has been retained and used as a guide for the replacement lip.

need to persuade one wing to move a little more than its opposite number if you are to enjoy symmetrical (and very visible) front gaps.
● The plenum chamber is the compartment beneath the front scuttle panel (just in front of the windscreen) through which air passes when the vent flap is open.

When the vent is open the plenum inevitably collects water, which should drain away through two rubber tubes into the inner wing cavity. The tubes can

and do get blocked, however, with the result that water gathers in the plenum and/or falls onto the floor.

The other weakness of the design is that the gap between the outer sill/rocker and the base of the wing gets blocked. Water then rots the top of the sill, enters it and does more damage. In any event, it's not a good idea to allow the water to drain over your newly repaired inner wing/sill. Although not original, you would be wise to fit longer drain hoses that lead the water away from the corrosion areas.

Two modifications are available: one comes in kit form from Moss and feeds the water out into the wheelarch through an extra hole drilled in the bottom of each splashplate. Sounds fine, but the kit seems expensive to my mind and, in any event, when the car is in motion air can blow up the forward facing drains and inhibit the escape of water. So option two might be favourite: it's shown in photograph 4-5-10 and, again, hinges on an extended drain tube. However, this method takes the tube straight on down through the top of the inner sill/rocker, where it turns in towards the centre of the car to exit the inner sill just below the line of the floor. It's probably a good idea to cut the end of your drain tubes at an angle that encourages the water to fall down and backward.
● The above idea has additional merit in that you need to be thinking about rust-proofing as your body repairs proceed. Granted, you should not actually apply the Waxoyl, or whatever protective treatment you are planning, until the shell has been painted, but the wax injection holes could be positioned now to advantage - before priming and other coats of paint are applied. The inside of the sills/rockers are going to require some holes, probably three, down their full length, and, if these are drilled from under the floor into the inner sill, they can be plugged with a unseen rubber bung after wax injection. To get to my main point, the front wax injection hole each side of the car could double as the outlet for your plenum drain tube, provided you position them correctly.

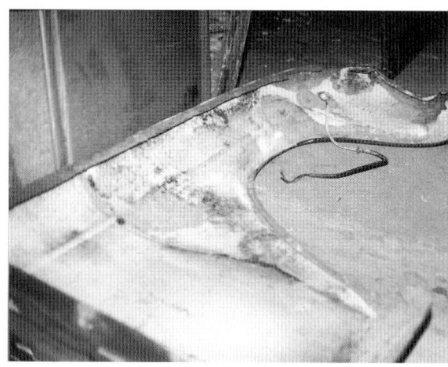

4-21. A Michelotti car wing, which doesn't look too bad. Note the side/parking lamp lead from the front of the wing that tells us this is a TR4A. This wing will need to be completely stripped of paint, using a chemical stripping agent such as (in the UK) Nitromors. The stripping of bodywork down to bare-metal is also strongly recommended. Not only does this remove the likelihood of a reaction between differing paints when it come to respraying, but it also enables you to see what's hidden by paint and filler, and enables you to take corrective action. Furthermore, you will get a far superior paint finish on a bare-metal foundation. A word of caution, however. Only use chemical stripper on single removable panels such as a wing/fender. Never use chemical strippers on the main bodytub or loose panels with seams, welded or otherwise. The chemical can get into the seams and never be properly removed - to the detriment of the metal and any subsequent coats of paint. It takes longer but the safest way to strip paint from the tub, or panels such as the doors, is with a heat gun and putty knife.

4-22.

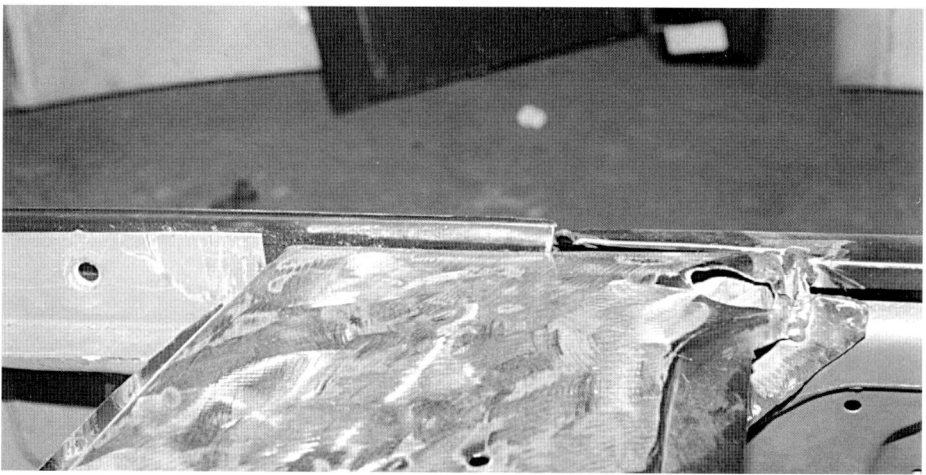

4-22 and 4-23 (above). It's understandable that you'd be keen to fit new wings to any TR on which you had spent a great deal of time and money. However, in the main text I mentioned that the best policy with new Michelotti panels generally, and wings in particular, was to repair the ones you have, for the fit of new panels will challenge even the most skilled of body repair experts. Here is an example of a new (in December 2000) front wing. The sad thing is that the main panel, which I consider to be the most difficult part to form, is a perfect pressing. The rear fit, though, is distorted by the inner pressing that forms the rear of the wing. I suspect that if the manufacturer used a TR6 rear pressing, the overall result would be superb.

SAND BLASTING

Too many restorers blast their bodytubs too early making an already weak shell very fragile indeed. Leaving the sand blasting until you have completed the major repairs has two benefits: your shell is at its strongest and, secondly, you are preparing the new (as well as the original) metal with a great 'key' for the subsequent painting operations. So, once the bodytub is complete, and all the new panels are properly welded in position, you should contemplate sand blasting for the first time. There may be the odd small area that you are uncertain about, and want to see the result of blasting before deciding to what extent new or repaired material is required.

The sand bounces off thick underseal, which, consequently, must be mostly removed. Use a blow torch (the type with a disposable gas canister)

very carefully, or better yet, an electric paint stripper, to soften the old underseal. This must then be scraped off to leave no more than a very thin black smear of underseal - which the blaster will remove. A putty knife or paint scraper will be essential, and be prepared for a real mess! If you are not comfortable with what is left after your first scraping operation, you can use

solvent/thinners/white-spirit and a rag once things have cooled down. If you leave the blaster too thick a coating to remove he will go through the adjacent metal before the blasting material can remove the normally thick underseal.

Do ensure the operator understands which areas you require blasting and which you do not. A really good operator will tell you what areas he will not blast. Experienced blasters usually avoid the flat parts of the larger panels - where they will only want to do the edges for fear of stretching the flat areas and causing rippling and distortion. Even with this point discussed and agreed, it is still a good idea to mask-off the scuttle and rear deck to prevent blasting. Do not allow outer panels to be shot blasted - wings, doors, boot and bonnet should not be blasted as they invariably end up rippled, although I have successfully had the edge (say, 1in or 25mm) of boot and bonnets blasted clean of rust.

Transporting the inner tub to the blaster on its chassis is safest but might mean having the body blasting completed before you start to finish paint the chassis.

Most blasting companies will also have the facilities to prime paint the body after blasting, which is an idea with some merit, particularly if you live any distance from the blaster. There are, however, some dangers to be aware of. The priming of the blasted body must take place quickly after blasting, an hour later would be good, for example, but you must not allow more that four hours to elapse between blasting and prime painting, because an oxide film (invisible at first) starts to form.

Even if you know there are areas to repair after blasting, it's still important to get the whole body primed quickly. Bear in mind, though, that your blaster can cover areas of poor blasting with a coat of primer which may not be compatible with your subsequent paint applications. If you are so far from the blaster that you feel it best to have the blaster prime your shell as well, do pre-agree the paint he will use and inspect the blasting work before he primes the car!

You will obviously need to remove the primer around any subsequent local repairs, but you must refinish (brush painting if you like) the stripped area as quickly as possible. We will examine the most preferable primers and cover a number of other painting details in chapter 6.

4-24.

4-24 and 4-25 (above). We have seen several pictures of this car as its body restoration progresses. In photograph 4-24 it is in the final bodywork stage, with the loose panels trial-fitted. They should be removed and painted separately, as picture 4-25 shows (note the loose panels against the far wall). The door openings will have had some sort of bracing securely bolted in place before the body was removed from the chassis. Note that the brown paper used for masking across the door aperture is clearly stuck to the door brace.

Chapter 5
Chassis restoration

SEPARATING BODY FROM CHASSIS

It's best to remove the engine's manifolds before contemplating a body-off lift as they could foul when the lower inner wings try to pass the engine. The six bumper dumb iron connections that pass through the body, together with the brake, clutch and fuel pipes, handbrake and speedometer cables, must all be at least disconnected, and preferably removed. Obviously, the seats and carpets will also need to come out (if you have not already done so) to allow access to the body mountings.

You will appreciate from our discussions on preparing a restoration plan that there are two methods of separating the body from the chassis. Let's first assume you have a reasonably solid shell, and that the floor and sills are perhaps in need of some attention but do not need replacing. Your first step must be to consider how you are going to proceed.

I would suggest removing the bonnet (which, on some cars is quite heavy), the boot lid, doors and all four wings before you even contemplate lifting the shell off its chassis. This has two benefits: firstly, it reduces the weight of the body, and it gives you a choice as

to how you are going to brace the door apertures, an **essential** step for one-piece bodytub removal.

Some do this by bolting dexion angle across the top inside of the door gaps from hood mountings on the B post to the bottom windscreen mounting bolts. Frankly, I think this method allows movement and does not get my vote. Photograph 4-3 shows some crossbraces achieved by tack welding mild steel flats. This method holds things rigid and also allows easier access to the inside of the tub. Although an improvement over the dexion idea, using steel angle for the crossbraces is an even stronger and, therefore, preferable option. Others prefer a slightly angled brace that bolts to two front wing mounting bolts on the outside of the 'A' pillar and to two hood frame mountings on the inside of the 'B' pillar. I have seen professionals use $1\frac{1}{2}$in or 2in diameter tube (suitably flattened at each end, of course), but a nice sturdy piece of mild steel angle (with the angle removed at one end) has certain advantages.

Another professional approach can be seen in photographs 5-1 and 5-2. My favourite method is to bolt an RHS or angle iron crossbrace across the doors to the screen mounting hole at the front

and to the hood mountings on the 'B' pillar at the rear. Properly done, this route allows you to offer-up the doors in due course without having to remove the braces. The choice is yours, of course, although you will not need to bother initially if your bodyshell is going to need new floors and sills and you decide to cut the shell in two and take the front and rear halves off in two parts. This really cuts the weights to be lifted when removing body from chassis.

You will need four people to lift a whole bare bodytub off its chassis in one piece, and six if the doors, wings, boot and bonnet panels are left in place. In both cases it's a good idea to have an extra pair of hands to disconnect/cut the one cable, pipe or attachment that always gets missed and only reveals itself as you try to part the tub from its chassis. Incidentally, it's called a 'tub' when all panels are removed, and a 'shell' when the external panels are *in situ*! Do not be concerned if some body mounting bolts have to drilled out or have sheared, as in photograph 5-3; that will be par for the course.

STRIPPING, SHOTBLASTING AND CHECKING THE CHASSIS

The now bodyless chassis is never a

5-1.

5-3. Few TR chassis are a pretty sight when they see the light of day for the first time in 30 plus years. As a matter of fact, this 'just-separated' IRS chassis does not look too bad, and is actually better than many. Nevertheless, it was still necessary to grind the heads off many of the body/chassis attachment bolts in order to release the body. If yours are like this you will need to carefully drill out the centre of each of the remaining bolts. Sometimes the heat and vibration caused by drilling will release the rusted bolt, but more often than not you will need to open the initial hole out with a second carefully selected drill that leaves the female thread intact, and then re-tap the hole in the mounting brackets. Any threads that do not clean up will need to be completely replaced by welding a new nut in place of the damaged one.

5-1 and 5-2 (above). Cross-bracing the door aperture. This may not be the most common way of achieving the essential rigidity of the body before removal from its chassis, but it's certainly an effective option. However, I prefer to be able to offer the doors up to the tub without disturbing the braces. There are several alternatives described in the main text, and it's vital that you adopt one of them before attempting to remove the bodytub from its chassis in one piece.

pretty sight, but let's hope it is no worse than your initial pre-purchase assessment. Swallow hard, but don't be too surprised; the chassis was never primed and received no more than a quick blow-over of black paint - and that was about 35 or 40 years ago, depending upon the car you are restoring. Make a start by taking lots of detailed close-up photographs before taking anything off the chassis. When you do start removing parts from the chassis use lots of welding wire to hold each sub-assembly, brackets and related shims together! Have plenty of tie-on labels to hand too, and religiously identify each sub-assembly as you take it off the car (*i.e.* LH or RH, front shims, outside LH side, *etc.*). Throw nothing away! Keep even the grottiest rubber bush or tatty shim, welding-wired into its respective place in the sub-assembly. I have know of occasions when hood frames were thrown out along with a tatty hood. I know you would not make a mistake like that, but it could just be a small bracket, or a few bolts that you forget to keep that cause problems later on - so throw nothing away, yet. Have some tough bags handy in which to place bolts, *etc.*, before wiring the bag to the sub-assembly. If in doubt, use a centre punch to 'dot' the relative position of brackets to the chassis.

As the removal of parts proceeds, you will start to get an idea as to how accurate your initial assessment was. Although you will have looked for evidence of accident damage when buying the car, take another look now. Use a small hammer to establish the extent of corrosion all over the chassis, hopefully revealing problems, such as those shown in photograph 5-4, sooner rather than later. Pay close attention to the rearward slanting square brace behind the front turrets. These braces are susceptible to corrosion at their

5-4. A repair patch removed from the bottom face of an IRS chassis. Note the remains of the cover/patch, curled up to left of the picture, revealing the corrosion underneath. The repair would have been up to UK MOT standard, in fact, and would not have been unsafe provided the welding was good. It would, however, have led to acceleration of the rust under the patch. It would have been better in the long run to either cut the whole section of chassis out (which is difficult with the body in place) or remove the lower flat part of the chassis section only. This car could have been sold to an unsuspecting buyer with a full MOT, yet further repairs would clearly have been required in the not too distant future. This underlines the need to look at the chassis before purchase!

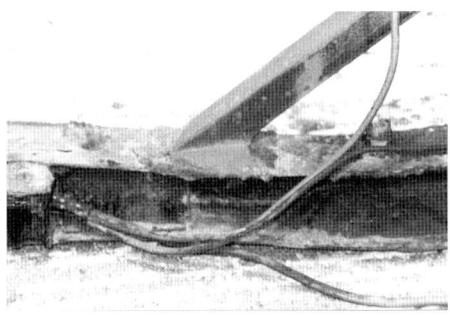

5-5. The lower/rearward end of a front turret brace showing clear evidence of significant corrosion, possibly accident damage, and definitely an unsatisfactory repair.

lower 2in or so, just above where they are welded to the chassis, as you can see in photograph 5-5. Moisture clearly tends to sit in the bottom of the rolled hollow (square) tube, and corrodes outwards. You'll need to bang them both quite vigorously to ensure they are absolutely solid. Although repair is quite easy, do ensure that both turret braces are solid enough to carry out their intended function for many years to come. The front turrets and the top of the turret braces will also require your attention, as can be seen in photographs 5-6 and 5-7.

When you have checked the extent

5-6.

5-6 and 5-7 (above). The first picture is a general view of the front left turret, while the second gives a closer look at the top of the turret, in particular a badly repaired top suspension mounting plate. The top plate and dome-shaped shock absorber mounting are prone to cracking and need to be very closely inspected for cracks, which, if found, must be properly prepared and welded. This is but one area where sand or shotblasting your chassis is particularly helpful, for many of the smaller hairline cracks will only become apparent after blasting. It's important to seam weld right round the periphery of the top plate, as has been attempted here, except that this is a safety-critical part of your chassis and the quality of the welding is vital. It's also important to seam weld right round the 270 or so degrees of dome to plate - which has not been more than toyed-with here. Also visible in this pair of photographs is damage to the rearward brace that is attached to the chassis, some 2 feet (600mm) to the rear of the turret. Such damage is typically the result of an accident and it's well worth examining this crossbrace for creasing and repair.

of corrosion and got everything off the chassis it would normally be time to get it shotblasted. However, while there are unlikely to be problems with a live axle chassis, corrosion in some IRS chassis can be so extensive as to make shotblasting a waste of time and money. We will discuss the usual IRS weak spots in more detail shortly, but let's assume for the moment that you have not had any unpleasant surprises and that your shotblasting operation can go ahead as planned. This can usually be done locally, though it's best to avoid the local shotblast companies which deal mainly with structural steel and/or 1in boiler plate. They could be too aggressive with the blasting operation and obliterate perfectly good parts of your chassis. Ask your TR restoration specialist, the most local TR restorer (who could even get work done for you), or your local TR Register group about where such work could be satisfactorily completed. Cost is usually about £100 or so, and is money very well spent.

Do not attempt any home remedies. Wire brushing and most of the other 'home remedies' merely polish the top surface of the rust.

One final but important detail about the shotblasting operation itself: ensure your chassis is painted within a few hours of shotblasting. We will also explore this point in more detail in chapter 6, but you must avoid allowing the surface of your newly shotblasted chassis to form even a very light film of corrosion. Paint it immediately after shotblasting, even if you know there is welding to be carried out on the chassis. You could use a weld-through primer but most restorers will get a coat of red-oxide primer on the chassis and be happy to wire-brush it off where/when welding is required.

The shotblasting operation will reveal the areas of damage or corrosion weakness that require attention. The beauty of the TR's chassis construction is that most enthusiasts can successfully tackle chassis repairs, particularly since there are a good selection of repair sections available.

Even if you have a superb chassis, ex-Californian, for example, it's wise to go over it with a fine tooth comb checking for cracks. The chassis normally corrodes and cracks due to fatigue in fairly predictable places, though, of course, such damage can occur anywhere. Cracks are mostly the consequence of the emphasis that was originally placed upon speed rather than the quality of chassis manufacture. Vee grinding and MIG welding will normally correct most cracks.

Additional plating to the main chassis members is not usually required, though some additional gussets will be required to most IRS chassis in order to strengthen steering, suspension and differential attachment points. Those readers considering a 'concours' restoration would be well advised to consider carrying out these safety improvements for, even if no cracks or corrosion is evident, this is still a once-in-a-lifetime opportunity to upgrade the known weak spots of the chassis as an insurance against any future problems.

A bare chassis allows excellent access to the known problem areas and, consequently, this is the opportunity to get any welding done well to guarantee a permanent solution. If your welding is not up to this standard, then it is cheaper in the long run to consign the repairs and modification to a TR specialist or a specialist welder. If you only half complete a repair now, and the problem re-occurs, it will be much more difficult and expensive to effect a proper repair with the body in place. If nothing else, it will certainly spoil the paint-work in the area that requires re-repair.

Bear in mind that the chassis is the absolute foundation of every TR. If it is not correct, you will be rebuilding your car on a potentially unsatisfactory base. You should need no additional encouragement to ensure the structure/welding is sound.

As well as the structure, the chassis dimensions are equally important, and, consequently, it is very important to have the chassis measured, or to measure it yourself before anything else is done to car. Most workshop manuals give dimensions of the chassis, and it is worth buying the correct one for your car for this reason alone. If there is obvious accident damage you may be wise to check the dimensions before shotblasting, for if the chassis is not true, then you probably need to plan a different repair solution, and the shotblasting could be a waste of money.

FRONT SUSPENSION CHECKS

Once the chassis has been shot blasted,

5-8. Here we see the front end of an early TR4. Note the 'Mickey-mouse'-eared steering rack mounting brackets and the crossbrace that goes between the front turrets. This one looks to have three mounting bolts at each turret, some have two each end. The outriggers and their mounting pads for the body are clearly visible higher up the picture.

look round the top of each turret, for, as we saw in photographs 5-6 and 5-7, there is a shallow bell-shaped pressing that accepts the top of the front coil springs. You will note three fairly short lengths of weld positioned roughly at 90 degrees around the pressing - these often crack. You would, therefore, be well advised to continuously weld right around the periphery of the bell/turret junction - about 270 degrees. Next, remove the bolted crossmember, shown in photograph 5-8, that joins the two front turrets just in front of where the engine was located. The turrets can be damaged by a side impact, in which case wrinkling of the crossmember will be evident. If yours is damaged find one from an undamaged chassis and use it as a jig to correct your chassis/turrets. Some turrets have two bolts each side, whilst later cars had three bolts each end. Clearly, you need one that is compatible with your chassis.

THE TR4 (LIVE AXLE) LADDER CHASSIS

If you find your live rear axle chassis requires extensive corrosion repairs to the main members - don't bother! Replacement chassis are around and it's probably more cost-effective to buy a

good secondhand replacement. Most ladder chassis have survived well and there is no point in making your restoration more difficult than it needs to be - unless you enjoy plating and welding that is!

The 1961 TR4s were made concurrently with the TR3B, and a similar chassis was used with 2in bolt-on additions to accommodate the TR4's body feet. There were steering differences too, but, since you will be very unlucky if you do need to find a fresh chassis, let's focus on the areas that require most attention in order to bring their original ladder chassis up to scratch:

- The rear gearbox mounting can crack. Occasionally hairline cracks will be found on either or both sides of the pads on the crossmember. The pads even can be missing.
- Live rear axle cars all have a pin going right through the base of each front suspension turret (see picture 5-10). The lower wishbone is attached, front and rear, to these pins and, consequently, they control the whole of the front suspension geometry. You will be well advised to check the pins' measurements, front and rear, and compare them to the chassis dimension drawing shown in your workshop

5-9. Here the chassis can be seen along with its mating body-tub. The outriggers can be seen on this (the right) side of the chassis although the body mounting pads are difficult to see. The metal dash-back can be seen in the background.

5-10. Early TR4 'eared'-type steering rack mounting brackets. The rack used with these brackets is 'solid-mounted', using an aluminium block that is actually superior to the later rubber-cushioned mounting. This rack can be identified by two features: it is about 10mm longer than the later rack, and has no 'D' shaped flanges welded to each end. For the most direct steering, fit your chassis with the later brackets (shown in photograph 5-11) and use the earlier solid-mounted steering rack.

professional. It's all too easy for the average amateur to doze' the pins into the correct position only to find they have distorted some other part of the chassis. TR Bitz, CTM and, indeed, all the contributing specialists (see Appendix 1) have jigs, and, for the relatively small expense will be able to correct this critical item. Overlook this small detail now and you will have major problems later. If in any doubt at least get an expert opinion.

• You need to be aware that the TR4 chassis has early and late versions of the steering rack and rack mounting. The earlier cars have vertical mounting posts, to which the rack bolts directly, through solid aluminium mounting blocks as shown in photographs 5-8 and 5-10. The later cars have a horizontally mounted steering rack designed to stiffen its locationing, but rubber mounting pads were also introduced to reduce shock loads up through the steering column (see photograph 5-11). Although the actual mounting framework varied, as we will see when we get to the TR4A, this method of rack mounting was retained throughout all further classic TRs. If you have an early TR4 (with the vertical rack posts), it is advantageous and quite common to introduce the later steering rack mountings and use a later steering rack. Take great care when purchasing spare steering racks and associated parts for the TR4, however, for the dimensions for the various racks, tie rods, etc., all vary slightly and it is important you buy exactly the right one for your car. Not all TR4 steering parts fit all TR4 cars!

• Body outriggers often crack due to fatigue and corrosion. There is a proprietary repair that involves cutting-off the old outrigger close to the chassis, and inserting a new replacement outrigger, designed with a slightly smaller diameter tube, that slips inside the old, now cut off, tube. The process is illustrated by photographs 5-12 and 5-13, and you will note that, when you weld round its circumference, the repair becomes almost invisible. The thicker walls of the repair tube ensure no strength is lost.

• The tail end of the main chassis members can corrode (photograph 5-14) and will, of course, need to be replaced.

• Differences between the TR4 and '4A include the fact that with the '4A,

manual. Around 30% of the older cars will have been involved in some sort of shunt, and those involved in a sideswipe could have had the parallel relationship of these pins adversely effected. Any problems must be carefully corrected to

ensure that both pins are not only parallel with each other but with the longitudinal axis of the car. Unless the restorer is comfortable with their skills, this particular issue is probably best corrected by an experienced

5-14. Inevitably, after 35 or 40 years even the most robust ladder chassis succumbs to corrosion at the tail end. Most restorers will make up their own repair pieces, but sections are available from TR specialists.

5-11. Late TR4 steering rack attachment brackets. These are the more rigid, and, therefore, better type of rack mounting brackets used on the TR4. They are available new, but, if you experience any difficulty getting hold of some, they are worth removing from an otherwise useless chassis and transferring to your earlier TR4. Note the 'D' shaped flanges welded to the rack itself, which allow the use of the rubber 'cushions' beneath the U-bolt securing clamps. You can, of course, re-use the solid 'ally' ones.

5-12 and 5-13 (right). Repairing the outrigger mounting tubes. In fact, these are the all-important rear spring hanger tubes, seen here prior welding the actual spring hangers in place.

you could no longer jack the car up from inside the cockpit, nor was the handbrake affixed to the chassis. Both details, on a TR4, can be seen in photograph 5-15.
● The design of the TR4 front suspension was such that the bottom wishbone mounting can seize onto the lower suspension mounting pin. Since the pin goes right through the front turret, you'll need to take great care

removing a seized bush (shown in photograph 5-16) without damaging the pin.
● The tail of a TR chassis cants upward, as picture 5-17 shows. It's unlikely that you will need to have to repair a ladder chassis this far forward but it is as well to be aware that the upward angle is by design. As a matter of interest, we can see the same upward angle in an IRS chassis in

5-15. The TR4 (and earlier TRs) jack can be positioned and the car raised from the inside of the car! This shot shows the main chassis rail with its slot-like jacking-point. In order to ensure the rear hydraulic brake pipe is well out of the way, Triumph looped the pipe around the danger area, as can be seen here. You must copy this pipe routing, for both originality and safety reasons. You may not intend to use the internal jacking method, but some later owner may think it a good idea - until he loses his brakes that is! To find the jacking point on your TR4 just remove the large rubber bungs from the floor of the appropriate side of your car, drop the jack down through the hole, engage the 'slot', and wind yourself up. The vertical tube on the left of the picture is the handbrake.

5-16. Another view of the TR4 front end. Note the brake light switch position and pipe routes. It's difficult to see, but the sleeve on the pivot, on the right side bottom pivot, has been left in place. The sleeve will require careful horizontal grinding to establish a longitudinal flat on the seized tube, and then progressively ground until the wall of the tube is just broken, whereupon the tube will loosen its vice-like grip on the pivot bar and can be removed.

photograph 5-29.

THE TR4A (IRS) CHASSIS

IRS chassis corrosion can be so extensive as to make shotblasting a waste of time and money. Strangely, these later chassis are more vulnerable to forward creeping corrosion than their earlier counterparts, and are much more likely to be in need of plating and welding. They are, consequently, in less plentiful supply and are, therefore, worthwhile repairing - but only up to a certain point. So what is the cut-off point, bearing in mind the corrosion moves forward from the rear? Certainly corrosion at or forward of the mid-point of a chassis, where the cruciform/'T-shirt' lies, makes it a candidate for replacement. In fact, you should probably seek advice if the corrosion extends to a point about 40% forward from the rear of the frame, as can be seen in photograph 5-18, for a new chassis then becomes highly likely. Obviously, you should consider the whole chassis but, significant corrosion in front of the cruciform, as shown in this picture 5-18, is very bad news. We will look at the alternative chassis options in a moment. Bear in mind, however, that accident damage could

also bring about the need for a replacement chassis.

You will recall from our discussion about examining the chassis prior to purchase, that we were very interested in accident damage in the single channel part of the chassis, just below the 'A' posts. Photograph 5-19 shows a typical crease while 5-20 shows the ideal. Unfortunately, any problem noted here might not be just a simple matter of correcting the distortion, for it could signal a more serious problem with the front suspension turrets and geometry.

The difficulties escalate in that it is not really possible to establish the extent of the problem or to correct it without a proper jig. So, if accident damage is suspected, checking and correction could be a matter best left to an experienced professional chassis specialist. In fact, the amateur could create more problems at 'point B', for example, than he solves by trying to jack-correct a distortion at 'point A'. So, creases in the single-leg section of the chassis may colour your whole approach to chassis renovation.

A replacement chassis may only be essential in a very small percentage of cases, but if your chassis has to go off to a specialist repairer, for any reason, it seems relevant to assess all the various options. Therefore, before looking at the repairs and improvements advised for a not overly corroded IRS chassis, let's look at the alternatives and their respective costs. Your main choices are:
(a) Brand new chassis: approximately £2000.
(b) Ex-Californian/dry state:

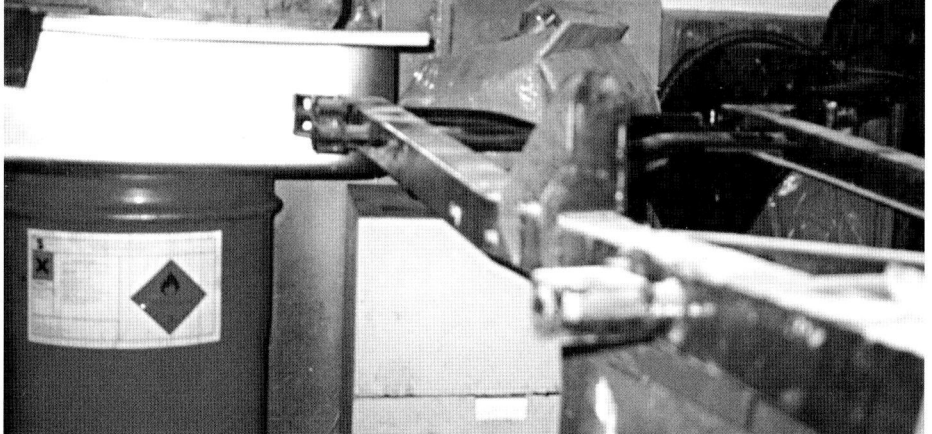

5-17. The upward slant of the last few feet of this TR4 chassis is clear to see.

approximately £1100.
(c) A professional chassis repair or exchange: approximately £1100.

A brand new chassis sounds great, and, for most purposes, is the way to go (if you can afford £2000). Be aware, though, that the new chassis will require your original front suspension turrets, and that these will be built into your otherwise new structure. The chassis will have the advantage of being slightly stiffer than the originals. However, potential concours contestants should also note, however, that, if noticed by

5-18. This shows the underside of an IRS chassis with the lower centre cruciform or 'T-shirt' pressing removed. The right side chassis leg has had the lower face repaired (it was almost certainly holed in the same place as the left side chassis leg is now), and a new rear suspension mounting arm has been fitted. The repair looks very good but would have been even better had the corner of the plate we see in the top right of the picture been extended backwards (towards the top of the picture) by about 2in (50mm). This would have ensured that it did not finish too close to where the T-shirt pressing will eventually finish. The two centre tubes are the exhaust pipes, of course, that most would remove to aid re-welding the replacement T-shirt pressing to the chassis - unless, that is, this restorer intends to plug weld through the T-shirt panel to the chassis.

5-19 and 5-20 (right). Buyer beware. The first picture shows a typical TR accident-damaged chassis leg, creased and bulging between the rear of the front suspension brace (shown in photograph 5-5), and where the central chassis cruciform joins the main chassis leg (just in front of the 'A' pillar). Clearly, this photograph is taken with the body off the chassis but, as I explained earlier, this bulge should have been detected when you carried out your pre-purchase inspection, even with the body in place. The crease gives evidence of some earlier frontal impact. Repairing the crease itself may not seem a major problem, but it is a body-off task and it may signal other, possibly more serious, accident-damage elsewhere. Photograph 5-20 shows how the same section of chassis should be - dead straight and flat.

the concours judge, even the minor differences from the original chassis will be marked down on the basis of non-originality.

Californian chassis are in such wonderful condition because, of course, the climate is dryer and the humidity lower than that of more temperate climes. Furthermore, the dry states rarely have any need to salt their roads - to the further benefit of the cars generally, and the chassis in particular. So, if you have concours aspirations, go for an ex-Californian chassis. All the spot welds are 'correct' and the chassis cannot be faulted from an authenticity point of view. If you are tempted to buy privately, though, do take care, for there are cars that have spent the majority of their lives in less agreeable (climate-wise) states and have been shipped to be broken or sold as 'Californian'.

EXAMINING AND REPAIRING THE IRS CHASSIS

When we were examining the car prior to purchase (chapter 2), the importance and vulnerability of the cruciform and rear suspension mounting points just forward of the differential was discussed. This is one of the IRS car's major problem areas. If yours is as corroded as that shown in 5-21, then everything in that area will need to be replaced. The only decision to make is whether you will do the work yourself, whether you will ask a specialist to do it, or whether you will get a fresh chassis. You may find the photographic sequence 5-22-1 to 5-22-10 helps you decide which route you want to follow. I would add the reminder that the integrity of the rear suspension mounting sections and the associated chassis members are absolutely crucial to the safety of the car, and, if you are in any doubt whatsoever as to your abilities, I do urge you to let experienced hands carry out this work.

There are difficulties in seeing the true extent of the corrosion within the 'capsule' where the box sections (that carry the trailing arms) are attached to the chassis main rails. Photograph 5-23, with its swollen T-shirt panel, should signal that it is essential you grind off both top and bottom stiffening plates - thus opening up the intersection of the various box sections. You can now properly inspect the condition of the sections previously hidden by the diamond stiffening plates.

You may be very surprised by what you see. You will almost inevitably find an absence of box section metal under the stiffening plates, and will realise that there was in fact no structural integrity at this crucial intersection of load carrying chassis members. This, in spite of your having closely inspected the area prior to purchase of the car, and in spite of numerous MOT inspectors having looked closely at it and declared the car roadworthy!

An early sign, incidentally, that all is not well in this area is when doors pop open as the car/chassis twists when

5-21. This picture shows part of an IRS chassis's bottom 'T-shirt' plate. An outrigger/rear suspension mounting arm exits the photograph bottom-left, while one main chassis leg exits the top of the picture. All the fore, aft and side loads brought about by acceleration, braking and cornering pass through this absolutely safety-critical focal point. The severely corroded condition of the pressed gusset plate bears witness to the vulnerability of this crucial part of the IRS cars. In fact, this bottom gusset has rotted away almost completely, as will all the internal interconnected chassis members above this plate thus reducing the structural integrity if this area of this car to nil. All this is bad news, but what is even worse is to note that someone has previously tried to make the car appear roadworthy by welding a top gusset over the top of the rotten material, as evidenced by the part-corroded strip along the rear suspension mounting arm. Who is he kidding? Even a thicker than average gusset welded to nothing provides no structural integrity whatsoever, and the owner risks a rear end chassis failure with possibly horrific consequences. This, therefore, is a crucial detail to examine very closely indeed when carrying out a pre-purchase inspection. If you miss this point you will certainly be in line for an expensive body-off repair at a later date, and you could be putting life and limb in danger in the meantime. If in doubt, get a second expert opinion.

traversing a bumpy road. Older rusty cars have been known to 'lose' a trailing arm box section completely, when the corroded and fatigued metal separates from the cruciform. Without putting too fine a point on it - this area is vitally important to the car, so do the job properly, and get the stiffening/'T-shirt' plates off and have a real good look!

The additional details to check/consider are as follows:

• Assuming you need to replace one or both box sections that carry the rear suspension trailing arms, it's important to position the new box sections at the correct angle (about 45 degrees) to the

5-22-1. The sequence in which you proceed with an IRS chassis repair is not always crucial, provided you remember the need to retain 'reference-points'. However, it is important is to get the angle of the rear suspension mounting leg correct, and some explanation of this is included in the main text. It's equally vital to ensure the integrity of the welding between each chassis leg and its respective chassis member is first-class before you give any thought to tacking the T-shirt pressings in place. Here we see that both T-shirt pressings have been cut longitudinally in half, and the left side of the chassis is being used as a mirror reference while the right side of the chassis is repaired.

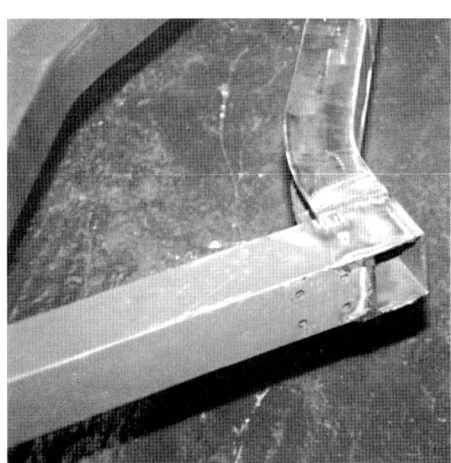

5-22-2. With the inside of the right side rear suspension mounting leg securely welded to the inside chassis member, it's time to repair the outer end. Remember the upward angle of the rear part of the chassis shown in photograph 5-29.

5-22-3. Do the same with the left side too!

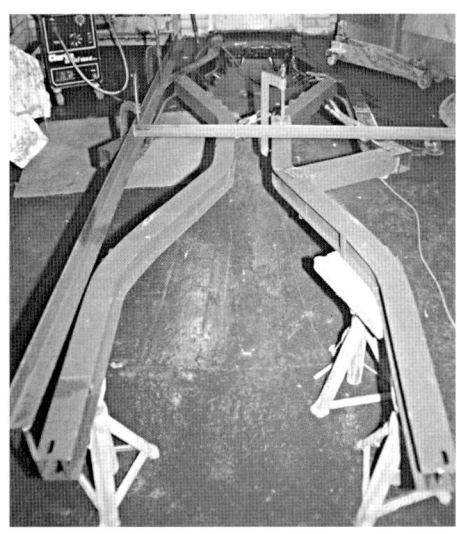

5-22-4. Like the TR4's ladder chassis, the IRS cars also had an upward slant to the rear of the chassis. Here we see an IRS chassis undergoing a major repair. Although it's inverted, you can see the tacked spacer ensuring the upward slant is maintained throughout the repair.

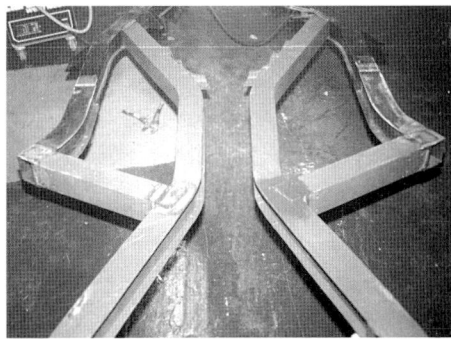

5-22-5. Some closing pieces can be added to the open chassis sections, almost whenever it suits you. However, it's vital to have the workshop manual's chassis dimensions to hand, and to align the two halves very carefully indeed.

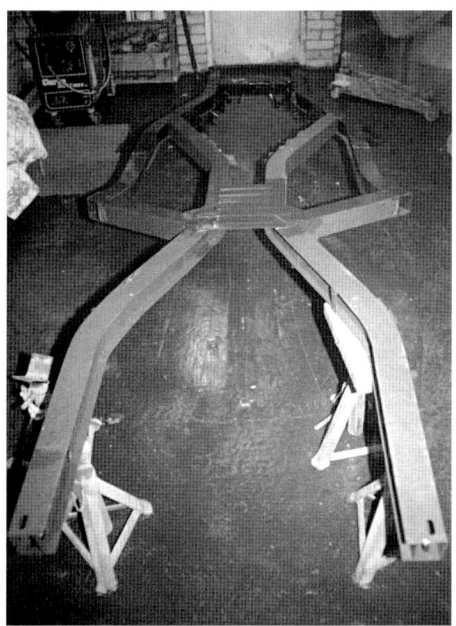

5-22-6. Securely tack the top T-shirt pressing in place.

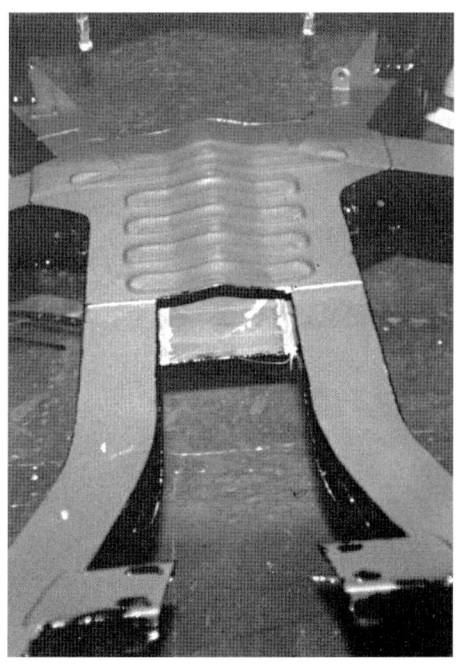

5-22-7. Turn the chassis gently over and tack the bottom T-shirt in place. Double and treble check the dimensions.

longitudinal axis of the chassis, when viewed from above. It is, of course, quite possible to either measure the outboard point of the box section, or use a plater's protractor to measure off the angle. Probably the simplest route to getting the new angle correct is to make up a

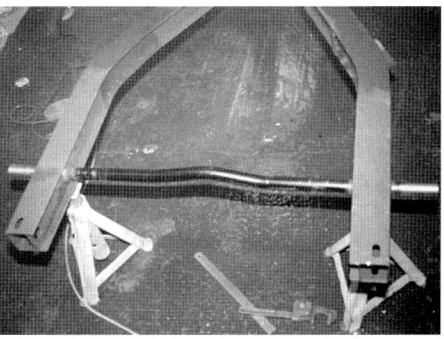

5-22-8. Give the rear of the chassis some stability by welding the rear cross tube in place.

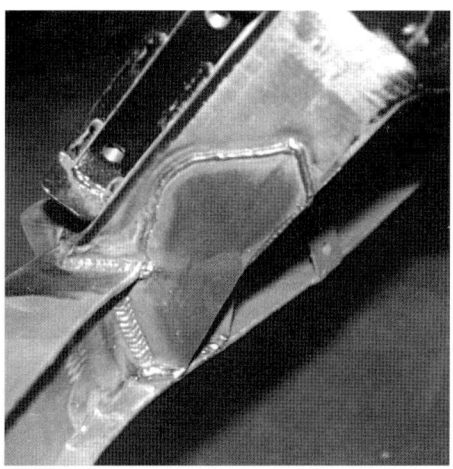

5-22-9. Securely weld the front and rear diff bridges in place, and recheck the chassis dimensions. Note the superb welding quality that is required, shown in this picture of the left rear end diff bridge.

5-22-10. Carefully weld the T-shirt pressings. Be sure to follow the 'diametrically opposite' sequence recommended in the main text, and only weld in shortish runs at a time, not much longer than 1in or so, to minimise distortion from weld cooling. Check your dimensions and finish welding the chassis.

5-22-11. Make and fit the extra gussets within the T-shirt pressings for your TR4A ... if you feel inclined, that is, or for authenticity.

5-23. There is evidence of corrosion in this picture of the top 'T-shirt' panel. The arrow points to a crack that is appearing central to a general area of swelling. The swelling is caused by corrosion under the plate expanding and lifting the plate away from the chassis members. Bulged or swelling 'T-shirts', be they top or bottom, are the first sign that all is far from well. You should proceed with due caution, for this area, along with the IRS mounting 'arm' sections, are the most prone to rust and the most expensive to repair (*in situ*) since you either have to take the body off the chassis to get at the corrosion, or cut out the rear floors!

(large) steel template using the old box section angle as a guide (before the pressed stiffening plate or box sections are removed, of course!). Check that the template fits both sides, and mark the 'top' very clearly.

A further suggestion that some might consider helpful would be to take your light gauge template down to your local engineering works and have them guillotine an identical template out of 3mm mild steel plate. You can then tack

5-24. The all important rear suspension mounting legs showing the equally important, but oft overlooked, internal stiffeners/spacers. When purchased, the smaller top channel section is only tack welded in place to allow you to remove it so that you can fully weld the internal edges of the main channel section to the structure of the chassis. When that is completed, you replace the smaller channel section and seam weld the edges to the main channel.

weld your template to your new box sections to retain their true position, while you first tack and then weld the new trailing arm mountings in place.

I know the rear suspension is shimmed, and, consequently, you have some lee-way, but I think it's best to get this part of the chassis rebuild 'spot-on'!

• The trailing arm chassis members have some subtleties that you should be aware of. The inside of the box section is more complex than it looks from the outside, because it has an internal stiffener/spacer to prevent the front and rear faces of the box section closing together when you 'pull-up' the bolts that carry the trailing arms. This spacer, shown in photograph 5-24, has an important secondary use in that it also spreads the stresses from the mounting bolts.

There are two types of trailing arm box section, and both have the matrix in place, but option 1 is designed for those who have elected not to remove their diamond-shaped pressed stiffeners. These box sections come with the rear closing channel loose (shown in picture 5-24). Consequently, you can position the front main channel of the box section inside the cruciform 'cavity', once the old/rusted legs are removed,

and weld it to the rest of the chassis members from the inside of the new main channel. Then you position the rear (smaller) channel 'half' of the box section, and weld that in place too. The second option for the properly spaced trailing arm box section comes pre-assembled and welded - but is only practical to properly weld in place with both diamond stiffening plates removed. In a bare chassis restoration I do strongly recommend you adopt option 2, and fall back to option 1 only when you are repairing a complete 'body-on' chassis.

• Now we come to the replacement of our two diamond-shaped pressed stiffeners, or 'T-shirt' panels as they are known. We discussed a 'hogged' chassis in chapter 2, and you are now at the point where, unless care is taken, you can spoil hours of work by hogging your own chassis.

The first prerequisite is that all is set up exactly as per the photographic sequence 5-22-1 to 5-22-11, that the workshop manual's dimensions are assured, and that both plates are solidly tacked in place. The hogging is actually caused by shrinkage, brought about by hot metal cooling after welding. You'll need to counter this shrinkage by only welding both diamond stiffening plates in short runs (1in at a time), and in a strict 'diametrically opposite' sequence.

To explain this last sentence. Say you start with a 1in run on the bottom of the chassis, on the left side. This must be followed by a 1in run on the top right side. You will then do a 1in run on the bottom right side and counter this by a top left side (diametrically opposite) run. This will involve a lot of chassis turning and the process takes time.

Nevertheless, don't be tempted to short-cut this diametrically opposite short-run welding technique, or you will twist and/or hog your chassis! Perhaps it would be prudent every so often to get out a straight edge and a tape measure to ensure the main dimensions are being maintained. I would certainly confirm these dimensions when you have completed one cycle of welds (i.e. one 1in weld in each corner of the plate). Accuracy to about + or - $1/4$in is acceptable, but any greater discrepancy and you'll need to have a beer and think about what you are doing.

• Although of no interest to potential concours contestants, some may be interested to know that it is possible to

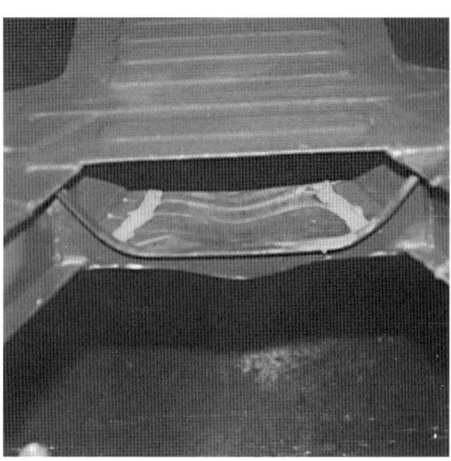

5-25. The TR4A was unique amongst the IRS cars in that it featured this extra broad U-shaped gusset within the 'T-shirt' central section of the chassis. It was dropped from subsequent more powerful cars, and is, therefore, unlikely to be missed (except by a concours judge!) should you elect to omit it.

use a TR6 chassis under a TR4A! There will be one noticeable difference, however, in that the 4A had a pressed saddle that braced the chassis just in front of the differential. This was obviously deemed unnecessary at some point, for it was omitted from TR5 and 6 cars, in spite of their extra horsepower, and so can safely be omitted from any IRS chassis bolted under a '4A. However, if you seek authenticity, you would have to make or find one, and attach it as shown by photograph 5-25.

A second difference which will not surprise you relates to the engine attachments. Four- and six-cylinder engines have different attachments, and would, obviously, have to be altered to suit the 4A's 4-cylinder engine if you used a TR6 chassis!

The final difference relates to the lower wishbone arm mounting brackets. The 4A's were bolted in place with one stud, but Triumph adopted two studs on the 6-cylinder cars. This is no bad modification, even if you are retaining a 4A chassis under your TR4A, so I'd advise you to drill the extra hole and fit the later type bracket. Even a concours judge is unlikely to spot this modification!

• One common variant related to North American TR4As involves the retention of the live rear axle. These cars are fitted with the later TR4 chassis (with rack and pinion steering), yet still retain the TR4's live rear axle and the

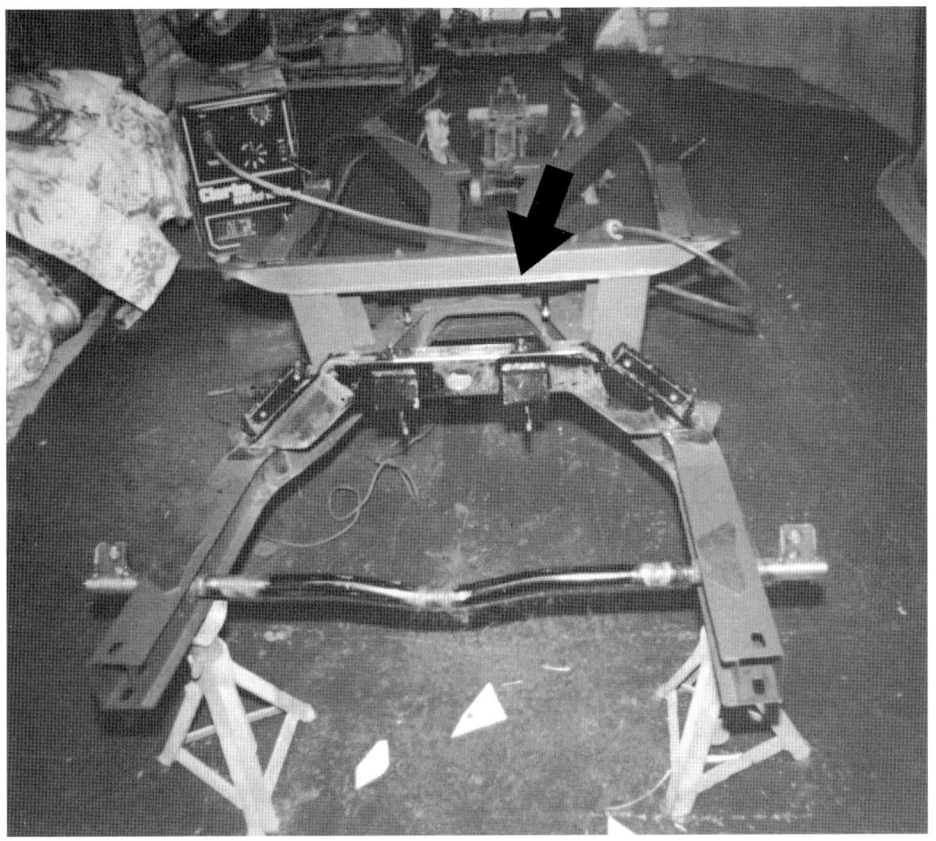

5-26. This picture shows both front and rear diff-bridges. From this shot the front one (arrowed) looks the simpler of the two, but, since it carries half the weight of the car through the rear coil springs, it needs to be absolutely solid.

5-28. The main diff bridge showing two welding repairs. Firstly, note that the right side pin head has been welded, but without the extra square strengthening plate advised in the main text. The second repair shows where pressure from the rear coil spring has cracked the front edge of the main diff-bridge (arrowed). As a result of the crack, the end of the bridge actually bent upwards slightly. The welded repair is clearly visible after the outer end of the bridge had been knocked back flat, but, if this was my car, I think you would also see an extra 6in long strip of 'L' shaped 16swg mild steel welded along the face and lip. If this section fails, the coil spring comes up through the body and you fly off the road moments later.

associated leaf springs. There is some evidence of the IRS chassis design too, in that these cars use the outside IRS trailing arm bracket mounting to affix the front of their leaf springs. These chassis can be converted to use the TR4A's IRS that was uniform in the UK, and ultimately used in the USA with the advent of the TR250. However, the American TR4A chassis were not fitted with a differential bridge - a channel that spans the differential and (with IRS) carries the weight of the rear of the car by providing the top mounting for the IRS rear coil springs. These bridges, shown in picture 5-26, are available new as a pre-welded sub-assembly, and would need welding to the chassis using the dimensions shown in the workshop manual.

• The diff-bridge can also corrode - sometimes badly, as seen in photograph 5-27. In such examples you also need to fit a whole new bridge. Failure to do will not only allow the coil/road spring to come up through the body, but it's also

5-27. The IRS rear diff bridge (or rear crossmember). Here we can see one end where a coil spring sits up into the 'cup', which has been badly repaired. We can see that the edge has been welded with no apparent effort to replace the corroded lip on which the whole of this corner of the car rests. The strength of the spring mounting depends upon the integrity of this lip for, without it, the end of the bridge can and will fold upwards and allow the coil spring to escape the bridge and poke up through the body! New diff bridges are available, and should be fitted if the rest of the chassis is sound.

highly likely you will lose control of the car, with unthinkable consequences. If an IRS car has been frequently used over rough roads, the differential bridge can split, inboard of the coil spring. The repair is simple in that (without the spring in place, of course), the bridge needs knocking down to form a flat channel again, and the splits vee'd out and welded, as per photograph 5-28. While not, strictly speaking, essential in every case, I must tell you that I would also strengthen the lips of the inverted channel in any car I was restoring where this problem had occurred!

• The last 4-5 feet (1500mm) of chassis may look particularly sad after shotblasting, and is vulnerable on all IRS cars. The tail end of the chassis, however, is available (along with the boot support cross tube), in various lengths, so find out the lengths in stock, cut off the most appropriate length to remove all the corroded section, and weld the repair section in place. Take account of the fact that the chassis tends to slope (slightly) down towards the front (photograph 5-22-4) from this rear section, and, as a result, the water runs forward from the rear towards the differential, rotting the chassis at the outer edges.

• The four differential mounting-pins are a known weakness on IRS chassis. Although all are susceptible to cracking, the two on the right side of the car are most prone to actually pulling away from their respective mounting points on the chassis. The most vulnerable pin of all is the front right side pin - attached to the larger crossmember of the two (that also forms the spring cups). This one takes most of the torque load as a reaction to that transmitted through the differential.

Today, most of these cars have seen repairs to one or more differential mounting pin. More often than not, these repairs have been of the 'get the car mobile and sell it' type. This usually takes the form of cutting a hole in the floor above the pin(s), and running a quick bead of weld around the top of each one that cracked or came adrift.

It's actually possible to fix the problem very satisfactorily, without taking the body off the chassis, using a repair-kit (the 'body-on' one!). Unfortunately, however, too few do.

The usual sort of bodge is unlikely to last very long so, if you notice anything amiss, or even if you don't, this is the time to carry out a proper preventative job, using the 'body-off' repair kit. The pins are available new if you should need them.

Photographs 5-30 and 5-31 show the types of repair kit that are available from all the premier TR specialists. The plates are best pre-welded to the head of the pins before welding the plates to the front and rear diff-bridges - thus effectively providing four double-strength mounting points for the differential. Simultaneously, you should create four complete 'turrets' by boxing in the lower brackets, as shown in photographs 5-32 and 5-34.

• The smaller bridge that goes over the rear of the differential deserves attention too. This bridge spans outwards between both rear chassis members, and carries the rear lever-arm shock absorbers. Regardless of whether or not this bridge is cracked, it is usual to take this unique opportunity to reinforce it by 'boxing-in' the channel section. Obviously, if yours is corroded or cracked, as per the example at 5-34, you must first effect a solid repair before

5-29. Taken with the chassis upside down, this picture shows how badly the main bridge diff mounting brackets can crack. Note the separation of what is, in fact, the right side bracket, and how important it is to reinforce it by 'boxing' it in if you are to prevent a recurrence.

5-30 and 5-31 (right). Two differential pin strengthening kits, both, in this case, from Revington TR. The former, with its large strengthening plates for the top of the main diff-bridge, is for body-off repairs and is referenced RTR7012/1. The kit shown in photograph 5-32 has smaller main diff-bridge plates, and is for body-on repairs (Revington number RTR7012/2). If you are considering a home/DIY job, remember that the repair work involves cutting the two top plates in half, followed by much overhead welding.

this further strengthening is undertaken. Even if you are planning rear telescopic shock absorbers, this is a valuable strengthening exercise. The telescopic shocks fit to the bottom of this bridge and, as a result, the loads still have to be safely dissipated throughout the chassis.

• Before you put the welding set away, you should give some thought to the rear gearbox mountings. These vary from gearbox to gearbox. If you plan to reinstall the car's original gearbox, then, clearly, no changes are called for and

you will (or should), find the flat plate gearbox mounting for the 'A' type gearbox. The same flat mounting is used for gearboxes with or without overdrive.

However, you may wish to add an overdrive to your gearbox; or you may elect to fit a later 'J' type gearbox and overdrive in preference to the earlier 'A' gearbox; or you may even be thinking of a proprietary five speed gearbox conversion (discussed in more detail in a later book).

Some of these conversions require

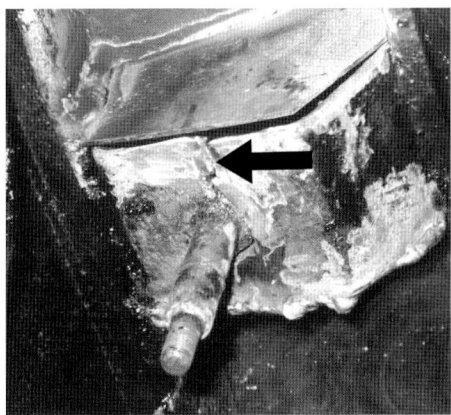

5-32 and 5-33 (right). The first picture shows a front diff-pin - another Achilles-heel of the IRS TRs. There are two pins hanging down from the front diff-bridge, and both are vulnerable to cracking, particularly in the higher-powered UK cars. The right side pin is particularly prone to coming loose from the front diff bridge due to the propshaft's torque being focused at this point. It is usual to fit non-original strengthening plates or gussets to prevent the problem or, as in this case, repair it. The picture is taken from beneath the car, with the diff removed, and shows that the repair is well advanced, with both new side plates welded in place to the front diff bridge, and the far side welded to the original cracked mounting plates (arrowed). Clearly, the next task is to weld the nearest new (inboard) side plate to the original bracket, thus closing the very visible gap, and then to weld the cracked original bracket together. The second photograph shows both front and rear diff pins, one rear driveshaft, and the partly completed repair with the cracked original bracket and the new inboard un-welded gusset clearly visible. You need to periodically check that the pins are still solidly fixed to their brackets, but you will be in no doubt when a pin pulls out of its diff bridge, as the differential will thrash and bang about as torque is applied to the rear of the car! Prevention is far better than cure, so do take a close look with a good light from time to time.

5-34. A rear diff bridge mounting pin, this time viewed from the top. The hole on the right side is for chassis tooling and not relevant, but you can clearly see that the mounting pin is cracked right round the top. The repair parts for the rear diff bridge pins are included in the repair kits, but you can make or buy two plates, about 1.5in (40mm) square, that span the front to back width of the rear bridge. They are the smaller rectangular plates/washers shown in photographs 5-30 and 5-31, with a circular central hole that will be used to plug weld through to the top of the pin. You must first locate and then completely seam weld each plate to the rear bridge so that the hole is central to the pin before the final plug weld is completed. This repair, or preventative step, spreads the stresses from the diff pin over a much larger area than Triumph originally thought necessary.

alteration to the rear gearbox mounting, so this is clearly the time to tackle the changes. Be advised that, although not popular, it is easy and fairly quick to change from 'J' type mounts to those that will accept an 'A' gearbox. The reverse of this may be far more popular, but the time and complexity involved in making the chassis alterations should not be underestimated. Again, you will be motivated by your own particular aspirations. Those with originality or concours in mind may well elect to switch to the earlier gearbox or overdrive unit. However, the additional reliability and the more readily available 'J' unit makes it the more usual choice. Variations of the 'J' type gearbox and overdrive unit were used on Triumph Saloons and Dolomites Sprints, so the 'J' unit may also be the cheaper option as well as the most reliable.

MODIFYING THE IRS LOWER WISHBONE MOUNTINGS

Prior to the TR4A the lower suspension fulcrums were, in effect, welded directly to the chassis frame, making any adjustments, particularly after an accident, very difficult. Indeed, an oxy-acetylene torch was required to heat and bend the erring component back to what looked like the correct position before you could try again.

The front suspension pillars were manufactured with a pair of fore-aft holes near the base of the pillar, through which passed a pretty substantial steel pin. A pair of plain diameters flanked the central part of the pin and carried the front and rear lower wishbones, while a pair of two-piece brackets secured the pin either side of the central pillar (shown in drawing number D5-1). Accident damage can result in the wishbone mounting becoming twisted in relation to the chassis side-member, and partially or even completely broken away from the chassis. The fulcrum pins are thought to be no longer available, but TR Bitz have them specially made and they are usually in stock.

With the introduction of the TR4A, two pairs of brackets were welded each side of the front suspension towers. These can be seen in outline in drawing D5-2, and in more detail in D5-3, and it will be noted that the brackets now allow for shims to be used to achieve the required geometry. However, these fulcrum brackets are only attached to the frame bracket with one $3/8$in stud, while the stresses fed into the rear brackets were only distributed throughout the chassis via one gusset, welded to the top of the frame. Both these details have subsequently been shown to be inadequate, and proved to be an Achilles heel of the IRS TR chassis (particularly the rear bracket). We touched on these in chapter 2 where you will recall looking down on each rear bracket through the inner wings.

Some of these brackets are susceptible to the tensile stresses imposed by reversing swiftly and then braking hard. Tired brackets even tend to part from the chassis! In fact, the whole arrangement proved marginal on the TR4A, and modifications are strongly recommended.

The front wishbone attachment brackets on the IRS cars also need to be checked for cracks or accident damage. Although they generally give less cause for concern than the rear brackets, they could have sustained earlier accident damage. However, the front wishbone brackets are stiffened to the steering rack crossmember by only a few mm of

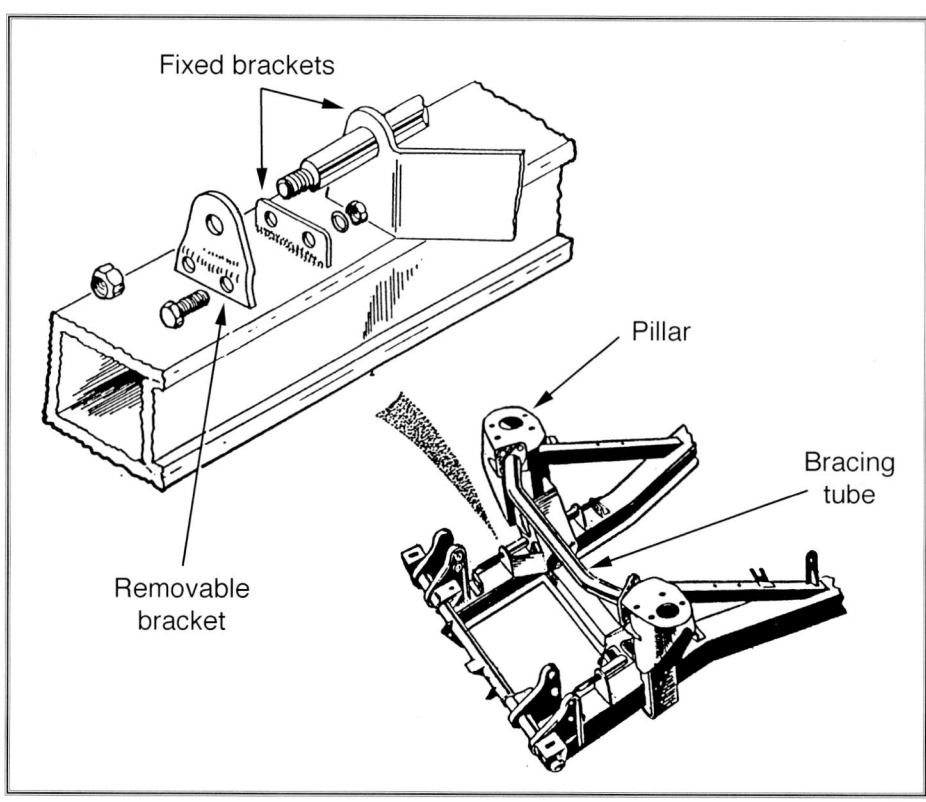

D5-1. General and detail (right) view of early TR front suspension lower mounting arrangement. (Courtesy TRaction - the magazine of the UK TR Register).

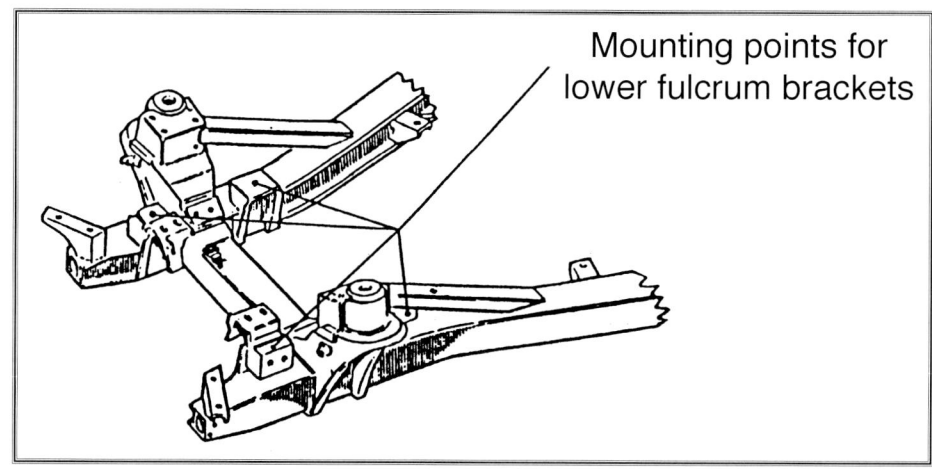

D5-2. The four lower mounting points for the front suspension in the IRS cars. Courtesy TRaction - the magazine of the UK TR Register).

weld, and it's 90% certain that, after shotblasting, you will be able to see that this small weld has cracked. You can, of course re-weld the joint, but it's better to add the new plate or gusset shown in drawing D5-4, and weld it so that it securely joins and mutually stiffens the rack's crossmember and the front lower wishbone attachment bracket.

Photographs 5-35-1 to 5-35-3 demonstrate why and where the extra plate is required.

The weakness in the chassis-mounted bracket was realised by Triumph, which issued designs, part numbers and fitting instructions for six $1/8$in (3mm) stiffeners shown in the drawings detailed earlier. To carry out

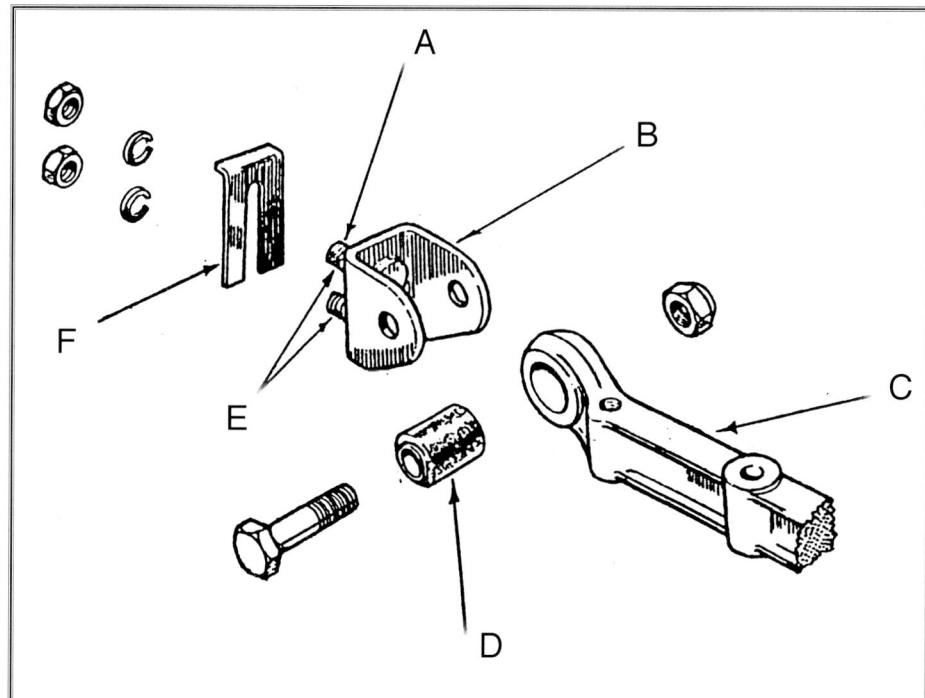

5-35-2. We see from a slightly different angle the front lower wishbone mounting bracket (in the centre), together with the steering rack mounting, this time without the steering rack in the way. The crack is arrowed and we can see the full area where a stiffening plate should be welded in.

D5-3. The lower mounting bracket details for the TR4A (1 stud) and the TR5/6 (2 studs). A. The 1 stud of the TR4A. B. Lower fulcrum bracket. C. Wishbone arm. D. Bush. E. The 2 studs of the TR5/6. F. Shims. (Courtesy TRaction - the magazine of the UK TR Register).

the modification to your car you need two of 88155846, two of 88155847, one of 88155531 and one of 88155532 - to quote the official Triumph part numbers (see photograph 5-36). All can be purchased from Revington TR, or indeed any premier TR restoration specialist, as strengthening kits with, you will note, pressed gussets for maximum rigidity.

The first step requires we get the strongest and most satisfactory mounting brackets welded to the chassis, which is probably best achieved by removing the TR4A's rear lower fulcrum brackets and checking the frame carefully. However, if you are sure the existing brackets and welds are completely satisfactory, it is possible to use the original brackets as the basis of reinforced mountings (with some additional mounting holes), see photographs 5-37-1 to 5-37-3.

Drilling extra holes will probably not be necessary if you replace the welded brackets completely. However, if you retain part of the original mounting points you are well advised to spread the considerable loads via additional studs, which, of course, require additional holes. Drill an additional hole

5-35-1. The TR4A steering rack (note the 'D' washers welded to the rack and the rubber cushion mounting), used, in fact, on TR4As, 5s, 250s and TR6s, with its traditional, but most undesirably cracked, mounting (arrowed).

below each original TR4A hole in preparation for fitting post-1972 TR6 suspension brackets. These can be identified by the four mounting holes shown in drawings D5-4 and D5-5, and the square backing washers they employ. The backing washers can be bolted through the original '4A holes, and then used as templates to drill the additional hole in each frame bracket.

5-35-3. The bottom front wishbone mounting bracket on the left side of the car. One strengthening plate has been added to the rear of the bracket, between the turret and the steering mounting crossmember, and the recommended rectangular plate (arrowed) added to tie the steering mounting to the top of the wishbone mounting.

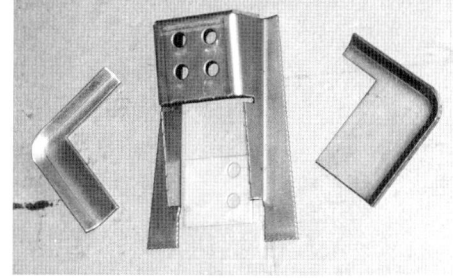

5-36. All the premier TR restoration specialists will supply you with strengthening gusset kits. This is one quarter of Revington TR's front suspension kit (RTR7017), plus an example of their substantial lower wishbone attachment bracket. Note the pressed radii on the edges of the gussets which add considerable strength. This particular kit can be welded to the car with the body *in situ*.

5-37-1, 5-37-2 and 5-37-3 (left to right). These three photographs show the logical steps in repairing and strengthening the left side of a TR front chassis area, just behind the bottom rear wishbone mounting bracket. The repaired chassis piece is dressed off, and a pressed strengthening gusset is added.

Assemble with the backing washers inside the frame brackets to increase the frame strength in this area.

From November 1972, all CR and CF models incorporated the latest thinking and, although the changes I am suggesting may not be original to your car's particular year of manufacture, the changes were an original Triumph design and were incorporated in the later cars for safety reasons. Need I say more?

With the chassis welding complete, you'll need to ensure that every tapped hole is clear (no doubt some drilling and re-tapping is inevitable). You are then set to repaint or powder coat the chassis, the various options for which are explored in chapter 6.

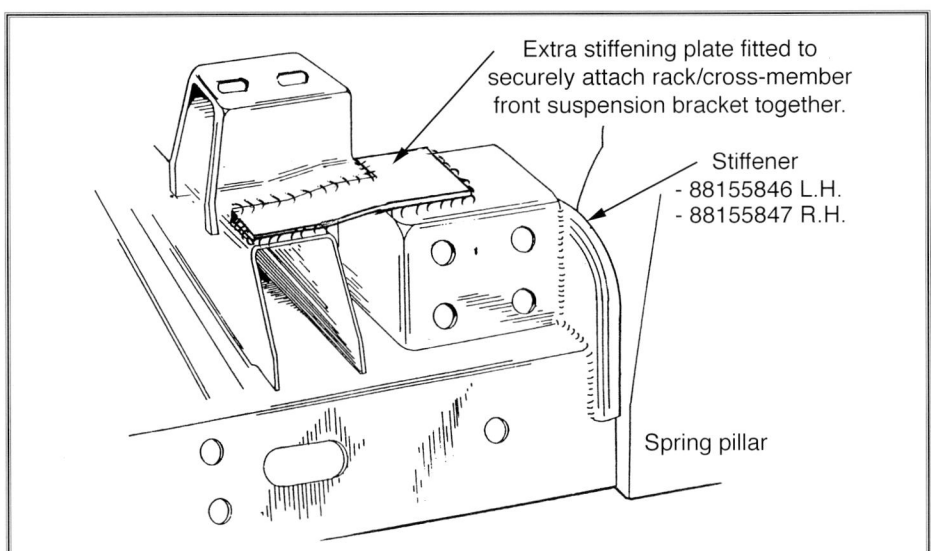

Extra stiffening plate fitted to securely attach rack/cross-member front suspension bracket together.

Stiffener
- 88155846 L.H.
- 88155847 R.H.

Spring pillar

D5-4. Strengthening the front lower left side pivot bracket. (Courtesy TRaction - the magazine of the UK TR Register).

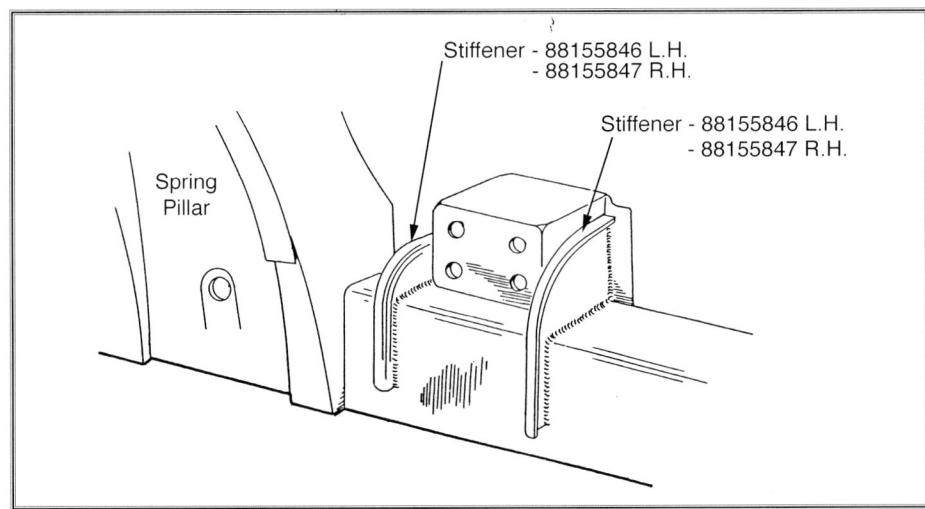

Stiffener - 88155846 L.H.
- 88155847 R.H.

Stiffener - 88155846 L.H.
- 88155847 R.H.

Spring Pillar

D5-5. Strengthening the rear lower left side pivot bracket. (Courtesy TRaction - the magazine of the UK TR Register).

Chapter 6
Painting, plating and rust prevention

GALVANISING

The repaired chassis is best painted after welding is finalised; galvanising is not recommended. I have heard it said that, with galvanising, two men carry the chassis to the tank but four carry the galvanised chassis away! The zinc builds up inside and outside of each section, but, unfortunately, this is not a guarantee of longevity.

The chassis is immersed in molten metal (mostly zinc), which can distort it. Furthermore, the acids involved in the pre-galvanising process do not seem to be able to escape from the chassis box sections, and are probably trapped in the tiny gaps between the folded flanges of various box sections, and within the many closed subsections of this complex structure. Whatever the reason, many galvanised chassis have rotted away from within, leaving the well-intentioned owner with only a zinc 'shell' that gives no strength to his TR. The final nail in the coffin, from my viewpoint, was to realise that zinc, when welded, gives off very toxic fumes. OK, so you are going to fix all the chassis problems this time round, and certainly before galvanising.

But what of the future, and - heaven forbid - possible accident damage that needs repair, or

6-1. The first steps of painting the underside are shown here. First, the primer has been applied - possibly 5 coats - followed by careful seam sealing round all seams. Did you spot that the outer sill on the left side of the picture (actually on the right side of the car!) has been left unprimed? It will be part of the final finishing of the exterior of the car, and is best left until that part of the finishing process starts. Consequently, this area, the interior of the car, and anything else that is to be painted at a later stage, has been carefully masked.

modifications, or upgrades that involve welding new or different brackets to the chassis. I think painting your chassis is the best all round and most

6-2. A further 3 to 5 coats of undercoat will have been applied followed by probably 5 coats of top coat to give a commendably high quality finish. It is very important to protect the car, but such a high level of finish should not be regarded as essential under the car - unless you are aiming at concours condition - particularly if you plan to 'Waxoyl' the underside in due course. Do not, however, attempt waxoyling until absolutely all of the paint work is finished. The sill on the right side of the picture has also been masked to allow finishing at a later stage - but note the precision with which the masking has been applied.

6-3. The shell has been turned over once the underside painting is done. Note the superb door gap strengthening jig that provides extra support to the rear half body via a coupling to the handbrake bracket. However, the main objective of the photograph is to illustrate the first steps of the second phase of painting - priming and sealing the inside of the car. It will be clearer in later photographs, but a close look will confirm that the top deck and 'B' post will have been masked off for they remain unpainted. You will appreciate that there are no 'loose' panels in place, nor will they appear for some time to come.

practical solution!

PAINTING YOUR CHASSIS

I have previously mentioned that, as soon as the metal work is sandblasted, it is imperative that the resultant bright surface is protected within a few hours (four maximum). If the blasting takes place on a wet or humid day, the chassis is best protected straight away, within the hour.

In either event, one suggestion you should consider is the use of a stoving wash-black etch paint. Do not use a high-build paint; you are looking for a thin surface finish that will prevent corrosion in the short term, which adheres very securely to the newly shotblasted surface. Your finish should be easily wire brushed off where welding to the chassis is subsequently required. The use of paint designed for stoving means that, when you weld, say, an inch or two away from the boundary of the painted surface, the heat effectively 'stoves' the paint.

However, before you decide, you may care to visit your nearest marine chandler to acquire a brushing metal primer and a gloss black brushing top coat. What's wrong with your nearest hardware store, I hear you ask. Well, nothing actually, but ship's chandlers are very experienced in dealing with the harshest environment in the world, and products they recommend might better protect your TR chassis in a salt-laden environment.

If you live an impossible distance from the coast, why not ask International Coatings' Yacht Division (01962 711177 (UK) or 1 908 686-1300 (US)) to send you its free booklet that explains in some detail how to prepare and paint steel boats? International's marine grade paints are of the highest quality, are safe to use, and can be applied by brush to give an excellent surface finish.

Incidentally, I specifically recommend brushing paints because spray painting a TR chassis at home is deceptively tricky, as in the average garage it is difficult to handle the chassis in such a way that all surfaces receive a good covering of paint. Furthermore, the volume of paint used to spray paint a chassis is far greater than you would ever estimate, and will probably require a high-build primer (which will have to

6-4.

or epoxy powder-coated finish.

Powder-coating is, as its name suggests, a process by which the finishing material is applied in a very fine powder. It is discharged from a special 'gun' and electrostatically charged in the process so that it 'seeks' your earthed chassis. The whole chassis is then put in an oven, the heat fluidises the powder, which then flows to form an excellent corrosion-resistant, smooth-surfaced finish. Good, eh? This electrostatically charged, plastic-like coating is, unlike paint, attracted to the edges of your chassis, a characteristic that makes it particularly suited to protecting chassis-like products.

Cost is a consideration; it may be in the region of £200-plus. Also be aware of a downside to powder-coating. As just mentioned, the electrostatic charge makes the powder seek the nearest earthed metal, which makes it very difficult to get the powder to penetrate right into the bottom of a tight-angled corner without first being 'pulled' to the nearest piece of chassis. As a result, the actual covering of powder in the base of any right-angled fold can be minimal. Nevertheless, the polyester coatings, in particular, are much more resistant to stone chips and, unlike paint, will usually withstand steam cleaning. The latter is a consideration if you live in or near a farming community, and wish to periodically steam/pressure clean the inevitable mud from the underside of your car. Paint will quickly be pressured off, polyester will stay the course, and probably offers the best long-term chassis protection.

Polyester coating will also smooth over a slightly pocked chassis, but is impossible to repair, although you can paint over any spots that have been damaged by welding, *etc*.

6-4 and 6-5 (above). Two views of the finished shell. Again, it is very clear from both these shots that very careful masking ensures that paint is not applied to those areas that constitute the exterior of the car, which will be painted by a professional painting contractor. When phase three - the final stage - of the painting process starts, the areas that are painted will be completely masked, allowing the painter to go through the priming, undercoating and finishing processes without harming or over-spraying your hard work.

be rubbed down between coats) to 'fill' the inevitable imperfections in the chassis. A very expensive and time-consuming exercise, and not recommended.

Powder-coating

If you don't wish to carry out the finishing process at home, or feel an even better chassis finish is essential, then your only alternative is a polyester

PAINTING BODYTUB AND PANELS

This may seem an inappropriate moment to mention a couple of details from towards the end of your restoration, but it's worth giving the final body rust protection and the hood frame a moment's thought.

Before moving on to the highly visible body protection, it's a good idea to consider where and how you intend to inject rust preventative wax into the cavities. You should now drill any access

6-6. The under-bonnet area painted to a very high standard. This detail is slightly hard to see, but in fact the masking for the scuttle is still in place, as is the masking that closes off the numerous holes in the bulkhead/firewall. If you are looking for an excellent under-bonnet finish in your car but doubt your ability to reach the desired standard, it can be sprayed separately from the rest of the car, so can be left to the professionals if your nerve fails you at the last moment!

holes that will be required. Furthermore, as is explained in more detail in chapter 17, the hood frame is best checked and repaired as necessary on the car. Heat and/or penetrating oil will possibly be needed to free the hood frame, so it's better that this is done before the body is painted, and certainly before trimming.

On to what you really want to read about here - painting the car itself.

Step 1: zinc primer

No matter which steel component it is, once repaired, it's absolutely essential that the dreaded tin worm doesn't get a hold again, and this has never been truer than with body panels.

Body panels are amongst the most expensive and time-consuming parts of the car to repair, so deserve the most comprehensive preparation and treatment when it comes to rust preventative measures. Whatever you do will form the foundation upon which all subsequent finishes are applied, so it's pointless spending hours and/or large sums of money on a wonderful paint job if, underneath, rust is re-establishing its hold.

This foundation is a two-part process, starting with the metal

preparation. On several previous occasions I have mentioned a professional sandblast finish with an immediate application of rust preventative primer. You can wire brush - grind, even - to your heart's content, but nothing removes the rust and prepares the surface of the metal with a superb 'key' like sandblasting does. It is not terrifically expensive either - some £250-£300 depending on location and the zinc primer you specify. Mentioned before, but well worth repeating, is that you must not allow the blaster to touch anything but the edges of flat panels like doors, boot/trunk lid, bonnet/hood, *etc.* The wings are very doubtful, too, but should be okay if just a 1in (25mm) edge is blasted. The problem is that the larger, flatter panels ripple, but this is not always obvious until the gloss paint goes on.

Your main problem will be getting the shell/tub to and from where it is to be sandblasted. Although we have touched on that already, we will look at this again in more detail later.

We have also discussed the importance of a good and timely primer coat on to a freshly prepared surface, and you are bound to be anxious to use

one of the best primers available. At the time of writing, two in particular deserve mention. Neither is readily available at your local DIY store, but both manufacturers operate a mail-order system, and their addresses are included in Appendix 1. The effectiveness of both products makes obtaining them very worthwhile. Both products must obviously be applied carefully to ensure that all edges, corners and joints - as well as any nuts and bolts - are adequately coated.

The first primer is made by Witham Oil and Paint and is called Unidox Zinc Rich Primer CR. This product is designed for application to bare steel with a wire brushed or (preferably) blast-cleaned surface. It contains a high percentage of zinc dust that results in a high zinc to steel contact which protects the steel by the cathodic (or 'sacrificial') action of the zinc. It is metallic grey in colour and is surface-dry in 20 minutes and hard-dry in about two hours, whereupon I would suggest a second coat. All oil and grease must be removed prior to treatment and the manufacturer recommends white spirit as the solvent. Application of the primer can be by airless spray, conventional spray, or brush, although brush application should ideally be limited to small areas only. Witham says that its product may be overcoated with conventional one-pack paint systems (*i.e.* cellulose) after a couple of days. Ask the manufacturer for a full data sheet and health and safety precautions when ordering your 1 or 2.5 litre packs. The cleaning solvent and (no more than 10%) thinner is TH2, and may be best acquired at the same time.

Called Bonda Rust Primer, our second shortlisted zinc primer is made by Bondaglass-Voss Ltd. This product is said to have particularly good penetrating and high wetting properties that help the primer to enter all the rust pores, hairline cracks, joints and fastenings. The manufacturer tells us that the product is based on a specially selected resin which, when combined with its excellent penetrative properties, allows the product to envelope each particle of rust with a tough water-repellent plastic coating. The coating makes an excellent bond to the base metal, as well as providing an excellent surface on which to paint. Not surprisingly, the manufacturer insists all

6-7. The four wings/fenders with the weatherproofing sealer applied to the mating faces after painting - ready to bolt to the body tub. As discussed in the main text, Dumdum is a never-setting sealer that most restorers would use. This looks like something other than Dumdum since it is considerably lighter in colour. The sealer is unlikely to be Sikoflex, or any other setting sealer for that matter. Whilst you have several hours to effect any adjustments with setting sealers, and these panels will have been on and off the car countless times and should fit well, you would be taking a risk applying a setting sealer to all four panels at once.

oil and grease be removed prior to applying the primer, and cellulose thinners are recommended for this purpose. It is also advised that any loose rust is removed by wire brush and/or sanding, and that the metal is as clean as is possible before application.

This primer has a red oxide appearance, a slight sheen, and can be brushed or sprayed. Two coats are normally recommended and are sufficient. The supplier points out, however, that almost all metal surfaces which have suffered from corrosion will resemble a mountain range when viewed in section under a microscope. Consequently, additional applications may be necessary where severe corrosion has occurred in order to ensure there are no peaks poking through the surface of the primer. The supplier also points out that several thin coats are preferable to one thick coat, particularly when brushing the product. Thinning is not usually necessary when spraying, but up to 10% 'fast' cellulose thinners may be added if required. The product accepts a wide range of subsequent coatings, including enamels,

oil-based, synthetic, two-pack and cellulose finishes. Sprayed cellulose topcoats can be applied within 6 to 24 hours or after 7 days (note the no-painting gap), but brushed cellulose can only be applied after 7 days.

Steps 2 and 3: etch priming and final gloss finish

These stages tend to roll into one, in the sense that the painter you contract to do the final gloss finish will clearly also undertake application and flatting back of the all-important etch primer.

The 'etch' part is important in that a gentle acid within this primer lightly etches the surface to provide a good bond for subsequent paint application. Obviously, it is important to carry out the preparatory seam sealing operation. This can be done by 'gun' although my personal preference is to use the brushing variety of seam sealer. You can really work it into the seams, although, if a neat edge is required (say, within the engine bay), you can pre-apply masking tape and, of course, peel it off a day or so after applying the sealer.

There are two alternative ways to

paint your TR and we will look at them in a moment. Firstly, however, I must emphasise that the way TR cars are constructed dictates that they must be painted with the panels (*i.e.* wings, boot, doors, bonnet, *etc.*) off the bodytub. This is particularly true of the wings, since it is imperative that the mating surface of both bodytub and wings are properly prepared and painted prior to assembly. They bolt together, so there should be no subsequent damage to any part of the car, provided appropriate care is taken, of course. Rest assured that the professionals always paint the loose panels off the car, and you should not listen to a paint shop that tells you differently. That said, there are some alternative ways to paint the bodytub:
• Paint the whole thing off the chassis and then bolt it to the chassis, or
• Paint the inside, underside and inner wings, bolt it to the chassis and then paint the outside.

The former method ensures no over-spray on the chassis, but you risk scratches on the bodywork. The latter method invariably leaves some over-spray on the chassis (unless you mask the chassis or use a water-soluble spray called Slime that does the masking job for you), but has the advantage of avoiding scratched or damaged body paint. Obviously, whichever method you adopt you should trial fit all loose panels before painting, but not finally fit the doors, wings, bonnet and boot-lid until the body is on the chassis, to avoid serious paint scratches during the first method.

Moving an unsupported body any distance, even with the door braces still in place, is dangerous and requires great care, so, although the second method may have disadvantages, it also has two advantages. Whilst not essential, it offers the option to paint the inside, underside and inner wings of the shell at home, which minimises transportation, preparation (the subcontractor is going to have to take the body off the chassis in order to fully paint the underside of the body) and painting costs. £2500-£4500 is the current ball-park cost to have everything (including loose panels before assembly) properly painted, the car reassembled to its chassis, and all panels replaced. The home restorer can save a large part of this cost by doing the inside/underside/inner wings himself, a further amount if he reassembles body to chassis, and even more if he takes the car to the subcontractor with all the loose panels off the tub and reassembles them at home after painting.

So, having investigated a couple of options, this is my recommendation. The following painting plan gives you the best value/quality for money, and should be integrated with the other details of your restoration. Since every car is different, it's impossible to cover every eventuality, but I hope that the following will give you food for thought.

• Carry out the body repairs and trial fit the loose panels at home. Remove the loose panels.

• Prepare areas to be painted at home and, with the crossbraces still in place, paint under, inside and around the inner wheelarches of the bodytub. Painting the engine bay is optional and can be left for the professionals if necessary.

• Drop the bodytub onto your finished chassis.

• Refit the loose panels, adjust gaps, and, finally, fix the body to the chassis. Remove the panels.

• Mask the chassis or arrange that the painter sprays the chassis in water-soluble Slime. This washes off after use.

• Take the chassis/tub and all panels to the painter for final preparation and painting.

• Carefully bring the lot home and store the loose panels well out of harm's way.

• Protect the body/paintwork and finish as much of the restoration as you can.

• As late as possible in your restoration, refit the loose panels.

Doing your bit

Assuming you have decided to finish the inside, underside and inner wheelarches of the bodyshell yourself, let us look at a few details.

Firstly, the matter of safety. Do not use two-pack paints without the necessary protective/breathing equipment. Ensure you budget for hiring, buying or borrowing the appropriate gear.

The materials you use must be compatible with those your professionals will use to finish the car, so talk to them and agree what you and they will use and where you should purchase your materials. You will probably find they can advise the quantities to purchase, too.

I do not think it matters whether you paint the underside or inside first, but, on the basis of minimising handling after painting, I would do the underside first (we will discuss the processes on that basis). Whichever route you take, do mask off the areas you don't want to paint. Study the photographs in this chapter to get an idea of the accuracy and extent of work involved. With the shell turned upside down, seal all welds and joints from the underside. A brushing seam sealer (approved by your painter) will do for the majority of seams, although 'Sikoflex' might be best in areas like wing surrounds and/or along the sills.

The painting phase/sequence is: clean/degrease, prime, stone-chip/guard (if you are going to; we'll discuss this process in more detail in a moment), prime again or undercoat and, finally, top coat. You will want to apply several coats of each paint finish, perhaps as many as five for each painting phase. There are some super 'etch' and 'high-build' primers on the market, but I would have thought an ordinary primer perfectly satisfactory for the underside, and indeed inside the car, particularly if you plan to apply a coat of stone-chip. Always start painting the difficult-to-get-at areas first; the undersides of brackets and channels, in the corners, and other hard-to-reach spots. The next phase is to ensure all the panel edges are well covered before the easy/quick/most-satisfying bit - filling in.

With the car returned to its normal stance you should follow a similar finishing sequence inside the boot/trunk, cockpit and engine compartment. Again, seam sealer is very important; use Sikoflex in the areas around the base of all four wings, at the base of the footwells, and in other particularly important areas susceptible to water and road grit, and brushing sealer everywhere else. The engine compartment is one area where you will want a reasonable paint finish, so I would leave spraying the engine compartment until last in order to allow you maximum time to get used to spraying techniques. I would never apply stone-chip to any part of an engine compartment, although some do apply it (to non-concours cars) over the cockpit floor and over the parts of the boot that are covered in flooring or carpet. If you are keen to get a particularly good finish within the engine compartment, consider using an undercoat of 'high-build' primer after seam sealing. This is thicker than usual primers and will help to cover any original or repair imperfections. You will need to rub down with wet and dry paper each of at least five coats, progressively reducing the grade of paper (start with 240 and end with 1000) for maximum benefit. Finish off with a coat of high-build primer-surfacer, before thinking about the finishing coats.

Other painting detail

If you decide upon a different painting plan, particularly one where the painter paints the whole body, you will wish to marry painted body to painted chassis once again. How, when and where? Plenty of good bodies have been damaged during transportation to or even from the painter's. Such damage is not completely irreparable, but is bound to be expensive and heartbreaking. It can also occur when moving the shell perhaps to or from having it sandblasted, of course, and you will have noted several references to moving the body on its chassis to prevent transit damage. That can be difficult if you intend to refurbish the chassis while the specialist is painting the body, so we had better establish the two main causes of damage to enable you to guard against them.

The most frequent is to allow the rear of the car to travel unsupported. The centre of the shell is usually securely strapped down, but, without its chassis, the rear 'overhang' of the shell bounces up and down during transit and stretches (fractures, in extreme cases) just in front of the 'B' posts. Support the shell under the boot floor with a couple of old car tyres of a suitable width.

The second opportunity for equally devastating damage can occur when a well-meaning driver goes to the other extreme and runs a commercial vehicle wagon strap (which ratchets down to secure a normal load) over the back of the car. He then, in effect, breaks the back of the car by pulling the rear down, which is particularly easy to do if the floor is unsupported.

The return journey also needs to be planned meticulously. Do not try to bring the finish-painted body home on its own; a finish-painted shell must have the chassis in place before return transportation, so gather your helpers and marry the painted bodyshell to its (preferably rolling) chassis at the painter's. If you try transporting a painted shell without its chassis, you will crack the paint. It helps if you pre-glue the body mounting pads to the chassis before taking it to the painter. As a little extra precaution, I would ensure that the doors, wings, boot and bonnet panels are never refitted by the painter, but transported home (very carefully wrapped and protected) off of the bodyshell. This eases the body to chassis marriage and allows you to do much of the mechanical reassembly with the loose panels stored well out of harm's way! Even after refitting the shell to its chassis, do not contemplate removing the door braces until your rolling shell is home and off the transporter.

Sooner or later you will need to address the question of how to affix the body panels. The 'how' applies not so much to the fastenings but the sealant between tub and panels that must be used if the job is going to last.

As already mentioned, Triumph created a corrosion problem when it fitted the various panels prior to painting. The panel interfaces remained unprotected and, except for in the warmest of climates, corroded. We have corrected one problem by ensuring our panels are at least painted prior to attachment. However, there is still plenty of opportunity for water to get into the interfaces between wings and body, and you would be well advised to ensure that these vulnerable areas are safeguarded by using a sealant between the panel joints.

But what sealant? The choice is more difficult than it seems for the joints between the rear wings and rear deck will continue to move, and a sealer that 'sets' will crack (as will any paint you apply to this area after affixing the wings). So, you need a non-setting sealer and will have to accept that TRs are best not painted after fitting the wings/fenders. Black rainwater gutter sealer remains flexible and is used on TRs, but it's essential you keep it low down in the seams. Modern bodyshops use Sikoflex and, whilst you can use it on your TR (and it is intended to be painted over), I should warn you that the panels in question will be very hard to remove at a later date. Dumdum is probably the preferred alternative, and

can be over-painted if you must, although, all things considered, it's still better not to paint the rear wings/deck at least after fitting. Dumdum is a black, non-setting sealer and, therefore, it's best to allow the panel joint to squeeze out the worst of the excess and to use a plastic scraper to remove the top $1/16$in (2mm) from each joint. Wipe over the joint with some petrol on a rag to ensure that no more than a thin black seam is visible.

STONE-CHIP PROTECTION

It is very much a matter of preference, but many an excellent - if non-concours - restoration has had a coat of stonechip to the underside, sills, front and rear valances, and even on the inside of the floors. Stonechip leaves a slightly mottled finish that can never be flattened, but does provide an excellent chip/corrosion-resistant surface for long-lasting bodyshell protection. Bodyline's 'Stoneguard' is a rubber-based product that should be applied, after sealing, over an etch primer and the covered by a further coat of primer. You can and should paint over stonechip with body colour which should ensure it is almost hidden from all but the closest inspection. You will need to discuss and agree with the paintshop the areas where the coating is to be applied. Do not confuse stonechip with underbody sealers that have similar names. These are usually black, cannot be painted over, and are not really recommended for classic car restoration.

There is also a clear stone-repellent film available that can be applied to the outside paintwork to protect cars that are likely to be subjected to really tough conditions (rallying, for example). This film, which is called Foliatec and is supplied in 175mm wide strips each about 1500mm long, can be stuck to vulnerable areas and peeled off as and when appropriate. Together with the cutting tool, this film costs around £20, and is available from TR Enterprises and the other TR specialists listed in Appendix 1.

BRIGHT METAL FINISHING
Chrome plating
Chrome plating is porous - and not a lot of people know that! Yes, it lets in water. When cars with chrome fittings were

originally manufactured, the top layer of decorative chrome was preceded by two surfaces; a layer of copper plate followed by a layer of nickel plate. This additional plating was designed to provide a non-permeable coating between any water that passed through the chrome and the underlying steel, thereby preventing rusting.

Plating with this copper base is unquestionably best, but the cost of copper has made it progressively more difficult to find re-platers who will triple plate on a copper base. However, if you are investing in the restoration of an immaculate TR you expect to keep for many years, then the additional cost of a copper based, triple plated decorative chrome finish could well be worthwhile. The next best thing is to specify a double coating of nickel, which is more readily available, but avoid the cheap chrome-on-steel approach which looks reasonable on the journey home from the platers, but rusts as soon as the car gets wet.

Whatever the quality of your chrome finish, it's worthwhile taking some precautions in order to extend the life of the plated parts. Firstly, keep them clean and wipe them over to remove the worst of any moisture as soon as the car is put away; this is particularly important if there is salt in the moisture. Secondly, use chrome cleaner to help keep the chrome bright, and, thirdly, do wax polish the chrome. The wax acts as a water barrier and makes the chrome sparkle!

While on the subject of chrome work generally, but bumpers in particular, the quality of reproduction bumpers is, frankly, disappointing, regardless of which model you consider. Consequently, I strongly recommend you stay with an original bumper wherever possible. If your original chromed parts are rusted, they can usually be repaired by welding in a similar section from a scrap bumper, provided the perforation is localised, or at least not too extensive. The repaired part is then polished flat and re-chromed to the extent that you could not guess from the outside what has been done. If your bumper has been dented, even badly, it is amazing what skills platers can employ to bring it back to life.

Obviously, if your (probably rear) bumper is very badly corroded, it may be beyond saving. However, do not make that decision yourself; take it to your favourite TR specialist or chrome restorer and seek expert advice. I have used Central Engineering Services (see Appendix 1) for several plating restorations.

If your existing parts are declared past it, you can, at least, start looking for an original replacement that is in salvageable condition. Your ideal, needless to say, is an ex-Californian part with minimal rust; this is more important than if it has a few minor dents.

The method I have recommended is not the cheapest option, and if your restoration is on a very tight budget then non-original replacements are probably the way to go.

Component preparation
A superb restoration and paint job can be made to look quite ordinary if the tiny details are not attended to. It surprises me how many classic restorations of any marque you care to name fall into the trap of not replating door catches, bonnet fastenings, large bolts, various brackets, wiper motors, servo cases, etc. Mind you, some go to the other extreme of fitting new replacements, which certainly complement the restoration, but at what unnecessary cost?

Replating many of the originally plated parts (such as those listed above) can be done, but it must be stressed that this is not worthwhile for small fastenings such as nuts and washers and small bolts/screws. Replating is a three-part process, starting with degreasing and followed by bead-blasting the parts to remove any rust. You could do these preparatory jobs yourself, since the task of bead-blasting each component is fairly labour-intensive, and you can buy a small bead-blasting cabinet for around £150 from Machine Mart. This may sound a lot, but you will be able to use the cabinet many more times, and the results will be far better than they would be trying to clean up dozens of rusty

parts with a wire brush, electronic drills, or whatever, which do little more than polish the rust! I have no doubt that the cabinet would pay for itself if you could share the cost with another enthusiast. Furthermore, new large bolts/screws can be expensive, and some of the original imperial bolts hard to find. However, most of the original steel bolts, particularly the larger ones, can be replated to a considerable financial advantage if they have had the two preparatory stages.

The actual plating process is called 'BZP' (Bright Zinc Plating) and is followed by a passivating process. This technique does not involve any significant heat so embrittlement of most steel is avoided. Nevertheless, it is prudent to avoid replating any highly stressed studs or bolts; for example, a cylinder head stud. The process is definitely worthwhile elsewhere and adds a new dimension of professionalism to a restoration project.

Assemblies such as door locks and bonnet catches can be rejuvenated in the same way as the fastenings mentioned above, although a little organisation on your part is required if you are to maximise the cost-effectiveness of the process. Plating is carried out by the load and a full load will be about 10 kilos. The cost of one load is about £25 and you will be charged for a full load whether you use it or not. So, you need to gather all the parts for your car into one load, arrange to pair-up with another restoration project friend, or persuade your local TR restoration specialist to put your bits in with his next load. If the last solution is used, prepare a list of the parts you are sending to the specialist.

A bead-blaster is also very helpful in preparing parts for painting, and will save your paint/powder coater much time and you cost! Whether you are doing the bead-blasting or contracting it to the painter, taking your parts to him piece-by-piece will run up a very large

bill. My recommendation is that you try to get all the blasting and prime painting and/or powder coating done in one, or two at the most, loads. This will save you hours of time and, if done in bulk, the cost per part will be quite small. Do check all parts before getting them finish painted or powder coated and correct any thread or more major faults first (e.g. re-bushing, welding, resetting, etc.). As you are dealing with a large number of parts, a photograph of what went to the powder coater will be helpful if you need to instigate a search for missing bits before they are lost forever.

RUST PREVENTION
That you must ensure that corrosion is kept to a minimum is beyond doubt. When and how is open to discussion.

Waxoyl, or something similar, is the preferred method/material. There are many who advocate that the wax injection be done when the car is absolutely complete, but I favour the double dose treatment.

I suggest you apply the wax to box sections and in the inaccessible corners/areas of the shell as soon as you are confident all painting is complete. You can actually apply a wax coat under components that will later be bolted over the waxed areas, ensuring protection where there is unlikely to ever be any by another route! I also wax the inside of the bulkhead/firewall, which you are unlikely to do once the car is finished. I also apply wax to each component as I assemble it, and finish off the whole car with a final spray.

I believe that, given the small cost involved, it is worth buying a compressed air injection gun, long reach tube and flexible hose. Machine Mart is one possible source. You must close all injection holes with a plastic bung, and be prepared to go through the underside/box section protection exercise every couple of years.

Chapter 7
The four-cylinder engine

BACKGROUND

In 1952, Ken Richardson was charged with turning Triumph's sportscar aspirations into a viable product, and, aside from numerous other problems, he needed an engine for the TR. As it happened, the Triumph engine factory was producing a 4-cylinder wet-linered Massey-Ferguson tractor engine. The engine had already been slightly modified and put to use in the 2088cc Standard Vanguard saloon/sedan, and the bottom end and cylinder block was thought quite suited to the TR.

Its 'wet liner' cylinder bores (photograph 7-1) came into contact with the coolant (hence the term wet liner) and were designed to be removable (photograph 7-2) for repair or replacement. This has both advantages and disadvantages, as we will see shortly, but it did mean that Triumph could very easily reduce the bore of the engine from 85 to 83mm, with the result that it could be offered in an 'under-2000cc' category car - at 1991cc.

The wet liner concept also meant that Triumph then, or you today, could alter the engine's capacity with ease. For example, TR3Bs and TR4As are fitted with the same liner, bored to 86mm, and, with the appropriate pistons, of

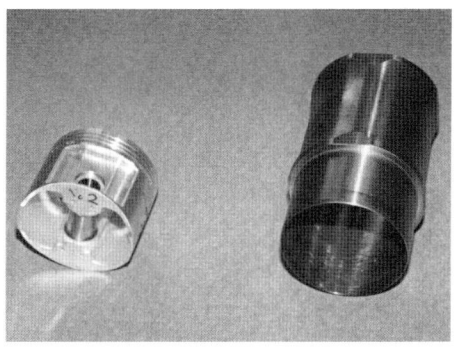

7-1. A piston and wet liner. These are best bought as a set and offer the huge advantage of never having to rebore the block of a four-cylinder TR engine. You can understand how easy it was for Triumph engineers to adjust the capacity of the Standard Vanguard engine to suit the TR.

course, this provides for a 2138cc engine. This is a very popular, if not the most popular, choice of engine size, and is generally known as the '2.2 litre' engine - which is slightly strange since there is also an 87.2mm liner set available giving 2198cc! In fact, your 83mm liners can be removed from the block, bored and fitted with appropriate pistons to both overhaul the engine and upgrade its performance. Very few would bother to salvage the old liners, however, since sets of new liners with

7-2. Although there are some precautions that one needs to take to ensure reliability, this is how easy it is to change a liner.

the correct pistons are so readily and competitively available.

All liners are interchangeable between all engines, and you can, today, buy piston and liner sets that open your bores to 89mm, giving 2290cc. However, there is, as they say, no gain without pain, and the wet liners are not without their drawbacks.

The base of each liner needs to be sealed to the block with a gasket. Each gasket, in fact, seals two cylinders, and is shaped like an '8', as can be seen in photograph 7-3. The liners are clamped onto these 'figure-8' gaskets (part number 112789) by a properly torqued down cylinder head and head gasket, so the length of the replacement liners is critical and must be uniform (more on this later).

FIRST CHECKS

Quite apart from the obvious things one checks upon purchase of a fresh car, you would be well advised to immediately drain the oil and drop the sump. You can then clean out any sludge and start the engine afresh (much better than merely changing the oil and the filter).

Occasionally an owner will notice a clatter within his engine that sounds just like a worn little-end bush. It is usually confined to low rpm and will probably disappear as the rpm increases. In spite of what it sounds like, do not rush into striping the whole engine - at least until you have checked one relatively simple shaft for wear. The shaft in question runs above and below the camshaft and is shown in photograph 7-4. It's actually driven by the camshaft through a bevel gear that is supposed to be securely keyed to the shaft. If you have this rattling noise it is most likely to be a worn key allowing the gear to move on its shaft.

The top face of the gear drives the distributor, via an offset slot, while the bottom of the shaft drives the oil pump via a spade machined on the end. A loose key will allow the shaft to flutter at low rpm and generate a light clattering sound, perhaps augmented by the spade moving slightly in the oil pump. The spade could also be worn and be responsible for generating the noise.

It's unlikely that you will be able to obtain a new shaft very easily, so you will need to re-key the gear to the shaft,

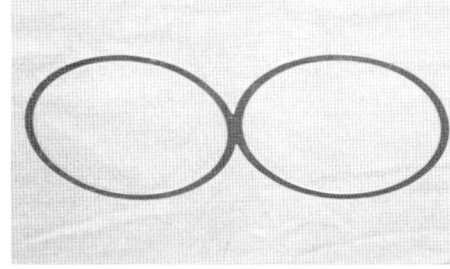

7-3. Generally shortened to 'Fo8', the gaskets can be obtained in steel, copper and aluminium. Steel ones were used originally, but tend to rust. Copper would be the material of choice today.

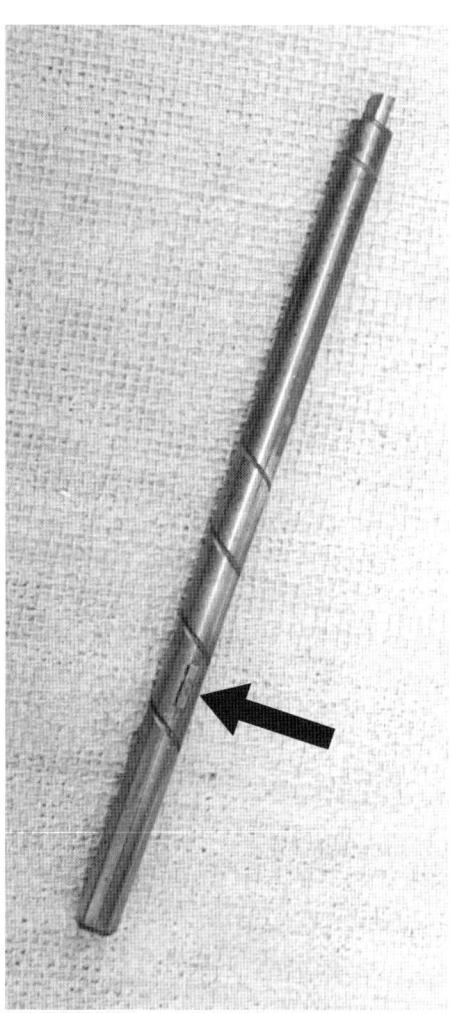

7-4. Often mistaken for a worn little end, a rattle at idle from a four-cylinder TR engine is more likely to emanate from a worn section of this shaft. The end tang (which drives the oil pump) and/or gearwheel key (arrowed) and/or the distributor drive slot (see photograph 7-14-40), can generate a rattle if worn, and need to be routinely checked when carrying out an engine overhaul. A worn little end is a very rare occurrence in a four-cylinder TR engine.

and take a close look at the spade for any signs of wear or polishing. Consider the situation carefully if you do find wear to the spade, for this is effectively the heart of your engine. Worn spades have been known to break off, resulting in a sudden and catastrophic loss of oil pressure. Your engine will continue to run, of course, but only for a very short while.

If you do need to strip your engine, another common problem concerns cylinder head removal. This, however, deserves a section all to itself!

REMOVING THE HEAD

Even with the rocker gear out of the way, Triumph cylinder heads often seem reluctant to be parted from their mating parts. Owners with six-cylinder engines have had to resort from time to time to a trick of stuffing a central cylinder with lots of thin nylon rope. While that may work with the six-pots, it should never be tried on Triumph four-pots as it can disturb the wet liners. Because of this, this rope technique deserves nothing more than a passing mention here.

In spite of the temptation, NEVER try levering the head from its block by putting something between them. You will damage either or both mating surfaces. NEVER try to 'shock' the head free either. Lots of patience and large quantities of penetrating oil will be required, so give yourself plenty of time if the head is scheduled for gas-flowing, skimming, etc.

So how do you get the darn thing off? Start by winding all the nuts sufficiently clear of the head (but not off the studs) so that a small circular 'dam' can be built around each stud using plasticine, blue-tack, or a similar, soft mouldable material. Resign yourself to a week of pouring penetrating oil around each stud at least twice per day, more frequently if you have the time and the studs are soaking up the oil.

After about a week wind a second nut down onto the original one and lock the two nuts together. You need two good spanners to achieve a solid lock. This can only really be achieved by unscrewing the bottom nut hard up to the top nut that you have held static. Remove the top spanner and try to unscrew the bottom nut and its stud. Most should come out, with some hard work, but it's another week of patience and penetrating oil on the rest before you try again.

With all studs removed, but with the spark-plugs in place, turn the crank over on the starter to unstick the head, or break the seal between head and block by very carefully tapping a wooden wedge between the outside of the block and the thermostat housing. Check all studs for stretching and discard any suspect ones.

THE CYLINDER LINER AND LOWER SEALS

Decomposing 'Fo8' (Figure of 8) gaskets, and/or cylinder head problems, are signalled by a mixture of oil and water in both sump and radiator. As I mentioned a few lines ago, the lower seal at the bottom of each liner is universally called an 'Fo8 gasket'. With the head removed, the next potential problem you face is that the gasket positioned at the bottom of each pair of liners tends to rust away, and, when you want to remove the liners, they appear to be fixed integrally to the block!

Occasionally the liners are no trouble to remove, but if yours are stuck fast you will need to drift them out from the underside with a block of hard wood. Clearly this is best accomplished with the pistons and conrods removed and the crank out of the way.

At about £250 for a set of pistons, rings, Fo8 gaskets and liners, it's rarely thought worthwhile reusing the old rusty liners, so, if the old ones get damaged upon removal it should be seen as no big deal. In fact, you probably won't save any money by reboring them anyway!

You do need to take a great deal of care not to damage the block, however, and, in particular, the fairly narrow seat that the Fo8 gasket sits upon. It's actually difficult to buy 83mm pistons and liners nowadays, since virtually every owner chooses to upgrade to the larger capacity - usually 86mm bore/ pistons. Consequently, you should treat with suspicion any 83mm pistons you are offered, at an autojumble, for example, since they are likely to be ex-MOD Standard Vanguard equipment. In particular, watch out for and avoid any 4-ring pistons, as these will almost certainly be Vanguard low-technology gear that will not give your TR the 'zing'

you will be trying to achieve! In short, buy modern technology/material in a new matched set for piece of mind, reliability and performance.

On the occasions when you don't want to disturb the liners, of course (head gasket change, decoke, etc.), they will, inevitably, be loose. If you accidentally disturb a liner, or liners, you will have broken the liner/block seal and will need to remove the pistons, conrods, and the liners, and fit new Fo8 gaskets.

If you do get the head off without disturbing the liners, some precautionary liner-clamps are a good idea while you work elsewhere on the engine. You can lay a piece of 0.125in or 3mm steel or boiler plate over the tops of two adjacent liners, but the special washers shown within the Assembling the Engine section will be fine. You may want to use at least four such washers, to be absolutely sure the liners cannot move. It's important not to move the crank until those washers are in place.

The 'deck height', i.e. the height between the top of the liners and the top of the cylinder block, is very important. Consequently, the cylinder liners, and/or the Fo8 gaskets, may also cause you some trouble when you come to reassemble the liners.

Fo8 gaskets come in two thicknesses: standard (0.013in) and a +0.005in version. In theory, these should enable you to assemble the cylinder liners to the correct height above the block. Most engine rebuilds give little or no trouble, and, if you have fairly consistent protrusions of between 0.002in to 0.006in above the block with standard copper or aluminium Fo8s, you should achieve a good seal when you clamp the head down. However, there will those who have difficulties in achieving the ideal or consistent deck heights, and, for those whose liners are too low, the first resort should be the 0.018in thick Fo8s.

There are variations in material to choose from too. Normally, one would use copper Fo8s, but steel gaskets, on the other hand, compress less, and can be used when the protrusion of the liner from the block is less than ideal. However, if your liner is flush (but not below the block) you would use a steel gasket to ensure the liner seals with very little compression of the gasket. On the other hand, if your liner(s) protrude by 5

or 6 thousands of an inch, you certainly would not want a steel and, therefore, virtually uncompressible gasket!

If you have a dramatic variation, of, say, 8 thousands of an inch at one end, and zero protrusion at the other, you would need to grind a little off the base of the worst liners to bring them into line.

There are two very important details to attend to before fitting the liners. First, you must clean all the scale from inside the edge of the block where the liner enters it. There must be absolutely no way you can dislodge particles of scale when fitting each liner to the block. If you fail to carry out this cleaning operation properly, you will almost certainly dislodge small pieces of scale, some of which will sit on top of your Fo8 gasket and prevent a totally watertight seal.

The second essential cleaning task must be to ensure that the base onto which the Fo8 gasket will sit is completely free of all dirt, grit, scale and old gasket. You really cannot be too careful here, and must ensure that the seat upon which the Fo8 gasket will sit is spotless.

The first you will know about any specks you left behind, or knocked off the inside of the water jacket, will be when you check the oil level after you first run the rebuilt engine and find oil and water mixed together (signalling a second rebuild, which doesn't bear thinking about).

On the theme of cleanliness, when you are assembling the liners, don't be tempted to knock them in too vigorously, if at all. Tapping/thumping the lining can dislodge bits of scale and your scrupulously clean base, awaiting its new liner, can soon become a dirt-trap.

I think you should use sealant when you fit Fo8s and liners. We will go into the detail within the Engine Assembly section later in the chapter, where you will note 'Wellseal' being used in several applications but under the Fo8 gaskets in particular. Not all the experts agree, but the majority run a very thin film of sealant round the base of the liner. No one would ever suggest silicone, but, something like Blue Hylomar applied very sparingly will help the bottom liner seal. A thick material, or the Hylomar applied too thickly, will actually prevent the liner from making a good seal with the Fo8 gasket and you'll be facing a second engine rebuild.

If you use steel Fo8s, do ensure they are the 'coated' variety (to reduce corrosion), and you should also seal them with Wellseal for the same reason.

OIL LEAKS, CIRCULATION AND CONTAINMENT

There's a tendency for the push-rod tubes in the cylinder head to leak oil (in fact, some engines tend to leak oil from every opening, especially from the rear crankshaft scroll/seal). There is a modification which, although non-standard, will prevent the perpetual oil weep from the original rear crank seal.

The lower half of the original seal can be seen in photograph 7-5, while picture 7-6 gives you a chance to compare the original with a modified crankshaft. You will note that the original scroll has been ground off the rear of one crankshaft. A kit is available, incorporating a split lip seal from a Land Rover, and is illustrated in photograph 7-7-1.

The split in the seal, which must be positioned pointing towards the top of the engine, fits into a specially-made aluminium carrier, available from all TR specialists, and provides a much improved rear crankshaft oil seal. You should get journal dimensions with the kit, but do check the instructions and/or enquire about where to radius the crankshaft to reduce the (however unlikely) possibility of crankshaft breakage.

When grinding the rear scroll off your crank, the grinder has an opportunity to put an additional radius into the crank (where the oil-seal diameter feeds into the spigot for the flywheel). This will smooth out the stresses and reduce the possibility of breakage.

You may feel I should be telling you the diameter to grind the scroll down to, but that's best left to your TR specialist who will know the latest lip seal that's in use, and the best diameter for it.

Ensure that your grinding subcontractor removes the crankshaft bungs and thoroughly cleans inside the shaft after grinding (to remove the inevitable debris that will have collected there during the life of the engine). You don't want rubbish from a previous life ruining your reground crank and new

7-5. This is one half of the original 'seal' located at the rear of the crankshaft. According to the workshop manual, the outer plate needs to be adjusted using the special gauge mentioned in the main text. In practice, however, those wishing to stay with the original, if less effective, rear oil seal, will try to line the outer plate gaps up by eye. Even if you get the gaps right, most TRs will leak some oil from the rear of the crankshaft. If you get the adjustment wrong, the rear bearing will leak really badly and you will need to remove the engine or gearbox to try again! If you must stay with the original scroll seal, then using the setting tool is advisable. It would be my recommendation, however, and that of most restorers, that you fit the more modern type of 'lip seal' shown in photograph 7-7.

7-6. Two crankshafts demonstrating how they look before and after the scroll has been ground off. It is, of course, the top crank that has been ground to accept the much improved type of lip seal shown in picture 7-7.

7-7-1. Most four-cylinder TR owners, even those bent on originality, regard this as a 'must' modification. The Land-Rover lip seal is far more effective at preventing the oil from leaking past the rear of the crankshaft. The mod requires a special seal housing, seen here in two halves. This picture shows the lip seal and its centre-sprung insert, along with the specially machined split lip seal housing. You can actually see the recess in the housing to accept the seal. The other feature of the picture is, of course, an early four-cylinder flywheel with shrunk-on starter ring-gear. This flywheel has been lightened by Revington TR from 28lb (13kg) to some 20lb (9kg), and balanced. It is depicted with the two important lock-tabs you must not forget.

7-7-2. Nor must you forget to ensure that the flywheel with the shrunk-on ring gear shown in photograph 7-7-1 is used with its matching 'bomb-looking' shrouded bendix starter motor, shown here.

bearings. Equally, you need to re-bung the shaft before assembly!

Incidentally, for the shorter stroked 4-cylinder engine, the standard available 'County' main and big end bearings appear quite satisfactory.

Bearing in mind the engine's propensity to leak oil, you would be well advised to use a sealant in addition to the appropriate gaskets when assembling the unit. Loctite's 'Multi-Gasket' comes highly recommended, but any RTV silicon will do an excellent job, provided you are very careful. Do not to allow surplus sealant to bubble into the inside of the engine or to form a lip along the inside of any joints. It's better to use too little sealant than too much, since surplus beads of sealant can block your oilways, with catastrophic results.

Replacing the sump in a manner that prevents or cures an oil leak deserves a few lines. An oil leak from the joint between sump (oil pan) and block is messy, and, unfortunately, is usually caused by our own enthusiasm in over tightening the retention bolts. This causes the holes to bend upward, or 'bell', toward the block - in effect taking the pressure off the sump gasket between the bolts and allowing oil to leak (absolutely everywhere!).

I have yet to hear of anyone successfully and safely curing such a leak without removing the sump, but, if you are of a mind to try injecting some sealant into the leaking area, remember that the faces of the sump and block are contaminated with oil. Furthermore, too much sealant will push the excess into the sump and thus into the oil system, possibly clogging it. So let's look at preventing the leak in the first place.

With the sump off the engine, and the mating faces carefully cleaned, saw about half the width off a length of angle-iron, clamp it in a vice and lay the underside of the sump flange on it. Tap the protruding 'belled' holes back down from the top. In an ideal world, after going right round the sump, you would lay the sump upside down on an engineer's table to ensure it is flat, but you may have to make do by checking for flatness using a straight edge.

Degrease the mating face of the sump flange, and apply enough Locktite Multi-Gasket or Blue Hylomar sealant to the flange to thinly cover the high parts and to fill the (numerous) depressions. Fit the gasket, pop a few sump bolts through about every third hole to ensure alignment, and lightly press the gasket into the sealant. Let the sealant become firm and remove any internal beads.

Thoroughly degrease and clean the screws and each tapped hole in the bottom of the block, and lay a bead of sealant around the outside edge of the gasket. Spread the newly laid sealant evenly over the gasket and offer sump to block. Ensure you have plenty of good spring, and the largest plain, washers that will fit, and, using a

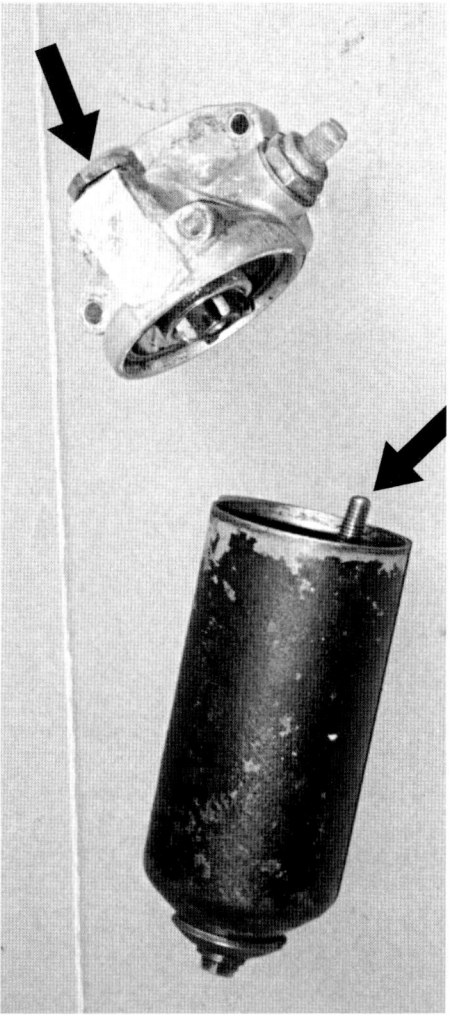

7-8. There are three types of oil filter, and, while the replacement filter elements are identical, the sealing ring and numerous other spares are different, making it important that you identify the filter system you have. The early 'bypass' filter arrangement can be identified by the ABSENCE of an hexagonal nut on the top of the casting that bolts to the crankcase. All later cars used 'full flow' filters which have an hexagonal nut on the top of the casting (arrowed). There are two types of full flow system, though, the Purolator and the Tecalemit. If you look closely you should find the manufacturer's name cast into the filter head, but, as a secondary check, the Purolator uses a coarse thread on the long central bolt (arrowed) while the Tecalemit uses a fine one.

proprietary screw-locking product (e.g. Locktite), fit and tighten each screw without delay. Torque to the recommended figure (20ft/lbs in my manual).

Moving on from retaining the oil to circulating it, you should note there are three different filter-mounting castings on the four-cylinder engines. The Purolator bypass design was superseded by the full-flow type, and, in turn, by Tecalemit's full-flow unit. It is very important you identify the one you actually have fitted to your TR and buy the relevant spares, filter, etc. The text and photograph 7-8 will help you identify yours.

One piece of reassuring news is that the Triumph engines have a reputation for self-priming, so those that choose to fill the oil pump with petroleum jelly are, more than likely, doing so unnecessarily. Far better to assemble the engine with a generous amount of a 50:50 mixture of STP and engine oil. Engine oil is, of course, better than nothing but the first time you start a newly rebuilt engine there will be a fair delay before oil-pressure is established and the more clinging the lubricant you used during assembly the easier the engine will turn and the less wear will take place.

There are alternatives, of course, and Wynns and Cam-Lubricant spring to mind. This procedure is particularly valuable if it is likely to be several months before the engine is started after a rebuild. It would also be a good idea to pre-fill the oil canister as far as possible before cranking the engine. It's not imperative, but it is good practice, particularly if your engine has been standing for many months (some stand for years) before start-up.

Turn the engine over, without the plugs in place but with a squirt of cylinder lubrication, until you are sure you have oil pressure. You can temporarily disconnect the oil-pressure gauge pipe while cranking to give you an early indication that the oil system is starting to build-up pressure, but don't forget to reconnect it when you fit the plugs and fire her up for real!

While talking oil/lubrication matters, one detail relating to originality may interest you. The TR engine block, as we have already discussed, was a development from the Standard Vanguard. Some Vanguard blocks still exist, and the odd one has found its way into a TR. There need be no detriment to the TR's performance, but its lack of originality may cause some prospective owners concern and depress the value of a TR they are contemplating purchasing. The Vanguard engine blocks should be easily identified by the

7-10-1. An example of the later starter motor, with its long bendix drive gear in evidence ...

7-9. If your engine is using the rearward dipstick location, to the right of the distributor drive, the engine almost certainly started life as a Standard Vanguard power plant.

7-10-2. ... and its compatible (bolted ring gear) flywheel.

different sequence of engine numbers, but, if there is doubt they can be identified by their 'incorrect' (in TR terms) dipstick position. The dipstick for a TR block should be just in front of the distributor pedestal, as shown by picture 7-9. However, you should also see a blank cast boss for a dipstick on the side of the crankcase just behind the dizzy pedestal. This was, of course, the position that was drilled for Vanguard applications.

OTHER BOTTOM-HALF SUGGESTIONS

• Tufriding the crankshaft is unlikely to be necessary, or worth while.
• Get each rotating engine part balanced individually - crank, front-extension, flywheel, and clutch assembly - and the piston/conrod assemblies balanced in the sense of equalising their weights.
The majority think an engine's rotating parts should be balanced in one piece, but forget that, if or when it is necessary to replace one of them, you are in fact destroying the whole balance of the engine. If your engine has been balanced as individual units (no doubt at a little extra cost initially), then you can

change the clutch, for example, without destroying the balance of the whole bottom end - provided you get the new clutch cover balanced before fitting, of course! The problem is made even worse should you ever need to exchange the flywheel and/or ring gear.
• Several different connecting rods were fitted to TRs originally, and they should not be mixed. If you do not have a full set and cannot find what you lack on the secondhand market, you will be forced to buy a full set of the only type now available - part number 211044. This set uses 'stretch' type bolts without tab washers. The early connecting rod bolts (part number 105312) should be used with tab washers but tab washers are not used with the later bolts (part number 138528). Stretch bolts are prevented from working loose by their tension after torqueing, tab washers would take up that tension and thus allow the bolts to work loose. Obviously, it's essential that the stretch bolts (138528) are never reused.
• The camshaft you select will significantly affect the performance, sound and drivability of the car. Remember, however, that the engine and its ancillary equipment needs to be planned as a package. A super cam is of

little benefit if the cylinder head, carburation, inlet manifold or exhaust systems are not all compatible. The camshaft aftermarket is very strong, and offers an almost bewildering number of options, so you should take advice before rushing out and buying the hottest one around.
The tappet setting on high lift cams is usually set for a greater clearance, which is why you will often hear a performance engine rattling at tick-over. This may not suit your tastes. It's likely that too hot a camshaft will make the car intractable and difficult to drive.
• Three different types of flywheels were used on the four-cylinder engines. However, there is nothing to prevent you fitting whatever is available - provided the starter motor you plan to use is compatible with the ring gear on your flywheel. For the sake of originality, be advised that a flywheel with shrink-on ring gear was fitted to TR2/3 and TR3As up to TS50000, and can be seen in photograph 7-7-1. The starter-ring has 91 teeth around its periphery, and can only be used with the early 'shrouded' starter motor shown in

photograph 7-7-2. The latter has a much shorter drive gear than you will see on the later starter motor shown in photograph 7-10-1.
• A flywheel with bolted ring gear, see photograph 7-10-2, was fitted to TR3As from TS50001, all TR4s, and all TR4As. Photograph 7-10-1 shows the compatible starter-motor with the later long drive gear.

CYLINDER HEAD MATTERS

4-cylinder engines respond well to tuning, and most of the results can be obtained by attending to the cam, exhaust and cylinder head. If the basic unit is sound, much can be achieved without taking the engine out of the car. Start by attending to the cylinder head. Gas-flowing and smoothing the passages at the same time as the head is being converted to run on unleaded fuel is highly recommended, and you will find some details on unleaded fuel conversion work in chapter 8. But before we get ahead of ourselves, let's look at the heads in a bit more detail, starting with an outline of the development that took place of this very important component:
• Although the TR's head was developed from the Vanguard cylinder head, a Vanguard head will not fit a TR.
• The original head required much development to extract sufficient power for Triumph's TR ambitions.
• The Vanguard cylinder head studs also required attention, no doubt as a consequence of the TR's higher power.
• The initially developed TR head subsequently became known as a 'low port' head, and was used up to engine TS9349 with 1.5in H4 SU carburettors. It can be seen in photograph 7-11.
• TS9350 saw the introduction of the 'Le Mans/low port' head designed to marry to 1³/₄in H6 SU carburettors.
• The 'high port' head was introduced at TS13052, and increased the distance between the respective centres of the exhaust and inlet ports. You can compare the high and low ported cylinder heads in picture 7-11.
• The TR4A head was introduced to TR4s at engine number CT21471. It has the number 511695 cast into it and is the best of the four cylinder tops.

All cylinder heads are interchangeable in the sense that all will bolt to the block quite satisfactorily.

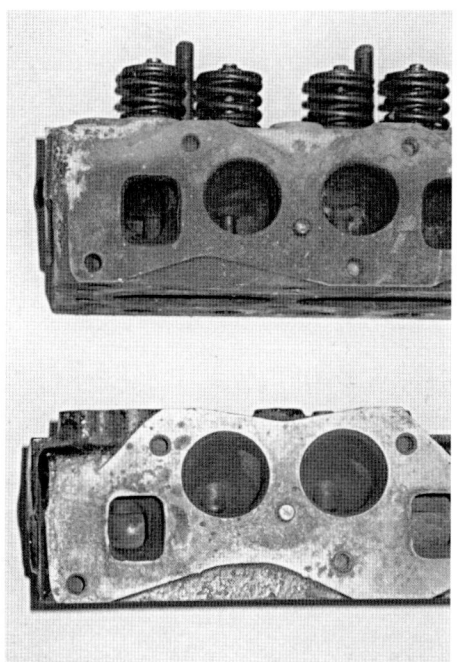

7-11. A comparison of the, so called, low (top of the picture) and high port (bottom) cylinder heads. The description refers to the position of the (circular) inlet ports, and it's clear that they are significantly higher in the bottom example.

However, the inlet manifold you have or select needs to be compatible with your chosen head. The low-port head, as fitted to the TR2 and early TR3s, can quickly be identified by the fact that all the ports are in line.

If performance is your only criteria, you are better off fitting the later 'high port' cylinder head, where the inlet ports are higher than the exhaust ports. This head can fit any of the four-cylinder engines, though there can sometimes be a slight interference problem at the front of the head on very late engines. In these cases the underside of the thermostat housing can sometime foul the top of the water pump housing.

Offer the head up to the block, and, if there is any interference, gently grind the underside of the head's thermostat housing until there is sufficient clearance to enable you to tightened the head down without it touching the water pump.

To identify the latest TR4A head, look for a bevel which has been cast along the edge of each combustion chamber - shown in photograph 7-12. As with many details in what is not an exact science, opinions vary as to the benefit of, and/or need for, this bevel. However, the majority of experts regard the bevel as the main reason for the superiority of the 4A's head, and that the

7-12. This is the latest and best of the standard TR four-pot cylinder heads, as fitted to the TR4A. It is, of course, a 'high port' casting, and its superiority over earlier high port heads was due to this cutaway cast into one area of the combustion chamber. This must have improved the flow of gasses through each combustion chamber, and the logical and subsequent development has been the gas-flow polishing of the heads, some of which can be seen in photograph 7-13.

7-13. The area where the four-cylinder head has been ground/relieved to maximise gas-flow and power output. Needless to say, although Carl Kiddell (of Revington TR) is pointing out one edge, the area needs to be addressed on both sides of all combustion chambers.

be those constrained by originality considerations.

The 4-cylinder engine's head should always be pulled-down after 500 miles and certainly no later than 1000 miles to make sure the Fo8 and copper asbestos head gaskets are tight. Use the workshop manual for the correct torque setting for your car. Clearly, you must also adjust the tappets following retorqueing.

ASSEMBLING THE FOUR-CYLINDER ENGINE

Although the engine is quite easily rebuilt at home, TR restoration specialists are very experienced indeed

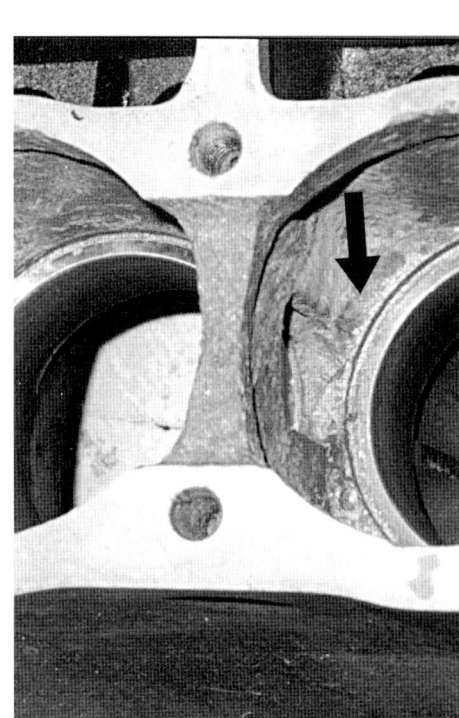

7-14-1. Most readers will expect to have to clean out the oil passages within the cylinder block. While this does need to take place, the first job with the wet liner engine is to ensure the cleanliness of the inside of the block. Any scale in the water passages MUST be removed, and it is ESSENTIAL that you do not disturb some and allow it to drop onto the Fo8 gasket seats (which must also be scrupulously cleaned). Finally, it is a good idea to blow the whole block out with an airline - but be very careful and protect your eyes.

later the head you fit to your engine the better.

Although this book is not about tuning, I cannot pass on without mentioning how easy the four-cylinder head is to improve. Photograph 7-13 will be particularly informative if you compare it to the best standard head fitted to a four-pot - that of the TR4A shown in 7-12.

Over the years most cylinder heads have been subject to skimming. Some gently, to merely restore their flatness, some more aggressively to raise compression ratios. Some have been skimmed several times, the end result being that it is difficult for the home restorer to be sure what the status of their head is, and how that compares with their particular wishes. A multi-skimmed head is not a particular problem for those who want a very high compression ratio. However, for those who seek smooth trouble-free 'down-to-the-pub-on-a-Sunday' type driving, this could pose a problem, since it's impossible to add metal to the face of a cylinder head. Your particular head may, therefore, give a much higher compression ratio (CR) than you wish.

Revington TR have a solution: a choice of four thicker-than-standard cylinder-head gaskets. The standard gasket is 1mm thick, but Revington TR also offers 1.2, 1.4, 1.6 and 2.0mm

thick options which progressively decrease the CR of the head. Because it's virtually impossible for the home restorer to select the correct gasket, Revington TR offer a measuring and selection service, whereby you send off your head, together with an indication of the CR you seek. Using measurements relating to the capacity of your combustion chambers, Revington TR will select the appropriate gasket for your head and CR.

As cylinder heads developed, it's not surprising that the valve and valves guides changed. So much so, in fact, that it became necessary to market a 'conversion' valve guide to accommodate some combinations of valves, guides and heads. Consequently, the ideal solution, when purchasing valve gear, is to actually take your head with you to the TR spares supplier. If that is impractical, it will not prove a major problem.

Try to identify your head carefully, and order the appropriate valves/guides, etc. - but check that everything marries up as soon as the parts arrive. If there's a problem, it can be easily and quickly sorted. Mind you, if you decide to have hardened inserts fitted in your valve seats to allow the use of unleaded fuels (chapter 8), then you can select the size of valve you prefer! Most will opt for the largest diameter of valve, but there will

7-14-2. After regrinding, do ensure that the machinist removes the screwed plugs (arrowed), and thoroughly washes the crank in a hot/high-pressure washer and blows it through. The purpose is twofold. First and foremost, this removes the grinding 'swarf' from inside the crank, while, secondly, it enables old oil sludge deposits to be cleared from the crankshaft's internal oilway.

7-14-5. ... and, still using lots of lubricant, ease the crank into place.

7-14-3. If you are retaining the original oil seal for the rear of the crankshaft, the first task must be to ensure that you have a matching pair of oil seal assemblies. They are stamped with an identification number and these must match. We talk about the theory and the practice of setting the original seals at photograph 7-5.

7-14-4. The engine block and main bearing caps are also made as a set and must have matching numbers (A54 in this case). Check that yours do indeed match, and, using lots of 50:50 mixture of STP and engine oil, fit the three main bearing half shells, making sure that the 'tangs' properly locate ...

7-14-6. Slip a pair of (un-tanged) new 'Standard' sized thrust washers either side of the central bearing. It's a bit of a fiddle, and very important that you get them the right way round. The grooved bearing face should be touching the crank (facing each end of the engine, if you prefer), while the written/stamped rear of the 'thrusts' need to face each other (on opposite sides of the main bearing, of course!).Check the end-float of the crankshaft using a DTI clamped to the crankcase, as shown here. Pull the crank right back, set the DTI to zero, push the crank forwards and read off the DTI. You need to establish your own crank end-float, and then to talk to a TR specialist, who will know what thrust washer sizes are available and which will best suit your engine. However, to get you into the principle of the operation, you need to establish a crank end-float of between 0.004in to 0.006in. Oversize thrust washers are sized such that, if your DTI shows, say, 14 thousandths of an inch end float, you will need to reduce that by 10 thousandths, to get to bottom tolerance. Consequently, you need to order a set of '+5' washers. It is, of course, possible to use one standard pair plus one '+10' pair, but this requires additional care to get the matching pairs correctly positioned. Once you have the correct thickness of washer, you will, of course, need to remove the 'Standard' size and replace them with your new plain halves.

7-14-7. Both pairs of thrust washers come in two halves. Each pair has a plain half, which we have already positioned either side of the central main bearing. So now it's time to fit the tanged half, shown here, on either side of the main bearing cap. The same rules of 'what faces what' apply and must be followed, so, if you are still in doubt, get a local TR club member to call in to check your work. You can just see the grooved faces (arrowed) ready to meet the crankshaft once the cap is married to the block.

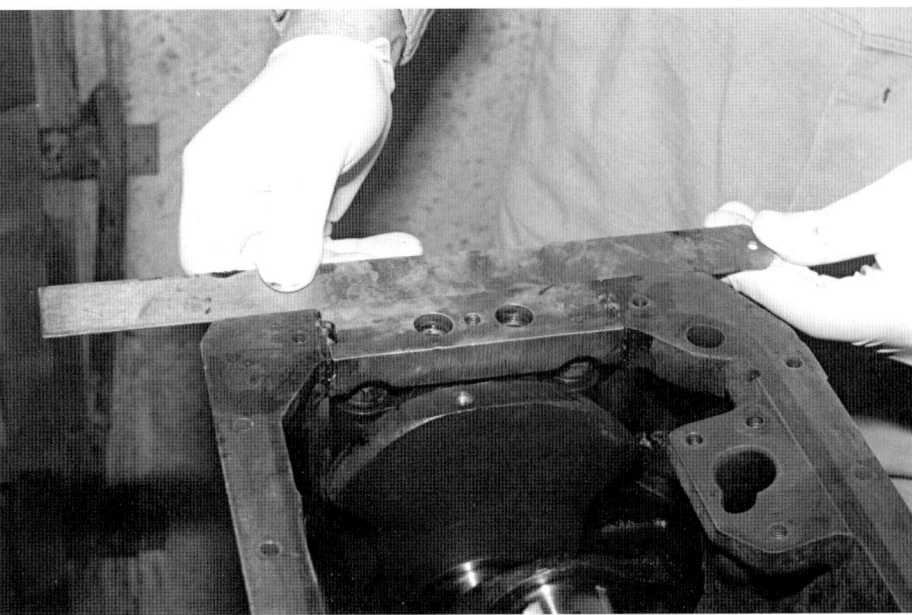

7-14-9. The front sealing block goes in next. Don't forget the 'T' shaped cork seals that go in at each end, and to get the front completely flat ready for the timing cover that will go on later. Did you spot the hole drilled as part of the crankshaft-balancing operation?

7-14-8. Use lots more lubrication on the crankshaft's journals and fit, not only the central mains cap (after which it's a good idea to double check the crank end-float for the last time), but the front and rear bearing caps too.

7-14-10. The rear main bearing cap has to be sealed on both sides with felt, which is best cut into 1in lengths and soaked for 30 minutes in Wellseal before being rammed (fairly forcibly) home. These need to get right to the bottom of what is an apparently bottomless void, one after another, until no more can be packed in. Cut the top off flush with the crankcase to allow the sump gasket to sit flat. It's a messy operation so you may be pleased to hear that Hammerite Paint Thinners is invaluable for cleaning the engine, your tools, and, indeed, yourself! After the clean up you need to turn the engine over.

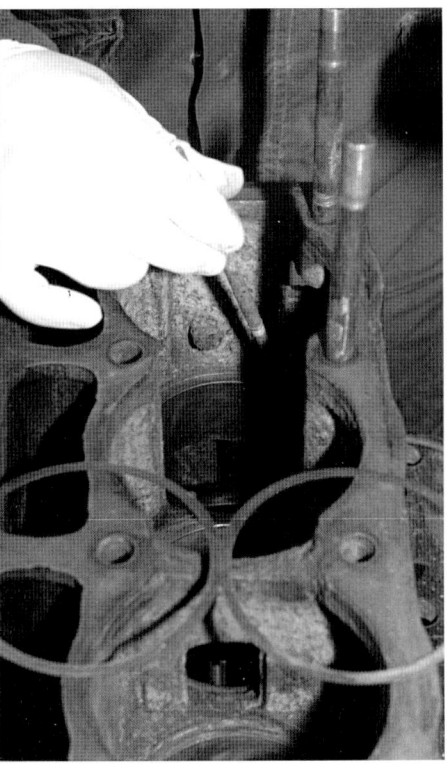

7-14-11. The reliability of the engine depends upon the integrity of the seal between liner and engine block, so a carefully applied ring of gasket dressing (in this case Wellseal) needs to be painted on the block's shoulder, on both sides of the Fo8 gaskets shown in the foreground, and ...

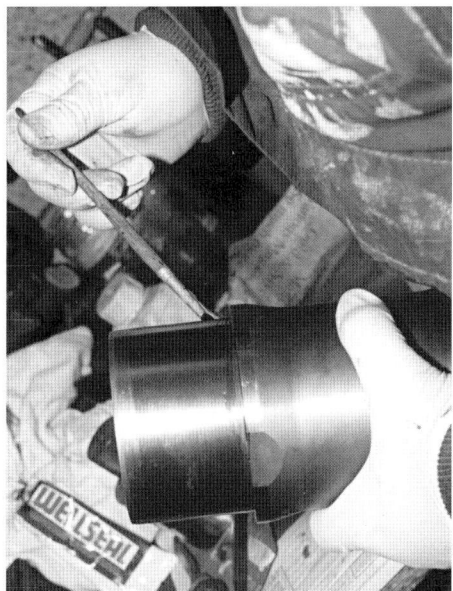

7-14-15. Conrods are numbered one to four, and it's a good idea to try and retain them in their intended position. When sending them away for balancing, therefore, tell the contractor not to obliterate the location numbers! The piston/conrod assemblies go in with the big end offset facing the camshaft side of the engine. Here we are looking forward from the back of the engine.

7-14-12. ... on the shoulder of each liner. You are best to avoid getting sealer on the outside of the bottom of the liner or on the lower bore of the block for it could make the liner very difficult to push home. As a matter of interest, the dressing is particularly important if you are contemplating using steel Fo8s, as it provides some protection from Fo8 corrosion. If you feel you must use steel Fo8s, do ensure they are the coated steel type, again to maximise corrosion resistance.

7-14-13. There is a special tool (shown in the workshop manual) designed for pressing the liners into place. Here you see it in use, though most will use a block of hardwood that is large enough to cover the whole of the liner's top flange. The 'deck heights' (*i.e.* the height of the liners above the block) are important in that they need to be consistent and within the limits laid out in the workshop manual. If you are concerned about your deck height(s) you could fit the studs, (temporarily), re-use the old head-gasket, drop the cylinder head on and torque the nuts down to about 70ft lbs, then strip the head and gasket off and re-check the deck-heights. Fo8 gaskets do come in differing thicknesses, as explained in the main text, and, if you cannot get the deck height correct, a suitable alternative thickness will be required. The two cylinder head studs are only shown in this picture because we couldn't get them out!

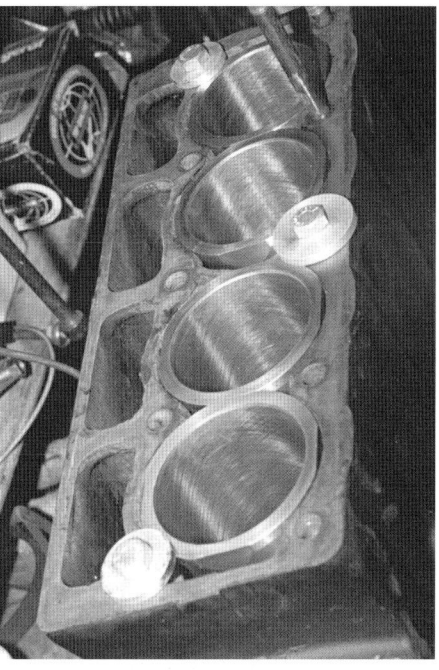

7-14-14. As an engine goes through its assembly sequence there is a lot of crankshaft turning, for one reason or another, and, in circumstances where the liner/block fit is loose, and/or the piston/liner fit is a bit tight, the liner can ride up out of its seat. This is not good as it increases the chances of getting dirt onto the Fo8 seatings. Consequently, we used these three washers to secure the liners, two at 1.6in (40mm) and one at 2in (50mm) diameter. All had an internal bore diameter sufficient to give clearance around a cylinder head stud - about 0.6in (15mm). Note the superb 'hatched-honed' finish in the bores of the liners - ideal for running in the engine without glazing the bores.

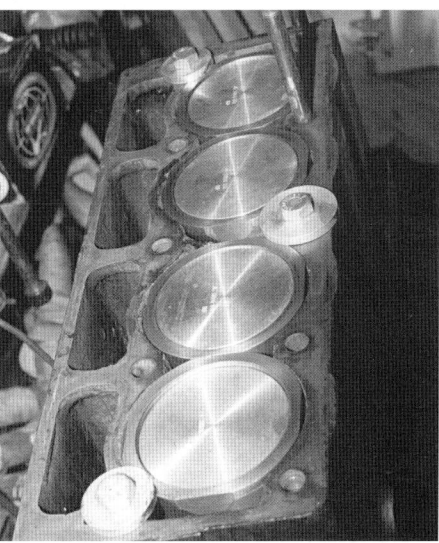

7-14-16. So now all four pistons are in place and it's time to turn the engine over again.

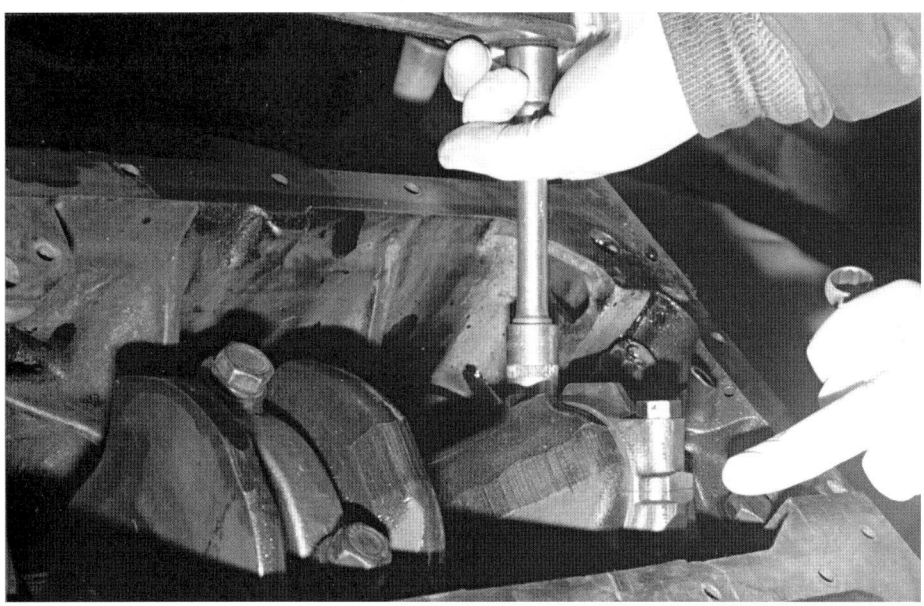

7-14-17. When you dismantle the conrods, take note of whether you have tab washers under the big end cap bolts. If you have tab washers then you can re-use the original cap bolts (which has significant cost advantages), though you must use new tab washers upon re-assembly. If there are no tab washers present when you strip the engine, you MUST discard the cap bolts and use new (stretch) bolts upon re-assembly. If in doubt buy and fit new stretch bolts and assemble them without tab washers.

The big end caps are located on the connecting rod by a tubular dowel through which one of the big end bolts pass. This prevents incorrect assembly, and, I understand, also reduces the stress on that bolt, so look for the tubular dowel. Torque the bolts up very carefully using the workshop manual's recommended settings. At this point it's worth spinning the crank over a couple of times, for, if you've got the big end offsets wrong, you will find that the crank will not do a full revolution.

7-14-18. It's on with some gasket sealer, the gasket, a little more sealer, and then the front engine plate, with, of course, the correctly torqued bolts shown here.

7-14-19. Lots of cam-lube on the cam bearings and lobes, then it's gently in with the cam. If it 'sticks', it is almost certain that a bearing journal is not quite in line with its bearing in the block, so use care not force. A length of light wire or string looped down through the block and under the cam may lift the cam sufficiently to allow it to slide home easily.

7-14-20. This is the cam fully home. It's supposed to be a little proud of the front plate ...

7-14-21. ... because the front cam bearing has to be bolted in place with the four slots facing outwards.

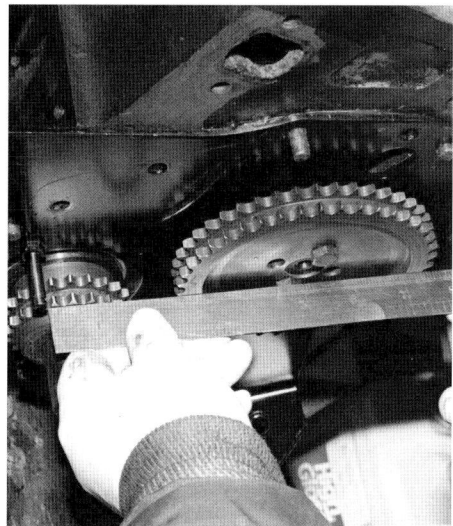

7-14-22. Put the camshaft sprocket in place. Bolt it down tightly, but don't worry too much about its timing marks - yet. Don't fit any tab locking washers either - yet. Push the crankshaft sprocket as far as possible onto the 'shaft, and, as seen here, lay a straight edge across the camshaft sprocket in order to gauge the extent to which the crank sprocket needs to shimmed outwards to ensure complete alignment of the timing chain. Use feeler gauges, note the recess at the crank sprocket, remove the crank sprocket, fit the appropriate shims, refit the sprocket and check that the two sprockets are now completely aligned.

7-14-25. It's not essential that you turn the engine over now, to finish the bottom end, for this can be done later. However, here, we wanted to get the sump on so we turned the engine over and fixed the oil pump studs, gasket and refurbished oil pump. I come from the school of thought that suggests that you should always fit a new oil pump. However, these engines don't generally suffer from low oil pressure (unless the crank is badly worn), and you can always adjust the pressure relief valve, so, refitting a pump that has been checked and found within the tolerances shown in the workshop manual is probably all right.

7-14-23. Set piston numbers one (*i.e.* the front piston) and number four to TDC (Top Dead Centre). A DTI is the ideal way, as shown here - but it doesn't, in my opinion, have to be quite this precise!

7-14-26. After a careful application of Hylomar to the crankcase, the gasket was positioned and a second, not over-generous, application of sealant was spread on the gasket. On went the sump and, mindful that oil leaks are actually created if you over-tighten the sump, we torqued the numerous bolts down to the workshop manual's figure.

7-14-24. Now we do need to get the relationship between the camshaft and the crankshaft right in order that the 'timing' of valve openings and ignition firing is correct. If you are fitting new sprockets (which rarely have timing marks) and are not familiar with timing an engine, the section entitled 'timing from first principles' in the workshop manual would be a worthwhile read. Put simply, you will need to rotate the cam until number one cylinder's inlet valve is fully open (fit one tappet and use a DTI). Using information from the cam manufacturer, set the crankshaft to the relevant position - normally about 105 degrees for a standard cam. Re-using your old sprockets is certainly a lot easier from a timing point of view, but they must be in first-class condition. Old or new, the crankshaft sprocket still has a keyway that orientates it with the crankshaft, but a new one is unlikely to have the edge scribed for alignment checks with the cam sprocket. With a used cam sprocket, you will see a centre-popped dot on both camshaft and camshaft sprocket. It's important that both dots are aligned and stay aligned during the subsequent assembly operations, since this orientates the cam with its sprocket. Now we need to get both sprockets correctly orientated with each other - which is where the lines scribed on the perimeter of the cam sprocket and the edge of crank sprocket come in. These need to be aligned off the engine, the new timing chain fitted round the sprockets, the sprockets/chain assembly offered to the engine, and the cam sprocket bolted in position. It's a good idea to use a straight edge, as shown here, to double-check that everything went together without losing sprocket alignment.

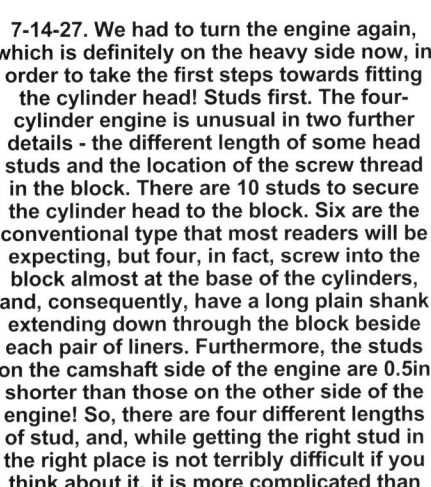

7-14-28. The opportunity was taken to have the cylinder head converted to be compatible for unleaded fuel. There is more on this topic in Chapter 8, but, briefly, hardened exhaust valve seats and the phosphor-bronze valve guides shown here were fitted. You will need a valve spring compressor to fit the valves and will find that all engines had double inlet valve springs. However, on cars up to TR4 number CT21470, triple exhaust valve springs were fitted. Thereafter, the TR4s and all 4As reverted to double exhaust valve springs.

7-14-27. We had to turn the engine again, which is definitely on the heavy side now, in order to take the first steps towards fitting the cylinder head! Studs first. The four-cylinder engine is unusual in two further details - the different length of some head studs and the location of the screw thread in the block. There are 10 studs to secure the cylinder head to the block. Six are the conventional type that most readers will be expecting, but four, in fact, screw into the block almost at the base of the cylinders, and, consequently, have a long plain shank extending down through the block beside each pair of liners. Furthermore, the studs on the camshaft side of the engine are 0.5in shorter than those on the other side of the engine! So, there are four different lengths of stud, and, while getting the right stud in the right place is not terribly difficult if you think about it, it is more complicated than your average engine.

You will note that we had to remove the three liner-securing washers, but reused two of them, a couple of old gudgeon pins, and some old head nuts to ensure the liners stayed in situ. If you are expecting to fit the head within a few minutes of fitting the studs, this precaution is unlikely to be necessary. However, if you expect there to be a time lapse between studs and head fitting then the precaution could be worthwhile. The well-lubricated tappets were dropped-in using the end of a finger.

7-14-29. Most new cylinder head gaskets spell out which way they should be fitted with the word 'top' stamped on one face. In fact, ours only used a part number but we were advised that the writing should be fitted upwards. If in any doubt take advice from your supplier, though, with most gaskets I believe the orientation is not critical. In theory, no extra sealant is needed with modern gaskets, but many a good four-cylinder TR engine has had Wellseal applied to both sides of the head gasket.

7-14-30. Torque the head nuts down in about three stages. Use your workshop manual to determine the final figure, say 100ft lbs, and go round in the prescribed sequence, starting with, say, 80ft lbs. Then go round again at 90, before finishing off at the recommended torque figure.

7-14-31. Rocker pedestal studs, pushrods, rocker shaft assembly and securing nuts come next.

7-14-32. Next we turn our attention to the front of the engine, and fit a cover securing stud and its fibre washer. A light smear of Hylomar followed by the timing cover gasket should precede the oil thrower on the front of the crankshaft, while the timing chain tensioner needs securing with a good sized plain washer and split pin.

7-14-33. Fit a new oil seal to the front of the timing cover, with the lip and pre-seal inwards. It needs to be knocked into the cover square using a flat block of wood. A light coating of Hylomar on cover and gasket is a good idea, but the cover itself has to be offered up to the engine mostly from the side in order to compress the timing chain tensioner. There are a variety of fastenings required to secure the cover, including four nuts and bolts. The only thing that requires particular attention is to ensure that the screws that go through the cover into the block are not over-length.

7-14-34. Provided the crank has been left such that number one piston is at TDC, when you fit the key to the crank and offer the fan hub extension up, a tiny hole in the lip of the belt-pulley should line up with the timing pointer on the front of the cover. This is a TR4/4A extension, earlier cars have a slightly different one. I would put a small blob of typewriter correction fluid on the rim of the pulley to aid dynamically timing the engine in due course.

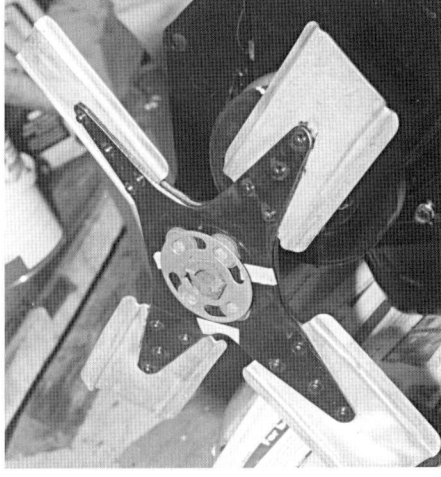

7-14-35 and 7-14-36 (right). Many TR owners fit an electric fan which may dispense with the actual fan, but the front crankshaft extension does need to be retained since it provides harmonic damping for the crankshaft. Nevertheless, the electric fan has a great deal of merit since the early TR fans were a major piece of engineering and, in theory, need balancing (by a balancing contractor) to get the adjustable balance weight (arrowed) correctly located. The design makes for awkward assembly as the weight has to be removed to get the various locking plates and tabs (seen on the left side blade and in picture 7-14-36) into place. The balance weight position may be best retained by drilling a $1/16$in (1.5mm) hole through BOTH weight and fan in order to ensure it can be correctly repositioned when the fan is finally bolted in place. However, in practice, particularly if you have had your engine balanced, you are better to replace the whole front pulley/extension/ fan assembly with a narrow belt kit, dampened pulley and electric fan!

7-14-37. The water pump housing on some early TR2s was different to that shown here, but the vast majority of four-cylinder engines used this housing, a paper gasket, blue Hylomar sealer and three differing length bolts to secure it to the block. Ignore the two Nyloc nuts that look as if they will be used to fix the water pump - the pulley will not provide sufficient clearance for anything other than a plain nut and spring washer ...

7-14-38 and 7-14-39. ... as these subsequent shots prove.

7-14-41. Note. An average of three shims are required, between the distributor pedestal and the block, to achieve the end-float specified in the workshop manual for the distributor shaft.

7-14-42. The oil filter mounting casting has one 'wrinkle' to watch out for. There is a small slot off the lower front mounting hole - to allow oil to pass up the outside of the stud. The idea is that this provides a take-off point for the oil pressure gauge pipe, which is connected to the stud by a banjo coupling. It is, therefore, most important that you fit a soft copper washer either side of the banjo to provide an oil-tight seal. You will see the banjo in the next photo.

7-14-40. Lining-up the tang in the distributor shaft with the slot-in oil pump drive was tricky. The offset slot for the distributor needs to be on the engine side of the centre, and to point at the angle shown here. There could be merit in fitting this shaft before assembling the oil pump (and fitting the sump), but, whichever route you take, be careful when you come to fit the distributor's pedestal. If it stands proud of the block by more than a millimetre, chances are you have failed to get the tang on the distributor's shaft properly aligned with the oil pump's drive slot. Never force the pedestal down! Start again (and again and again) until you feel two clicks as the shaft is offered up. The first will be when the drive gear engages the cam and is easily achieved; the second one you are looking for is when the tang enters its slot in the top of the oil pump. Obviously, a long screwdriver to adjust the oil pump slot is a prerequisite. If you fail to carry out this operation properly you will start your engine in due course without any chance of oil pressure ... with unthinkable consequences.

at rebuilding the Triumph 4-cylinder engines, and/or converting them to unleaded operation. You may, in fact, find that it's £1000-£1200 well spent, if only because the responsibility and warranty for the engine rests with a reputable supplier.

Cost-out the parts and machining for a home rebuild. It's quite likely that you will not be able to shave any significant sum from these figures for a full rebuild, even by doing the work yourself.

Since a picture speaks a thousand words, with thanks to Michael Metz for providing the 'model', I have used a pictorial sequence with associated text

starting at 7-14-1 to explain the fundamentals of assembly, for those still anxious to do the work themselves.

FITTING THE ENGINE

It's not unknown for the four-cylinder engine to be sitting too low due to the age or type of engine mountings in use. The four-cylinder engine always sits low and it is normal for you to have to jack the engine up to change a fan belt. So, do not concern yourself if that is your situation.

However, if the engine sits lower than it should, it will wear a groove in

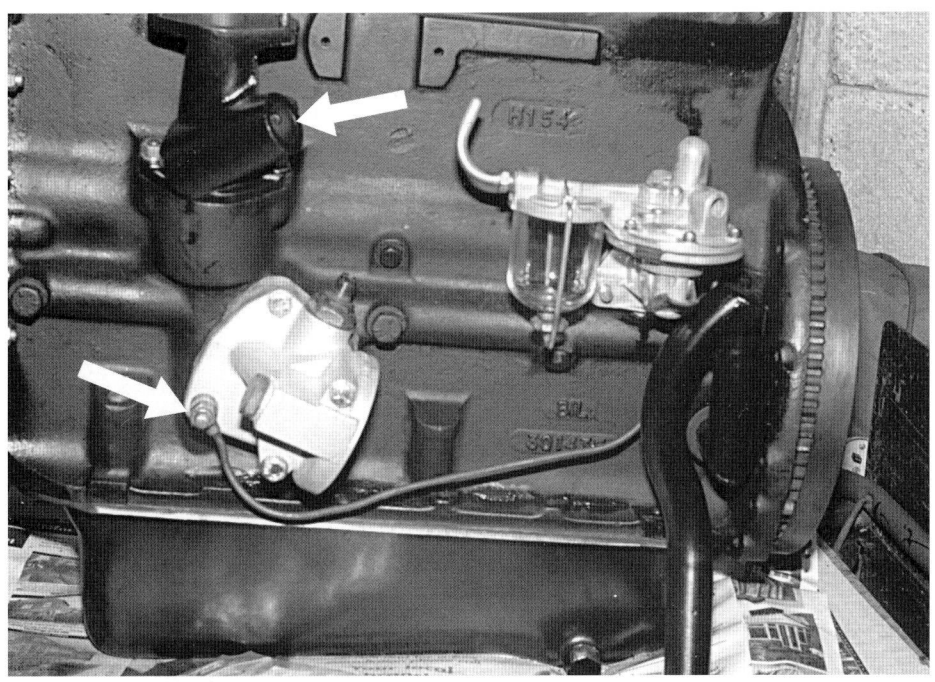

7-14-43. The crankcase breather, fuel pump and glass-bowl filter, and the oil filter mounting casting, make the left side of the engine look positively finished. Note the oil pressure gauge banjo (arrowed) and copper pipe which couple to a flexible line and thence to the dashboard area. However, we still have the oil filter and housing, the tachometer drive (arrowed) to the distributor's pedestal, and, of course, the distributor itself. However, all are best fitted once the engine is in the car.

7-18. The two exhaust manifolds for these cars - the TR4 (nearest the camera) offers reasonably good gas flow, while the best of the four-cylinder manifolds is the TR4A, with its twin exhaust outlets which you should just be able to pick out in this shot. Note the support studs that come down from the inlet manifold to the two flanges cast onto both exhaust manifolds.

the steering rack and make a lot of unpleasant noise due to the front crank pulley rubbing on the rack. That you do need to worry about!

The first thing to check is to ensure that the engine mounts have been installed with the end marked 'top' actually at the top. For reasons that I cannot explain, they are quite often installed upside down. This is enough to lower the engine and cause the problem. If this proves to be the case with your car then the remedy is obvious!

If you still have a problem, do not worry for the remedial work is not as expensive as it sounds - provided you've caught the situation in time. You can use several large washers, positioned under the engine mountings, to lift everything up until the pulley just, but consistently, clears the rack. The TR4A/5/6 washers used for securing the differential are ideal (part number 134234).

ANCILLARY EQUIPMENT

Distributors
The OE distributor used on the four-cylinder engines, up to and including the TR4 with 2.2 litre engines, was Lucas model DM2P4. TR4s with smaller engines, and all TR4As, used a Lucas 25D4.

It is quite possible to look-up the original Lucas part number for your car, but, since they will have often been replaced, it would be a surprise to find that yours matched with the original specification. Furthermore, the part numbers changed when the engine changed cubic capacity, and some very minor spring and/or weight changes in the advancement mechanism are the only basis for many of the variations in part number.

If in doubt, use a 25D4 for standard applications. For those concerned about a pre-TR4A vehicle, you can also use the '4A's 25D4 distributor with confidence - for it will suit all standard-tune four-cylinder applications. Clearly, those tuning their engines will take the advice of those helping them assemble a complete and compatible package.

Inlet manifolds
Six were used, and all are listed,

photographed and discussed in chapter 10.

Exhaust Manifolds.
The standard four-cylinder cast manifolds are reasonably effective, and the one that came with your car should not be thoughtlessly discarded. The three types, in chronological order, are as follows:
TR2 and 3, originally fitted to the low port cylinder heads, and with a single exhaust pipe.
TR3A and 4, intended for high port heads, and using a single exhaust pipe.
TR4A/high port, with a rather more swept pattern, and requiring twin exhaust pipes.

Those used on the TR4 and TR4A are shown in photograph 7-18. All are interchangeable, in that any exhaust manifold will, in fact, fit any head, high or low port. Clearly, therefore, unless originality issues restrict you, a TR4A exhaust manifold would be the unit of choice.

However, if you have to buy an exhaust manifold, consider going one stage further and buying a fabricated tubular 'extractor' manifold and exhaust system. These systems are usually required to maximise the benefits of head tuning, but I view them as a general improvement.

Whatever system you go for, I would recommend a stainless steel system, particularly if the car is to be used relatively infrequently. Mild steel systems do cost less, but rust from the inside, even when the car is idle!

SOME COOLING DETAIL

The majority of cooling detail is pretty straightforward, so I do not propose to take up too much time or space on routine matters. However, one detail I will mention relates to the car's tendency to overheat in hot ambient temperatures. I have already made reference to the use of electric fans, so bear that in mind.

There are two changes to the radiator that, to my mind, offer even greater benefits. The main causes of overheating are the restricted airflow through the radiator, the inevitable furring up of the core with time, and the reduced water flow brought about by the hole for the starting-handle - shown in picture 7-15. Sorry, it may not be original but at the first re-coring opportunity, do dispense with that starting-handle hole. It will improve the effectiveness of the radiator by some

20%. It will also make the re-coring job cheaper too!

If you also ensure that the radiator repairer uses a more highly efficient core than usual, for example a 'Pack' constructed core, you could further increase the cooling effectiveness of your radiator by an additional 15-20%, for very little additional cost.

If your car is not already fitted with a ducting kit, you should fit the appropriate one in order to dramatically improve the air flow through your radiator.

Except for the hottest of climates, you will have almost certainly resolved you car's overheating problems by now. However, an aluminium high capacity radiator is the next level solution and you should certainly fit one before you give any thought to fitting an aluminium cylinder head. Unfortunately, they bring a significant cost penalty, but are available through Cambridge MotorSports.

The usual thermostat/top hose arrangement is shown in photograph 7-16 - which may be of help when reassembling this beast! However, you are very unlikely to see the really complicated initial arrangement (shown by photograph 7-17) that Triumph used on the very first four-cylinder engines. Nevertheless, I thought you might like to see it for comparative purposes.

7-15. As you can see, the insertion of the starting handle hole closes off at least four of twenty vertical water passages, and is, therefore, best omitted when you next re-core your radiator.

7-17. Now that is complicated! As a matter of interest, this is the second TR ever built ... TS2, in the course of refurbishment at TR Enterprises.

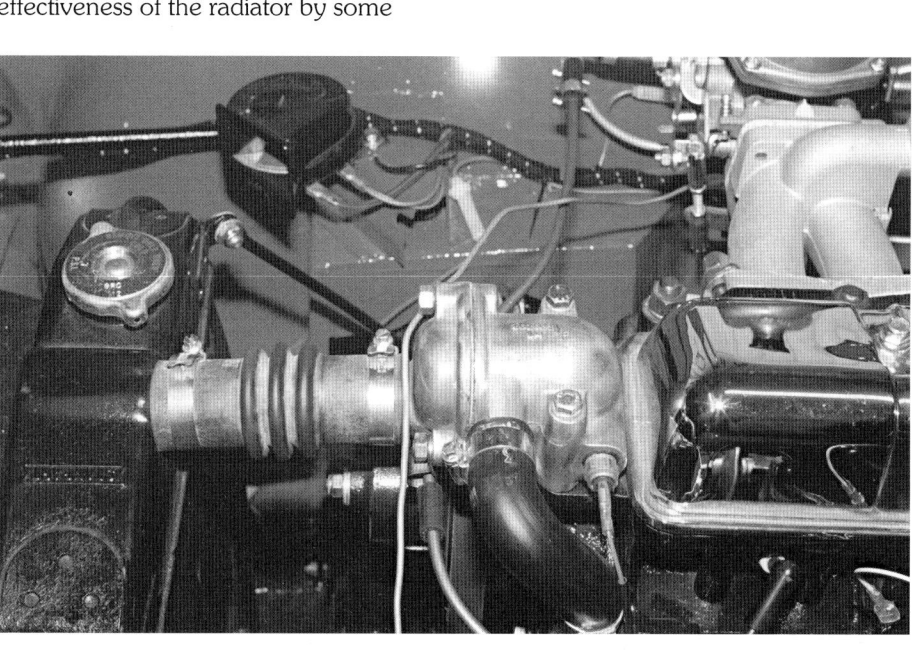

7-16. This is a late TR4 thermostat housing and top hose arrangement, which, although complex by today's standards, is much simpler than the very early four-cylinder arrangement shown in photograph 7-17.

Chapter 8
Modern oils and fuels

RUNNING-IN/BREAKING-IN AND ENGINE OILS

One area where modern developments can work against owners trying to improve their engines relates to the lubricating oil they initially select. When you're running-in (breaking-in) the engine in your TR, you can actually harm your doubtless expensively rebuilt power unit by over-pampering it, initially, with synthetic engine oils. Strange but true.

Synthetic and semi-synthetic oils have superb anti-wear characteristics, and it's worth considering them (after a while), although views on the suitability of synthetic oils for classic car engines are very polarised, both for and against. However, everyone agrees they must be avoided for at least the first 6000 miles, and possibly the first 9000 miles, since they'll delay the bedding-in of cylinders, rings and bores. Used too early, synthetic oils are likely to promote bore-glazing before the cylinder walls are smooth, and prevent pistons and rings achieving their best gas-tight seals - because, as strange as it seems, they are too slippery and prevent the running-in process from taking place effectively! So, by using synthetic oil during the running-in period you will end up with an under-performing engine that may burn more oil than you would expect from a newly reconditioned engine, however carefully you have driven it during this period.

Let a good purpose-made running-in mineral oil from Castrol or Penrite do its job during the initial 500 miles, and allow the bores to be smoothed off and the rings to seat. Change the oil and filter at 500 miles. Most of the rest of the running-in process occurs within the next 2500 miles. Therefore, to give your engine the best start in life, change the oil and filter at 3000 miles and then again, I suggest, at 6000 miles, and use a very good mineral oil for each refill. Castrol Classic 20W/50 (Castrolite to us old 'uns) or Penrite Classic 20W/50 are ideal after the 500 mile mark.

The concern of those opposed to the use of synthetic oils in classic engines usually relates to the vigorous detergents used in many synthetics. Certainly, there is a real danger that a well-coked engine with many thousands of miles under the flywheel can lose compression, start burning huge quantities of oil and lose performance if introduced to a synthetic oil high in vigorous detergents. However, it is my opinion that a classic engine which has just completed, say, 6000/9000 miles since a complete rebuild, filled with a low detergent synthetic oil does bear consideration and I have followed this policy with my own cars.

While talking about running-in a newly reconditioned 'classic' engine, let's just touch on the best rpm band to use during this critical period in your engine's life. In short, keep rpm between 2500 and 3000 for the first 500 miles and 2500 to 3500 for the next 1500 miles or so, and do ensure (to state the obvious) that the fuel mixture is correct and not causing bore wash through over-richness.

OIL THERMOSTATS

Mineral oils are formulated to perform best at between 90 and 110 degrees C (194-230 F). When they become too hot they thin, and thicken when too cold. At both extremes they give less than optimum lubricating performance.

If you have elected not to have an oil cooler fitted, then you need read no further, since this section does not apply to your car. However, for those with, or thinking about, an oil cooler it seems a good idea to also consider an oil 'stat. These go in the line to your oil cooler and will make the oil bypass the cooler when it's not up to temperature. Obviously, this will accelerate warming up of the oil and assist initial lubrication, particularly in cold climatic conditions. Oil 'stats are widely available with push-on or standard $5/_8$in threaded unions, and will enable you to have an oil cooler in circuit all the time and available when oil temperature rises as the result of hard work or hot weather. At a stroke, overheating and overcooling your oil are eliminated. Picture 8-7 shows any who are unfamiliar with oil 'stats what to expect.

USING UNLEADED FUEL

By now most UK TR owners will have become used to filling up with unleaded fuel of one type or another, and have, no doubt, found it necessary to retard the timing by a couple of degrees or so. Probably most have given some thought to having hardened inserts fitted into the cylinder head exhaust valve seats. It's unlikely that TR engines will run indefinitely on unleaded fuels without some action, although this may well be necessary later rather than sooner.

Let's look at the situation in a bit more detail, starting with the undeniable fact that you will probably have to retard the timing slightly immediately you make the change from leaded to unleaded fuel. The exhaust valve seats are, however, much less clear cut and longevity will depend on a number of factors, but largely the vigour with which you drive the car. They were originally machined straight into the cast iron head and are, therefore, made from material that will not withstand continuous vigorous driving using unleaded fuel, but don't panic. If you've been using leaded fuel in your engine for a number of years a thin but very worthwhile protective lead deposit will have built up on the working surfaces. This will, depending upon how you drive your car, last for maybe thousands of miles. Obviously, if you do a de-coke, drive flat out for hours, or tow a caravan, the 'lead effect' is dramatically foreshortened, but, with light driving at, say, 50-55mph, it could last for several years.

In due course you will have to adjust the tappets with increasing frequency, signalling the start of valve seat recession. But so what; tappet adjustment takes but an hour from start to finish and, if you're covering only some 5000 miles per annum, you could go many years with just an annual tappet adjustment. Do not worry that you are doing your engine irreparable damage, and running the risk of needing a new and very expensive cylinder head. Eventually, when the time comes to have the head modified, the valve seats that have been recessing due to the use of unleaded fuels will be machined out and replaced with a hardened insert. By adopting a 'wait and see' policy you are doing your engine no damage whatsoever.

Then there are numerous additives for unleaded fuel that further delay valve seat recession, although no additive will protect or perform as well as leaded fuel. These additives (the full name is Anti-Wear Additives or AWAs) will also be most effective in light to normal driving conditions. In the US, leaded additives have been readily available at every autopart store for some 15 years or so, and a distribution network and agents are becoming established all over the UK even as I write. Sodium, phosphorous, potassium and manganese components form the basis of most of these additives, which will, unless you drive fairly hard, add years to the life of your cylinder head. Use a reputable make and always stick to the same brand. Never mix additives with leaded or lead replacement (more in a moment) fuels.

A number of additive products underwent comparative tests at MIRA in late 1998, and four were initially declared as having met the pre-set valve seat recession criteria. Since then, additional products have been submitted for tests and several products have been added to the list of those proven to delay the onset of valve set recession. At the time of writing the full list is as follows:
Additives with octane boosters (treatment costs about 8 pence per imperial gallon of fuel)

- Millers VSP-Plus
- Castrol Valvemaster Plus
- Nitrox 4-Lead

Additives without octane boosters (treatment costs about 3-4 pence per imperial gallon of fuel)

- Red Line Lead Substitute
- Superblend Zero Lead 2000
- Valvemaster
- Nitrox 4-Star

On the face of it, it seems there's little point buying the more expensive 'with octane booster' product. However, if your car needs the higher octane rating of super unleaded fuels (see section on anti-run-on valves), you may find a cost saving is possible by using standard unleaded 95 RON fuel with the octane boosting additive. Its makers claim the octane booster increases ratings by 2 or 3 points, which brings the resulting combination back to leaded fuel octane. You would do well to study all the respective manufacturer's claims and the chemical constituents of each product. As I understand the information released to date, Superblend showed the lowest valve seat recession during tests and uses potassium as the basis of its protection. Red Line's product is based on sodium and has been in use in the USA since the eighties. Valvemaster bases its product on the chemical properties of phosphorous. Send off for more information from a short-list of suppliers. Once you've started to use a lead substitute product, it's wise to regularly check tappet clearances, and keep a record of any adjustments necessary until you are confident that VSR (valve seat recession) is minimal.

Then there's lead replacement petrol - LRP - which replaced the vast majority of UK four star leaded fuel pumps from autumn 1999. LRP fuel will probably be satisfactory for light driving, but cars used at high speed could experience some recession, and will still need to have the cylinder head attended to - eventually.

Obviously, the situation changes if and when you come to an engine rebuild for other reasons; clearly, it makes no sense to refurbish the bottom end and clamp the old head back in place. No, this is when the time for procrastination is over and an unleaded head conversion called for. Many automotive machine shops are capable of creating the cavity, and inserting a hardened valve seat insert at each exhaust valve position in your cylinder head, but I think it makes sense to entrust the machining work to one of our premier TR specialists. The original BL valves are of very high quality, although some non-OE replacements supplied in more recent times are not so good. When the head work takes place a specialist's advice may be required about whether to replace or retain your valves. Most will elect to do the job properly and have new OE valves, or special 'unleaded' valves with hard chrome flashed stems fitted. In any event you should have phosphor bronze valve guides fitted, but the message is, don't rush to spend your money too soon. Wait until it is essential, or you are inside the engine for other reasons.

'UNLEADED' CYLINDER HEAD

So, how do you modify a cylinder head so that it is suitable for hard or sustained fast driving using unleaded fuel? The process is the same for aluminium heads and cast iron ones, and involves machining a recess for the hard-sintered valve seat insert used for each exhaust valve and shown in photograph 8-1. This is definitely not a DIY job, but, since it's a topic that will be relevant to every reader at some time, I thought it would be of interest to establish the work and cost involved.

The machine shop needs to select the appropriate insert for your head, which means not only choosing the correct grade of sinter, but the appropriate sizes (bore and outside diameter), too. The size issue is relatively self-explanatory: you need a bore that is compatible with the throat size of the particular cylinder head you are about to machine, and an outside diameter that will accommodate the exhaust valve in question. There are hundreds to choose from! What most of us will not, perhaps, have appreciated is that there are also at least three grades of sintered insert to choose from. For unleaded petrol/gas, it is usual to use a mid-range insert, but if one were preparing a cylinder head for, say, propane, LPG or natural gas, it would be necessary to use a harder grade of insert. The 'HM' (high-machinabilty) grade consists of a blend of finely dispersed Tungsten-carbide tool-steel, and alloys of iron which the makers say provides machining characteristics comparable to cast iron, yet the insert is hard enough, and, therefore, suitable for naturally aspirated and turbocharged engines.

The first step in the process is to remove the old valve guides and fit new ones. This is important since virtually every subsequent operation will rely on a mandrel that will be positioned in each valve guide to ensure the accuracy of each machining operation. The

8-1. These are the sintered insert rings as received by the cylinder head reconditioner. A huge range is available, but this is how the hard basic ring looks before being pressed into a machined recess formed where each exhaust valve sits. They are more complex, metallurgically-speaking, than they look.

machining can be carried out by numerous pieces of 'kit'. Where high volume/repetition production is involved, the machines can be very sophisticated indeed, and correspondingly expensive. Photograph 8-2 shows how it is more likely to be carried out in a low-volume 'classic' car-focused restoration business such as Bailey and Liddle (see Appendix 1 for details).

Next, the old valve seat is

8-2. Whatever machine and holding fixture the restoration company uses, a high degree of accuracy is required to ensure the true vertical movement of the cutter while the head always stays absolutely horizontal. This machine has been especially modified to ensure these requirements are met, and that the speed of the cutter is compatible with the machining of both cylinder head recesses and the subsequent work required in the sintered exhaust valve seat inserts.

8-3. The cutter can be seen forming number 2 cylinder's exhaust valve recess, while, in the foreground, the result of number 1 machining can be seen.

8-4. Here, the insert can be seen standing proud of its recess for a few seconds. The hammer blow required to overcome the interference between insert and bored recess is quite considerable. Fortunately, the insert has a special chamfer on one end to aid entry into the recess.

8-5. In the foreground the insert has been machined flush with the combustion chamber, while the next insert is being machined to the profile of the exhaust valves provided by this TR owner. You can establish whether your valves seem likely to be up to the rigours of unleaded fuel by a quick magnetic check. If the valve attracts a magnet it will be too soft for use with unleaded fuels and must be replaced with one that contains more stainless/nimonic materials, which will not attract a magnet. Not a lot of people know that!

8-6. The anti-run-on valve; two, in fact! It is unusual to have to fit two, but it is an option for high-compression engines.

machined away, as can be seen in photograph 8-3, but with great care, for it is important to ensure the outside diameter of the hole is absolutely correct for the selected insert. In fact, the hole needs to be a prescribed amount less than the insert outside size, and, to ensure this, Bailey and Liddle actually bore the hole twice. The first cut is never quite to size because the cutter warms up and expands. Consequently, the boring tool is slightly adjusted after the first holes have been bored and before the second, much finer dead-size cut. The depth of the bore is also important and is regulated to a shade less than the depth of the insert; once the insert is in place, it will be slightly proud of the combustion chamber. More on this in a moment.

Next up is driving the inserts into their recessed bores, as per photograph number 8-4. The picture is slightly deceptive in that the mandrel mentioned earlier is in place to ensure the insert can only be driven home square to the valve guide. Although already an interference fit, the insert plays its part, too, by expanding into the bored recess, thus providing a dependable valve seat that will not move even at the elevated temperatures in a combustion chamber.

You may be surprised to learn that there are still two machining operations to carry out. The first, shown in photograph 8-5, involves the same set-up (including the all-important but unseen guide mandrel) and brings the top of the sintered insert down to the level of each combustion chamber. The second requires selecting a cutter that matches the profile of the exhaust valve to be used, and machining out the inside of each insert until the valve sits properly in the head/insert/combustion chamber - nothing to it, really! The final operation is carried out by hand to blend-in, where required, the base of each insert with the respective exhaust passage.

The cost of fitting new valve guides and unleaded compatible exhaust valve seats to a 4-cylinder TR head will range from about £120 for just fitting inserts to your stripped and pre-cleaned cylinder head, to about £250 for the comprehensive service of fully stripping, fitting inserts, suppling all parts and re-assembling your 4-cylinder head ready to bolt to the block.

ANTI-RUN-ON VALVES

I am anxious not to cause any alarm, but it might be wise to mention that, as the fuel octane rating you use in your TR reduces, engines with a compression ratio of about 9.5, possibly 10:1, can start to experience 'running-on'. That is to say, the engine continues to turn over, usually very roughly, after the ignition switch is turned off. Sometimes the running-on period is a matter of a

few seconds, but occasionally can be longer.

This never happens with modern EFI (electronic fuel injected) cars for the injectors cease to open once the ignition switch is 'off'. The 6-cylinder TRs with PI are also very unlikely to suffer from run-on since the fuel pump stops pressurising the fuel and opening the injectors. However, carburettor cars have a reservoir of fuel in the float chambers, and air drawn through the carburettors by the engine revolutions will continue to carry fuel to the cylinders - for quite some time!

A reduction in fuel octane may not be the only cause of run-on. Your cylinder head may be in need of a de-coke and have carbon deposits that glow and act as a substitute for the spark plugs. However, in the context of a change from 98 RON (leaded fuel octane rating) to 95 RON (unleaded octane), if you start to experience running-on your first step should be to start adding an octane boosting additive to your unleaded fuel. If running-on problems persist, try switching to super unleaded fuel, which has an octane rating closer to that of leaded fuels.

If running-on still persists, you should try fitting anti-run-on valves. These electromagnetic valves 'close' when the ignition is 'on' and are ineffective in that mode. However, they are coupled to the inlet manifold and, as soon as you switch 'off', the valve(s) will automatically open and allow air into the inlet manifold. This dilutes the fuel/air mixture, hopefully, to the point where

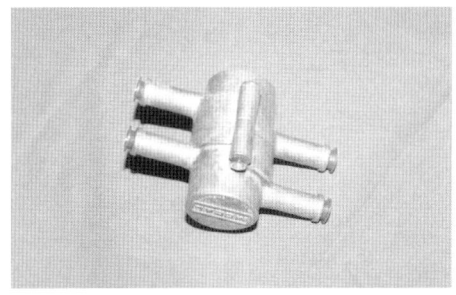

8-7. This is a typical oil thermostat that allows hot oil to circulate through an oil cooler when necessary, but to bypass the cooler when the oil temperature is insufficient to warrant cooling. This particular example has four ends that accept plain hoses fixed by jubilee-like clips. Some 'stats have screwed end couplings that necessitate corresponding couplings on the end of the oil lines. I think 'plain end' 'stats are easier to fit (particularly retrospectively) than those with screwed ends.

your engine has insufficient fuel to run-on. Photograph 8-6 shows an anti-run-on valve.

The valves are available from Rover dealers and most TR specialists at about £35 each, and the part number is ADU9535. You should initially try one, which will usually do the trick, but resort to two, as this owner had to, if your first valve does not work. They work best when mounted vertically. If you still have problems, look for other reasons, like compression ratios in excess of 10.5:1.

Chapter 9
Clutches, gearboxes and overdrives

THE CLUTCH

You may have heard that some TR clutches can be a problem. Well, of course, any car's clutch can be a problem, and those TRs with six-cylinder engines do have a, sadly, deservedly 'fragile' reputation when it comes to the clutch. However, let me reassure you that the clutch used with the four-cylinder engine will enjoy a long life provided it is not abused. It has a good and consistent life, and pedal pressure remains constant throughout.

The cover plate may be of an old type 'spring' design, see photograph 9-1, but is rugged and serves its purpose admirably. The workshop manual gives all the advice you need when fitting a clutch, so I do not propose to take up space unnecessarily, other than to add a few details to aid the longevity of your new clutch:

● The two pins mounted each side of the fork should be round. The pins can be seen loose and *in situ* in photograph 9-2, and they should be replaced if they have flats on them.

● If you are experiencing clutch drag or gear engagement difficulties, before the gearbox is removed, do ensure that the clutch slave cylinder's push rod fork and clevis pin are connected to the middle

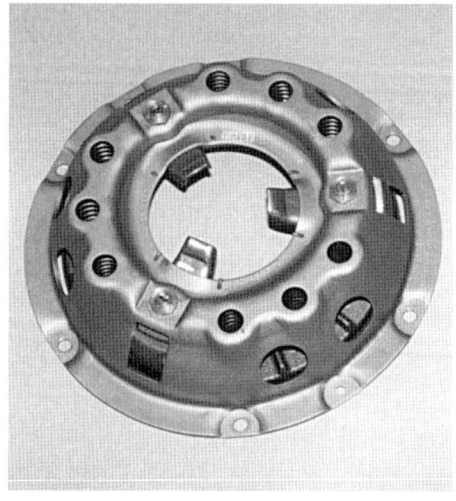

9-1. The four-cylinder engine's clutch cover can be distinguished by its nine pressure springs and three release fingers. This unit has few vices and, given proper installation and reasonable care, should give long and very satisfactory service.

hole (of three options) in the side lever/ crank shown in photograph 9-3. The bottom hole will result in insufficient clutch separation, while the top hole would increase clutch separation but with significantly increased pedal pressure.

● Take particular care when pressing

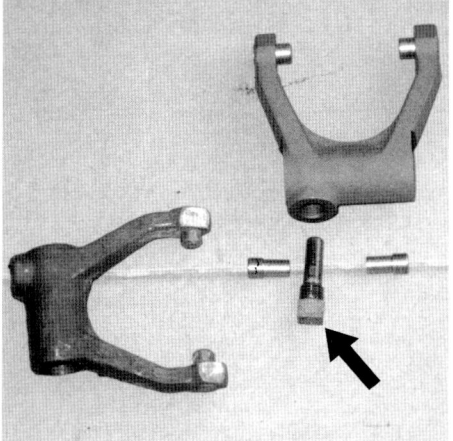

9-2. Much has been said about the clutch release fork, at least in the context of six-cylinder TRs. Here are two examples, along with the hardened locating pin (arrowed) that should be replaced every time you are inside the bellhousing, even if you have a four-cylinder TR. The picture also shows two replacement pins that engage the sliding sleeve. While you cannot see the wear in this photograph, these pins do become 'flattened' and should also be replaced in the fork (since the 'flats' reduce the movement of the sleeve).

the thrust bearing to its carrier. The thrust bearing, shown in photograph 9-4, needs to slip onto its carrier with **slight** interference so that the operation

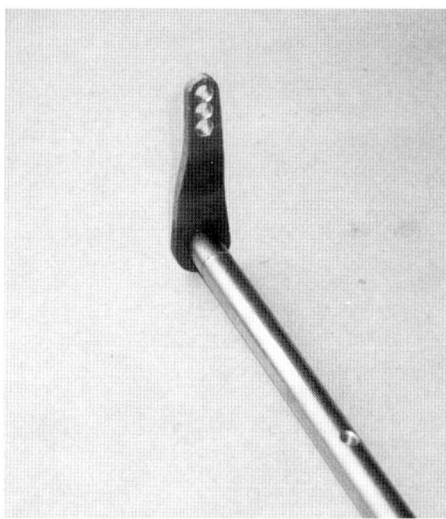

9-3. This is a general view of the cross-shaft, included to show the three holes in the actuation arm. All TRs use the central hole.

9-4. The clutch release bearing and fork are important to the satisfactory operation of the clutch. You will find information in the main text as to how to install the thrust bearing, and on the precaution of increasing the strength of the fork to cross-shaft pin. Here, (arrowed) a 0.25in (6mm) diameter hole has been drilled through the fork and the cross-shaft, and a high-tensile bolt and (just-visible) new nyloc nut has been fitted. There are alternatives explored in the text but, if you follow this route you should ensure that the plain shank of the bolt comes almost through to the outside of the fork. You should also lock-wire the new pin. Most professional TR restorers carry out a similar modification to improve the reliability of this vulnerable part of the TR4/4A clutch. However, their hole will rarely be more than 3-4mm in diameter, with additional security gained by driving in a 'roll pin', see photograph 9-5. Incidentally, the larger than average hole in the bellhousing flange directly to the right of the cross-shaft is provided for a locating dowel-pin on the rear of the four-cylinder cylinder-block.

can be completed with minimal pressure. The wrong technique or heavy-handed pressure can shorten the life of the thrust bearing and necessitate your removing the gearbox prematurely. This is best avoided!

Ensure that both the outside of the carrier and the bore of the new thrust bearings are spotlessly clean, and that there are no burrs, high spots or anything that will increase the pressure needed to press the bearing onto the carrier. Lubricate the two interference faces and use a block of soft wood to spread the pressure over the whole face of the bearing. Set the bearing and carrier 'square' in a vice and slowly squeeze the two parts together - never shock (e.g. hammer) the bearing onto its carrier - and, if resistance increases, stop, investigate and take remedial action before resuming.

• Although far less prevalent on the four-cylinder cars than their six-cylinder successors, it's still not unknown for the pin that holds the clutch fork onto its gearbox cross-shaft to break. The pin (identified by an arrow in picture 9-2, and shown *in situ* in photograph 9-4) is hardened and tapered, and, for some reason, very rarely breaks off cleanly. More often than not it breaks at 45 degrees. The problem with an angled break is that it allows the fork to move on its shaft but only by about 15 degrees. As strange as this may sound, this movement is rarely sufficient to make an absolutely sure diagnosis without stripping the car and testing the pin. Indeed, more than one TR has been stripped, fitted with a new clutch and the whole car put back together with the prime reason for the car's problems left uncorrected! The slight movement of the fork on its shaft allows the clutch to partially operate, but it will probably feel very 'heavy'.

Furthermore, upon strip down, the fork will appear secure on its shaft, which is why numerous TR gearboxes have been remarried to their engine with a new clutch in place but with no worthwhile improvement in operation. In fact, the pin is so difficult to get at, and the proper orientation of the fork/shaft is so important, that the assembly warrants the 'dual-pipe test' whenever the gearbox is out. Also, the cost of the pin is such that it's worth replacing it as a matter of course every time you take a peak inside your car's bell housing!

You will be wondering what on earth is the dual-pipe test! Take two pieces of pipe or tube, each about 12in (300mm) long. Fit one over one leg of the fork, and one over the shaft's external actuation lever, and test one pipe against the other to see if the fork really is securely pinned to its shaft. Even 2 or 3mm of movement is too much, and necessitates a new pin and a re-test.

• If you are unlucky enough to experience a broken clutch fork/cross-shaft pin you may appreciate our exploring some solutions. The pin in question, as I mentioned earlier, usually shears at about a 45 degree angle, thus making it impossible to just remove the cross-shaft. If your cross-shaft is worn and needs replacing anyway, then the easiest and quickest solution is to cut the shaft adjacent to the fork on the external lever side of the fork. You then remove the sub-assembly in two parts, salvage the fork and fit a new cross-shaft (part number 136354). However, if the shaft is not worn we should try to salvage both shaft and fork by drilling the pin out ... except the pin is hardened and a 'spark-erosion' operation will cost more than the replacement parts! So, for a salvage attempt on the basis that you have nothing to lose, start by removing the square head and a short section of the shank of the pin. Put a small piece of thin tube in the resulting hole to protect the thread in the fork (or drill a hole through the centre of a suitable screw) and, using a (hardened) pin-punch, try to break-up the protruding part of the original pin. If that fails to allow the shaft to exit its fork, you could try drilling a 3 or 4mm diameter hole into the other side of the fork, diametrically opposite the threaded boss, and use your pin-punch to break-up the original pin from the other end.

• The pin-shearing problem is not so frequent with four-cylinder TRs and, therefore, a solution is not quite so urgent. Nevertheless, the time needed to remove and replace the gearbox just to replace a sheared pin makes me recommend you do, in fact, add some additional strength to the fork/cross-shaft. You can, for example, insert the extra 0.25in (6mm) diameter bolt that can be seen pinning the fork to the cross-shaft in photograph 9-4. You may prefer to drill a smaller hole, though, and fit a 'roll pin'. They come in varying sizes

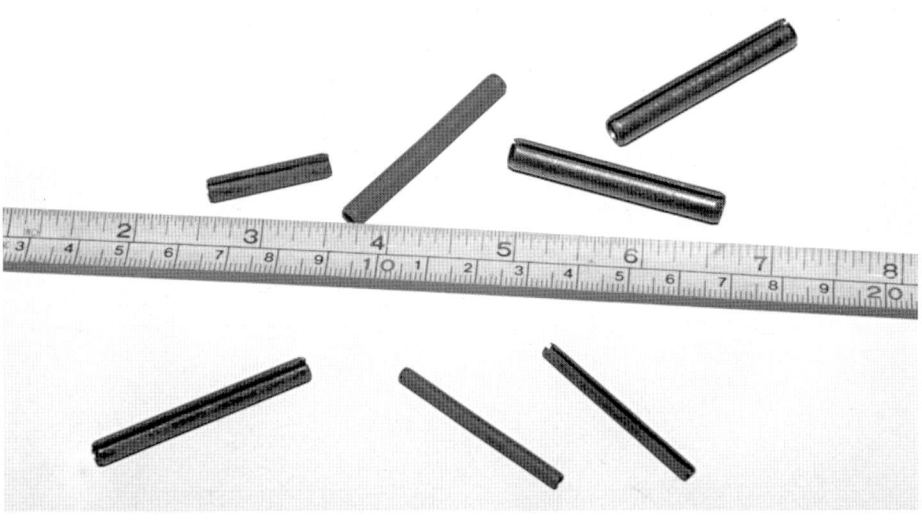

9-7.

9-5. Some examples of 'roll pins' ... mostly too long for this application but, nevertheless, useful for identification purposes. Extra length can always be ground off after fitting, provided you protect your gearbox from grinding dust. Note that the drill size should always be smaller than the diameter of the roll pin you plan to use, and you should seek advice as to the size of the hole required for your particular pin. These examples are 2, 3 and 4mm in diameter, the 3mm probably being the optimum for four-cylinder applications. Roll pins are no longer available in the UK in 'imperial' sizes.

9-6. For comparison, here are two 'A' type gearboxes with overdrives - identified at a glance by the large brass sump nuts. The one on the left is the variant from a saloon (2000 and/or 2500) or a Mark 1 Stag as revealed by the horizontally-mounted solenoid and vertical mounting studs. Were this gearbox from a TR, the solenoid would be mounted vertically as per the unit on the right. You will have noted the flat rear platform for the rubber Metalastic mounting pad on the right unit, confirming this to be of TR origin. Note, too, the solenoid lever and through shaft, and how vulnerable they are.

THE GEARBOXES

The TR4 and 4A should, strictly speaking, only be fitted with the earlier 'A' type gearbox and/or overdrive unit, as shown in photograph 9-6. However, there are those who may have purchased a car with a later ('J' type) gearbox/overdrive already fitted, or those who feel that the cost, availability and reliability benefits of the later transmission warrant some loss of originality. Consequently, I propose to review both Triumph gearboxes here. Pictures 9-7 and 9-8 will help you identify each of the gearboxes with their respective overdrives.

Stripping and reassembly of your gearbox is a job for an experienced expert, and is, therefore, outside the scope of this book. If you doubt this, take a look at photograph 9-9, and consider that even the majority of professional restorers will not usually do more than the basic gearbox operational repairs. Instead, they will send the 'box to a specialist who is repairing them all day every day. That said, there still is a lot to consider, starting, I suggest, with a review as to which gearbox should be fitted to which car, and whether you have the correct 'box for your car.

Triumph used a prefix numbering system that tells us whether the gearbox was originally assembled to a TR, and

9-7 and 9-8 (above). Three gearboxes, all with overdrives fitted. On the far side of the first photograph we have the correct TR2 to early TR6 'A' type gearbox and overdrive. The central gearbox is a 'J' type, correct for later TR6s, but which will fit most earlier TRs with care. Note the extra support for the gear change casing. Nearest the camera, the vertical mounting tells us this is a saloon gearbox, confirmed by the fact that the speedometer drive exits the 'box high on the casing and horizontally. The TR speedometer drive will be low down and angled at about 30 degrees to miss the tunnel cover, as can be seen in both other examples.

what type of gearbox it was. Your car's commission number will not be reflected in the gearbox number, which comprises a prefix and number, and is stamped in various positions on the left side of the gearbox. However, as we will discover, there are lots of good reasons why the case of your particular 'box

and possibly the 3 or 4mm examples seen in photograph 9-5 will provide you with the piece of mind, and your car's clutch with the extra strength needed to ensure a long and trouble-free life.

9-10.

9-9. I thought you might like a look at what's inside a gearbox. In fact, you can take the top (not shown in this shot), of the gearbox off and peak at the contents without getting yourself into too much trouble. The overdrive is also missing from this picture, which should emphasise the fact that gearboxes (and overdrives for that matter), are a speciality in themselves, and, unless you have experience, or the assistance of an experienced specialist, they are best left to the experts.

9-10 and 9-11 (above). Comparative views of two bellhousings and first motion shafts. On the left side of both pictures is a Triumph Stag gearbox that is similar in many ways to the TR gearbox shown on the right. Although the splines are the same, the spigot for the Stag can be seen extending about 2in (50mm) too far for immediate TR use. A specialist can correct this by substituting first-motion shafts, which puts you in business. I wonder if you have spotted a less obvious but important detail? The TR bellhousing flange is only about half the thickness of that of the Stag. In fact, the TR bellhousing flange is actually broken for about 45 degrees along the top edge, reinforcing the wisdom of choosing, whenever possible, the later, thicker flanged, stronger Triumph gearbox, whatever your intended application. All Triumph applications use the same interchangeable casings, and you'd be particularly well advised to swap your thin flanged TR casing for a thick, say, ex-Saloon one, if you plan even modest increases in performance.

may indicate that it comes from another Triumph model.

As parts become both more expensive and more difficult to find, it becomes increasingly common practice to use components from sister cars to repair TR gearboxes. Consequently, the case, or some of the internal parts within your 'box may well be non-original! But don't panic. Few will know and even less will care. When it comes to it, what does it matter if, say, your 1st gear countershaft was from a saloon 'box. If your thin-flanged bellhousing has cracked, surely most will be pleased to get the car back on the road and somewhat less concerned that the case is now an ex-saloon, thick-flanged one, particularly as the thicker flange became a Triumph gearbox improvement right across the whole model range.

The difference in flange thickness can be seen in photograph 9-10 and, to

a lesser extent, in 9-11.

I understand that the issue of originality prohibits such variations for some owners, but, for the majority, the message is do not be overly concerned if your gearbox case numbers are non-TR in origin. Four-cylinder, three-synchro 'boxes were prefixed TS and UF, four-cylinder four-synchro ones CT, LE, LF, MD, ME, MG, MK, VA and VF, while the six-cylinder 'boxes carry the prefix CC, CD, CF or CP. Factory reconditioned units carry a GR prefix.

There are some very bad quality components on the market that may not be spotted by the home restorer, but which will be all too obvious after hours of work, once the 'box is in the car and put to use. In this context, see my notes under 'Rear axles', about service-exchange units being preferable from a reputable dealer.

You can, of course, fit complete ex-saloon gearboxes with perhaps four-synchro and/or overdrive, and I will give you more information on this with some pictorial help in just a moment. However, if you are of a mind to delve into your gearbox, do not do so thinking you may be able to convert a three-synchro gearbox to a four-synchromesh 'box. You, or perhaps more likely an expert, can add overdrive to either type of gearbox provided you have the correct overdrive assembly and the tail-shaft and adapter plate for your gearbox. More on this, too, in a moment.

However, before we get into the unusual, let's explore some of the much more usual gearbox and overdrive issues that you can at least confirm at home, some of which may be following up suspicions formed when we first inspected the car prior to purchase:

● Drain the oil and inspect it closely. A slight 'brassy' look is normal. If the oil is very grey in colour, or if grey-coloured steel chips are obvious, remove the top cover casting and look for damaged gears. You may need to revolve a number of them, but it is likely you will find missing or at least chipped teeth. Check second gear for play. If present, the thrust washer is probably broken, which will have caused further damage to both the gear and the main shaft. A thick, grey sludge means the layshaft and/or gears have disintegrated (we will probably have noticed the telltale 'hiss' on our test drive). Brass pieces signal broken synchro rings or bushes, which will also have been obvious on our test. Any or all of the above imply you need a major overhaul, or that an exchange or replacement 'box is on the cards.

● When refilling the repaired, exchange or replacement gearbox, the quantity of oil for a normal gearbox is 1.5 pints or 0.85 litres. A box with overdrive, on the other hand, will need 3.5 pints or 2 litres. Use ST90 gear oil for all types of standard gearboxes, but, when filling the overdrive gearboxes, do allow plenty of time for oil to fill the overdrive. It's best not to use synthetic oils in an overdrive gearbox.

OVERDRIVE MATTERS

The two types of overdrive under discussion are shown in photographs 9-12 and 9-13.

Problems and solutions common to 'A' and 'J' types

It's not the objective of this book to act

9-12. You will get few clearer views of an 'A' overdrive. Note the vertical actuating solenoid on the left of the unit and slightly angled (downward) speedo drive right of centre.

9-13. The tail end of a 'J' type overdrive with, not shown, a 'J' type gearbox. Note that the flat rear mounting 'pad' just forward of the drive flange signals this is a TR overdrive unit, while the rectangular 'sump' at the bottom of the picture, together with the position of the solenoid, declares this a 'J' model overdrive unit. Mind you, Laycock de Normanville kindly removed any doubt by fixing an identification plate that says 'J' type overdrive!

as a workshop manual, or to cover all eventualities and problems. Nevertheless, there are some frequent overdrive problems that we should explore.

First and foremost, watch for the classic overdrive problem where the overdrive switch on the steering column rotates and earths out, thus permanently engaging overdrive, with potentially expensive consequences. So, if your column switch is loose, fix it ... now! As a preventative step, whatever you do before reassembling a car you are rebuilding or re-clutching, treble-check that the overdrive inhibitor switches atop your gearbox are functioning reliably and consistently. You could have one (if your overdrive functions on 3rd and 4th gears), but those gearboxes that also enjoy overdrive on 2nd gear will have two such switches. Use a battery and light bulb, or a multi-meter, to check for electrical continuity when the requisite gear is engaged, and, equally important, no continuity when non-overdrive gears are engaged. It is particularly important that there is no continuity when reverse gear is engaged.

While you are there with the relevant equipment, take a moment to check that the reverse light switch is working.

A sudden and complete non-operating overdrive probably signals an electrical problem, but one that most owners of classic cars should be able to cope with. At first, many will think this sounds like really bad news, but, in fact, the problem could be fixed quite quickly and cheaply and it really is worth exploring the situation yourself before you go off to a specialist.

The earlier 'A' type overdrives are notorious for the way the solenoid valve operates: the design tends to allow water, dirt and oil to gum them up. This certainly is a problem that virtually every owner can check for and rectify. You will need to take the gearbox cover off, and, using your workshop manual and/or the accompanying photographs, identify the solenoid and its through shafts. Jack up the back of the car and safely secure it, mindful that, eventually, the rear wheels may be rotating, and changing rpm, too, either or both of which can cause the car to jerk off conventional axle stands. You might, therefore, want to support the chassis with ramps, or find some alternative, but very solid, method of getting the rear wheels off the ground.

For the first check, we only need to have the ignition switched on, so there's no need to start the engine, although you will need to engage, say, third gear and flick the overdrive switch in and out. Obviously, you should see the solenoid and its mechanism operate each time you alter the switch position. If nothing appears to be happening, try the same test in, say, top gear, and then use your multi-meter (on low volts setting) or a 12 volt bulb and an earth lead to detect whether power is being presented to the solenoid. If power is not reaching the solenoid, you need to work backwards until you resolve the electrical problem. More than likely, however, you will find power is reaching the solenoid, and you will need to free off a seized/frozen mechanism with penetrating oil, or possibly replace the solenoid. Once you feel the problem is going to take more than a couple of minutes to resolve, pull a low tension lead from the coil (and wrap a little tape around the termination), to save the ignition system from prolonged use.

If the solenoid mechanism is working, we need to look 'downstream' for the problem. Again, with the car still safely on its particularly stable stands, but this time with the engine running at a shade above tickover rpm, loosen the operating valve plug. Once third gear is engaged, oil should bleed past the loose plug. Allow a few moments for any trapped air to bleed, but, if no oil is forthcoming, the pump is probably not working, so re-tighten the bleed plug. Let things cool off somewhat and drain the gearbox, looking carefully at the oil. Refresh your mind as to the points made in chapter 2 on listening to the gearbox before purchase, and (earlier in this Chapter) what the colour of the oil tells us.

Bear in mind that the same oil circulates around both gearbox and overdrive, which means that a gearbox problem can and will circulate contaminated oil through the overdrive and damage the overdrive unit. If the oil does not look too bad, remove, inspect and clean the overdrive filter. If you now remove the pump body plug, the base of the pump will be exposed. Tap it gently. Put the 'box in neutral and have a partner turn a rear wheel so that the propshaft turns and the pump moves up and down freely. If it doesn't, or if the pump sticks again, you need to talk to your friendly TR specialist, overdrive repairer (see Appendix 1), and bank manager!

A running car could experience a couple of overdrive difficulties that are rather puzzling to those not experienced with this type of mechanism. The first concerns the very slow uptake of the overdrive. We will discuss the exceptionally fast and average engagement of overdrives in a moment, but when you need to wait several seconds before the overdrive unit cuts in you have a very slow unit. This is almost certainly due to a worn pump. It's worth checking for clogged filters (refer to your workshop manual) but, thereafter, you'll have to decide if, how, and when to resolve the problem of a worn pump, particularly if the overdrive stays 'in' once it engages.

You can usually take your time and fix this problem at a convenient moment, provided the overdrive has or will disengage when required. Do not drive the car anywhere if overdrive is not disengaging. However, if overdrive gear is eventually there when you want it, although the might pump be so worn that the return springs cannot be compressed and the overdrive fails to engage, or hold 'in', you can at least take your time fixing it.

There is another reason why the overdrive take-up can vary. It may cut in okay sometimes; you may feel it is trying but never really makes it; sometimes it feels as if it has actually dropped out ... but hasn't; this almost certainly signals worn brake ring linings in the overdrive unit. The conical brake-ring linings wear and eventually fail to properly hold the conical clutch when it is pushed backwards by the pump. Consequently, the clutch fails to lock and the drive fails to be directed through the sun wheels. You might feel you can tackle the former problem, but the latter is really not a job for the inexperienced. Furthermore, you are likely to lose overdrive completely in the very near future, so a call to a specialist is appropriate.

The 'A' type overdrive

Photograph 9-12 shows a genuine TR 'A' type overdrive *in situ*. One of the most frequent 'A' type faults is that the valve in the right side of the overdrive, which holds the overdrive 'in', becomes blocked for want of servicing. Not a tremendous problem (cleaning the filter will usually restore normal service), provided you notice that overdrive is not disengaging. However, if you fail to notice that the car suddenly has very high gearing all of the time, and engage reverse gear, you'll find the back of the car will rise up (as if the handbrake has been left on). The 'J' type overdrive is protected and will slip before anything breaks, but the 'A' type will break and require a professional rebuild.

If you have your 'A' type rebuilt, always have an improved/modified uni-directional gear fitted, as it is much more robust. Furthermore, the 'A' type is not strong enough to withstand the torque generated by a hard-driven TR in second gear. The factory realised this and, late in the 'A' type's life, stopped putting overdrive inhibitor switches on 'A' type second gears. In fact, overdrive was not reintroduced on second gear until the CR/CF TR6s. If you do have an 'A' type overdrive, and can engage it when in second gear, do treat the gearbox/overdrive unit with care or, for insurance, replace the second gear inhibitor switch with a blanking plug next time you have the gearbox cover off. Conversely, if you have a 'J' type overdrive, you can use overdrive in second gear and may even wish to fit a second gear inhibitor switch if you do not already have one.

There were actually two types of TR 'A' type overdrive units, and, as the saying goes, not a lot of people know that! Photograph 9-6 does show two different types of 'A' overdrive but, unfortunately, only one is a TR 'A' type. The large brass nut located below what is the accumulator protrusion clearly identifies all 'A' units.

The picture helps to illustrate my next point: there were two sizes of accumulator. The very early units had what turned out to be a larger oil accumulator, which 'bangs' the overdrive 'in' pretty fiercely. After some time the protrusion into which the sump drain nut is screwed was reduced to the size shown in this picture - thus reducing the size of the accumulator and softening the take-up of overdrive. Obviously, this is not applicable if you plan any track racing, since I doubt you would want either the extra weight or the reduced revs an overdrive unit brings. However, if you intend to use your 'A' overdrive in competition/rallying, you might want to be selective by using an early casing with a 3/4in (20mm) deeper protrusion above the brass nut rather than the shallow protrusion shown in photograph 9-6. The casings with the deeper protrusion are usually more robust. Furthermore, if the brass sump plug sits on a 3/4in (20mm) protrusion, there's a chance it is the earlier, stronger, harder, quicker unit with the larger accumulator. I am sorry to say that an expert will have to get inside the overdrive unit to establish that it has the larger capacity accumulator. However, the latest 'A' overdrive units with a relatively short protrusion (perhaps 5mm), will certainly not have the large accumulator, so will not be so desirable for competitive use.

Photograph 9-6 serves an additional purpose in that, because of the considerable amount of highly specialised work involved in converting a saloon gearbox/overdrive to TR specification, there is very little, if any, saving in using the non-TR 'A' unit shown in this picture. While it can be done - and you will not know the difference at the end of the exercise - it's as well to pay the apparently substantial sum for the real thing and be done with it!

An ex-saloon gearbox is not, however, without its uses, since, if your TR 'A' unit has internal or casing

9-14. It may sound strange when you learn for the first time that the exhaust system you order is dictated by your gearbox/overdrive. This picture shows the mid-point mounting for a single-pipe free-flow exhaust system, and perhaps explains why you need to sort your gearbox details out before you order your exhaust system! Perhaps more important, in the context of a chapter on gearbox matters, is the detail of this 'A' type overdrive speedo drive point. It's angled down at about 30 degrees so we know this is a real TR installation. The flat 'A' type rear mountings are pretty clear, too.

9-15 and 9-16. The first picture shows the non-original, but much improved, PVC moulded gearbox cover for a TR4A. In the second shot, an extra access door has been added to allow service work on the speedo drive. Mild steel would be most owner's choice of cover material, affixed with self-tappers. This cover is actually a special fibreglass moulding made *in situ* before the hole was cut in the base PVC.

damage, then a good ex-saloon 'box will be a much cheaper way of acquiring the replacement parts you need. Indeed, you could transfer the lot and, if the saloon's 'box is in good shape, that's not such a bad idea!

The 'J' Type Overdrive
The 'J' type gearbox and overdrives were introduced late in 1972 for the 'CR' UK cars, and an example of the overdrive is shown in photograph 9-13. Few US 'CF' series cars actually had overdrive fitted, but it was, nevertheless,

the same gearbox.

If your car does not have an overdrive fitted then this 'J' type is the easiest and most reliable unit to target, but you will need the 'J' type of gearbox to go with it. The 'J' overdrive was fitted to several Triumph cars of that era and one or two examples appear in the photographs 9-7 to 9-8 to aid your identification.

One further advantage of the 'J' type overdrive units is that the speedo drive gear on the rear drive shaft of the gearbox can be changed, thereby adjusting the speedo-drive ratio to suit the TR's 15in wheels. The other Triumph models all had smaller wheel sizes and, without the ability to change speedo gear ratios, will give some strange speedo readings! The earlier 'A' type gearbox and, more particularly, the 'A' type overdrive units, did not enjoy this flexibility. Consequently, using an 'A' type gearbox/overdrive unit from, say, a 14in wheeled Stag in your TR, will result in either a very expensive and specialist weld/re-hobbing operation, or a re-calibration of the speedo. The latter can be accomplished for about 10% of the cost of the re-hobbing, so will be most people's choice!

If you are using a non-TR gearbox/overdrive, you will have to consider the drive flange, and either have the one you get with the non-TR 'box altered, or get an ex-TR rear drive flange. The alteration is not particularly difficult, a slight skim is taken from the non-TR flange recess, the flange is turned through 45 degrees, and the holes redrilled on a slightly bigger PCD.

If you wanted to fit a non-TR 'J' type gearbox and overdrive unit to a pre-1972 TR, this can be done quite successfully, but requires an adapter kit to allow the rear gearbox mounting to sit securely and comfortably in your TR.

Some welding to the chassis of suitable mounting plates may be required, which are, of course, non-original in respects to both gearbox and chassis.

So, as a potential purchaser, you do need to reassure yourself that the overdrive fitted to your prospective purchase is as original as you feel important, and that any chassis modifications have been carried out in a professional manner.

It is worth making the point that the 'J' type gearbox and overdrive is a much better unit than its predecessor. The first gear is a little taller, to advantage, and the overdrive solenoid is more reliable for two reasons. Firstly, the overdrive on the earlier 'A' type is operated by a genuine solenoid, whilst the later 'J' type is more of an integral electromagnetic valve. Secondly, the earlier unit operates through an external lever/bellcrank that is, along with its driveshafts, somewhat exposed to the elements. You can just see the mechanism on the far gearbox/overdrive shown in photograph 9-6.

It's unlikely to be a major influence on your decision, but you should be aware that the 'A' type unit is notoriously susceptible to oil leaks. The overdrive units run at 400-450psi and so need to be designed to retain high

pressure oil over a prolonged period. The 'J' type wins comfortably in this respect - although it would be better still if it had been designed with horizontal joints for superior oil retention.

A very useful tip from Alan Wadley concerns the servicing of 'J' units. He tells me that in his experience, many owners do not appreciate that the 'J' overdrive has two filters, both of which need cleaning from time to time. Most owners know about and attend to the first (suction) gauze located under a ribbed 'sump'. However, there is a large plug above the suction filter with a second (pressure) filter above that. The plug is the largest of those in the base of the 'J' and, of the two filters, this plug covers what is, in fact, the more important filter. However, it rarely gets the attention it deserves and should, perhaps, be added to your annual 'super-service'.

In conclusion, a couple of relatively minor but helpful details are shown in photograph 9-14 (how the exhaust system mountings are effected by the overdrive you choose), and photographs 9-15 and 9-16, which illustrate the improved gearbox covers that are available these days.

Chapter 10
Carburettor induction

IDENTIFYING YOUR CARBURETTOR

Early TR4s, like the TR3 and '3A before it, used two H6 SU carburettors, each with a 1.75in diameter choke, measured at the throttle disc. Photographs 10-1 to 10-6 show H6 carburettors, with additional information regarding installation. At car CT21470 the TR4s, and all subsequent TR4As, switched to the 1.75in Zenith-Stromberg carburettors, shown in photograph 10-7. In view of this mixture of manufacturers, it seems prudent to start this review of carburettors and their overhaul by establishing just which one you have, and whether it is appropriate for your car.

When SU carburettors were originally manufactured, a thin triangular aluminium tag stamped with the part number easily identified them. The tags were secured by a float bowl cover screw. Most tags have been lost over the years; one or two may have been discarded as otherwise identical carburettors from another vehicle (which would carry a different identification number) replaced the original TR carburettors.

If your early carburettors have been lost or irreparably damaged, don't despair. Your chances are slim of finding

10-1 and 10-2. A pair of 1.75in H6 SU carburettors on a 'log' manifold. This is actually an example of the third type of inlet manifold listed in the text, and we see it in place on a lovely 1959 TR3A. The rocker cover has clearly been changed for the second shot. Nevertheless, this is the same car in both pictures.

10-2.

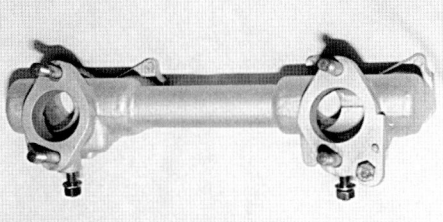

10-4-1. This is an example of the first type of inlet manifold listed in the text, designed for 1.5in SU carburettors. It was only ever fitted to TR2s with low port cylinder heads. It's easily identified by the two carburettor mounting studs, since all subsequent inlet manifolds use four.

10-4-2. The third type of manifold (shown here) is, in fact, very difficult to tell from the second type. I had the advantage of being able to read the cast part number 302119 on the bottom. Had this been the second type of manifold, it would have had 302006 cast underneath.

10-3. An identical induction set-up to that shown in photographs 10-1 and 10-2, but this time on an early TR4. The manifold is another example of the third type listed in the text. Note the 'ears' cast into the face that bolts to the cylinder head. The carburettors are the ever popular and effective 1.75in H6 SUs.

10-4-3. A less cluttered view of a TR4 inlet manifold. This time we can see a central boss cast onto the top of the now familiar 'log' balance pipe, enabling the manifold to be identified as an example of the forth type used. The reason for the 'ears' is also a little clearer. The car will have been fitted with H6 SU carburettors and the same air filter arrangement as we saw in the earlier pictures.

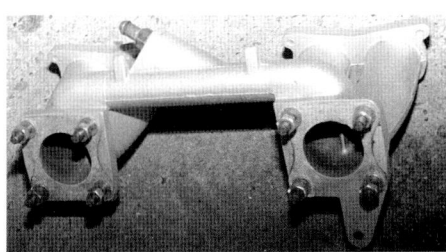

10-4-4. This photograph shows a close-up of the fifth type - from the normal viewing angle ...

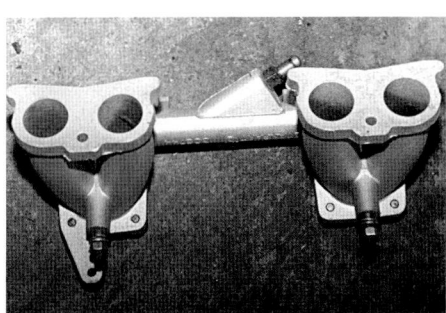

10-4-5. ... but if you wanted a worm's eye view, and to see the two support studs, this is the picture!

a pair of actual original carburettors, but there are still a large number of identical carburettors about, and a visit to a salvage yard which has some cars from the 1950s and 1960s, particularly BMC/ BL models, is likely to resolve your problem. Alternatively, look in the relevant BMC/BL motor clubs' advertisement columns. You will, of course, need to change the jets and needles but, since you will almost certainly be refurbishing the whole unit(s), this will be no hardship.

Fortunately, it's still possible to obtain virtually every TR SU service component. The supply of components

to overhaul Zenith-Stromberg carburettors is also pretty good, and you should be able to rebuild your original carburettors with few problems. Like the SU situation, there are alternatives for any major breakage or omissions, and I would suggest Stags as a potential source of replacement 1.75in Strombergs.

The TR2 used twin $1\frac{1}{2}$in (still measured at the throttle disc or the inlet manifold end of the carburettor body) H4 SUs. These are easily identified by there being only two carburettor to inlet manifold securing holes. To the best of my knowledge, these were the only (TR) SUs to use only two fixing studs, all the rest used four. The correct identification tag number is AUC721.

The TR3 increased the size of the

choke to $1\frac{3}{4}$in, which automatically gives them the SU designation of 'H6'. The twin configuration was retained, but these carburettors were secured by four mounting studs, and designated AUC786 up to 1958. To be absolutely correct for these early TR3s, the fuel inlet pipe is secured by a screwed fitting.

The TR3A, post-1958, and the TR4 (up to CT21470) used a very similar carburettor, but the fuel supply pipe was pushed over a short pipe cast into the float chamber, see photograph

10-5 and 10-6 (right). Two shots of the same TR4. The H6 carburettors in close-up are interesting. Not only do we get a good view of the fourth generation 'log' type inlet manifold (note the tapped vacuum pipe connection), but we can appreciate the overall length of the H6. It's worth comparing them with the HS6s shown in photograph 10-9, for you will then understand that the 'S' (in HS) really did stand for 'short'! Note that the petrol feed pipe to the rear carb is looped over the front air filter.

10-8. These should carry the tag number AUC878.

After what I'm sure must have been much soul searching, Triumph designed its own carburettors, and switched to a different carburettor manufacturer ... Zenith-Stromberg. Easily identified by the much 'dumpier' body, the change was clearly brought about by the tightening emissions regulations and to ensure they could be met without any loss in power.

Many TR owners view the Zenith-Stromberg as inferior to the equivalent SU. It was, perhaps, never as easy for the home enthusiast to adjust and tune, probably by design, for it was pre-set at the factory. In fact, the Zenith-Stromberg needs to be viewed in the context of providing equal power as the SU, but with fewer emissions. In fact, those who have switched to SUs from the original Zenith-Stromberg (without further engine modifications) have found no difference in the car's performance. Having said that, it is interesting to note that Triumph actually used Strombergs up to 1973 for the 2000 Saloons, but switched to SUs for the larger capacity six-cylinder Saloons thereafter!

On balance, the HS6 SU is probably the carburettor of choice for your TR4/4A - although you are best avoiding SUs with waxstats on the bottom, since the carb and engine/

exhaust are in such close proximity in the TR. The resulting heat on the SU can incorrectly adjust the waxstat!

If you're experiencing fuel supply difficulties when the engine is hot, whatever your carburettor, it's a good idea to consider a heatshield between the carburettors and the manifolds (shown in photograph 10-9). This is particularly important when using unleaded fuel, since this boils at a much lower temperature than leaded fuel.

Those seeking a pair of HS6 SUs could well use ex-Saloon components (post-1974 2500TC or 2500S), though a change of needles will be required to suit your engine capacity and tune.

IDENTIFYING YOUR INLET MANIFOLD

A total of six (slightly) different inlet manifolds were used for the four-cylinder engines. In sequence they were:
First type - TR2 'log type' balance pipe for low port heads and 1.5in H4 SU carburettors seen in photograph 10-4-1.
Second type - TR3 'log type' balance pipe for low port heads and 1.75in H6 SU carburettors.
Third type - TR3/3A 'log type' balance pipe for high port heads and H6 carburettors (photograph 10-4-2).
Forth type - TR3A/B and TR4 'log type' balance pipe for high port heads and H6

carburettors (picture 10-8).
The fifth type was used solely on the TR4 - 'Curved' balance pipe for high port heads and for 1.75in carburettors - either 'HS6' SUs or '175' Strombergs (photographs 10-4-4 and 10-4-5).
Sixth type - TR4/4A 'curved' balance pipe for high port heads and 1.75in HS6s or '175' Strombergs.

The last one was probably the most

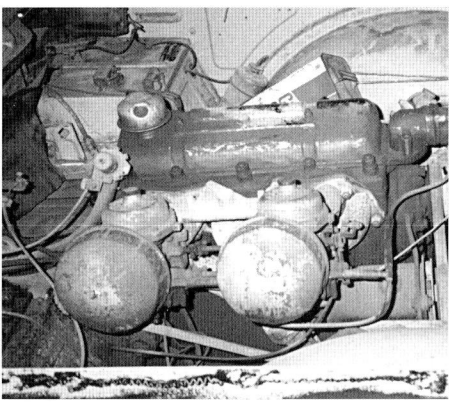

10-7. A higher swept arc-type balance pipe has replaced the earlier 'log' inlet manifold (note that we can no longer see the manifold studs). This is, in fact, an example of the fifth type of inlet manifold listed in the text and, although some were fitted with H6 SUs, this one has a pair of Stromberg CD175 carburettors. The carbs were the same size as the SU carbs (1$\frac{3}{4}$in venturi), but the lower dash pots make the Strombergs very easy to identify.

10-8. A later TR4, but this time fitted with H6 SUs, with the push-on fuel inlet pipe connection. Note the neat fuel overflow pipe arrangement, using plastic pipe connected via a short length of sleeve. Did you identify the inlet manifold as a fourth type? As an aside, it's worth drawing your attention to the two (arrowed) air inlet holes, shown clearly in each inlet flange. Not every restorer appreciates the need to keep these open, and it is, therefore, important not to close them over when fitting the air-filter and associated gasket.

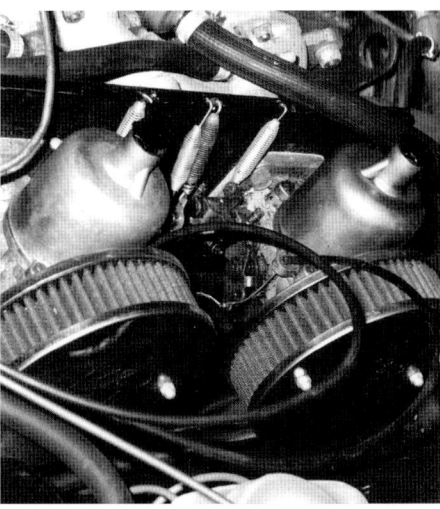

10-9. Here, a pair of unremarkable HS6 SU carburettors is fitted with a pair of (highly effective) K and N air filters - something you would do well to contemplate. K and N air filters provide a less restricted air flow into the carburettor than 'normal' air filters, so you will also need to change the SU needles. However, the main purpose of the picture is to draw your attention to the heatshield mounted between the carburettors and the manifold. This installation would be even more effective if the engine side of the shield was covered with a reflective thermal insulation. The heatshield doubles as a fixing for the carburettor control springs.

efficient inlet manifold of the entire range. It's arched balance pipe and the number 307455 cast underneath it make this inlet manifold easy to identify. Although not correct from an originality point of view, you could fit this later inlet manifold to your TR3/3A/4 (high port heads only) in place of the earlier straight 'log type' balance pipe inlet, for improved engine breathing and running. TR3s/3As will also need to fit the (S for 'short') HS6 carburettors (shown in photograph 10-9) and, due to space limitations, the upward offset air filters. The task is also slightly complicated by your having to reposition one heater hose through the bulkhead and to fit a longer choke cable.

PRELIMINARY OPERATIONAL CHECKS

The optimum performance of each carburettor, and therefore of your car, depends greatly upon condition, very fine adjustment and balance. All these details are difficult to explain, and even more difficult to illustrate! You should, therefore, read this chapter ever mindful of the close mechanical tolerances required throughout an efficient pair of carburettors, and that a workshop manual will be a particularly invaluable aid to carburettor rebuilding.

The very first check to carry out on any carburettor is to establish whether the, almost inevitable, throttle spindle wear has reached an unacceptable level. You may need to disconnect the various return springs to make a true evaluation. The test is simple - do the throttle spindles move up, down, in or out within their housings? The smallest movement is possibly acceptable but if you can see a gap opening and closing, you may as well skip the next few sections and cut straight to refurbishing the throttle body! If your spindle wear looks acceptable, but you are unhappy with the idle, performance or fuel economy of your car, read on.

Before you resign yourself to rebuilding your SU or Zenith-Stromberg, we need to consider the simpler carburettor adjustments and diagnostics first. Since the carburettors we are discussing are simple in concept and in detail, some even earlier basics should be first given consideration before you try adjusting your carburettors.

The initial step is to look for and correct any obvious mechanical defects, starting with the condition, adjustment and operation of the choke, fast idle and throttle linkages.

Not so obvious is the smooth operation of the SU pistons in their housings, but they are definitely worth

checking as dirt or corrosion can adversely effect their operation to the serious detriment of the carburettor's performance. Remove the (three) top cover securing screws and correct any obvious contamination by the gentlest means possible. If there is nothing too obvious, or you have tried the car after what you thought was an adequate cleaning of piston and bores, remove the cover(s) again. This time look for signs of (slight) interference between piston and bore. It may only be a small single 'high spot', but it could be enough to slow or even hold the piston's movement resulting in some very strange performance characteristics! You do need to polish the bore at the point where the piston 'binds', but this must be done carefully with either very fine emery paper or metal polish. Remove only just enough material local to the high spot, remembering this needs a slow 'do a bit and try it' approach.

If you are still uncomfortable with what you think is a carburettor problem, give thought to servicing matters in general, and the condition of the ignition

ENTHUSIAST'S RESTORATION MANUAL SERIES

system in particular. It's far more likely that ignition components will need attention than, say, carburettor balance. Do you have a filter fitted in the fuel line to the carbs, and, if so, has it been replaced in recent history? If you do not have a fuel filter in line, first clean out the two carburettor float chambers of the inevitable dirt that will have collected. Then check that the fuel cut-off (needle) valves in the float chamber tops are opening and closing fully when they should, and then fit an in line fuel filter.

If your needle valves are not working to your complete satisfaction, or you have been experiencing flooding, consider not only replacing your needle valve/seat assembly, but upgrading them via the use of 'Grose Jet' valves. They are not, strictly speaking, original, but are much more effective and reliable than the original valves. The Moss part number for H and HS type SU Carbs is GAC9201X, whilst Zenith-Stromberg carbs carry part number GAC9200X.

With or without Grose Jets, you need to check that fuel levels within the float chambers are set at a sensible level, and are more or less equal in each carburettor. Use the workshop manual to check float levels. Alternatively, with the piston/needle assemblies removed again, and aided by a battery powered torch/flashlight (do not use a mains powered light as it gets too hot to use in close proximity to fuel) look down into the jets for the fuel level. You'll almost certainly need to ruffle the surface of the fuel by blowing gently. The fuel level should be approximately 5 to 6mm (1/4in) below the top of the jet. If it isn't, you'll need to give your floats, float pivots (you'll be amazed how they can wear) and, of course, the needle valves themselves, remedial attention.

When significant engine wear occurs, the inlet vacuum will reduce and the induction requirements of the engine will change. It's possible to tweak the carbs to partly compensate for this, but the car's performance will be below par and, in any case, proper carb adjustment is hardly possible when the engine wear is advanced.

Are the tappets correctly adjusted? By now you will have got the message to check that everything else is correct before you start altering the carburettor settings, particularly the balance.

As the name implies, the dash pots

in both SU and Zenith-Stromberg carburettors are designed to dampen/slow the piston as it moves up and down in the carburettor bore in response to the inlet vacuum created by the engine and driving conditions. As you increase throttle opening, the engine demands more air, which increases the vacuum within the inlet manifold and the carburettors in particular. Consequently, the piston rises, presenting a narrower section on the control needle and allowing more fuel to be sucked into the incoming air flow.

As far as the damping effect is concerned, I'm sure you will appreciate that the thinner the oil in the damper/dash-pot, the faster the piston will rise and the quicker the injection of fuel. So thin oil sounds just the business? Well, yes, provided you are not already over-fuelling the engine. It's usually a matter of trial and error, so start with 20W (SAE 20), or somewhere in the middle of the range, and subjectively decide what seems best for your engine. Any subsequent significant carb, needle, ignition or engine changes may require you to re-trial the damper oil. ATF fluid is the thinnest oil and would be categorised as having a 5W (SAE 5) viscosity. It will allow your piston to rise in the shortest possible time. You will find a 3-in-1 oil in a red can has a 10W viscosity rating, while 3-in-1 in a blue can is 20W. In the UK, Hermetite offers a special carburettor damper oil at SAE 20 viscosity. I dislike engine oils as the viscosity thickens as the temperature increases. However, despite my reservations, many successfully use 15W-40 or 20W-50 engine oils at the thickest (slowest rise) end of the range.

Finally, don't over fill the dampers; about 12mm (0.5in) above the top of the piston is sufficient.

ADJUSTING THE IDLE SPEED

Don't try to get your TR to 'tickover' at too low an rpm. Obviously, it depends upon the level of tune and the car in question, but, in general terms, consider 700-900rpm as about the most suited idle/tickover speed.

If this is difficult to achieve, look first for the obvious mechanical causes. The jet/choke linkage position is the first, while obviously you should have a small clearance between the fast idle adjusting

screw and the fast idle cam. If all is well here, but you are still experiencing difficulty in achieving a consistent idle, check your induction system for vacuum leaks.

Start with a close visual examination of the carburettors and the inlet manifold. Do not forget the servo valve and/or vacuum piping, if fitted. If nothing is obvious the next step is to start the engine. Set it at a fast idle/tickover and spray the various joints and spindles with an aerosol of carburettor cleaner (Moss part number MRD1023). This is best done with a plastic 'nozzle' on the aerosol button, with a partner watching the exhaust for a changed (usually darker) emission, whilst you listen for a slight change in engine tone. A systematic approach is usually helpful, and I would start with the manifold to head joint and spray test each possible source of a vacuum leak progressively nearer the carburettor spindle(s). Do not spray carburettor cleaner into Zenith-Stromberg carburettors without first removing the diaphragms, as the carburettor cleaner will quickly render the diaphragms useless. This does not apply to SU carbs, although you are not likely to reveal a vacuum leak from the inside of the carburettor!

Chances are that your vacuum leak test will reveal at least one worn throttle spindle, which will need repair before you progress to carburettor tuning and balancing. We will explore how to carry out this repair shortly, but now it's time to check and adjust the carburettor balance.

BALANCING TWIN CARBURETTORS

This operation should be carried out before any attempt is made to adjust the choke mechanism. The procedure is explained in detail in the Triumph Repair Operations manuals. It is largely the same for both types of carburettor, and revolves around the changes in engine speed that occur as the mixture is altered.

The air cleaners need to be removed, the inter-carb throttle linkages loosened, and the tickover/idle set at about 800-900rpm. Using either a small screwdriver or the carb's in-built piston-lift button, raise one piston about 3 or 4mm (0.15in). The engine will respond in one of three ways:

10-10 and 10-11. It really is a very good idea to take lots of pictures as you dismantle your car. You'll never be able to get every tiny detail on film, of course, but these pictures would help me reassemble this pair of HS6s.

● An immediate increase in engine revolutions will signal that that carburettor is adjusted to give too rich a mixture. Expect the increase to be about 50-100rpm, so, although a partner watching the tachometer could be useful, your clearest sign will be a change in engine note. Close the main hexagon by one flat and try again.

● A reduction in engine revs signals that that carb is currently presenting too weak a mixture, and the adjustment hexagon should be lowered by one flat and the test repeated.

● A slight change in engine rpm (a momentary hesitation), quickly followed by a return to the previous rpm, indicates that that particular carburettor's mixture is correct.

Adjusting SU carburettors is relatively straightforward, but it's as well to mention that if you have Zenith-Strombergs, you should buy or borrow a special tool that passes down through the top of the carburettor. The tool stops the piston from turning (which will damage the diaphragm) and, via a hexagon key, adjusts the mixture. These procedures are effective, but you cannot better a modern gas analysis tune-up that will check CO, CO2 and unburned hydrocarbons and balance the carbs too.

If you are following the DIY route, you need now to adjust the throttle settings to provide equal or balanced air flows through each venturi. You can buy a proprietary balancing tool but quite satisfactory results can be achieved by using about a 12in length of 0.25in bore rubber or plastic tube as a stethoscope. Listen for the 'hiss' of passing air at the inlet to each carburettor, and adjust the throttle butterflies to achieve an identical sound on each one. This means you have equal air flows.

Before any choke adjustment can be made accurately, the carburettors must be synchronised and balanced, and the choke cable disconnected from the carburettors. The correct adjustment of the 'choke' or fuel enrichment mechanism of any carburettor is of great importance. The later Zenith-Stromberg uses a conventional choke (flaps which pivot to restrict air flow through the carb venturi thus increasing the flow of fuel). The earlier SUs do not use the conventional method. Instead, they (depending upon the type of SU) either draw the lower jet downward to increase the area between needle and jet, or use a bar that pivots up under the air pistons, restricting air flow while increasing fuel flow.

REPLACING THE THROTTLE SPINDLE

Well, having tried everything else, there will come a time when you decide that the throttle spindle(s) need replacing. We will look at this operation to establish whether it is really necessary, and to ensure that it will provide the cure you are seeking.

Wear between the body and the shaft results in 'play', revealed by simply wiggling the shaft in its body. As unlikely as it sounds, this wear will result in a vacuum leak which will cause an inconsistent (often rough) tickover, poor performance and poor fuel economy. The greater the wear the more pronounced these consequences. Some wear is to be expected, but you will be unable to adjust the carburettor to compensate once the 'play' becomes 0.005in.

As I explained earlier, carburettor cleaner sprayed (both sides) where the shaft exits the body will tell you what you do not want to hear. If the tickover changes for a moment, your shafts and/or bodies have unacceptable vacuum leaks and need rectification.

There are some excellent workshop manuals available that make detailed instructions superfluous here, but let's explore a few tips and the general principals as to what might be involved. If the wear is not too bad, the solution may be as simple as replacing the throttle shaft(s). Identify the top of the butterfly plate(s) with felt tip pen or typewriter correction fluid, before closing the splayed ends of each butterfly grub screws and removing the screws, butterfly(s) and shaft(s). Offer an unworn length of shaft to each side of the carburettor body and test for body wear by moving the shaft up, down, in and out. Any movement over and above the very minimum will almost certainly mean body and spindle wear. If the movement is minimal, a new throttle shaft of standard diameter should solve the problem satisfactorily.

If movement is clearly present but judged not excessive, consider using an oversize throttle shaft. These take up slight wear in the carburettor body, but are best fitted by your local engineering shop, each body needs to be through-reamed to a specific size that is slightly larger than the diameter of the new shaft. The most drastic solution is required when the carburettor body is too worn for oversized shafts to be effective. In these circumstances, the body will have to be cross-drilled, reamed, and fitted with a pair of phosphor bronze bushes, or service exchange service for a re-bushed body. If your carburettor bodies have got to this state, I recommend you go the service exchange route as re-bushing to achieve a smooth operating, standard-sized spindle is best left to the professionals.

When reassembling your carburettor(s), remember to refit the butterfly the correct way up, and to splay the butterfly's securing screws as soon as you are sure the butterfly fully closes the carburettor venturi.

Chapter 11
Front suspension and steering

Numerous important changes/ improvements have been established by the TR fraternity over the years. Certainly, when the car is undergoing a complete restoration, the opportunity should be taken to not only restore the car to its original status, but also weld a number of additional strengthening brackets and gussets to the front suspension of the TR4A. Such structural improvements can mostly be accomplished when the chassis and body are united, of course, though few would disagree that they are easier with the body removed from the chassis.

I consider these welded changes to be chassis related, so have covered them in the chapter devoted to chassis restoration and improvements.

The main focus of this chapter is on matters to do with maintenance, improvement and/or repair of standard TR4s and TR4As, although owners of IRS cars should read it in conjunction with chapter 5, for it might be necessary to also carry out some of the structural changes.

REASONS FOR A SUSPENSION REBUILD

There are several reasons why you may feel that the front suspension or steering

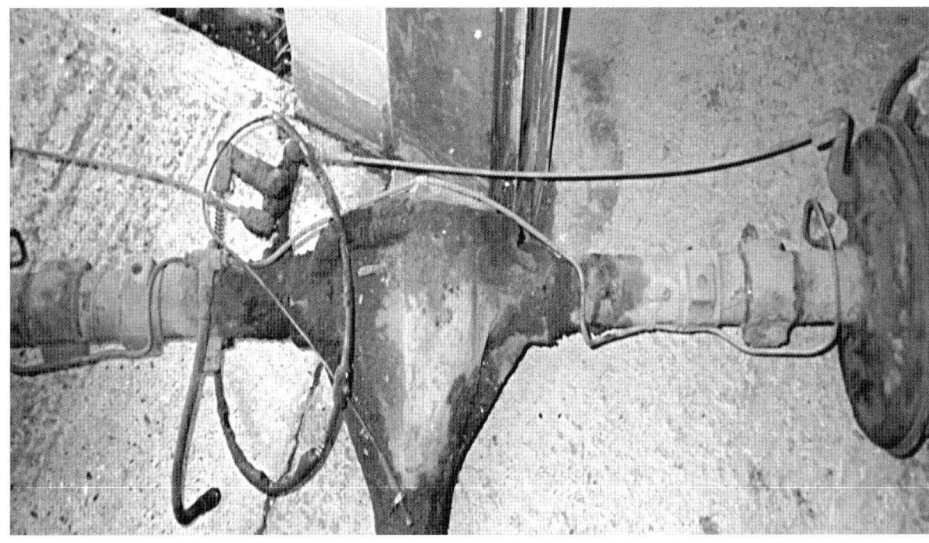

11-1. Note the similarity of many of these parts. They're not all 'handed' but you need only assemble one wrongly for it to mean that there will be a second incorrect one on the other side of the car in the not-too-distant future. Note the holes in the lower wishbone spring pans – they're ideal for removing and replacing the telescopic shock absorbers.

needs some attention over and above routine maintenance. Stiffness in the steering, or mechanical noises in the front suspension when changing direction and/or when braking hard and/ or reversing are not unknown, and all must certainly receive immediate attention. In this context, the springs, shock absorbers, wheel bearings, hub, ball joint, trunnion bolt and bushes, and top and bottom wishbone bushes all deserve close investigation, and there are four particularly important details to be aware of since you need to:

- Check the lower chassis and suspension mountings for evidence of fatigue or accident damage.
- Ensure all suspension mounting bolts are of adequate length so that none are relying on the threaded part of the bolt as a bearing surface
- Check that the steering rack mounting pads on later cars have been pushed sufficiently outwards on assembly to prevent rack movement.
- If your steering is stiffening, establish where the fault lies. Any stiffness in the steering should be taken very seriously; consider the situation particularly carefully if either of the bottom trunnions are suspected of being at fault. They are known to snap after first exhibiting symptoms of stiffening.

There's more on each of these matters as this chapter progresses, but first let's consider the front suspension and steering on a less critical level.

Overhauling TR suspension, front or rear, is not, generally speaking, difficult, so I do not intend to duplicate the information given in the operations manual. There are a few pitfalls with the front suspension, and we will explore these in some detail in just a moment.

Guard against getting handed parts mixed up; they look very similar when off the car, as photograph 11-1 shows. It may be sensible to tackle one half of the front suspension at a time. I have bought several 'incomplete restoration projects' from inexperienced owners who have stripped everything in sight, piled it all into one huge box and then realised they have lost all reference to what goes where and in what order. Mind you, it's very hard to finish the front suspension before the chassis is fixed in a complete restoration, when all the various sub-assemblies are likely to have to come off the chassis before it can be repaired. In this event take lots of photographs of each subassembly *before* you start removing bits of car! Identify the parts by name, number or position and tie a label to each, as per photograph 11-2. Make some sketches of things you cannot photograph well and keep the information in separate folders for easy reference.

Buy a copy (it does not have to be new) of the parts manual for your car. When taking a subassembly off the car (and certainly when you take the subassembly apart), take a photocopy of the relevant page in your parts manual

11-2. It is obvious what parts we are looking at, but note and follow this example of identifying and labelling each component. Front suspension parts are particularly easy to mix up, confuse or get the sides muddled, which makes this job very worthwhile. Some components are handed, so mark the 'top' or even 'this side up' on each part. Note, too, that the various fastenings have been temporarily replaced: this really is a good idea.

and mark the copy up with additional information, such as assembly sequences, angles and spacers, and even which way round the bolt-head/nut goes. The parts manual will usually have the assembly sequence information shown in an 'exploded' illustration, but 6 or 12 months later that may be insufficient. If you do not plan to refurbish a subassembly - say, the front suspension - immediately, try to remove it from the chassis in the largest complete piece you can, and only strip it to component parts when you are ready to refurbish it. As you strip major assemblies from the car, try and replace fastenings in their respective places.

Unfortunately, the foregoing advice is the exact opposite of that elsewhere in the book, when refinishing components are dealt with 'in-bulk' for maximum cost-effectiveness. You'll appreciate, however, that there's no point in saving money by bulk refinishing components if you have no idea what goes where!

IMPROVING HANDLING

TRs are noted for having good handling characteristics, so, assuming your car is operational but not handling to your satisfaction, let us first look at some of the most common reasons why before

we go into the detail of a complete front suspension rebuild.

Inevitably, there will be some reference to rear suspension details, as poor handling cannot be solely down to the front suspension. Since it is hardly practical to separate them in this context, I hope you will forgive a slight overlap. If your front suspension work involves removing and/or replacing the front springs, do read the relevant operations manual and take note of the pointers that follow later in this chapter.

The TR4
The complete early suspension assembly can be seen in photograph 11-3. There are all sorts of chassis/steering improvements that can be contemplated but, in general, we will focus here on the more mundane standard details.

First up, the lower wishbone arms on all ladder chassis cars (TR2/3/3A/4) are not shimmable, as photograph 11-4 demonstrates. If your chassis is in any way out of true, then the car is unlikely to handle well, and the only solution is to get the chassis repaired; it's likely to be a body-off job.

The upper fulcrum pin (part number 200659, photograph 11-5) on all cars deserves your close attention during assembly since the same pin can

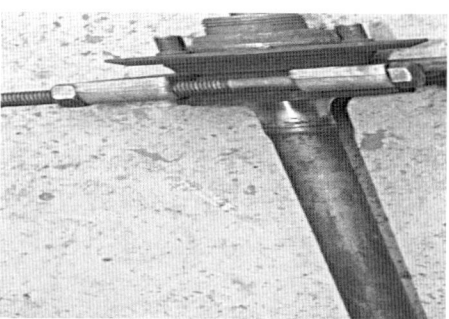

11-5. The two ways of assembling the top fulcrum pin. The main text details which is which, but, very briefly, the lower example is how it sits on early cars and the top one the later cars. It may be hard to see, but can you spot the worn 'necking' on the right side of the top one, making it suitable for the scrap bin only?

11-3. A good view of a sidescreen TR front suspension assembly. Note the fully tubular top wishbone and compare it and its top ball joint to the later example shown in photographs 11-6 and 11-7. Sharp eyes may possibly spot the brake caliper differences - with this earlier car's bridge pipe connecting the two halves of the caliper. Later calipers were internally drilled to carry the fluid to the outer piston without a bridge pipe.

11-4. A nice view of a beautifully repaired and powder coated ladder chassis, identified by the non-shimmable 'through' lower wishbone pivots and steering box mounting.

be fitted two ways, depending upon the model. If you are rebuilding your car, get it the right way round before you fit the bodyshell as it is ten times as difficult to correct with the body in place. If your car is complete and operational, but does not feel right, or if you have trouble adjusting the camber angle, probably the best thing to check first is that the upper fulcrum pin is assembled the right way round. More details follow shortly.

While discussing putting the front suspension together the correct way round, note that the word 'Top' is stamped on the upper rear wishbone arms. Not only does this mean the arms fit to the top wishbone assembly, but it is also intended to ensure that they are fitted 'top way up'. Put another way, the word 'top' should be visible when looking down on the assembled front suspension. The arms are handed and, if you follow this suggestion, you will fit the right arm on the correct side of the car. The front arm is not handed and can be fitted either side.

The TR4A

Triumph's shimable front suspension can be seen in photographs 11-6 and 11-7. From the introduction of the TR4A, Triumph revised the mounting of all lower wishbones to the chassis. Two shimmed brackets, each with a removable bolt passing through a rubber-to-metal-bonded ('metalastic') bush, were introduced. This made adjustment, stripping and reassembly a much easier process, although the resultant bottom suspension mounting is less rugged than the earlier non-shimable design.

It is in these lower wishbone mounting bracket areas that most of the chassis modifications, mentioned earlier, emanate from. If your IRS car handles poorly, have a four-wheel alignment check carried out. This is a job for your professional TR restorer since there are various shims to adjust, both front and rear. If all is still not well, you need to rectify the car's general tendency to rear end steer by fitting polyurethane bushes to the rear trailing arms and better rear shock absorbers. Superflex bushes are recommended in the former case and Koni or Spax telescopic shocks in the latter. The shock absorbers will require a pair of special mounting brackets, but these changes will transform the overall handling, and the rear end in particular. We will look at these in more detail in chapter 13.

Still not happy with your car? Then it's the front suspension we focus upon next, starting with the bottom wishbone pivot bushes, which are the sturdier 'metalastic' type with a steel inner sleeve. You will have to press them out in the vice and, whilst direct replacements will be appropriate after years of service, there should be no need to upgrade the bushes. However, the top wishbone bushes come in two halves and will probably push out without too much effort. They are much less satisfactory and polyurethane/ Superflex bushes in the top wishbones

Errata

Dear Reader, due to a production problem the wrong images appear on pages 124, 125, 126 and 127 of our Triumph TR4 & TR4A Enthusiast's Restoration Manual. This errata sheet contains the correct images together with the relevant captions. We at Veloce Publishing offer our sincere apologies for this error and any inconvenience it causes.

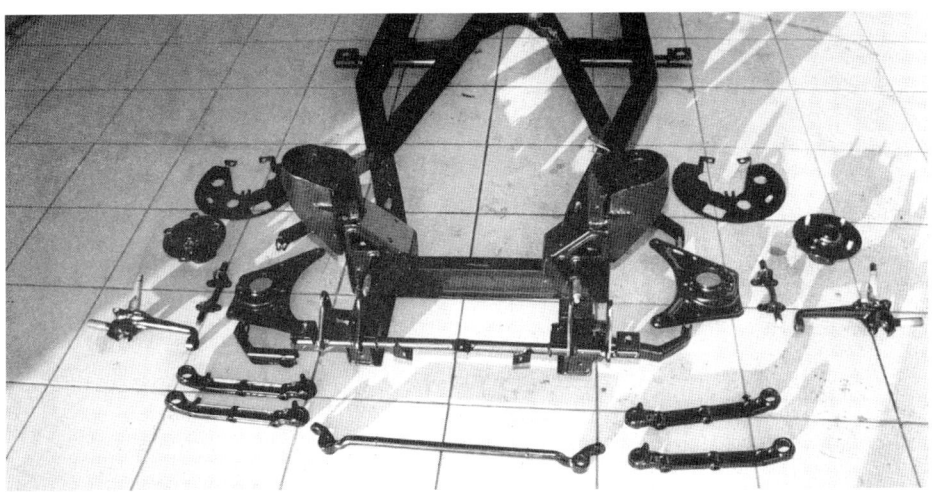

11-1. Note the similarity of many of these parts. They're not all 'handed' but you need only assemble one wrongly for it to mean that there will be a second incorrect one on the other side of the car in the not-too-distant future. Note the holes in the lower wishbone spring pans which facilitate removal and replacement of the telescopic shock absorbers.

11-2. It is obvious what parts we are looking at, but note and follow this example of identifying and labelling each component. Front suspension parts are particularly easy to mix up, confuse or get the sides muddled, which makes this job very worthwhile. Some components are handed, so mark the 'top' or even 'this side up' on each part. Note, too, that the various fastenings have been temporarily replaced: this really is a good idea.

Picture 11-3 overleaf >

11-4. A nice view of a beautifully repaired and powder coated ladder chassis, identified by the non-shimmable 'through' lower wishbone pivots and steering box mounting.

11-5. The two ways of assembling the top fulcrum pin. The main text details which is which, but, very briefly, the lower example is how it sits on early cars and the top one the later cars. It may be hard to see, but can you spot the worn 'necking' on the right side of the top one, making it suitable for the scrap bin only?

11-3. A good view of a sidescreen TR front suspension assembly. Note the fully tubular top wishbone and compare it and its top ball joint to the later example shown in photographs 11-6 and 11-7. Sharp eyes may possibly spot the brake caliper differences - with this earlier car's bridge pipe connecting the two halves of the caliper. Later calipers were internally drilled to carry the fluid to the outer piston without a bridge pipe.

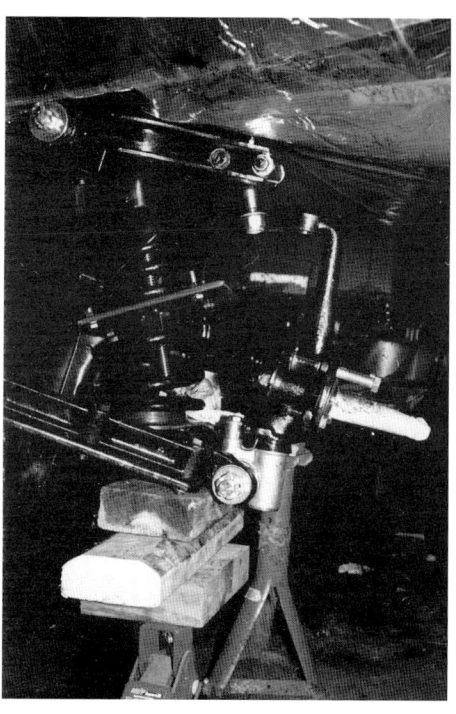

11-8. This picture shows the front swivel pin with an internal front spring compressor in action. The vertical link is free to move as required and the top ball joint is positioned ready to be coupled up when everything is nicely located. The trolley jack at the bottom of the picture will lift the assembly while the top ball joint is connected.

11-6. Shimable front suspension differs from earlier cars. The turret brace is well in evidence, and you will note two body mounting holes in the brace. Note the grease nipple to lubricate the top ball joint. There is a second nipple each side in the bottom trunnion, and it is most important that it is regularly greased. All four grease nipples should receive attention every 3000 miles.

11-7. The front suspension from an IRS car with rack and pinion steering, is clearly quite different from the sidescreened car's arrangement shown in photograph 11-3. The two-piece channel section top wishbones are also very clear.

11-6. Shimable front suspension differs from earlier cars. The turret brace is well in evidence, and you will note two body mounting holes in the brace. Note the grease nipple to lubricate the top ball joint. There is a second nipple each side in the bottom trunnion, and it is most important that it is regularly greased. All four grease nipples should receive attention every 3000 miles.

11-7. The front suspension from an IRS car with rack and pinion steering, is clearly quite different from the sidescreened car's arrangement shown in photograph 11-3. The two-piece channel section top wishbones are also very clear.

are strongly recommended as they will improve handling and last longer, with minimal increase in road noise.

While you have the front suspension apart I suggest you fit a pair of slightly uprated lower springs. The TR4A did not have a front anti-roll/sway

bar, and you should fit one of the sort used in the TR6. This tightens up the front end dramatically and is completely reversible if you subsequently need to restore originality. We will discuss solid steering rack mounts shortly, but, if you are still concerned about your car's handling, it is time now to look at the upper fulcrum pins in more detail.

The upper fulcrum pin

The two ways that this pin can be fitted are shown in photograph 11-5. This is a frequently made mistake, so it's worth checking yours, even if you aren't unhappy with your car's handling or steering.

On early cars (TR2 to TR3A), the pin is positioned as shown in the workshop manual. You can take off a wheel and feel the fulcrum, which should be fitted with the curve radiusing inwards, away from you. To help further, the curvature of the pin seems the correct shape relative to the turret, as it seems to be following the rear contour of the turret. On the TR4A, it looks as if the pin has been assembled the wrong way round as it seems to run against the turret's curvature when correctly fitted. It should curve outwards towards you.

The pin on a TR4 could go either way! In order to change the front geometry, Triumph switched the position of this pin in 1962, and changed several other details simultaneously at TR4 chassis number CT6343 (wire wheels) and CT6390 (steel wheels). If, therefore, your car is about that commission number, you could do worse than take professional advice from a TR specialist if you have doubts about handling, or before you reassemble the front suspension.

To expand on the changes; note that early TRs had no caster angle built into the suspension geometry. From the above chassis numbers, a three degree castor angle was introduced, with the result that the top of the vertical link leans backwards slightly, and is nearer the rear of the car than the bottom. The situation is actually helped by the simultaneous changes that Triumph introduced. These will give you a clue to which design of suspension your car is intended to have, as an improved/different top ball joint was introduced and the trunnion became handed.

Be aware, however, that the one component that does cause more

problems than any other is the upper fulcrum pin.

With the above suggestions in mind, you will probably have transformed the handling of your TR. If, however, a more rigorous refurbishment is required, read on ...

IMPROVING THE STEERING

Regardless of which model you have, take great care if the steering is, or becomes, tight in any way. While this is not a very frequent problem, the consequences are such that it is worth alerting you to it.

The potential consequence of ignoring stiffening steering is that one vertical post, seen in photograph 11-8, snaps clean off at the top of the threaded portion. In the first instance, suspect one or both of the lower swivel pins, or trunnions, as they are officially known. There are three types which vary with caster angle, but all do the same job of allowing the steering to swivel where the lower wishbones pivot. The best initial test is to jack up both front wheels and take hold of either road wheel and swivel it. It should move from

11-8. This picture shows the front swivel pin with an internal front spring compressor in action. The vertical link is free to move as required and the top ball joint is positioned ready to be coupled up when everything is nicely located. The trolley jack at the bottom of the picture will lift the assembly while the top ball joint is connected.

full lock to full lock without stiffness or binding. If it is hard going, take one track rod end off and try to deduce which swivel pin, if either, is causing the trouble, and drop that one for individual examination. With the suspect isolated you should strip the trunnion and establish that there is no untoward wear. Use liberal quantities of lubricant (more on this shortly) to prevent re-occurrence during reassembly. Fully tighten the cross bolt/nut and liberally grease the trunnions at frequent intervals in future. The workshop manual will tell you that you should oil the bottom trunnion, but the oil drains out, so you're better advised to use grease, but frequently.

TR4s used the nicely direct steering 'rack' as standard. These are easily replaced and are not expensive, so I suggest you exchange your rack almost as a matter of course when rebuilding your car, or if you are in any doubt whatsoever about the smoothness and operation of your rack.

The early TR4 racks were mounted on two tall ear-like brackets which, not to put too fine a point on it, were very Mickey Mouse-like. The rack was very securely mounted to the floppy 'ears' by commendable solid aluminium blocks and U-bolts. We saw a picture of these rather flexible early rack mountings in chapter 5, but, since they are so relevant here, I repeat the illustration here as 11-9-1.

At CT20063 (LHD) and CT20265 (RHD) the rack movement allowed by these vertical eared brackets was improved by using a much more rigid rack mounting via a horizontally-mounted chassis plate. Photograph 11-9-2 should refresh your memory. The overall length of the system, ball joint to ball joint, remained the same as on earlier cars but, simultaneously, both track control arms increased in length so the rack had to be shortened. This is one point to note, should you ever go looking for a TR4 steering rack, for there are two non-interchangeable types!

However, all was still not absolutely wonderful as the original solid aluminium mountings were replaced by rubber bushes held captive by a U-shaped clamp, and the later/rubber bushed rack can move within the mounting rubbers after a couple of years. This movement can be improved and/or delayed by ensuring the U-clamps are pressed apart before the nuts

11-9-1. The early rack mountings allowed for a very solid rack to mounting arrangement; trouble was, the 'Mickey Mouse' brackets were not as rigid as they should have been and were replaced in later TRs.

11-9-2. The post CT20063/CT20265 method of mounting the steering rack. If you are refurbishing an early TR4, the improvement in steering effected by these much more rigid mountings makes them worth fitting to you car, if originality constraints allow.

are tightened. A turnbuckle tool is helpful (see photograph 11-10), or pre-tensioning can be done by weld clamps.

Many individuals fit a pair of the original aluminium/solid mountings to later cars. This modification gives a very direct feel to the steering at the expense of increased harshness, but is completely

reversible if not to your liking, or you wish to restore originality.

Significant steering column play at the wheel in a TR4 is probably due to the securing bracket on the inside of the bulkhead/firewall having fatigued and broken. It is a one-piece pressing made from 18swg material, available as part

11-10. The later steering racks are mounted on rubber bushes, but all too rarely are these bushes installed correctly. They do need to be spread outwards prior to the two 'U'-bolt fastenings being tightened in order to remove the (slight) sideways rack movement that can otherwise occur. There is a proper tool that works like a turnbuckle on both rack clamps simultaneously, which is shown in this picture. However, the trade normally uses a pair of wide nosed mole grip-like welding clamps to pull each 'U'-shaped clamp outwards before individually tightening each.

number 815834SB from all our premier TR restorers. As an aside, we will touch upon this very same bracket when we talk about left-hand to right-hand drive conversions later in the book.

If you are rebuilding your car for *Concours d'Elegance* purposes, then you have little choice but to make a welded repair to the original bracket, or replace it. Either way, a great deal of work is involved in creating sufficient space to carry out the necessary welding if repairing a running car. If a total refurbishment is being done, and you are not planning to enter *concours* competitions, consider making up a bracket with a much stronger 'bridge'. My original bracket had more or less disintegrated, and I fabricated a completely new bracket, mostly from 16swg material, but with welded in 1in x 0.125in steel for the all-important column bridge/support. Furthermore, I supported the column with a second 0.125in (3mm) cross packer, to ensure that however tight I pulled up the 'U' clamp nuts, there was no chance of distorting the new bulkhead bracket.

Alternatively, for those reluctant to strip or weld beneath the assembled dashboard, I guess a new bracket can be fabricated from a section of aluminium or steel angle and bolted in place. However, I think for something as important as this bracket I would

consider this to be no more than a temporary measure to get me through the fun months, stripping the dash and welding a stronger-than-original replacement during the winter months.

ADDITIONAL TIPS AND SUGGESTIONS

- Check your vertical links carefully as, believe it or not, it is possible to bend them in an accident. If your wheel rim rubs on the top ball joint, a bent vertical link is the most likely cause.
- On early cars, the wishbone bushes need reaming after being pressed into the wishbones. Few home restorers will have a $^5/_8$in reamer, so you will need to find a (probably small) local engineering business that can run a reamer through each of the bushes. If you pre-arrange the task, it can probably be carried out while you wait.
- Ball joints and wheel bearings should be replaced almost as a matter of routine. However, there is one very important detail to beware of when fitting a replacement wheel bearing kit - the felt oil seal is always too thick. The current felt is not to OE specification and needs to be cut with a razor or similar sharp blade to approximately half its thickness. If you fit the felt washer as supplied in the kit, you will find it impossible to tighten the wheel bearing nut properly. You may think you have done the job well and the torque wrench may 'click', but the over-thick felt will have stopped the bearing spacers seating as intended.
- The front wheel bearings need a certain amount of float, as the workshop manual calls for, to allow for the bearings to warm up and expand, but to do so without seizing/freezing. As a consequence of assuming all 'play' is due to this clearance, many home restorers fail to recognise a couple of mistakes when reassembling the front hubs. Firstly, your outer bearing ring (the 'A' ring) must be an interference fit in the hub casing. If it 'falls' in there will be an unacceptable degree of play in that front wheel, which no amount of bearing replacement or adjustment will eradicate. You can use the correct grade of Locktite to hold it in its housing, but personally I would find a replacement hub as soon as possible. The second fault that new TR-ers think is of little consequence is to overlook a worn

bearing seat on the stub axle. The inner (or 'B') ring should, of course, be a sliding fit on the stub axle but, for a variety of reasons, a previous owner could have had an inner ring rotating for a while, and this will have worn or polished a witness mark, even a groove, on the stub axle. It's tempting to think that a new pair of properly adjusted bearings will resolve the resultant play in the front wheel, and you may be lucky, but in all probability the play will remain, or return after a short while, because the 'B' ring is moving ever so slightly on the shaft. Like the sloppy outer bearing ring in the hub, that movement is multiplied many times to give play in the front wheel.

- The trunnions that form the lower steering swivel are supposed to be oiled as part of the car's routine servicing. I mentioned a short while ago that you should liberally lubricate the trunnions upon reassembly with trunnion oil, and frequently grease them thereafter. You may be interested in one professional 'dodge'; provided you liberally oil each trunnion with Hypoy EP90 oil on assembly, you can use a conventional grease during each service, secure in the knowledge that this oil will keep the grease soft.
- Earlier I recommended replacing the rear lever arm shock absorbers with Koni or Spax telescopic units. Whilst the improvement might not be as dramatic, many TR owners advocate a similar change at the front. The original front shocks are, of course, the telescopic type, but are non-adjustable. However, both Koni and Spax are adjustable and, consequently, can be fine-tuned to suit your driving and car use. Spax are adjustable *in situ* but you will need to take the usually more expensive Koni's off the car to adjust them.
- The shank of a bolt is that plain portion between the underside of the head and the point at which the threaded section of the bolt starts. There is a danger that, at some earlier date, a bolt or bolts with too short a shank length have been used to assemble the front and/or rear suspensions. The consequence of this is not immediately apparent but, over the years, a threaded area of the bolt bears against the bracket, wears prematurely, and introduces play into the suspension mounting point(s). This is clearly very undesirable, but a more serious

consequence is that some lower fulcrum bracket failures are attributed to the snatching loads imposed by the resultant play in these suspension components. Therefore, do ensure you purchase bolts of sufficient length to provide a complete unthreaded surface right through the assemblies, even if you have to add an extra plain washer to take up any surplus bolt shank.

• All rubber bushes throughout the front suspension will need replacing if you are carrying out a full rebuild. However, the OE upper fulcrum pin bushes in particular are - not to put too fine a point on it - useless. I would advise fitting - admittedly non-original - polyurethane bushes throughout the front suspension. If you do not wish to fit polyurethane bushes throughout the whole front suspension, you would be well advised to fit them to the top - unless you fancy a little job each year! If your car is not handling to your satisfaction this would be a worthwhile step, whatever model TR you own. Superflex front suspension bushes are recommended, at the expense of slight additional road noise.

• Take care not to tighten the inner fastenings until the suspension is loaded and the car assumes its road-going stance. If you tighten the bolts too soon you will eventually force the bushes to flex into areas they were never intended to and they will shear. On the other hand, make a careful note somewhere that the fastenings remain loose, because you must not forget to fully tighten them once the car is on the ground.

• It's not a great idea to leave your TR suspended on its new front suspension bushes for several years while you sort out the bodywork. You certainly need to stand IRS cars on their suspension while you sort out panel fit, so why not leave the old suspension in place until the car is nearing the end of its restoration journey, before fitting new rubber suspension bushes?

FRONT COIL SPRING COMPRESSOR

With the engine and body in place, as would be the case with a running car,

11-11. Three of the various spring compressors available. Top is a proprietary internal compressor ideal for use on TRs. Right side below is another internal/front unit that has been slightly modified. The original 'ears' were cut off and the end replaced by a thick piece of steel drilled with a clearance hole for the threaded rod. The four bolts are placed so as to centre the plate on the coil spring. This unit can be seen in action in photograph 11-8. Bottom left is one of a pair of external compressors; these must be used in pairs and can be seen in use in chapter 12 (rear-suspension).

you probably won't need a coil spring compressing tool, since the weight of the car/engine/body assembly should be sufficient to compress the road spring using a trolley-jack. Note the specific reference to a trolley-jack; only this type of jack has the stability to allow you to contemplate this task in reasonable safety. Do not try compressing a road spring with any other type of jack, and, in any case, only if your car is virtually completely assembled.

If your car is largely un-assembled, you will almost certainly need a coil spring compressor. Photograph 11-11 shows various types of spring compressor and in photograph 11-8 one can be seen in use. You can buy or make one, but an internal one is recommended in view of the space restrictions. If you wish to buy one, it should be from a TR specialist such as Revington TR. Spring compressors can be made at home from something like 0.5in UNC studding. However, appreciate that the forces within a coil

spring under compression are considerable, and you must ensure that your compressor is made from material that is comfortably up to the job. Remember, a flying coil spring can cause much damage.

With an external compressor you will need to control and compress the lower wishbone in order to squeeze the spring up against the top spring/fixed chassis 'cup'. Better yet, you can safely unbolt the four fastenings at the bottom and one nut at the top to release and remove the shock absorbers. The shock absorber comes right out through the bottom wishbone, leaving plenty of room for an 'inside' (the spring) compressor.

The 'inside' compressor basically consists of thick plate steel with a hole in the centre for a threaded rod to pass through, with large nuts and washers top and bottom. Slowly, evenly and under control, release the spring tension after it has been removed from your car.

Chapter 12
Rear suspension and 'live' axles

REAR LEAF SPRINGS

The 'live' or 'beam' axled TR4 was fitted with the rear axle shown in photograph 12-1. This went right across the full width of the car, and was, in turn, suspended on a pair of leaf springs. The majority of TR4As used the quite different 'independent rear suspension', and we will study this in the next chapter.

The leaf springs used in the TR4 served both to locate the rear axle, and to provide the rear suspension. The arrangement was very common in those days. However, Triumph did something that I believe may have been unique, in that they elected to fit different strength springs to each side of the car (a harder spring was provided for the driver's side). The TR leaf sprung rear suspension provided reasonable handling for its day but, if you were fitting new rear springs today, or just switching the car from LH to RH drive, this original design could pose you some handling problems if you neglect to change both rear leaf springs. There is a suitable spring available today which is a satisfactory compromise between the various options that were originally manufactured.

When you have the body off your

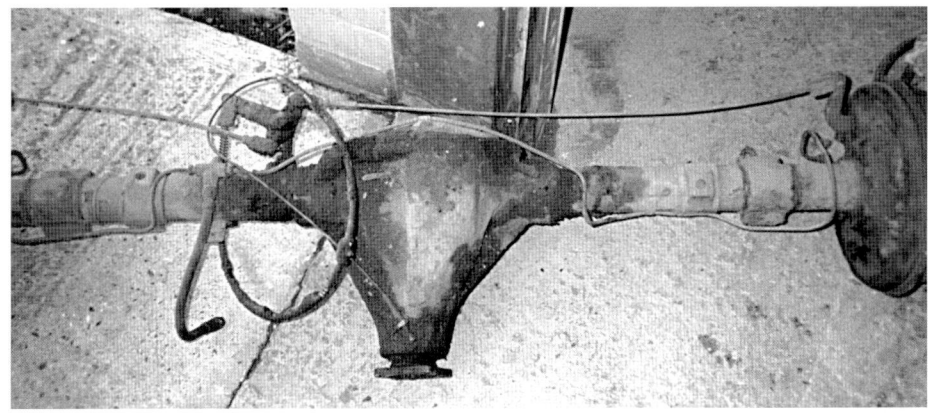

12-1 and 12-2 (right). The TR 'live' or 'beam' Girling rear axle. One reason why the TR4's handbrake is more effective than that of the TR4A, is the 'T' shaped handbrake compensator, clearly in evidence here. TR4s (and a small number of US live-axle TR4As) also had shorter, straighter cables, than the TR4A design. The beam axle's hand brake cable is a single 'bowden' type, with a compensator, that gives about a 2:1 mechanical advantage, mounted on the rear casing. Note how the hydraulic brake pipe hugs the diff before being steered away from any chassis interference by its route along the front of the casing and over the spring pads. The second shot gives a better view of the compensator bar bent through 90 degrees.

TR, although it may not be at the forefront of your thoughts, do ensure that all the rear axle fastenings are free and well lubricated to ensure they do not seize/freeze in future. The front attachment pin that locates each spring to the chassis is particularly vulnerable, and difficult to remove if rusted. This pin is almost an interference fit in the 'eye' bush located at the front of the spring. It seems to rust particularly solidly, and very quickly, to such an extent that no amount of heat or straining will remove them with the body *in situ*. Improved accessibility makes the job just possible with the body off.

At the risk of offending you, I will very briefly mention that MGBs have exactly the same problem, and, in my experience, you may just as well get stuck in with a 'Junior hacksaw and/or grinder - for you are never going to push them out!

Many TR4 owners drill a hole in the quarter panel in order to get a punch to the pin in the hope of getting it out. No doubt a few succeed, but the real object of this piece is to emphasise how important it is to get the pins out, needed or not, when you have the body off, and to really put lots of copper-slip on the pins and in the eye of each spring before reassembly. If you need to take the axle out at some later date, after the body has been replaced, it will be easier! In fact, I also spray these 'eye' bolts annually with a very fluid Waxoyl spray - just to make sure!

I mentioned that the 'majority' of TR4As had IRS. This requires explanation, for everyone knows the '4A as the first of the IRS cars. In fact, a TR4A aimed primarily at the US market, was built with a live rear axle and leaf springs. It was felt that the reduced cost, extra comfort and the predictability of a solid axle would sell more cars than would the improved road holding of the 'IRS' cars. The live axled TR4As can be identified from the commission number's prefix, or, of course, by a quick peak under the car. The normal TR4A prefix was CTC, but the 'non IRS' TR4As were prefixed with 'CT' (also, commission numbers commenced at 50000).

Not surprisingly, the shock absorber links and rear (leaf) springs differ from those of preceding TRs, and were part numbered 142155/6 and 212113, respectively.

The TR4 used a similar Girling live axle to the TR3 and is shown in

photographs 12-1 and 12-2. However, you should note that the TR4 (and the non-IRS US-spec TR4A) axle is slightly wider than the TR3's Girling unit. The handbrake cables are also different.

THE GIRLING REAR AXLE

Tackling problems associated with the rear axle's differential is really best left to experts, and, consequently, I do not propose to even try to outline remedial work within the diff. You should, of course, remove the axle from your TR and carry out any hub/oil-seal/bearing work by all means. However, when matters concerning the differential are concerned, pass it to the transmission specialist in your area. He will be able to draw on years of experience to get the shimming right, and the work will be done in a fraction of the time that you would take.

However, I favour the service-exchange approach, via your favourite TR specialist. I recommend this because you will always know where you stand, price-wise. Even if you get a quote (they are always estimates, by the way) for rebuilding your axle from your local specialist, it will always be subject to what he finds upon strip down. Invariably, worn components will come to light that really need to be replaced and, as the work proceeds, the costs could mount up.

All TR restorers will do a service exchange unit and, naturally, the replacement axle carries a warranty. You should be aware, however, that the price of the exchange units is kept attractive by the restorer using as many of the original components as his experience shows to be practical. Nevertheless, there are several advantages of using your specialist TR restorer to supply your exchange unit, for there are a couple of details particular to TR axles to watch for. A restorer's experience may help you establish whether you have a problem, and what the solution might be.

There are, of course, plenty of opportunities where rear axle and brake problems can be resolved at home, and we should discuss the main areas that may require your attention. The workshop manual will cover the routine operational sequence and detail, but I think the following additional points may help.

12-3. The first operation is to remove the 6 x $^1/_2$in AF setscrews, as described in the main text, and to withdraw each hub and half-shaft assembly. This is the hub/half-shaft result ...

REMOVING AND REASSEMBLING THE HUBS

- It's possible to remove the complete drum and brake assembly, with the respective half shaft, in order to gain access to a seized rear brake. You can also remove the drum and brake components if you wish to replace the hub bearing or seals. In either event, the six $^1/_2$in AF setscrews that secure the bearing housing to the axle-flange will need to be removed. However stubborn they are, this must be done carefully, to avoid rounding the corners. A six-sided socket from an impact wrench is very helpful here, because it has flat faces. Most socket spanners, on the other hand, grip on the corners and have 12 recesses. Pictures 12-3 and 12-10 show the locations of these six potential problems.
- Never attempt to remove a hub from its half-shaft with the latter still in the axle. You will damage the opposite wheel bearing if you strike the hub/puller in an effort to shock the hub from its half-shaft. Instead, the following advice and photographic sequence should be of help.
- As you withdraw the hub, half-shaft, and back plate assembly, watch for and retain the shims from between the back plate and the axle tube. A couple of re-sealable plastic bags are a good way to keep left and right sides separate, secure and well identified - for they are unlikely to be identical.
- The inner seals will probably remain

12-4. ... while this is how the Girling axle flanges will look once the half-shaft and hub are clear. Note the very distinctive circular end-flange on a Girling axle - the early TRs had the slightly fragile Lockheed axle with square end flanges.

12-5. Separating the hub from its half-shaft is a task for those with powerful equipment ... a power press I hasten to add. First, loosen the axle nut, and then apply as full a circumferential support as possible to the hub. Both aspects can be seen here.

12-7. This is the penultimate step, with the hub off its taper and the bearing housing (and oil seal) revealed. However, there is no point in coming this far without renewing the hub bearing - whether it is obviously needed now or not. So, we need to remain at the press for a second operation on each half-shaft, as shown in photograph 12-8.

12-8. Using the same set-up as with the hub, we need to remove the inner (or 'B') ring off its shoulder. While it may not be a problem when removing the old bearing, it's just worth mentioning that on no account should you exert any force whatsoever through the rollers (or where applicable the balls), of a bearing when assembling it to its shaft or housing. Always press on the ring itself, in this case the inner ring!

12-6. Now the hub is supported on the bed of the power press, while the press is brought to bear on the end of the half-shaft. Note the nut is left in place, for two important reasons: firstly, to prevent damage to the threaded end of the half-shaft, and secondly, the taper will 'let-go' very suddenly (and with quite a bang). So, without the nut, the shaft would fall to the floor, potentially damaging the diff-end of the half-shaft!

12-9. You will be rewarded with the inner-ring coming off its shoulder and, if you left the nut in place, with the shaft not falling to the floor!

within the axle tube, in which case they will need to be hooked out.

- You will need to separate each hub from its tapered half-shaft. There are two ways to do this. Method one necessitates, and I do mean necessitates, a proper Triumph 4-stud hub puller, such as the Churchill M86C. Even with this indispensable aid it will be very hard work and, while you may be able to buy, borrow or hire one, I strongly recommend you make arrangements to have your trusty partner/TR restorer remove the hub(s) from the half-shafts for you! Fortunately, there is an alternative that necessitates, and again I do mean necessitates, a power press. Because I believe this is the preferred route, I have provided photographic sequence 12-4 to 12-9 to help you. Watch out for the bang!

- Upon reassembly, use Loctite if either the 'A' (outer) or 'B' (inner) bearing rings are even slightly loose on the shaft, or in the hub, respectively.

- Check whether there dual-lipped oil seals are available yet. I was given to understand that they were coming, and will find an unworn area of axle to seal on. Sounds a very good idea.

- Completely pack the hubs/bearings with grease and smear a little right round each seal.

- The tapered hub bearings need to be shimmed to provide the correct end float, using a set of shims between the axle ends and the brake back plate. Note that the brake back plate must be finished before any attempt is made to set the end-floats. So, paint the back plates and allow the paint time to harden (or get them stove-enamelled), before you start. It's important that your axle does not overload the opposite hub bearing by feeding axle loads from one side of the car to the opposite bearing. Consequently, the right amount of 'play', or end-float, is important.

The half-shafts will expand as the axle warms up. Too little initial end-float

12-10. We have jumped ahead several reassembly steps, but, one very important detail that will not be obvious from anything we have discussed so far, is to use a fully painted and cured back plate when setting your end-float with a DTI. End-float tolerances are discussed in the main text.

12-11-1. The general view of the TR4 rear suspension and leaf spring arrangement.

12-11-2. This closer, sideways view might be helpful when it comes to refitting the Girling axle to the car. In case you should compare your rear springs to these, I guess I had better tell you that these are 'competition' hardness ... good luck Jennifer!

12-11-3. This shot of the front location point of the leaf spring is interesting because the large washers either side of the rubber 'eye' bush are, in fact, non-standard. However, they are recommended for all but concours enthusiasts, since they improve the locationing of the springs and, consequently, the rear axle. These were supplied by Revington TR. Note the body mounting point.

12-11-4. The large extra washers are not required at the rear end, but you may find this picture of the spring-shackles helpful. Note the very carefully repaired cross tube extension.

can overload the bearings or even bring about seizure, while too much can bring equally serious consequences. This is, therefore, a task you should subcontract if you do not have the necessary skills, experience, or a DTI (dial test indicator).

• Start with the same thickness of shims each side (about 0.08in), reassemble the half-shafts, hubs and back plates, and fully tighten all setscrews. Check the end-float between the back plate and the hub assembly, using a DTI as shown in photograph 12-10. This 'short-cut' is not recommended as you near your final readings, but you will see that we used a G-clamp to pull the hub together to check the initial shim adjustments. Re-shim until 0.004-0.006in end-float is achieved each side. As far as possible, the shims and end-float of one side should roughly equal the those of the opposite side.

• When reassembling the brakes, check you are about to use the correct rear wheel cylinders and that they are in first class order. Frankly, for something as important as your brakes, it seems silly to re-use old cylinders. Ensure the new ones are identical with each other, and, to minimise rear brake lock-ups, are compatible with your rear drum size. I recommend the following:
0.7in is the best balanced cylinder bore diameter for 9in diameter brake drums, while;
5/8in is the best balanced cylinder bore

diameter for 10in diameter brake drums. However, many cars have successfully used the smaller cylinder on the larger drums in an effort to reduce the probability of rear wheel locking.

• Don't forget to torque the axle nuts to the manual's recommended figure

(about 135lb ft), re-fit the split pins, and fill the axle with (Hypoy 90EP) oil.

• Be frugal with subsequent rear hub lubrication. Over enthusiasm with the grease gun will lubricate the brake drums!

• When the time comes to reassemble the rear axle and suspension, the photographic sequence 12-11-1 to 12-11-4 should provide a useful reference.

Chapter 13
Independent rear suspension and differential

TRIUMPH'S IRS SYSTEM

Most TR4As enjoy a rear suspension set-up that allows the two rear wheels to move independently of each other, which should provide for a more comfortable ride and better roadholding. A relatively small number of US TR4As were manufactured with the '4's live rear axle, but, in the main, the TR4A was manufactured with Independent Rear Suspension (IRS).

With a live rear axle, when, say, the left wheel moves up and down, this movement is unavoidably transferred to the right wheel because of the nature of the axle's beam-like construction. Consequently, the angle of the right side wheel to the road varies, which can have an adverse effect on the roadholding capability of the right side wheel. Hence the desirability of IRS, where this effect is minimised, if not eliminated. Furthermore, IRS offers the designer the opportunity to reduce the un-sprung weight on the rear wheels by mounting the differential on the chassis instead of in the rear axle. This also improves the roadholding at the back end.

The TRs in question have a type of IRS called 'trailing arm'; the rear wheels and hubs are kept in place by two

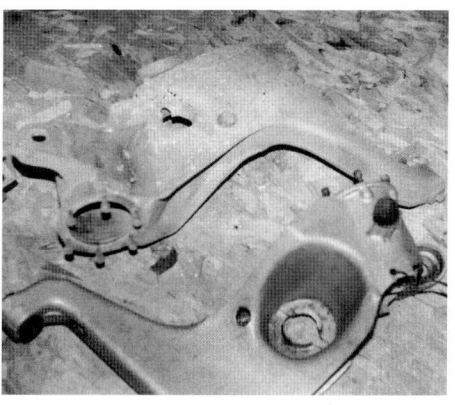

13-1. This is a nice illustration of the trailing arms, and the difference refurbishing makes. The top trailing arm is as it came off this '4A, whereas the lower arm has been thoroughly cleaned, rebushed and finished by being sprayed with a clear plasticoat.

trailing arms (shown in pictures 13-1 and 13-2). These are supported upon a pair of coil springs, which you can see in photograph 13-3. A pair of shock absorbers controls the suspension's movement.

On each side of the diff is the IRS equivalent of a halfshaft, officially called the 'outer axleshaft assembly'. Although picture 13-4 shows a modern/upgraded version, it will, nevertheless, serve to identify the component in question.

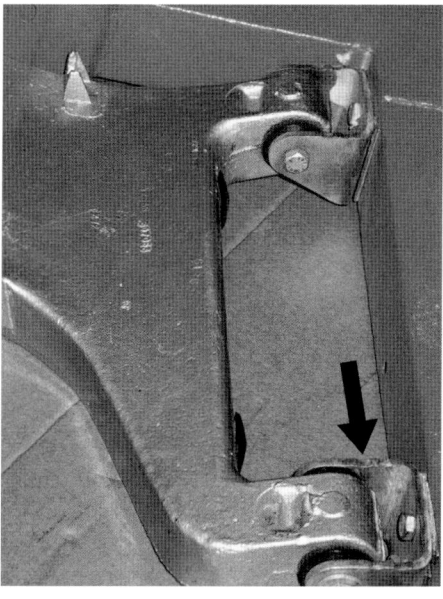

13-2. An excellent view of the rear suspension trailing arm, its mounting brackets and the all important chassis mounting member. Note that both mounting brackets have identification notches (arrowed) on the top edges (always mounted to the top). The trailing arm bushes are polyurethane and are mounted with the bolt heads facing inwards. These bolts will be impossible to remove at a future date if assembled the other way round - precluding camber adjustments, *etc.*! So always fit the heads of the bolts so that they are 'looking' at each other.

13-3. The complete IRS rear suspension. The top bump stop is clearly evident, and tells us we are looking at a post TR4A trailing arm. Can you spot the outer handbrake cable attachment point?

13-4. This may look familiar at first but, in fact, it's not quite what it seems. This new driveshaft and hub are one way you can uprate your rear driveshafts using Revington TR's rolling 'splines' - which provide four sliding ball bearing type interfaces down the length of the driveshaft. Clearly, this eliminates friction and any tendency for the splines to lock, even under higher-than-standard torque conditions. The assembly fits through the TR hub in the usual way.

13-5. The trailing arm *in situ*, nicely contrasting with the rest of the rear suspension. Note the original shock absorber and linkage, but as yet no driveshaft. When you come to fitting your driveshafts, carefully tighten the six nuts seen here, and to no more than the torque figure shown in your workshop manual.

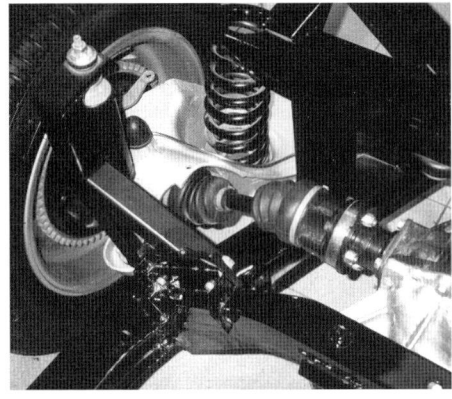

13-6. Another overview of the rear suspension but with TR Bitz's excellent telescopic shock absorber and mounting bracket. The shock is well located since it is attached to the trailing arm right at the point of maximum movement, thus giving maximum control. The bracket design is good too since it 'picks-up' on the original lever arm mountings and exerts no stress whatsoever on the body.

An inner universal joint terminates in a flange that is bolted to the rear axle drive flange. An outer universal joint terminates in an outer axleshaft that passes through the rear hub housing. The hub(s) are mounted to the trailing arm, as shown in photograph 13-5.

With the differential effectively fixed to the chassis, and with the rear hubs moving as road conditions dictate, the rear driveshafts need to vary (slightly) in length and angle, hence the provision of a sliding spline in the middle of each shaft, and a universal joint at each end. Photograph 13-6 should help you

envisage the arrangement, although again, the driveshaft at the centre of the shot is a modern/upgraded one. We will be discussing these features in more detail a little later!

A difficult to resolve downside of IRS is the now infamous low rear end, particularly noticeable under hard acceleration (sometimes termed 'squatting'). Triumph engineers must have been faced with a dilemma: fit softish rear springs to make the ride as comfortable as was decent for a sportscar (with lots of attendant rear end droop), or go for hard springs to prevent rear end dip under acceleration, but with the attendant teeth-chattering suspension. Opinion today is that the original choice of suspension for the TR4A, at about 280lb/in, was too soft. This is borne out by the fact that by the time the TR6 was introduced, the rating had increased by some 25% to around 350lb/in. Most TR4A owners upgrade their rear springs and use TR6 springs. However, the '6 is also well known for its rear end squat under acceleration, and many TR4A owners fit 390lb/in springs ... which do chatter the teeth at times!

THE TRAILING ARMS

You have almost certainly already read the chapter on chassis repairs to the IRS mountings, so I propose to do no more than very briefly re-emphasise some of the most vital details regarding the mountings for the trailing arms. However, I make no apologies for

raising some topics again, since we are talking about matters that could have serious consequences if they are not fully absorbed.

To 'recap', the chassis section rots badly right at the point where the where the trailing arms mount to the chassis; to make matters worse, the structure rots from the inside out. Many a, so-called, repair has been carried out by the owner or his garage, which has involved merely plating over the top of the corroded section, often to get the car through its annual MOT examination. Often the car is still sub-standard since the new metal has been welded to very little. Worse, in the case of the trailing arm attachment members (new ones are shown in photograph 13-7), there are still no solid internal spacing-tubes. Many a trailing arm mounting bracket has been reassembled to a 'repaired' and apparently strong chassis section, but, without proper spacer tubes within the chassis members, the trailing arm bolts just squeeze the new plates together without ever tightening in the intended manner. This very unsatisfactory situation is compounded by inexperienced repairers re-using the original, but now too short, bolts to secure the trailing arm mounting brackets to the useless chassis leg!

This really is a very dangerous area to bodge, overlook or get wrong. Rather like the steering or brakes on a car, if the trailing arm mounting point(s) 'let-go', the car could go straight into an oncoming vehicle or the ditch with no warning or time to react. If there is any

13-7. Yes, we have looked at a very similar picture in the chapter on chassis repairs. Nevertheless, since this is one of the most vulnerable yet crucial parts of an IRS chassis I make no apologies for including this second view as a reminder of the importance of these two structural members (and particularly their internal stiffeners/spacers) to the integrity of an IRS chassis.

swelling whatsoever of the chassis members in the area of the rear suspension mountings, replace them, and please do so with the proper pre-assembled spacered product specifically made for the job (shown in photograph 13-7).

The differential bridges snap just inboard of the pocket where the rear coil spring sits in the suspension/diff-bridge. This would result in the rear springs coming up through the body! Sadly, these weaknesses can be difficult to detect. Look again at pictures 5-27 and 5-28, and for any sign of weakness, corrosion or repair to your car. Take precautions if there is any doubt in your mind as to the structural integrity of your diff bridge.

Home restorations rarely include having the four (notched) mounting brackets, seen in photograph 13-2, crack-tested. This should be done if you plan to re-use the originals. For safety reasons, I would advise you to buy new replacement brackets. There were different combinations of brackets for different models. Initially, bracket 141399 (identified by 1 notch) was fitted

as the inside mounting, and 141398 (2 notches) on the outside.

Although outside the TR4A production run, it may be as well to mention that a 3 notch bracket (part number 1555502) was fitted to later IRS (CR/CF) cars. You must use the later brackets if you decide to use a later car's trailing arm casting(s). It's easy to fit any of these brackets upside down, so note that all notches are positioned upwards (see photograph 13-2).

The original rubber bonded bushes (part number 137599) fitted to carry the trailing arms were very probably too soft. Those fitted to the TR5s were harder, but later cars reverted to the softer bushes again! Any original bushes left in your car are likely to have deteriorated with the passage of time and will need replacing. The question is, what to fit now? The latest standard bonded rubber replacements are made from an even softer rubber compound than the originals, which does reduce road noise but will not improve handling. They are also very likely to wear out quite quickly (particularly those fitted to the inside of the car). On the other hand, there are special uprated TR5 rear bushes that will fit the '4A. They are harder than the original '4A bushes and should improve the handling, but they are really difficult to fit. Nylatron bushes are harder still, and, probably as a consequence, seem to transmit too much road noise. Superflex seem to have got the balance between ease of fitting, hardness, handling and road noise about right for most IRS owners. Superflex bushes will improve the drivability of the car, and it should be routine for every new IRS TR owner to change them.

The easiest way of removing the old bushes, which after years in place can be reluctant to move by conventional means, is to heat the bush until the rubber catches fire. By this point the metal sleeve will offer little resistance to being pushed out, and the remaining rubber is then easily removed.

The polyurethane replacement bushes (Superflex) can be equally difficult to reassemble if you are unaware of a couple of tips. They are shaped like a cotton-reel with a small lip at each end that makes them reluctant to enter the trailing arms at all, never mind entering them square! Take a few

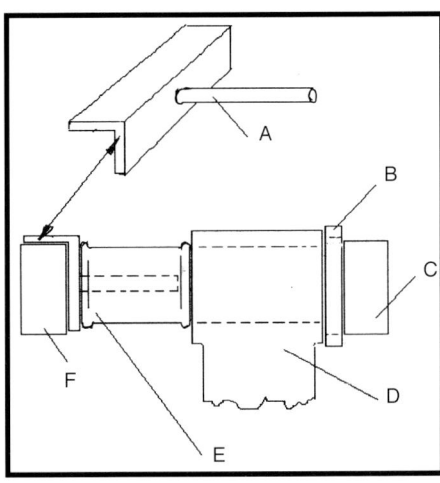

D13-1. Guiding a new trailing-arm bush into position. A. Suitable bolt welded square to angle arm base. B. Spacer (short piece of pipe). C. Vice/vise jaw. D. Trailing-arm. E. Polyurethane bush. F. Vice/vise jaw.

minutes to make the angle-iron/bolt aid sketched in drawing D13-1, it will be well worthwhile. Obviously, the bolt shank needs to be only marginally smaller than the bore of the new bushes. The aid holds the bush square to the trailing arm while you use your vice to squeeze the bush into its housing, aided by pre-warming the bush in hot (but not boiling) water and liberal doses of washing-up liquid. Do put lots of copper slip on the bolts before fixing your refurbished trailing arms back on the car.

Look out, too, for cracks in the rear trailing arms caused by stress and age. They most frequently go in the two places highlighted in photograph 13-8. The trailing arms are also vulnerable where the six hub-mounting studs screw into the aluminium arm (see picture 13-5) as they can pull out or the thread can strip. You will need expert help from your favourite TR specialist to heli-coil the casting with $5/16$in UNC threads. Note that the original thread into the casting is UNF, but coarse threads are best into soft material like aluminium. The outer end of the studs should ideally match the original UNF thread, but you may have to accept a UNC outer thread too.

If the casting or threads are particularly badly damaged, you might be better off getting a replacement trailing arm. Although they look similar at first sight, ex-Stag and ex-Saloon units do not fit. Any replacement must come

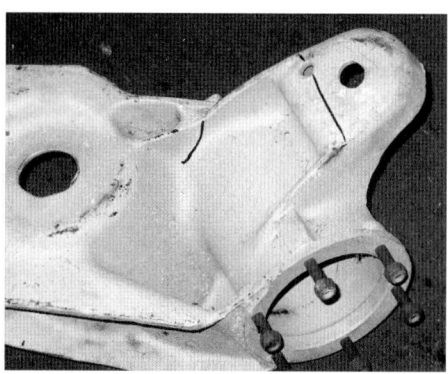

13-8. The IRS rear trailing arm with the two most common crack points highlighted. Don't confine your inspection to the areas shown, but be sure to inspect and even crack-test both arms where shown.

from a TR. However, while they may look identical, there are even some differences between the various TR units too. The TR4A arms, for example, do not have a bump stop fitted to the arm; they were fitted to the underside of the body. The TR5s and TR6s had provision for a bump stop on the trailing arm itself. The later (CR/CF) TR6 arms were cast with a slightly different camber angle, but are perfectly usable on an earlier IRS car provided the compatible 3 notch mounting bracket is also used.

You should find the casting date shown on the body of the casting to help you identify which notched mounting brackets to use. If you have trouble re-establishing the rear suspension geometry after a rebuild, the chances are that you have either put a notched bracket in the wrong place, mounted one upside-down, or not used the correct brackets for your particular casting(s).

THE DIFFERENTIAL

All TRs have a tendency to leak a little oil. It's almost a trademark of the marque! The front bearing of the IRS differential is a case in point, and it's not unknown for TR owners to overdo the initial remedy. If your front diff oil seal leaks too much oil, check that the breather hole in the rear cover is not bunged up, before you start on the oil seal itself. Over the years, oil and dirt collect and can close the breather, leaving the diff without a breather as it warms up.

The only alternative for the trapped but expanding air is through one of the

three oil seals. Either of the side seals are possibilities, but the most frequent route is via the leather front seal. All the seals are, of course, lower than the breather, so they will allow oil to escape instead of the intended air. If you clear the breather hole you will take the pressure off the oil seal that is leaking. Take care not to remove the split-pin from the breather plug as it's quite a job to put it back. Also, take care not to drop dirt into the differential as you clean the breather vent.

If you still have a leaking front oil seal after clearing the breather, then I'm afraid it's a case of replacing the seal. As I mentioned, it is a leather seal which requires special treatment before fitting. The seal must be soaked in engine oil for at least 24 - and preferably 36 - hours before fitting. You can warm the oil a little from time to time during the soak to help its uptake, but do throw that oil away at the end of the softening/ soaking period. Fill the diff with fresh oil, as per the workshop manual, after you have fitted the new seal.

The IRS differential either works or it doesn't. If you are intent on the best repair possible, a service exchange route is probably your best bet. A straight rebuild is £240 in the UK and, if you have ground to a standstill, then it's almost a certainty you will also need a new £175 crown wheel and pinion. US readers should have no difficulty in finding a complete secondhand replacement, though these are somewhat more difficult to find in the UK.

Fortunately, there are alternatives. The TR4A used two differential ratios. The standard one was 3.7:1, but there was an optional ratio of 4.1:1. If you have just broken a 4.1 ratio axle, you may see this as an opportunity to simultaneously increase the car's 'legs' by fitting the higher of the two ratios - particularly if you have to, or plan to, increase the capacity of your engine. There are several cheaper solutions than a rebuilt unit, but in all cases you will need the front and rear parts of your existing differential, so don't be tempted into parting with them!

It's not always appreciated that Triumph was commendably frugal, using the same differential ratios (indeed the same basic rear suspension) on a variety of cars. Other ratios were available, but the two rear axle/

differential ratios that interest us are 4.1:1 and 3.7:1. The ratio used in your car can identified from outside the diff by marking both hubs (wheels off the car first, of course) and the drive pinion flange with felt-tip pen or typewriter correction fluid. With the gearbox in neutral, get a friend to turn the drive flange 11 revolutions while you and another helper ensure both hubs turn the same number of revolutions. If the hubs revolve (to all intents and purposes) 3 complete turns, chances are you have a 3.7 ratio in your differential. If both hubs turn fewer than 3 revolutions (a fraction less than 2.75) you almost certainly have a 4.1 ratio in place. From inside the diff it's even easier, in that you need do no more than count the crown wheel's teeth, with the following information in mind:

37 crown wheel teeth signal a 3.7 ratio
41 crown wheel teeth signal a 4.1 ratio

Fortunately the 3.7 and 4.1 ratio differentials were also used in several other Triumph vehicles of the era as follows:

TR250 .... 3.7
TR6 (US Carb) 3.7
Stag 3.7
2500 Auto Saloon 3.7
2000 Manual Saloon 4.1

Photograph 13-9 shows the unique rear casing for the TRs we are focused upon. If you have broken this rear casing, or your front mounting has broken, then the following proposal is no help, and you must either search for replacements (possibly via the USA), get your broken parts repaired, or switch to the TR6 rear casing and mountings (which are available new).

However, for the majority, the core differential, pinion, crown wheel, drive flanges and main casing in the above cars are, in fact, identical with our IRS TRs, although you should note the pinion spacers can vary (more in a moment). The front mountings and rear cover plates may vary from car to car, but if you have your complete TR differential unit (of either ratio) and wish to fit a different ratio or a replacement differential, you can do so via the appropriate non-TR core unit.

You may be curious as to why I mention that, on the one hand TR

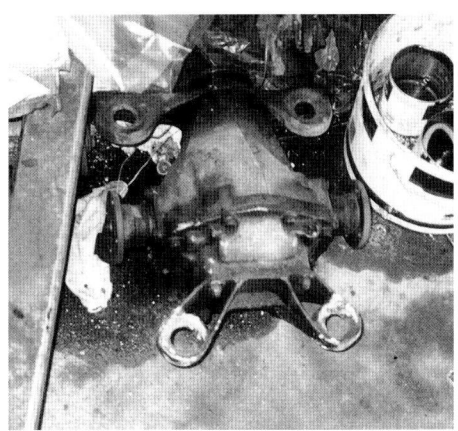

13-9. The rear mounting arrangement for a TR4A differential. This uses two pairs of cone-type mountings identical to those used on the front mounting of all TR IRS differentials.

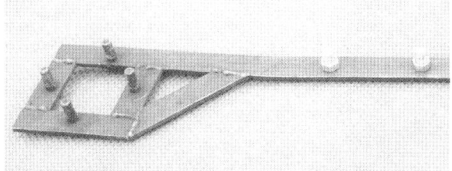

13-10. A means of locking the differential pinion and/or driveshaft flanges. The four fastening studs are, of course, for securely attaching the arm to the pinion in question, while you address the 1.125in AF nut. Note that there appears to be a slight 'set' in the arm. This is not an illusion and serves to illustrate the force often required to move these nuts.

differentials are hard to come by, and on the other, list two TRs as potential sources of 3.7 ratio axles. The reason is that all repatriated TR250 and TR6 cars from the USA come with 3.7 ratio differentials. However, the six cylinder engines in UK tune are quite capable of handling a 3.45 rear ratio, and many cars do have the diff ratio increased to give them longer legs. Consequently, the six-pot TRs are a potential source of 3.7 ratio differentials, or at least the cores for the assembly. The Stag and Saloons have a front extension that is very easily removed but, to return to the pinion spacer differences, use a collapsible spacer. This needs to swapped for the TR's fixed spacer and pre-loaded. This is a skilled job that should be left to professionals, such as First Gear (details in Appendix 1), or your TR specialist.

You need to check that the ratio of any replacement core you are considering is suitable and that it runs smoothly - after which it's merely a matter of swapping front and rear fittings to achieve the replacement you need. Be cautious about purchasing a replacement differential that exhibits signs of weeping oil seals, for, all too often, a weeping seal signifies a worn bearing. However, if the replacement is competitively priced, or your diff is otherwise in good shape, we will briefly explore changing oil seals, although there are very good reasons to ask an expert to tackle the task.

For those interested in finding out what's involved, there are three oil seals, one in the pinion and two in the

driveshafts. Removing the driveshafts from a car is obvious, from both the manual or by looking at the car. If the diff is still in place, do not be too hasty to remove it for, as inconvenient as it sounds, it's often better to loosen and subsequently tighten the $1^1/_8$in AF nuts with the diff on the car. You can then use the car's chassis to hold things still while you tackle the 110ft lbs of torque required for the substantial nuts. However, you also have to hold the drive pinion still as you loosen or tighten its retaining nut! A special long, strong, bar, that bolts to all-four pinion drive-bolts, is essential. Take a look at photograph 13-10 for an idea of what's needed, and then leave the job to a specialist! If you persevere, there may come a moment when you wonder if you are turning the tommy-bar in the correct direction. I can only reassure you that the nuts do use a conventional right hand thread!

Four bolts on the housing flange are all that stand between your taking the whole inner axleshaft assembly to the bench. If you wish to replace either the axleshaft bearing or the oil seal, it's first necessary to remove the flange from the shaft. Use a three-legged puller, and expect to have to exert considerable force (a very strong puller would be a good idea).

You would not be the first to find the shaft/flange appear to have become 'welded' together. In this case, the power press at your local engineering works will rectify the situation, but don't wait until after you have damaged your shaft's spline and/or flange - use the press first, before the damage occurs!

The oil seal and housing can now be pulled off and the oil seal carefully tapped out of the housing. Drive the

axleshaft through the bearing and throw the used bearing away, for it must not be re-used. Tap a new bearing onto the shaft by carefully striking the inner ('B') ring only, in order to avoid damaging (or 'brinelling') the tracks inside the bearing. When reassembling, don't forget to check the metal protector cup for damage, and put it back against the flange before putting the housing and well-lubricated/soaked oil seal into position.

When reassembling the diff and diff mountings to the chassis, ensure that the nose of the diff points ever-so-slightly downwards, or you run the risk of starving the front pinion bearing of oil and causing some expensive damage. Before you get to that point, however, do ensure that the rubber diff mounting cones are all in good shape. Frankly, for what they cost, you are better off replacing all eight.

Finally, for completeness, the right side front diff mounting pins are prone to break loose from the chassis, especially when faced with the torque of a six-cylinder engine. While not nearly so prevalent with four-pots, it would be wise to strengthen all four pins (in the manner detailed in the IRS section of chapter 5) whenever you are forced to remove your diff for other reasons.

One final recommendation for you whenever working in the area of the differential: always check that the four bolts that secure the front end of your diff to its mounting/cross bracket are tight!

THE DRIVESHAFTS

There are a couple of common errors made when reassembling the rear driveshafts to the differential.

Firstly, it's best to feed the bolts through the flanges from the inside of the car, so that the head of each bolt is 'looking at' the diff, and the nuts are on the outside of the universal joint flange. It's good engineering practice to always use new nyloc nuts (never re-use a nyloc nut) or new spring washers under all plain nuts; if you follow this principle it's very unlikely you'll have a problem. However, if you are unfortunate and a nut comes off one of these particular bolts, it will almost certainly drop away unnoticed. This is far from ideal, of course, but the alternative is even less desirable. If you've put the bolt in from the outside, there is just a possibility that the bolt will exit the coupling and jam in the universal joint!

Secondly, the left and right driveshafts carry the same part number (RKC454), and can be interchanged. This is not a bad idea since you will then be driving on the other side of each spline. If this is on your mind I suggest you mark each shaft as you remove it to remind you which side of the car it came from originally.

Many restorers do elect to reposition **parts** of each shaft to the opposite side of the car in order to drive on the other side of their splines. I'm not sure I would regard this as good engineering practice, so think about it carefully. Fortunately, for those with driveshaft problems and who are thinking of this as a solution, Triumph used many of the same components on the Stag and the 2000, 2.5PI and 2500 Saloons. The TR driveshaft assemblies, however, are different from the other Triumph models, in that the lengths of the outer shafts (from the sliding spline covered by a rubber gaiter to the outmost universal joint yoke) vary. However, these differences do not affect the interchangeability of the majority of components used in the sliding splines, or other parts within the rear driveshafts for that matter.

All the components within each driveshaft need checking for wear, if you are to avoid or are already experiencing, the infamous Triumph IRS rear end 'twitch'. This is easily resolved provided your driveshaft sliding splines are not overly worn.

It's worth taking a moment to explain the reasons behind this alarming trait. If the lubrication in the splines dries out, if dirt finds its way passed a (split?) gaiter, or if spline wear has occurred, the torque from the engine can, in effect, prevent the splines from sliding as suspension movements dictate. Obviously, the lower gear you are using, or the larger capacity of your engine, the higher the torque transmitted to the rear driveshafts and, consequently, the more pronounced the problem. When the torque causes the driveshafts splines to lock, rear suspension movement (which would normally cause the driveshafts to slide and change overall length), is either prevented completely or severely restricted. In due course, a sufficiently large road surface bump or a reduction

in torque (when you lift off the accelerator), 'unsticks' the splines and the rear suspension takes up its unrestricted position, causing the rear of the car to 'twitch' quite suddenly, unexpectedly, and very noticeably!

Cleanliness and lack of wear of the splines is vital to the satisfactory performance of IRS. To examine the splines, first pull back the gaiter. TR4As have a threaded collar, a steel washer and a cork washer on the female part of the sliding splines. The collar must be unscrewed and slid away. These parts were omitted from most of the other Triumph IRS driveshafts, which used two wire/cable-tie 'clamps' round the gaiter. Thorough cleaning, examination for wear, and testing of each spline's sliding action is necessary. If all looks well, apply a little torque, first one way and then the other, whilst you try sliding the spline longitudinally. Wear or a feeling of roughness when doing this sliding test, suggests a replacement is required.

Try using some parts from another sliding assembly (noting the respective differences outlined above), rechecking for smoothness, greasing the spline liberally and placing your new assembly on the opposite side of the car. This applies the driving torque to the other side of the splines.

The driveshafts rarely break. They can lock up if left un-greased, but it's more likely they will wear and 'clonk' when taking up drive or on over-run. One consequence of worn and clonking driveshafts is an abnormally short life for your universal joints.

Although there are numerous rear driveshaft upgrades, space dictates we must leave these to a later book. I must, however, mention that GKN Driveline (who made the original driveshafts) now use a bonded resin coating, 'Rilsan Fluidglide', on the splines of new original driveshafts. This, it is claimed, eliminates the infamous IRS 'twitch' by ensuring the splines no longer stick, even under load. Furthermore, the coating longevity is reputedly enhanced by the provision of grease nipples to lubricate the splines. The new driveshafts cost around £300 and come with new universal joints.

During reassembly of your original driveshafts, do note that the halves only engage in one position. Be alert to the importance of absolute cleanliness, of lubricating the splines all over with a

heavy duty molybdenum grease (e.g. Castrol SM3), of using new gaiters, and of sealing the assembly to prevent the ingress of water and grit.

THE UNIVERSAL JOINTS

IRS cars unquestionably suffer from the consequences of using six universal joints to transmit power from the gearbox to the rear hubs. You only need a small amount of play in each universal joint for it to seem like an eternity before action at the clutch pedal is translated into motion! Worse still, that motion invariably starts with a 'clonk'!

Whilst, strictly speaking, we are discussing the rear suspension universal joints, which are quite accessible, the universal joints at each end of the IRS propshaft can only be accessed with either the gearbox or differential out of the car. Consequently, they should also be on your list of 'while the diff is out' jobs! It's worth mentioning that the universal joint circlips will be far easier to remove if you spend a few minutes with a 10mm wire brush and your drill cleaning up the 'mouth' of the yoke. As with the driveshaft splines, it goes without saying that everything must be scrupulously clean upon reassembly.

There are two types of universal joint on the market. The original TR4A used sealed universal joints (without grease nipples); later, grease nipples were used on the inner universal joints; and, later still, grease nipples were incorporated into the outer universal joints. Sealed universal joints were reintroduced for the TR6.

Whatever your car and whatever was originally fitted, the driveshaft universal joints should always be of the highest quality you can buy and always have a grease nipple. GKN are the universal joints of choice in view of the quality and size of the needle-rollers used, but you may need to go to an 'AE' (Turner and Newell) distributor to get them.

A PVC cover can be fitted to any IRS car but was only originally fitted to the '6. I find mine flaps about and I personally question its value but, in theory, they act as a dirt shield.

All universal joint grease nipples should receive attention from a grease-gun every 3000 miles or so. However, the outer pair of universal joints on each driveshaft need even greater care and attention. These two units experience the very minimum of flexing when in use, which you may think is an advantage and should extend their lives. In practice, however, the grease gets pushed out of the narrow angle through which the joints move, internal wear becomes focused on a narrow band and water gets in, making these universal joints the most prone to rust, stiffness and seizure.

You might be surprised to hear that universal joint stiffness also increases stress on the diff mounting pins. Therefore, annually - perhaps each spring when you are preparing your car for the season ahead - it would be a good idea to exercise the outer pair of universal joints through their full arcs. This can be accomplished by disconnecting the driveshafts at the inner ends, and rotating the outer universal joints through the widest arc you can whilst thoroughly greasing them. If your universal joints are the sealed type, take the first opportunity to change them for high quality, greasable units.

REAR HUBS AND BEARINGS

The IRS rear wheel hubs are further areas that require care, attention to detail and a certain amount of expenditure.

Going straight to the most vital detail; on the end of each rear outer axleshaft there is a threaded portion that can snap off, and allow the wheel to come off the car. The reason this happens is that a crack develops at the root of the threaded section, which eventually fails allowing the end of the shaft and its wheel-retaining nut to part company. Additionally, there is likely to be the inevitable wear (signalled by play) in the rear hub bearings.

This problem can be resolved by having the existing stub axles crack tested, or spending around £275 on a pair of re-machined shafts. The re-machined shafts are as good as new in that they are freshly machined, albeit from used driveshaft stubs. However, it will take a 100 tonne press to split the bearings off your morse-tapered stub axle. If you try to do this at home you are very likely to reduce the shafts to scrap by 'belling' or 'tuliping' the flange. Furthermore, while the workshop/operations manual explains that it is essential to replace the collapsible

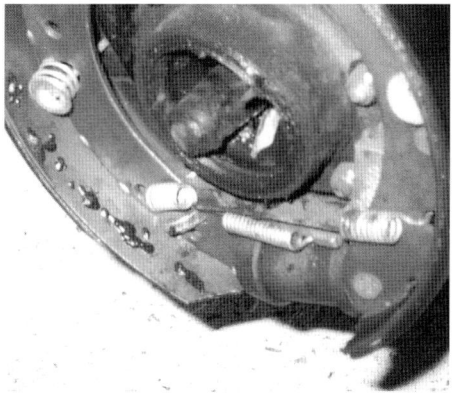

13-11. Cracked for some time, by the look of the fracture, but this is the consequence of the threaded end of the shaft shearing, taking the retaining nut, washer, studded driving flange, brake-drum and the all-important wheel with it. Some of the grease from the hub bearings can be seen splattered on the brake shoes, whilst, out of shot, is the chewed-up key and keyway. Strangely, and very fortuitously, I was only going about 10-15mph round a roundabout when there was a load bang, but just moments before I had been travelling a great deal faster.

spacers, bearings and oil seals as a set, it does not, in my view, put enough emphasis upon the importance of also replacing the adjusting spacer (ULC2188) and the tab washer (139057).

In short, there are so many opportunities for the home restorer to get this job wrong, and these parts are so important to the safety of you and your car, that I very strongly recommend you go the 'service exchange' route. All service-exchange work on rear hubs for the industry is carried out by TR Bitz, and includes crack-testing of the shaft, new bearings and such other parts as are required. The cost - at £75 each (exchange) - does not make it worth your while even contemplating anything else. Consequently, I do not propose to tempt anyone into a DIY attempt by an operational description here. In fact, I take the other view and emphasise the importance of not even trying to start the operation, for you'll more than likely damage the shafts and render them valueless.

You may be surprised to hear me suggest that, provided you do not try to get inside the hub, there is nothing to stop you using an ex-Stag, 2000/2500/2500PI hub assembly on your TR.

13-12. Another excellent telescopic shock absorber conversion arrangement. This is the CTM design, a company perhaps more widely known for its work repairing and/or building new TR chassis. These conversions are usually supplied with AVO adjustable shock absorbers.

A BRIEF SUMMARY OF THE MAJOR UPGRADES

Whilst this book is primarily aimed at original restorations, I must briefly mention two IRS upgrades.

First and foremost, fitting telescopic shocks to the rear (an excellent upgrade which will transform your car). There are several makes to choose from but, if you are selecting adjustable shocks, do ask about the method and ease of adjustment. Some need to be removed from the car; some can be adjusted on the car. However, it's probably the design of the mounting bracketry that's the more important issue when it comes to fitting telescopics to a TR.

There is no one universal method of mounting the shocks, each retailer/specialist has its own ideas and bracket designs. Avoid mounting brackets that in any way touch the body of your TR. The mounting bracket should be designed to contain all stresses within the chassis structure, not through the body. Ensure that those you are looking at are fit for your intended purpose: brackets designed for racing will be light but may not stand up to the rigors of thousands of miles of carefree motoring.

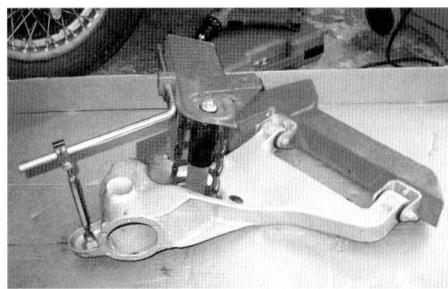

13-13. Revington TR's anti-roll/sway bar and rear shock absorber.

13-14 and 13-15. You will need a method of compressing the springs, particularly if you are assembling your rear suspension without the weight of the body to help you. Photograph 13-14 shows one of a pair of rear spring compressors, whilst 13-15 shows two rear spring compressors in action. I am of the opinion, however, that a single central threaded bar compressor, up through the middle of the spring, will serve you better and allow more space for getting to the task.

The design must allow for the use of fuel injection pumps, filters and pipework. I have not looked at every design available as yet but would suggest that the TR Bitz and CTM designs are worth exploring. These are shown in photographs 13-6 and 13-12.

Rear anti-roll/sway bars are also worth a quick mention, though it's my intention to discuss upgrades/improvements in more detail in a follow-up book. However, I came across the demonstration exhibit shown in photograph 13-13 at Revington TR, and felt it offered such a simple assembly method that, at the last minute and in spite of a lack of space, I must mention it in passing.

SPRING COMPRESSORS

This is pretty routine stuff so, without going into detail, I'll just mention that you will need a spring compressor for the rear springs, as shown in photographs 13-14 and 15. There's not much room to get at things so enquire of your TR specialist if he offers a central compressor.

Chapter 14
Brakes

BACKGROUND

Although the situation stabilised somewhat during the TR4/TR4A/5/250 and early TR6 production runs, overall, the number of brake variations is somewhat confusing. It's not my intention to go into the graphic detail of the brakes fitted to TRs produced either side of the TR4 and '4A, but you may find a summary both interesting, and possibly even helpful when seeking spares.

Basically, the vast majority of rear brakes are 9in drums and are more-or-less identical. The position of the back plate may vary, but there is continuity running right through the major part of classic TR production.

The front brakes are not so straightforward. Initially, the TR2 used drum brakes but the TR3 introduced an 11in diameter front disc that was fairly quickly changed to a slightly smaller diameter ($10^{13}/_{16}$in) disc on the TR3As. The respective calipers were also different and, needless to say, were changed simultaneously. A further change of caliper was introduced with the TR3B, but a period of stability then existed through to mid-TR6 production, when a metric version of the caliper was introduced.

The point I wish to make is that the discs or the calipers on your car may have been changed from the original specification. This poses no safety problem if they have both been changed to compatible pairs of the earlier or later type. However, you may decide to fit new discs, for example, and, quite correctly, choose those $10^{13}/_{16}$in that are OE for your car. If your pads overlap the top of the disc, you'll need to fit the 11in diameter discs or find a pair of TR4/4A calipers. If the brake pipe fitting seems either very loose or very tight, check that you are not mixing metric and imperial threads. Forewarned is forearmed!

THE BRAKE LINES

Most experienced restorers will appreciate that the original 'bundy' brake pipes, being predominantly steel, are prone to corrosion. If you are carrying out a classic car restoration you should note the advantages of copper brake pipes and braided flexible hoses.

The copper brake pipe kits are available for all TRs and, although not absolutely original, all but a restorer aiming for concours standard should definitely use copper pipes. The material is not actually copper, it is cupro-nickel, but it has the same corrosion-resistant characteristics.

You do not need to worry about flaring tools, for the pipes come ready-flared. They will arrive coiled (for ease of shipping) so you will need to straighten them. Put one end in a vice, suitably wrapped for protection, hold a rag round the pipe adjacent to the vice and, starting with a 45 degree pipe-angle behind your rag/point of straightening; pull hard down the full length of the pipe. If you do not introduce a bend but try to pull the pipe straight, you will not achieve a truly straight pipe. Then there are, of course, various radiused bends to position correctly if the pipes are to be both safe (i.e. not kinked) and look their best. Putting the radius in is best achieved using one of the large varieties of pliers available (in 45 and 90 degrees) from most auto-factors. These are recommended and will make a world of difference to the appearance of your finished piping. Photographs 14-1 and 14-2 will give some additional help with the installation.

Flexible hoses

You will not need me to remind you that; (a) flexible hoses are a safety-critical part of your car, and; (b) for the small extra sum involved, stainless steel

14-1. Some interesting detail on brake pipe installation. Clearly, you can fit many of the brake lines prior to fitting the body - if you are careful. As a rule-of-thumb, don't fit any of the pipes on top of a chassis member. In this picture you can see that the lines have been securely attached to the sides of chassis members. These lines are made from 'copper' material and we can see the pipes for the front 'section' and the rear section are not coupled together. This, therefore, is either a dual-circuit car, like a TR5, or an upgraded TR4/4A that is being fitted with a dual-circuit braking system for safety reasons. Note the unusually long copper pipe connecting the front caliper to the flexible hose. The extra length is absolutely no problem provided it is routed so that the line will not foul on any part of the body or suspension when the steering is on any part of its lock. Worth a double check before the car goes out for the first time!

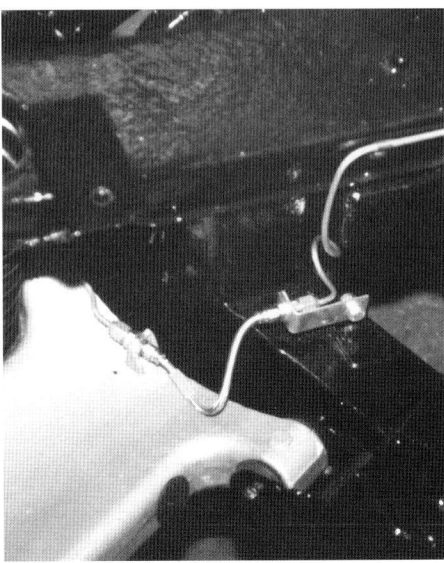

14-2. Some detail for the rear brake line installation on a TR4A. Note how this caring owner has 'lost' some excess pipe length, mounted the pipes to the chassis and routed the braided flexible hose.

braided hoses (shown in picture 14-2) are better than the originals on two counts. Firstly, they are more resistant to abrasion. Secondly, they are more resistant to the inevitable, very slight, expansion that takes place when you brake, and will give your brakes a more 'solid' feel. This is particularly important with the IRS cars where there are four flexible hoses within the system rather than the usual three on earlier TRs.

I'm sure that this next comment is totally unnecessary but, if any of your flexible hoses are swelling visibly when you put your foot on the brake pedal, do not drive the car until you have replaced them. The 'normal' degree of expansion I spoke about a sentence or two ago will be quite invisible!

BRAKE SERVO PERFORMANCE

Brake servos weren't fitted as standard to TR4s or 4As - but they can be. Although a servo does not actually increase the stopping power of the brakes, it will reduce the pedal pressure required to bring about the braking effect, and there are a couple of scenarios where fitting a servo would be beneficial.

Most of us, for example, might only use our TRs as a second car. For most of the time we are probably cossetted in the relative luxury and servo assisted comfort of a modern saloon. When we do drive the TR, the brakes will probably feel very heavy indeed, and a brake servo would redress some of the comparative difference. Alternatively, a driver who finds applying the necessary pedal pressure an effort in a TR would also appreciate the benefits of a brake servo.

The usual approach is to fit a 'remote' type servo, such as a Girling Powerstop (which is available via most TR specialists), or a Lockheed type 6, on the vertical part of the bulkhead/firewall, as shown in photograph 14-3. This type of servo was fitted to most MGBs from about 1968 to 1974 and used ones are, therefore, in fairly plentiful supply. Furthermore, a 'repair/

service' kit is readily available - although you will find yourself paying more for the service kit than a secondhand servo! However, bearing in mind the importance of one's brakes, and that a malfunctioning servo can apply the brakes when you don't want them applied, a new one seems, on balance the better idea.

If you feel your brakes do need to be improved, before you start to seriously consider any of the details that follow, do take a couple of hours to ensure your existing brakes generally, and the servo if fitted, are functioning to their maximum effectiveness. Check the servo is operating by running the engine for a couple of minutes (to build up vacuum in the servo) and then switch off. Place your foot on the brake pedal and you should hear a 'chuff' noise. Leave your foot on the pedal and start the engine; you should feel the pedal depress if your servo is working satisfactorily. No 'chuff' and/or depression means you should start to question the effectiveness of the servo.

Carry out all the obvious maintenance checks. It might be a very good idea to replace the vacuum hose that leads to the servo before trying the foregoing test again. If the servo is definitely working but you still feel the on-road braking leaves something to be desired, take the relatively simple precaution of connecting a second manifold take-off point into the vacuum hose that feeds the servo. As unlikely as it sounds, particularly when you look at the balancing pipe installation, a second vacuum take-off feed to your brake servo can improve the effectiveness of the servo and brakes.

The task will involve removing the inlet manifold and welding a second pre-tapped take-off point to a convenient spot on the manifold. If your brakes are still not up to your needs, read on!

GENERAL BRAKE TIPS

- Remember that brakes are a safety-critical item, and you need to treat the components accordingly. If in any doubt whatsoever, ask a professional, and remember he will always err on the side of caution, as indeed should you. A completely new, or a factory reconditioned, unit is usually the best option when it comes to brake parts.
- When removing the rear drums, let-

14-3. A brake servo is not a standard fitting on either of the cars we are focused upon. However, although 'non-original' it is a very valuable extra. Here we see a Lockheed Type 6 remote servo mounted on the passenger side bulkhead/firewall. Unfortunately, this location necessitates an additional pair of lengthy brake pipes running more or less across the width of the engine compartment, but that is a small price to pay! One detail shown clearly in this picture is the position of the white (flying saucer-looking) air valve. Unfortunately, you will see many cars, particularly MGBs, with this valve incorrectly positioned. It should point downwards, anywhere between '8-o'clock and 4-o'clock', to aid bleeding, as in this example.

off the handbrake and slacken off the adjuster located on the backplate.
• When bleeding the brakes, always start by bleeding the wheel furthest from the master cylinder. This means the left rear wheel of all cars regardless of RHD or LHD. I get on well with the 'Easy-Bleed' single-handed system, although many feel it brings too much moist air into contact with the brake fluid.
• Many restorers feel it appropriate to replace the rear wheel cylinder seals, and certainly it is likely to be important that the rear wheel cylinders receive attention. However, on average, replacing the seals meets with no better

than a 50% operational success rate and I would suggest, for the cost involved and the relative importance of one's brakes, you replace the cylinders completely with genuine Girling replacement parts. This is particularly true if your rear wheel cylinders need honing.
• Your best policy with questionable calipers is to do a service exchange deal. If you really must explore the units further, do not split them. The experts feel there is too much opportunity to get the subsequent re-torqueing incorrect, so not only will you find it difficult to buy the internal seals, but also the new bolts (with built-in plastic locking tabs) will be hard to find too.
    It is practical to change the piston seals once the calipers are off the car. Remove the circlip and dust boot on the later types of caliper and extract the pistons, making sure you know which piston came from which bore, and that they are not interchanged. Carefully prise out the seals, ensuring no bore damage occurs, and thoroughly clean the pistons and calipers in brake fluid or methylated spirit (wood alcohol). Assemble new seals to the caliper bores, lubricating with clean brake fluid. Assemble the dust boots on early types of pistons, and carefully locate the lip in the groove in your caliper. Push the pistons home squarely. For the later types of caliper, fit new dust boots, and don't forget the circlip in each caliper. When refitting the caliper to the car, be sure not to forget the lock tabs and the pad retaining pins (yes, they really are forgotten from time to time). Bleed the whole system.
• Stuck master cylinder pistons are not unknown, and some thoughts regarding repair may be helpful. The master cylinder is a safety-critical component and may be best replaced. If you do so I suggest you use a genuine OE replacement part. Still want to recover your old unit? Okay, but do get the bore of the master cylinder honed before re-assembly, and clear all dirt and rust and then soak the whole assembly in penetrating fluid, such as 'Duck-oil' or WD40, for several days. If the usual tapping (best with wood, of course), and/or using the return spring to encourage the piston out fail to do the trick, try the 'Easy-Bleed' system. This uses brake fluid pressurised by tyre pressure (at no more than 20psi),

14-4. Cross drilled brake discs are an aid to cooling, although the effect is fairly minimal. I'm not comfortable with cross drilled holes with significant countersinking at each side of the cross-drilling as it reduces the pad to disc contact area. If you cannot buy discs with plain holes, of about 0.125in (3mm) diameter, buy un-drilled discs and have your local engineering shop drill plain holes to this pattern on a 'dividing-head'.

although, when attempting this, don't forget to close the pipe connection with an old union and folded pipe! If the piston is still stuck, and you really are reluctant to scrap the master cylinder, try a grease gun coupled to the pipe connection. You are best to remember that rebuilt cylinders only work satisfactorily about 50% of the time, so you are best to buy new if you've got to this stage!
• Upgrading brakes will be one topic explored in some detail in a later book, but, very briefly, cross-drilled TR discs (photograph 14-4) will help cooling, and are a first level improvement worth considering. Be aware that some brake pad materials only work at their best when warm, so are unsuitable for many applications outside competition. Nevertheless, you may care to look into alternative pad materials, but be aware that Mintex M1144 does take time to warm up, though it is popular for TR competition applications. Kevlar 'Green Stuff' is becoming very popular too. A significant upgrade in braking terms is to fit Wilwood alloy calipers to your current discs (about £500 from TRGB), or, alternatively, approach Revington TR for information about its complete brake disc and caliper upgrades.
• Those keen to improve their rear

brakes should explore Alfin alloy rear drums from TR Bitz, as shown in photograph 14-5.

THE HANDBRAKE

The handbrake on the TR4 was good. It was mounted on the chassis and came up the right side of the propshaft tunnel. Partly due to the length of the actual handbrake (lever), it enjoyed an excellent mechanical advantages. The compensator shown in photograph 14-6 offered a further mechanical advantage, while the uncomplicated design of the cables (photograph 14-7) added to the overall effectiveness of the '4's hand/parking brake.

The TR4A's handbrake, however, was moved to the top of the propshaft tunnel, its length was reduced, and it operated with two cables instead of one, without the aid of a compensator. This resulted in reduced mechanical efficiency. We will look at compensatory upgrading for TR4As in a later book, but the most common problems contributing to an unsatisfactory handbrake are as follows (and you should check that **all** the following are in first class order if you are dissatisfied with your 4A's handbrake):
- worn linings
- seized brake shoe adjusters (the square drive peg on the rear of the backplate)
- seized and/or worn rear cylinders/levers - particularly when the cylinder cannot slide fore and aft on the backplate
- corroded and/or stretched cables
- worn or distorted drums
- worn clevis pins.

14-5. Only some 30% of braking effect comes from the rear, so it makes sense to spend the majority of your 'brake improvement' cash at the front of the car. Nevertheless, these aluminium finned rear drums will increase rear drum cooling, provided you are sure the original drums are getting too hot.

14-6. This shot shows the handbrake compensator on a TR4 and indicates the mechanical advantage it adds to the operation of the handbrake. Note the handbrake cable return spring and the hydraulic brake piping arrangement.

14-7. An interesting close-up of the backplate in TR4 configuration. The components remained largely the same, but the backplate orientation and fixing holes changed for the TR4A and subsequent IRS TRs.

14-8. I thought this TR4A aluminium handbrake cable cover was likely to give you better support when, like me, you lean on the propshaft tunnel. However, it may make carpeting the tunnel a shade more difficult.

Chapter 15
Miscellaneous matters

ELECTRICAL SUGGESTIONS

The repair, renovation and maintenance of a car's electrical components needs to be addressed, if only because the majority of motoring breakdowns are, in fact, electrically related. The problem is that one can fill a book detailing fault-finding and rectification of the numerous electrical components that make up even our relatively simple cars, and we just do not have the space.

However, there is a 181-page electrical maintenance handbook available for the TR250/6 cars, and much of its contents remain applicable to the TR4/4A models, so I commend it to you. It's currently available direct from the author and details are included in Appendix 1 under 'Electrical'.

The following list of pointers and basic improvements, however, may be helpful, particularly for new TR owners:
● Never buy a car without a set of TR dashboard dials/instruments, even if you recognise they are not original to the car in question. The common and main problem of all TRs is the non-availability of the instruments. It's not recommended that you swap the instruments on TR2, 3, 4 or 4A. Not only is the clamping arrangement of the 5in instruments different, the wiring to

the smaller units could require some major surgery. Instruments from the Sidescreen and Michelotti TRs (4 and 4A) appear, at first sight anyway, generally similar, but they are very different in detail. Consequently, you are better off with a set of TR dials from about the same era to swap/bargain with, than with no instruments at all. Nevertheless, finding the correct dials will be very difficult indeed, particularly if you have not established a partnership-type arrangement with a TR specialist.
● Similarly, if you are about to buy a 'basket case' TR4 or 4A, do check that you not only have a starter motor with your purchase, but that it is the correct one for your engine's flywheel. Starter motors have become very scarce indeed. There was an earlier type of 'shrouded' starter motor that engaged a 91-tooth 'shrunk-on' ring gear. Photographs 7-7-1 and 7-7-2 show the pairing. This starter motor gets its name from the sort of 'shroud' covering the gear that engages the flywheel. The TR4 and TR4A used a motor best identified by its long, exposed (no shroud) bendix gear and shaft, engaging a 90-tooth ring gear bolted to the flywheel. Photographs 7-10-1 and 7-10-2 show both these components. If you have a starter motor, particularly if it's a good one, but

of the incorrect type for your flywheel, it may be easier to change your flywheel than find the correct starter motor! If you mismatch starter and flywheel they may still work - but only for a while. It is, of course, quite unacceptable to some owners, but there are ranges of high torque aftermarket starter motors available today for the TR4 and 4A. You need not be without a method of starting the engine, therefore, provided you do not mind fitting a modern, very efficient, lighter, lower current consumption unit. We will look at these modern units in more detail at a later date.
● The power generating department is, of course, important for any car. In an infrequently and/or little-used TR, however, it has an even greater influence on reliable, and therefore enjoyable, motoring. I make no apologies, therefore, for discussing it from various 'angles', starting with checking the original dynamo (shown in photograph 15-1) generally, and the brushes in particular. Temporarily fit a bare 'jumper' wire between terminals 'D' and 'F' on the regulator, and clip the negative lead of your voltmeter to the centre of this jumper wire. Clip the positive voltmeter lead to the earth on the dynamo and check the voltage with

15-1. A typical early TR dynamo and 'wide' fan/drive belt. Also of note in this photograph is the 4-2 fabricated tubular exhaust manifold.

the engine ticking over at about 800rpm - it should be 15 volts. A reading of about 5 volts will signal a faulty dynamo winding. No reading at all suggests the brushes require replacement, though you could have a broken wire from the dynamo to the regulator, so a continuity check is prudent before you 'tear into' the dynamo.

● In today's traffic it becomes almost a necessity to fit higher intensity headlamps. They are, of course, another non-original detail I have been tempted into mentioning, but they are almost indispensable in today's driving conditions. Sealed beam units are available, but I recommend 'Quad-optic' replacement units, which can be fitted with halogen bulbs giving a slightly stronger light straightaway. Furthermore, you can fit the blue-tinted Xenon bulbs either immediately or in due course, thereby increasing your illumination by a further 30% without a corresponding increase in current. However, it's prudent to consider additional wiring capacity and a relay at the same time, to maximise output without straining the car's original fuse/wiring/switch capacities to breaking point.

● If you wish to fit a modern accessory (in-car audio, for example), bear in mind that such equipment **must** have a negative earth electrical system. You can fit a new (larger or reconditioned) dynamo, of course, but it is possible to re-polarise the original one. All new dynamos come without polarity so, if you are about to fit a replacement, or wish to alter the polarity of your existing dynamo, the first step is to ensure that the battery is disconnected. Fit the dynamo to the car but don't connect the wires up yet. If you are altering the

polarity of your existing dynamo, remove the electrical connections/wires. Temporarily connect a length of 28/0.3 wire (insulated, of course) to the smaller (field) terminal on the dynamo and hold the other end against what you want to be the live terminal of the battery for a few seconds (five should do the trick). Disconnect the temporary wire and restore the original leads to the terminals of the dynamo. You have now fixed the polarity of your dynamo.

Where you have altered the polarity of the system, give very careful thought to all the other electrical components on the car before reconnecting the battery. The ammeter will work, but will show a discharge when in fact you are probably charging nicely, so the terminations at the back of the ammeter will need to be reversed as soon as possible. The starter should not prove a problem, in that it should work with either polarity, as should the lights and the wiper motor. The coil, however, will require an immediate switch of polarity.

You are unlikely to have electronic ignition on a positive earthed car, but could now contemplate one of the aftermarket kits once you have negative earth. In any event, you should go through the electrical fittings on your particular vehicle with care. If you have an audio system pre-fitted before the polarity change, you will at least need to reverse its polarity, but, in truth, you'll probably need to replace it with a negative earthed unit. When in doubt ask your local auto electrical specialist.

Having gone through all that detail related to dynamos, the fact is, however, that any car that needs to be converted to negative earth may be better served by fitting an alternator. This is particularly true where the car will be used infrequently, and/or the owner is thinking about fitting an overdrive and/ or upgrading the headlamps! Read on.

● More power in the generating department is essential if more powerful headlamps are being contemplated, or if an overdrive is to be fitted, particularly if the car is used infrequently. It's not that the overdrive solenoid needs all that extra amperage, but it will lower your engine revolutions and reduce your dynamo's generating capability. Space here is limited so I will have to leave the detail for a later book. However, your TR4/4A's polarity and generating

15-2. Modern alternators are becoming more compact, as this picture confirms. This very neat installation was devised by Revington TR to provide the extra power required by its EFI (Electronic Fuel Injection) conversions. However, there is absolutely nothing to stop you following this alternator installation, even if you are not planning EFI. You should remember, however, that compatible 'V' belt pulleys would be required for the crankshaft and water pump, and that you will need to increase the capacity of the cable from the alternator.

capability can be updated in one step by fitting an alternator. The TR4/4A dynamo has a maximum output of 22 amps at 2000rpm. The point to note is that a dynamo's maximum output is dependent upon significant rpm for an extended period if the battery's charge is to be replenished; and that's without the drain of, say, high capacity headlamps. An ex-TR7 alternator provides greater generating capacity at much lower rpm and is one possible route to getting more power.

Photographs 15-1 and 15-2 compare the original dynamo installation with an alternator installation. The latter uses the deceptively powerful component available from Revington TR. Take a look at picture 15-3 too, and note the cost advantages of this ex-TR6 alternator route. Beware, however, of the knock-on consequences outlined below of changing to an alternator.

● The modern alternator fan/drive belt is a lot thinner than the original TR4/4A drive belt shown in photograph 15-4. Consequently, new crankshaft and water pump pulleys will be required at

15-3. At first glance you may wonder why I have included a picture of a very nice SU carburettor installation. However, if you look below the carbs you will, in fact, spot a neat alternator installation - an ex-TR6 16 ACR I would guess.

15-4. I haven't measured it, but the standard TR fan/drive belt used on all four-cylinder engines must be about twice the width of more modern belts. Here is an original one on a TR4.

the same time as any change of generating method. An advantage of this is that the new 'thin' crankshaft pulley incorporates a harmonic damper which reduces the crankshaft's harmonic cycles. Furthermore, lest you still need convincing, the new 'V' belts generate less friction, less heat, and, therefore, consume less power. It's the way to go!

• Speaking of drive belts, new owners should note that the original 'wide' drive belts were meant to fit and to run fairly loosely, in order to ensure reasonable longevity of the water pump and dynamo bearings. There is plenty of belt-to-pulley contact area, so you do not need to run the wide belts tight to be sure of driving well. Another issue to consider, where wide belts are concerned, is that any engine tuning that increases the usable engine rev range will decrease the life of the belts. So tuning your engine will almost certainly necessitate a change to a thinner drive belt; and, while you're changing the drive-belt, what about an alternator conversion?

• If your horn sounds when you go round bends, the chances are that you have the steering column too far down inside the outer column.

• For maximum longevity, first crimp and then solder the electrical terminations. US readers can buy a

product called 'D5 De-Oxit' which, I understand, cleans and de-oxidises old electrical terminations very effectively.

• A very light smear of copper-slip or petroleum jelly as you push your electrical connections together will aid conductivity and ensure corrosion is kept in check. This is particularly true of connections within the engine bay.

IMPROVING SECURITY

The incidence of car crime has fallen in the UK, lulling many into a false sense of security. This decline may be true in the case of the opportunist thief, but most classic cars tend to be stolen for breaking. This is a major topic, so let's take a few moments to consider the most obvious and fundamental types of car theft in an effort to help you weigh up what security measures are the most cost effective.

Theft from within the car first. High-security (circular) door locks are an absolute waste of time on open car. You are better off removing temptation from sight and using a conspicuous steering-lock. Never leave a locked box or other container on view, for obvious reasons; the place for valuables is in the boot/trunk. However, don't forget that the Michelotti boot lid can be opened when locked, although I'm sure you will agree that it would be silly of me to tell the bad guys precisely how ... Nevertheless, Michelotti boot lids need relatively minor modifications to guard against unauthorised entry.

A spacer between the boot lid skins will make the handle much less prisable, and a large washer welded to the end of the latch pin makes it most unlikely that anyone will succeed in 'forcing' your boot/trunk lid. The cars are so easily entered via a slit in the hood, or by a flat piece of metal down the outside of the window, that it's hardly worth fitting improved locks to the doors. Better to fit a good lock (part-number AHA8532S) to your boot, and leave the rest of the car with its original, if ineffective, arrangements!

We are all aware of the opportunistic thief who strikes when your car is left on the drive, or outside a shop 'for a moment'. The moral of this is: more care with the keys, less heartache! An immobiliser will help but only if the keys aren't to hand. Although the immobiliser I have seems easy to circumnavigate, it would take time and should, therefore, deter this type of thief. Although most cars stolen in this way are recovered, they have usually been vandalised and an attempt made to disguise their identity. It's a good idea to hide something in the car (*e.g.* a business card) or to keep photographs of a couple of unique features on your car (*e.g.* a special carburettor or seat mounting, *etc.*).

The next most easily deterred thief is the joy rider, who is bound to be looking to make a fairly quick getaway, albeit with your car! Security etching on the glass is not going to deter him, nor may a steering lock, since I understand that these thieves are able to remove all but a select few very quickly indeed. However, for those whose cars have electric fuel pumps, a well-hidden fuel cut-off switch may delay the thief sufficiently to make him decide to try an easier target, particularly if the car also has an immobiliser.

My immobiliser cuts off the feed to the starter but I believe immobilisers are available that also cut off the ignition and/or fuel supply. I would personally prefer to fit two separate devices so that potential thieves have two obstacles to overcome, so I suggest you fit a commercial immobiliser in addition to your own fuel/ignition cut-out.

Unfortunately, the majority of carburettor TRs use a mechanical fuel pump which precludes the use of a security device!

It's very hard to put off the professional thief that wants your car for its parts, or in order to 'ring' it with another identity. I've even heard about a car, fitted with an immobiliser, that was stolen from a double-locked garage, even though the keys were kept safely indoors. In this case, the police established that the car had been broken within 24 hours of the theft. The thieves had winched the car onto a transporter, giving witnesses the impression that the car was being taken away for repair.

Your only defence is not to advertise your address, and to have the car fitted with a vehicle-locating device, such as Tracker or Securicor's Trackback. These devices are the most expensive precautions you can take and, although I speak without personal experience, I believe they can pinpoint the location of your car very quickly indeed.

Make a note of all the serial numbers and try to clearly but unobtrusively mark the chassis and body parts with some identification. A few centre-popped initials may enable you to prove to the police that a particular part is from your car.

Take particular care if offering your car for sale. Don't allow potential purchasers to see it in the garage, and don't tell them about its security protection until the deal is concluded and you have received the money.

Because car anti-theft devices are becoming so effective, often the only simple way a thief can steal a car is to break into the owner's house and steal the keys first. This is happening on an ever increasing scale, which is partly why the car theft statistics are coming down - since a car stolen by this route is now officially categorised as burglary. Such cars are often still broken within a few hours, but this trend extends your area of car-care to the house generally, and to where you keep the keys to your car(s) in particular. Therefore, as far as is practical, it's a good idea to keep the car's location as private as possible. Indeed, along with weighing-up car security measures, you may be wise to consider comparable security measures for your home as well!

Finally, a few thoughts on immobilisers, the first of which is get one fitted! There are basically two ways to achieve this, and we'll talk about the professional installation company first.

Immobilisers cost between £100 and £200, and even up to £500, but this does include installation. I don't feel the more expensive immobiliser/alarm systems are value for money. How many times have we all ignored flashing lights or a blaring horn as being a false alarm? Nevertheless, whatever level of system and whatever fitting route you choose in the UK, you must only select a 'Thatcham' approved system. This means that the equipment has been tested and approved by the Motor Insurance Research Centre located at Thatcham.

The professional installer will give you a certificate upon completion of the job that could get you an insurance discount, or put you on better terms with the insurance company should the worst happen. I believe you will only get a certificate if a professional installer fits your immobiliser, which is one reason

why you need to have an accredited company supply and install the system. You can add sensors to some systems (such as level sensors that detect the vehicle being lifted, or hot-wire ignition sensors), and you should discuss your options with a couple of Vehicle Security Installation Board (VSIB) accredited businesses.

Alternatively, you could install an approved system yourself, which is not without its advantages. Firstly, you can - and indeed should - 'bury' the wires within the car's main harness to make detection of the immobiliser very difficult indeed. Secondly, you can take the precaution of using male and female connections at the points where the system interfaces directly with the car's wiring, to give you the option of bypassing the immobiliser circuits in the event of its failure. This feature is particularly valuable in roadside situations. I recall one situation where someone could not leave the cross-channel ferry since their car's alarm was locked 'on', apparently by the ship's radar! Obviously, you need to ensure that the bypass connections are not obvious (hidden under some black tape?) and located so as not to compromise the security of the car.

BONNET RELEASE CABLES

You may be wondering what's so special about the car's bonnet release cable. Have a look at the car's rear-mounted bonnet catch and picture how difficult it will be to open the bonnet without a serviceable release cable. A broken or seized bonnet release cable is not an infrequent problem; and the consequences will be frustrating, time consuming, and potentially expensive.

Please do follow my advice, starting with the obvious: lubricate both the cable and the latch assembly. It's worthwhile going to the trouble of separating the inner cable from the outer, and applying lots of 'copper-slip' before feeding the inner cable back inside the outer. Feeding a used inner into the outer can be frustrating, but I assure you that it's even worth buying a new inner/outer cable assembly and lubricating it properly before fitting it to your car.

I strongly recommend you arrange some form of secondary or emergency release mechanism; a discussion with

15-5. Bonnet/hood releases. The photograph shows a simple, effective secondary/emergency bonnet/hood release, achieved via one extra hole in the side of the catch assembly and one extra hole in the arm just behind the normal release arrangement. During manufacture, the 'skin' of the catch assembly metal becomes work-hardened, and each hole may first require a small ground spot to break through the 'skin' of the metal. The additional cable is a cut down original, routed through the bulkhead/firewall from an additional bracket fixed slightly in front of the right side 'A' post. It works so well that it has become my standard method of opening the bonnet/ hood. The gauze-topped cylinder is an anti run-on valve.

your local TR group will provide a wide variety of ideas. My method was to fit the second bonnet release cable and bracket shown in picture 15-5, with a second bonnet release pull fixed to the right side of the car. An improved version from PDI (see Appendix 1) can be seen in picture 15-6.

It's important that you fix the second bracket to the right side 'A' post very securely indeed; you'd be surprised just how much strength is occasionally required to release the bonnet catch. Mind you, one significant benefit of a right side release catch is that you can (with an open window) press down on the bonnet (above the catch), simultaneously pulling on your new right side cable toggle. You will find the bonnet releases very easily; so easily, in fact, that I now rarely use the 'proper' release cable on the left side of my car.

Photograph 15-5 shows how I married my second cable to the release catch.

Well, so much for prevention. What do we do if the release cable is already broken? The good news is that, unless your car consumes vast quantities of oil and/or water, you should be able to use the car until the problem is resolved. I have, however, heard of owners having to drill a hole in the bonnet to activate the release catch. Hopefully one of the following suggestions will help you avoid such desperate measures!

Assuming the cable has seized rather than broken, first of all, have a helper push down on the bonnet, perhaps an inch forward of the rear edge, as close to the catch as you can judge. If this works the most likely problem was a poorly lubricated cable or catch, but a poorly adjusted catch or bonnet stops can bring about the same symptoms. If this initial step proves unsuccessful, but still assuming the inner cable has not actually broken, try unscrewing the outer cable's securing nut. Ease the inner/outer cables out of the mounting bracket and, again with your helper pushing down on the bonnet, give both inner and outer cables a good pull. Still no luck? Time, then, to visit your nearest friendly garage with a car lift/hoist, for an 'underside attack' on the problem.

The first approach is a 'long-shot'. See if you can lever the catch arm towards the right side of the car with a long rod. Take great care with this, for you will be very close to two power terminals, one on the rear of the starter motor, the other being the positive battery terminal. The latter sits just a couple of inches (50mm) from the catch arm. Consequently, a stout wooden pole might be best.

It's possible to unbolt the hinges at the front of the bonnet from the underside of the car while you have it on the ramp, and this will most likely result in the rear catch unfastening. However, and particularly if you have a LHD car, you may prefer to remove the glove/cubby pocket first, and try to reach the catch arm through one of the bulkhead/firewall holes. Remember the proximity of the battery termination, and that the catch arm needs to be levered towards the right side of the car (the kerb-side on a LHD car). You'll probably have to remove several air hoses from under the dashboard/fascia of later cars to stand any chance of success. If you are able to get a screwdriver to the catch, have a helper take the pressure off the catch arm by pushing down on the appropriate point of the bonnet. Do ensure that your helper pushes down quite close to the rear lip of the bonnet if you wish to avoid a dent.

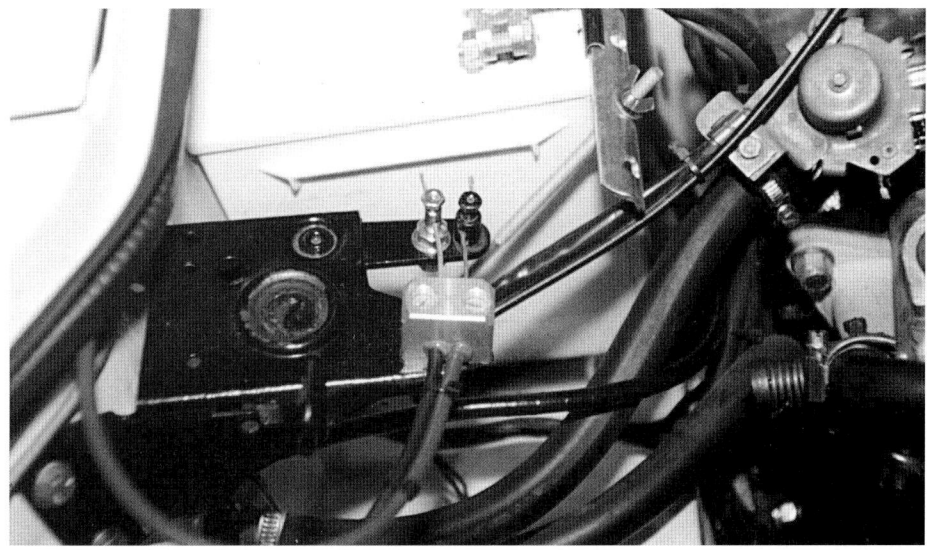

15-6. This slightly more sophisticated, but very neat, solution is available from PDI (Prestige Developments and Injection).

Chapter 16
Interior trim

RESTORING THE WOOD VENEER

Most TR4s didn't have a wooden fascia/dashboard since it was an optional extra that, I believe, few exercised. The TR4A, on the other hand, had a wood veneered dashboard/fascia that screwed onto a metal back. It's made up of a plywood base with a thin hardwood veneer stuck to the visible face. The veneer is then finished with a coat of clear varnish (some satin finish, some gloss) in order to seal and protect the veneer and, of course, to add to the aesthetics of the cockpit.

If your base plywood and/or veneer is obviously damaged, there is nothing for it but to purchase a replacement dashboard/fascia - they are readily available in the original finishes, as well as some, to my eyes, very attractive burr-walnut finishes. However, the purpose of this section is to explore the possible salvage of a fascia that looks cracked and split.

The veneer itself, beneath the varnish, may not be as bad as it appears at first sight. The varnish can crack, allowing dirt to get into the cracks and onto the veneer, making the fascia appear a lost cause. It may not be, and, since you have nothing to lose, try

careful, slow and gentle stripping of the varnish off the front of the veneer once you have the dash out of the car and all the fixtures and fittings removed from it. You could well find International Coatings' (free) booklet on yacht paint and varnishing very helpful (see Appendix 1).

You will need a mild varnish-stripping chemical that will soften the varnish. A flat bladed wallpaper stripper, or similar tool (not too sharp or you endanger the veneer beneath the varnish), should get most of the varnish off if you have applied sufficient stripper and left it on long enough to do its work. For any remaining stubborn varnish spots, apply a second coat of stripper and gently scrape again, before finally wiping down with white sprit to clean the dash and remove the worst of the dirt that will have become ingrained in the veneer.

Carefully inspect the veneer at this point; it may turn out to be cracked and will need to be professionally re-veneered. If you have managed to remove most of the 'crazing', it's probable that your dash/fascia can be returned to its original glory by gentle cleaning (with white spirits) until the dirt is gone. Avoid sanding, if possible, although, if you feel the surface of the

veneer will benefit from a light hand 'dusting', it is possible to use a very fine paper on a flat block to gently freshen-up the veneer. It's essential, however, that you proceed slowly and with caution.

Most of those TRs that were fitted with a wood dash/fascia originally had a high-gloss finish, with only the very late examples using the gentler 'satin' finish. This is your chance to apply whatever finish you feel appropriate for your restoration (i.e. gloss or satin). A chandlery is one possible source of the clear polyurethane exterior varnish you will require. Applying the varnish in several thin coats using a model maker's spray is likely to give the best result, but you could also experiment with a foam brush on a scrap piece of furniture before taking the plunge!

SOUND DEADENING FELT AND CARPET FITTING

The first order of business is to equip yourself with a good quality, generously cut carpet and sound deadening kit, such as you will get from the premier TR specialists mentioned in Appendix 1. You will need several sharp blades, or a Stanley knife, and two types of adhesive: an aerosol of spray-on adhesive (500ml) and a ($1/2$ litre) tin of contact adhesive. The former will allow perhaps 5 to 10 minutes adjustment time before it sets, while the latter, as the name implies, sets on contact. The second, but equally important, point to note before starting work is to appreciate that these adhesives can be both your friend and a problem if, for example, you are careless with their application. Ensure you have plenty of working space around the car, and remember that the aerosol adhesive can be carried on the wind or by a draught, which could result in adhesive over-spray all over your car. Never, therefore, spray adhesive outside!

When it's unavoidable that you spray directly onto the car, move the car inside and ensure that draughts are minimised. Ascertain which solvent will remove surplus adhesive without damaging car, felt or carpet. My first choice is white spirit (known as mineral spirit in the US), but you may need to resort to petrol (gas) to remove some modern adhesives. Have some solvent(s) handy, for mistakes are best corrected as quickly as possible.

Assuming you are trimming right through the car, remove (or do not fit in the first place) the steering wheel and the 'H' dashboard/fascia support, and undo the door-check strap bolts (one per door), but leave them in place until you need the door wide open. Prior to

fitting, it really is a good idea to lay all carpets and felt out flat overnight. Try to minimise having to drill or even screw through carpet since the drill, the chuck, or the screw, can 'pick-up' a carpet thread and pull out a very unsightly line of weave. Always use a very small pilot drill if you have to drill through a piece of carpet (about $1/32$in diameter or less than 1mm), and roll back the carpet and open the pilot hole first. Always stick several layers of masking tape on top of the weave to protect the carpet from the chuck when your drill 'breaks-through'. This will have the added advantage of telling you where your drill hole is! Don't laugh, it really is all too easy to lose the hole in the carpet and no fun at all when you are working at the bottom of a deep footwell!

Always use a (usually conical) 'cup' washer under the screw head when fixing the carpet with a screw. During the course of this chapter I will refer to a number of small washers, fittings and clips that not every reader will be familiar with. Therefore, it seemed a good idea to correctly identify most of your requirements, so I hope that photographs 16-1 and 16-2 will help, while drawing D16-1 identifies the respective felt, carpet and trim panels for a TR4A. The TR4 differs slightly in that its handbrake comes through the floor on the right side of the tunnel, while the TR4A handbrake is mounted atop the

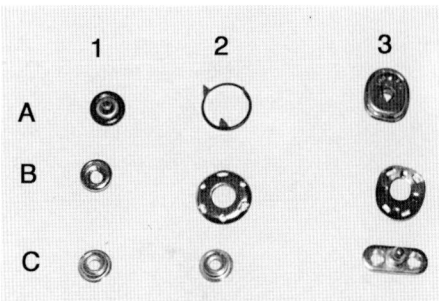

16-1. TR4 trimming fastenings. Column 1 shows the 'snap' fastening components used inside the hood. Column 2 the carpet clips. Column 3 shows the constituent male/peg and external female parts of the 'lift-the-dot' fastenings used around the rear of the hood. You will note some common usage with the later car's fastenings shown in picture 16-2. An aid for fixing the lift-the-dots will be found in chapter 17.

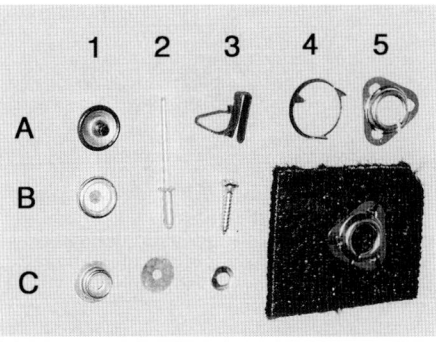

16-2. TR4A fastenings. Column 1 shows the three types of 'snap' fastenings used at the rear of the hood. Column 2 the pop rivet and its essential washer. Column 3 the panel fastening clips, chrome screws and cup washers. Columns 4 and 5 show the two-piece carpet clips which, after assembly either side of the carpet, clip to the base fastening in the bottom left of the picture.

prop tunnel.

With one or two exceptions the sequence of fitting is not absolutely crucial and you will note that, on several occasions, the photographs show a slightly different sequence to the one I am proposing in the text. Nevertheless, the drawing and photographs should help you sort the basic sequence of fitting. Photographs 16-3 and 16-4 show a couple of the preparatory steps needed for some carpet sets.

Finally, in general, always pull surplus carpet, or smooth any wrinkles, from the centre of the car outwards.

Start your trimming with carpet 1, as per D16-1, the one with the substantial 'U'-shaped cut-out. This

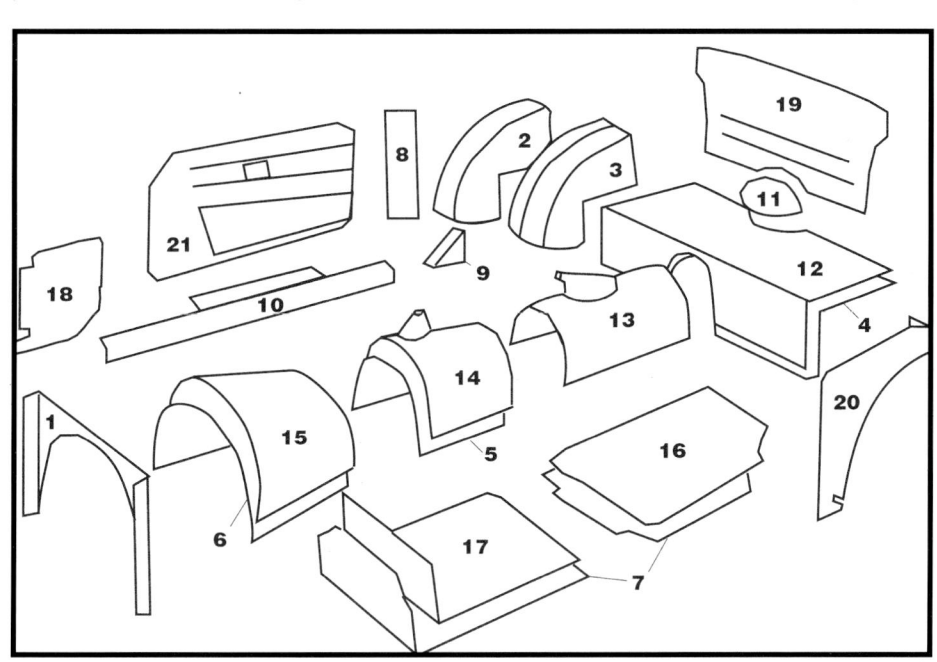

D16-1. Fitting sequence for felt, carpet and trim panels.

needs to be stuck to the bulkhead/ firewall using aerosol spray adhesive, with holes for speedometer and accelerator/gas cables neatly cut before you finally smooth the carpet flat. This will ease you into the trimming task and is one of the simpler carpets since there is no underfelt required.

The rear wheelarches are your first serious trimming task. Your wheelarch kit will include two pieces of $1/8$in (3mm) foam (2) which need to be stuck to the wheelarches to deaden the road noise and to give the subsequent cover a more luxurious feel. Apply the spray glue to the wheelarch, wait for it to become very tacky (to almost finish 'flashing-off'), and then apply the foam to the wheelarch. If you spray the glue directly onto the foam, or position the foam too early, you run the risk of the foam 'taking-up' the glue and then going rock-hard as the glue dries.

The foam pieces need to be undersize so that they do not reach (by about 0.5in or 12mm) the rear and floor panels. The vinyl covers (which we will be applying shortly), must stick to the car, not to the foam. Photograph 16-5 shows the work underway, but with the all-important edge trimming yet to be completed. Cut any surplus foam away at the corners too, since one thickness of foam is more than sufficient!

Let the adhesive set first, of course, and then draw a line with felt-tip or marker pen on the outside of the foam 4in (100mm) from and parallel to each inner wing, starting at the top/rear and finishing where the wheelarch meets the floor. Turn your vinyl wheelarch cover (3) inside-out, and offer it to the wheelarch to ensure that any seat belt mounting point, usually welded to each wheelarch, does not cause the loose inside edge of the piping/beading to bulge. You may need to move the cover just slightly, and/or trim a fraction off the inside edge of the piping. With the cover still inside-out, very lightly spray the whole of the inside of the cover, concentrating most of the adhesive round the edges of the cover. Allow this to 'flash off' for as long as you dare to minimise the take up of glue into the foam, but allowing some adjustment time. Do not spray the adhesive onto the foam.

Apply the vinyl arch cover, concentrating initially on getting the piping/bead to lay along your felt-tip

16-3. Some sound deadening felt has been fixed to the top of the tank - which is not the good idea it may at first seem. Fuel and water have been known to leak from the filler cap hole in the rear deck. The felt soaks up the fluid and both increases and prolongs the fire-hazard if it's fuel, or adds to the possibility of corrosion if it's water. The place for that piece of sound deadening felt is along the front of the tank. The picture is interesting for a second reason - fixing the carpet to the propshaft cover behind the handbrake. Obviously, every car can be completed to individual preference, but my main text recommends you do not fix the propshaft cover until you have glued the carpet to it. Third point of interest, I wonder how many noted that the triangular gussets on this car have been cut away adjacent to the centre of the wheelarch? It really is a good idea to completely replace, or at least make good, these load-carrying stiffeners when you are doing your panel work and welding. Some restorers even weld an 18swg sheet across the full front of the tank, to stiffen the bodyshell and act as a firewall.

16-4. This TR4A carpet set provides separate handbrake and gearbox gaiters. Most carpet sets have these already sewn into the relevant carpets. You will hardly need me to tell you that you must fix the gearbox cover before starting trimming, but you may be interested to know this is a modern plastic moulded version, which, though tiresome to fit, offers excellent longevity compared to the original moulded board.

16-5. Back to the rear of the car; this is part way through the first step of covering the rear wheelarch, the thin foam stage. Note how the foam has been carried backwards almost as far as the back of the tank, which will also help deaden road noise. The excess foam lying along the floor, and the edge of that running round the bottom of the wheelarch, is about to be trimmed away to provide a gap of at least a 0.5in (12mm), where the wheelarch abuts the rear shelf pan. This apparently minor adjustment is important, since it allows the vinyl cover to be glued directly to the wheelarch. The final trimming operation will be to remove the excess (arrowed) that runs in an arc around the wheelarch. Note the advice in the main text about keeping the foam as free of glue as possible to stop it losing its soft 'luxury' feel!

line, starting at the top and working towards the bottom/floor of the car. Your next job must be to get the outside (4in wide) strip of the cover to lay smoothly and straight over the upper part of the arch from top to bottom. With this almost to your satisfaction, flip the inside-out lower part of the cover over the lower inside of the wheelarch and ensure that this, too, lays pretty smoothly over the foam. Some final adjustments should still be possible before the glue sets, enabling you to remove any minor wrinkles from the cover.

You need to allow about 1in (25mm) of vinyl to carry-over and stick to each of the adjoining panels, but the most important part of this work is the long radius over the top of the wheelarch. You will need to snip the 1in overlap every inch or so around its periphery, so that it lays unwrinkled against the inner wing. Take great care not to make these cuts too deep initially, for they could show when the job is finished. Better to try a short snip first,

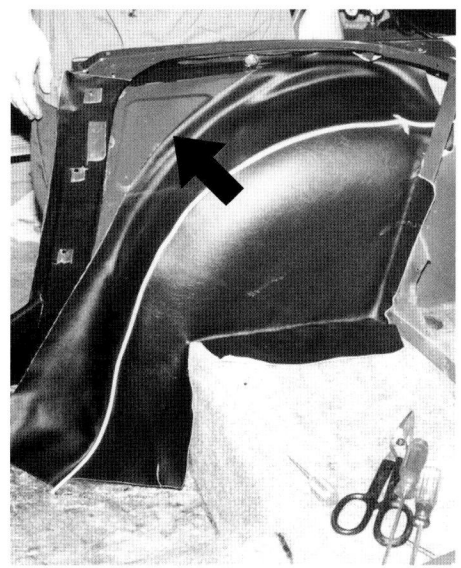

16-6. The wheelarch covering is about 90% complete. All TR4s and '4As had white beading, which needs to be carefully aligned to the inner wing, with as much vinyl as possible turned round the edges of the corner. These turned 'lips' will lay flatter if they are cut radially (arrowed) when they run round a radius, such as a wheelarch.

even if you have to extend it a bit later. The corners of the cover (where they meet each adjoining panel) will also require trimming. A single cut at 45 degrees to the angle is usually sufficient to allow the surplus vinyl to overlap while still laying flat. These cuts aren't too critical since carpets or panels will cover them as trimming proceeds!

Photograph 16-6 illustrates the second step of one of the most difficult parts of the trimming work. You would be well advised to carefully cut provisions for any seat belt mountings, as shown in picture 16-21, and to smooth the vinyl cover down before the glue finally sets.

Next up are some of the sound-deadening felt pieces, that need to be stuck in place with spray adhesive. The first pieces to position are those above the differential and on the adjacent vertical heel board. I will explain why shortly, but I would not glue the felt that goes over the fibreboard propshaft tunnel cover in place. Instead, glue the smaller gearbox cover felt (mostly behind the gear lever, but numbered 5 in D16-1) in place. The final piece of glued sound-deadening felt you should attach at this stage covers the front or main part of the gearbox cover (6).

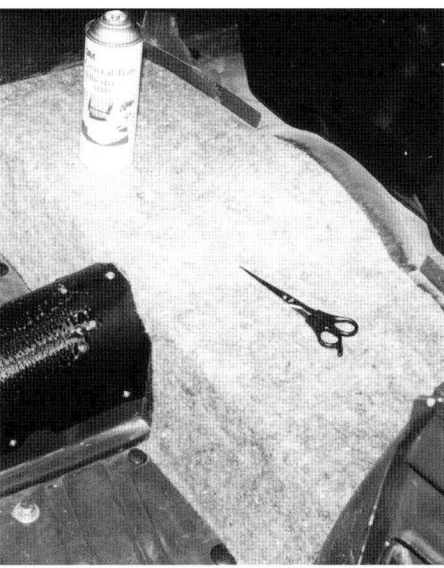

16-7. The sound deadening felt going in on the rear shelf using the aerosol of spray adhesive shown. The scissors need to be newly-sharpened if you are going to cut neat edges to the felt and for any carpet trimming that may follow. The cover for this '4A's handbrake cables has just been glued, ready for the sound deadening felt. In the main text I suggest you may get a better carpet fit by gluing the carpet to the cover with the cover flat, outside the car. However, there is no 'right' way of carrying out the trimming, and you should do what you think best.

Photographs 16-7 and 16-8 help you understand what has to be done.

Fit the rubber gaiters around the gear lever/shift. You can cut the four footwell felts (7) to shape, as the pictures show, but do not glue these in place. In fact, once cut to size, these footwell pieces need to be removed and placed to one side for the time being. Make sure that the felt is cut away (photograph 16-9) to allow the 'H' dash/fascia support casting mounting feet and the seat runners (photograph 16-10) to be bolted in place in due course.

Spray-glue and fit the two 'B' post vinyl strips (8) so that they wrap around the door frame lip (they will eventually be covered by the furflex door-seal), yet extend back behind where the quarter panels fit. It's a good idea to cut away where the fastenings will come a little later (as photograph 16-11 shows), or possibly to make a small hole with an awl.

We can now finish off the preparation at the rear of the car by covering the two triangular gussets at the

16-8. Cracking-on now. The gearbox cover and prop tunnel felts will have been glued in place, but the floor felts will have been only laid in place and cut to size, but not glued, as explained in the main text.

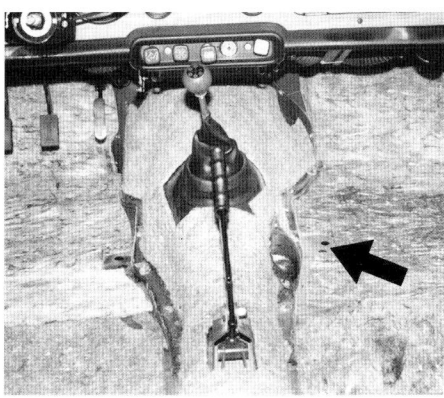

16-9.

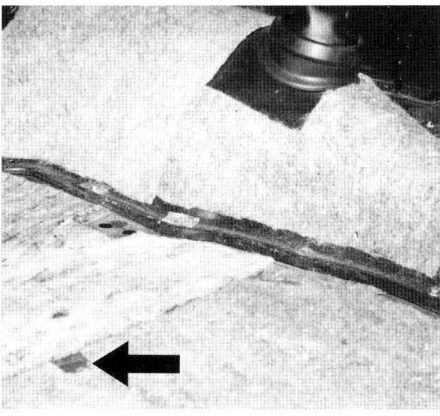

16-9 and 16-10 (above). Two views of the felt in place. Have you noted the fairly generous cut-outs for access to the mounting holes for the 'H' support bracket, and provision for the seat mounting bolts? Both are arrowed. Note, too, that the steering wheel has been removed for (slightly) easier access to the footwells. I imagine that any access holes in the gearbox cover will have corresponding holes cut in the underfelt very shortly, if not in the carpet.

16-12 and 16-13 (right). This carpet set included a special underlay for the sill carpet and wheelarch covers which, at least as far as the sills are concerned, is a definite plus and will give the sill a more luxurious feel and deaden noise, too. Here we see that the 'B' post corner gusset has been trimmed and the underlay glued in place over most of the sills. Can you spot the rear wiring harness - correctly positioned before the carpet was laid, and now sneaking under the carpet for added protection?

16-11. The 'B' post cover in place. Note the cutaways to allow each quarter-panel to be easily screwed/clipped in place in due course. However, the covering is better applied perhaps 1in (25mm) further forward. This allows it to be wrapped around the lip onto which the furflex seal will eventually be pushed.

base of each 'B'-post. These have a board stiffener inside each vinyl covering which needs to be bent over to lay along the top edge of the triangular gusset. Use contact adhesive for strength when fixing these particular trims.

Sill carpets (10) are next. There is usually no sound deadening foams or felt to worry about with these, just where to position the carpets relative to the sill, although the trimming kit shown in photographs 16-12 and 16-13 did actually include an underlay, just to confuse you! Underlay or no underlay, it's not difficult to position the sill carpets since the front of the triangular gusset at the base of each 'B'-post provides the longitudinal reference. Once you have established which carpet goes which side if the car (this will quickly become clear if you lay them roughly in place), you will note that part of the top of each sill carpet is finished off with a piece of vinyl or tape. This is intended to go over the sill lip beneath the furflex door seal that you will eventually position around the

door opening.

Your first point of reference is to marry the rear of this tape to the front of the 'B'-post gusset we spoke of earlier. You will also need to think about positioning each carpet relative to its sill. The plan here is to butt the carpet as tight to the top/outside edge of the sill as possible, without allowing the carpet to 'turn-up' towards the door - which, in due course, would prevent the furflex from fitting as intended. The vinyl strip or tape will, of course, 'turn up' towards the door, but that is as intended for it's thin enough for the furflex to slip over without a problem.

These carpets need to be glued with contact adhesive, which, although stronger than the spray-on adhesives, allows very little time (if any) to adjust the fit. I always use 'Trim-Tack' adhesive, which does give you a few moments grace to sort out any wrinkles! A tip you might find helpful is to put the sill carpets in place in 'step' sequence. By this I mean, stick down the top of the carpet the full length of the sill, before turning your attention to the full length of the vertical face, and finally the surplus inch or so that sits on the floor. The end result is shown in photograph 16-14.

Now to carpet the heel-board and rear-shelf, both of which are situated behind the seats and numbered 11 and 12 on drawing D16-1. Spray glue over the small oval-shaped piece of carpet, and locate it on the existing felt over the

differential bulge. Position is not critical, but if you want to double check all is well, you could offer-up the (not glued as yet) main rear shelf carpet to reassure yourself and make any adjustments. Spray glue over the main rear shelf carpet and pop that in place. The vertical heel board carpet is next (using spray adhesive), and you should expect/allow about 1in of surplus carpet to run forward onto the rear of the floorpans. Photograph 16-15 shows where we

16-14. The sill carpet looks great and gives the impression that the trimming really is starting to take shape. Regrettably, however, this carpet set stops the sill carpet at least 12in (300mm) short of the front of the sill, and also omits the vinyl strip that was originally fixed to the top of the sill carpets. As a consequence, there is nothing to turn over the bottom door lip, and the furflex door seal cannot, therefore, restrain the carpet, as was originally the case.

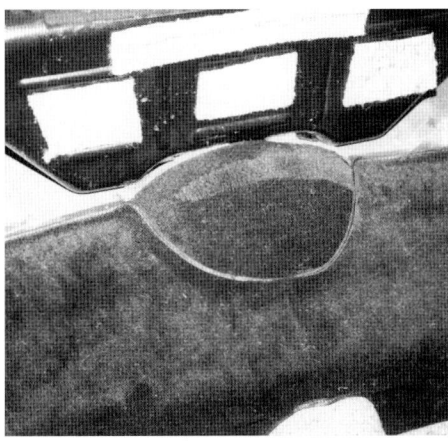

16-15. The hump of the differential was first covered with the oval carpet from the set, with the rear panel/heel board carpet glued in place shortly afterwards. Surplus felt has been stuck to the front of the tank to act as sound deadening ... a very good idea.

16-16. The propshaft carpet glued to the underboard, shown by the absence of wrinkles. I would prefer to see both seat underfelts removed from the car as, currently, they look to be getting towards the point of becoming immovable!

have got to so far.

Forward a few feet is the propshaft tunnel (13), where there is a choice to be made. Many a TR has been successfully trimmed by having sound-deadening felt stuck to the fibreboard cover and the carpet pulled over the handbrake and stuck in place. However, this 'traditional' method tends to result in the carpet sitting loosely on the prop tunnel, so I am going to recommend an alternative that I think our premier TR restorers now use pretty much as standard. It does mean that the sound-deadening felt is dispensed with here, but the neater appearance of the resulting installation more than makes up for this.

Unscrew the fibreboard prop tunnel cover from the car, lay it flat on the bench and find the rearmost centre point (across the width of the car). Lay the prop tunnel carpet face down on the bench and find and mark the centre point at the rear of the carpet. Offer the centre of the fibreboard cover to the centre of the carpet and roll the fibreboard from side to side marking the carpet where the outside edges of the fibreboard cover come. Remove the fibreboard cover and re-mark the carpet with two lines, each about 1.5in (say 40mm) nearer the centre than the original outside edges of the fibreboard cover. Contact-glue just the area of the carpet inside these two lines and, making sure that the centre points are aligned, stick the fibreboard cover to the

carpet (with both flat on the bench). The two outside lips of this cover/carpet assembly should not be stuck together, which means you should be able to lift both edges of the carpet to re-screw the fibreboard cover (and, now, propshaft carpet) back in place. If you are in any doubt, hopefully photograph 16-16 will help.

The gearbox cover now gets our attention, starting with the smaller rearward piece (14) that should be positioned over the gear lever and its underfelt. The main gearbox cover carpet (15) has a reputation for being difficult, but you should find (already fitted) (or can easily rivet) four male press studs to your gearbox cover. If you have added sound deadening felt this will complicate the issue slightly, but only to the extent of having to cut a 1in (25mm) or so clearance around each stud in the felt. The special auto carpet clips are virtually invisible rings that are pushed through the carpet and turned over, whereupon they clip to the bases riveted to the gearbox tunnel. Incidentally, if you are fitting the male studs and the associated carpet clips together, they are exactly the same as those you would fit to hold the floor carpets in place, and can be seen in photographs 16-1 and 16-2.

We now need to position the four sound-deadening panels for the floors (item 7 on our sequence drawing) and, in particular, cut four 1in (25mm) diameter clearance holes in each felt - in

the rear felts these are for the seat runner mounting bolts and, in the front pair, for the carpet clips. I would use a sharp pointed instrument like a scriber or awl to find where the holes should go, and then cut them with a blade outside the car. You need to be more careful when it comes to cutting holes in the actual carpet, but with the rear pair of felts and carpets held in place by your seat runners, you will appreciate that gluing the rear pair of felts is quite unnecessary.

The forward footwell felts (7) and carpets (17), are best spray-glued together, but I suggest you refrain from gluing the felt to the floor in case you wish to remove the footwell covers for cleaning, drying-out, or to vacuum the footwells. Instead, you should rivet four press-stud bases to the floor each side (don't forget the washer for the other side of the rivet!), and secure the carpet/ felt with carpet clips. The two forward ones are really on the bulkhead/firewall and are, therefore, best riveted in place before you fit the steering wheel and pedals! Take care getting the alignment of bases and clips right. I found it best to rivet the male snap fastening to the floor and to then use a very strong needle pushed through the carpet to establish the centre of the female clip. Photographs 16-17 and 16-18 illustrate footwell carpet fitting.

Last but not least, the two front kick-panels (18) on the outside of each footwell need to be glued to the fibreboard backing panels and screwed in place. Pretty straightforward really, except it's a good idea to have an inch or two of furflex door-seal handy as you do need to get the carpets just right fore and aft. Too far back and you will not get the furflex properly in place, too far forward and you will have a (possibly difficult to see) gap between carpet and seal. Photograph 16-19 is interesting ...

INTERNAL TRIM PANELS

I have not described how to remove the trim, as it's pretty self-explanatory. However, one detail that may help is how to remove the old door panels, and the internal door and window handles in particular.

Window handles are actually pinned in place, but the pins are usually hidden by the trim panel, which is pushed outwards by two coil springs

16-17.

16-19. The central, almost 'U'-shaped carpet has been previously glued to the bulkhead at the front of the gearbox cover, and the side footwell carpets have been glued to the mill board backing and are being located prior to screwing in place. Note how the access to the footwell area has been improved by temporarily removing the door 'keeps' (just to the left of the top awl) which is a good idea provided you don't allow the door to open too wide and damage your paint. Might be even better to install the check straps simultaneously with the doors and just remove the (single) connecting bolt as and when you need extra access.

16-20. The 4A's rear panel/tank board screwed into position. Read the main text to appreciate the importance of centralising the first hole/screw and the sequence thereafter. If you align the central panel line, you will see the central screw does indeed fall dead centre to the differential. It's a matter of choice whether you fit the side trim panels before or after the tank panel, but, should you choose to fit the sides after the tank panel, it's a good idea to leave the end tank panel screws out until the sides are in place.

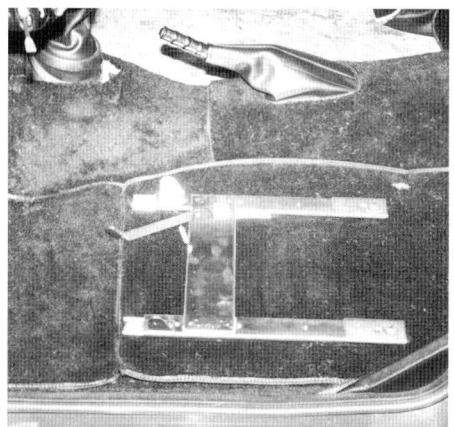

16-17 and 16-18 (above). Two views of the floor carpets which are placed in the footwells but not glued, because of the possibility (that's a probability in the UK!) of the carpets getting soaked and having to be removed and dried before corrosion can set in.

positioned behind the door trim panels. To release the two pins per door, push the trim panel inwards at each handle revealing a cross hole in each square drive, and push each pin out with a small screwdriver. Try not to lose the pins, although, when we get to re-assembly, I will tell you a little trick of the trade, so all is not lost!

Moving swiftly on, the rear or tank panel numbered 19 on our sequence drawing is the first trim panel to fix in TR4As or TR4s with a Surrey top. The

soft top TR4s had a seat back that we will discuss in a few pages time. The patterns on your panels may differ slightly from that shown in some of the attached pictures, but that will not detract from the validity of the sequence or method of application. Start by carefully measuring the tank panel to find the top dead centre point. You need to apply equal care to find the top centre of the rear deck of the car and, if there is a hole pre-drilled from an earlier life, whether it is indeed dead centre. If the rear deck hole is dead centre, then drill the tank panel (judge the height carefully) to allow you to screw through the tank panel with a chromed trim screw and special chromed conical/cup washer (available from any TR restoration specialist). If the rear deck centre hole is not dead centre, ignore it and drill both panel and deck dead centre! Sadly, in the majority of cases, the holes in the rear deck will be non-symmetrical, and you will almost certainly have to drill new holes in both panel and deck.

Whichever you have to do, make sure you only position one screw at a time. Work outwards from the centre, alternating fixing screws from side to side to keep the panel position as even, flat and symmetrical as possible. You will

only have two screws to fix each side of the centre fastening since the outside screw each side is best left off the car for a few moments. Photograph 16-20 shows the end result but, incidentally, when drilling through this, and indeed the other vinyl panels, it really is a good idea to protect the vinyl from the drill chuck with a couple of layers of masking tape. It's a very skilled trimmer that can exert enough pressure to get through the rear deck metal and still stop the chuck from touching the vinyl when the drill breaks through. It will help if you make sure your drill tip is sharp and, for the cost involved, new ones really are worthwhile. Be aware of and guard against the possibility of snagging the drill tip in the layer of foam beneath the vinyl. The result is the drill caught in ball of foam and a torn/ruined vinyl panel. It's also worthwhile, though a complicated process requiring three hands, to use a piece of metal to compress the vinyl/foam while drilling each hole. A 1in (25mm) 'washer' with about a 2 or 3mm diameter hole should help, and also ensure that the chuck does not touch the vinyl. The masking tape is still important, however - to prevent the washer marking your vinyl.

Offer up the two rear quarter panels (numbered 20 on the drawing and also shown in photograph 16-21), to the inner rear wings above the wheelarches. Align the vertical edges; again, it could be useful to have a couple of inches of furflex door seal to hand to ensure that the vertical edge is the correct distance back from each 'B'-post. The furflex will need (eventually) to go fully onto the 'B'-post before it touches the front of each quarter trim panel.

The trim panels are held on with three chromed screws and conical or 'cup' washers around the top, and a couple of hidden clips lower down. The key detail that may not be clear if your car has already had its trim panels removed is that each rear/inner vinyl 'tail' from each of these panels needs to be tucked behind the outside ends of the tank panel we put in place a few minutes ago. Consequently, it is only at this point should you fit the outside screws to the tank panel. If your quarter panels are fitted using the clips I mentioned, you should never hit them with anything hard, a clenched fist should be sufficient and will not damage the panels. Care is required when fitting the front top screws to each panel. If these two screws (one each side) are too long you will mark the deck panel by an outward 'bubble' in your paintwork, which would somewhat spoil that day's work!

The first step with the door trim panels is to buy and cover the inside of the door with heavy-duty polythene sheet, as shown by picture 16-22, to protect your door-trims from moisture. I hold my polythene sheets in place with masking or 'duct' tape around the edge, but many restorers use a spray-on adhesive. Either way, fix it to the inner faces of your doors and then make two holes to allow the door handle and window-winder drives to poke through.

Assuming your door trim panels have their holes pre-cut (photograph 16-23), your next task is to position the twenty or so right-angled trim clips in the pre-punched holes in the hardboard backing to the door trim panels (21). These can really try your patience when you fix and position them for the first time, and there is much to be said for the 'one-clip-at-a-time' approach. A further complication is that you will need to choose your moment when to 'screw' (by about half-a-turn) the two cone-shaped springs into the hardboard trim

16-21. The vinyl wheelarch is glued down, the hidden/turned up edges around the inner wing will have been slit to allow them to lay flat without crinkling, and the quarter panel has been screwed in place. Note how the seat belt mounting has been opened up and a seat belt bolt temporarily screwed in place.

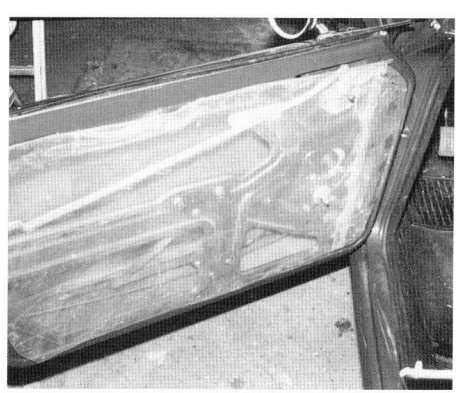

16-22. Door trimming. Step one is to get a piece of heavy-duty polythene sheet on the inside of the door to protect the door trim panels from any water your car may encounter - from rain and washing too!

panels. The top or small ends fit into the door handle and window winder holes to hold them in place while you fix the trim panels to the doors.

If you have positioned all the panel retaining clips in one go, your next step is probably the worst part of trimming a TR - getting all the clips to align with their respective holes in the door. Obviously, you need to offer the panel up to its respective door and try to get, say, the top pair of clips into their door holes. This at least holds the panel in place while you work progressively away

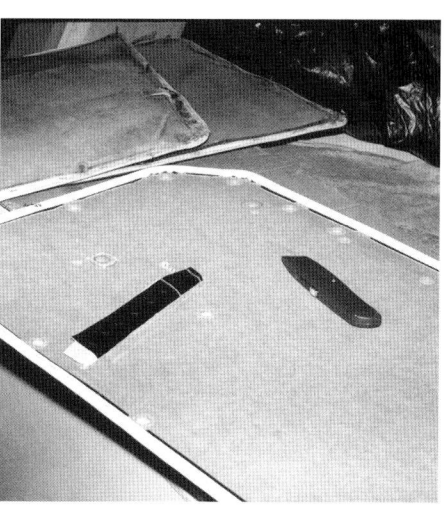

16-23. A preparatory step you may need to carry out with some door panel sets, is to cut the holes in the backing board for the window-winder and door handles. Some panels have the holes pre-cut, which is a definite advantage in view of the risk you run of accidentally cutting the vinyl trim when getting through the board backing. If you do need to carry out this task, use the old trim panels (now you see why I told you not to throw anything away until the car is completely finished) to locate the board holes you need to cut. You will need to cut the vinyl eventually (for the square drives for window and door handles), but these holes need to be more accurately located with the door trim in place on the door, and will definitely be in a different spot to any hole you accidentally cut when preparing the board. Conclusion: favour any trim sets that have door trim board holes pre-cut!

from each top corner, manipulating each clip with some thin-pointed pliers until it can be persuaded to enter its relevant hole in the inner door panel. The rear edge of the door can be worked on in reasonable comfort, but to tackle the bottom row there's no alternative but to lay on your back. A mirror might help with aligning the front clips.

Although it may seem that I'm making a simple job sound more complex than it is, give passing thought to positioning the clips one at a time, and then fitting the two coil springs to the door and window openings.

After that it's all plain sailing, beginning with the holes for the two square drives which will not yet have come through the vinyl since the holes are rarely pre-cut. However, four light taps with a hammer on each edge of each square drive will effectively 'cut' the hole you need in the vinyl, and each square will come through the panel. If you cannot bring yourself to hit the square drive quite hard enough, no-problem, a light tap will mark the vinyl enough to enable you to cut the hole with a blade.

The large plain escutcheons (washers to you and me) go on each square drive next, whereupon we come to the final 'pinning' of the door catch/window winder handles. Take a length of welding wire of the correct diameter, and mark the length of the pin you'll need to cover the complete diameter of the relevant handle. Cut the wire half through with a junior hacksaw, push the half-cut end into the arm (once you have aligned it with its square drive holes) and wiggle the welding wire until it breaks off at the half-cut.

This is the earliest that you should fit the furflex door seals. Bearing in mind there is still some climbing in and out of the car to do, it actually makes sense to postpone fitting them until the last moment. However, you must be absolutely confident that your door glass is nicely aligned with the windscreen/windshield and that the doors will shut nicely with the seals in place.

SEAT BELTS

The static seat belts shown in picture 16-24 are available from many sources, but you may be interested to hear that Securon makes a range of aftermarket inertia seat belts which available through the premier TR outlets in the UK. Two models are applicable to the TR range.

Without the complication of a folding hood frame, the TR2, 3 and 3A will accept Securon's model 514/30, mounted atop the wheelarches and aligned across the width of the car. In practice, a slight inclination of the reel towards the outside shoulder is ideal. The TR4, 4A, 5, 250 and 6 all have a folding hood frame to complicate the issue. In these cases, you could give consideration to Securon's model 500/30, which aligns fore/aft at the bottom of the inside wheelarch, with a pillar loop located at the top of the wheelarch, as per photograph 16-25.

REBUILDING THE FRONT SEATS

There were three different seat types fitted to TR4s. The first two are so similar as to be interchangeable (for only

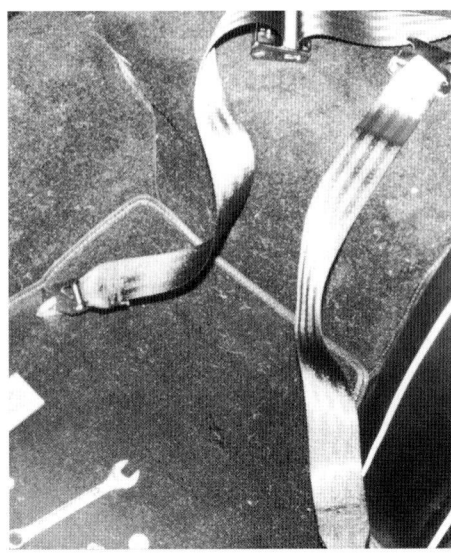
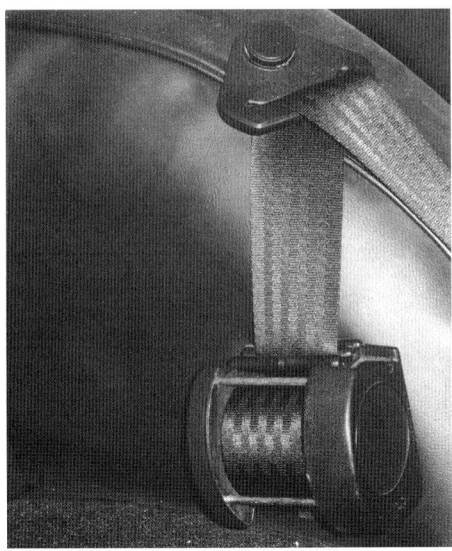

16-24 and 16-25 (right). Towards the end of trimming you will need to tackle the seat belts. Photograph 16-24 shows the static/lap variety on the left side of this TR4A, while picture 16-25 may be of help to those considering inertia/reel belts but are wondering how to fit them (I did). The solution, which works very well, was a pair of Securon Pn500/30 belts mounted as shown here.

the seat covers differed). At first glance, the earliest TR4 seats look identical to those of the TR3A. The main construction was identical, being from pressed steel panels (photograph 16-26), with the back of the passenger seat (only) pivoted to tip forward (16-27) to aid access to the rear. The '3A seat covers, with their horizontal pleats (photograph 16-28), were retained initially.

The seat pan for the TR4 seat was still pressed separately from, but affixed to, the back of the seat, while the seat cushion was still removable, as is shown in photograph 16-28. Changes were made to the springs, runners and back, however, making the TR3A (and B) seat non-interchangeable with a TR4 seat.

At some point a vertical pleated cover was introduced, though this was mainly used in cars heading for North America. The later seats were pretty much the same as the first TR4 seats which draws me to suggest that, if necessary, the early and late TR4 pressed steel constructed seats are interchangeable.

The third type of TR4 seat, sometimes referred to as the 'Herald' type, is shown in photograph 16-29. It introduced the concept of one-piece tubular frame construction, and dispenses with the separate seat cushion used in the earlier designs. In spite of the

16-26. The early TR4 seat was identical to that of the sidescreen cars. It's made up from steel pressings welded rigidly together. This is the driver's seat.

innovation they were not popular since they failed to 'hold' either driver or passenger. This might explain why they were only fitted during the latter part of TR4 production, from mid 1963 to late

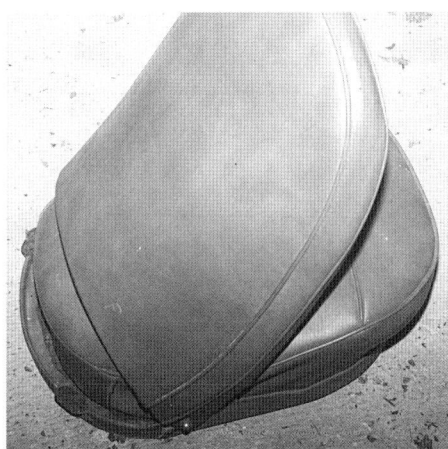

16-27. The early TR4 passenger's seat will fold forward, pivoting at the bottom of the rear panel, to allow easier access to the rear of the car.

16-28. The base cushion clips to the back of the seat pan, and is easily removed. The construction of the seat cushion is (a mass) of springs, as was the technology of the day. Atop is a wood platform, horsehair padding, and, of course, the cover.

1964. They did, however, improve access to the rear of the car by the whole frame tipping forward, pivoted from the front of the base.

The TR4A retained many of the features of the 'Herald' seat, but improved the support, or 'hold' offered, via improved seat cushions with, of course, correspondingly different seat covers.

Your attitude to restoration will obviously be influenced by the degree to which you wish to retain the originality of your car. I found the original TR seats far from comfortable on all but the shortest of journeys, and will suggest how to replace them completely in a later offering. This book, however, is focused upon restoring the cars to their original specification and condition, including the seats.

There are those intrepid DIY-ers who will even entertain making their own seat covers. This is something I don't intend to explore, on the basis that experts have spent years developing and proving patterns and manufacturing techniques, and, consequently, it's my recommendation that you buy a good set of specialist manufactured seat covers. These are one of the most visible parts of your restoration, and will affect the enjoyment/comfort of the car, so I feel you are courting disappointment not to take advantage of some of the excellent covers that are available.

How do you establish what is a good set? I would only shortlist suppliers who are both specialist TR restorers and, ideally, make the covers themselves.

16-29. TR4s adopted the basis of today's seat construction - a single tubular-framed unit - in about 1963. Access to the rear was provided by hinging both seats at the forward end of the frame. Although the basis of the design was retained, all TR4A seats used improved foam moulding beneath the covers to provide a firmer 'hold' on driver and passenger.

However, even that statement may warrant revision, for there are two quite different approaches to front seat restoration (depending upon the construction).

RE-COVERING PRESSED STEEL TR4 SEATS

You need to strip both seats back to the metal 'frame'. This, of course, consists of a series of welded pressings. I strongly recommend, however, that you only strip one seat at a time, in order that you retain the other seat as a reference. Furthermore, I would also recommend you throw nothing away until you are sure the job has been completed to your satisfaction. If you do feel compelled to work on both seats simultaneously, take notes, pictures and draw sketches as you proceed. Note, too, that the folding passenger seat has one or two slight differences in detail, so don't concentrate all your attention on one seat and forget to record the detail of the other. Once stripped to the frame, it's likely you'll find some cracks around the mounting holes. These need to be welded before the seat is cleaned up and repainted.

The cushions that fit in the seat bases offer a number of restoration options, and I would suggest that only those very keen on originality retain the original sprung/horsehair base.

Furthermore, only those with some experience should attempt refurbishing them at home. I will outline how it's done, of course, but, if you're determined to retain the original seat cushions, then, frankly, your best route is to get a professional to carry out the work. They are very 'springy' and tend to give a less comfortable ride than the non-original wood/foam substitute that we will explore in a few moments.

Re-covering the original cushion requires you obtain a re-covering kit. This will have the new cushion covers in the colour and material of your choosing. It will also include a pair of horsehair mats which you will need to lay on top of each spring base, and a cotton pad, which needs to be laid smoothly over the horsehair.

The first step is to turn the new cushion cover inside-out. Some enthusiasts apply a little spray glue to the cushion base to get it to stick to the cotton pad - though **never** to the skirt. You should note, however, that there is then a good likelihood that the cotton pad will bunch up, and possibly even disintegrate. So, while applying some adhesive may seem a good idea, you are almost certainly better off without it. (You may not think so, however, as you struggle to hold everything still while you turn the cushion over and pull the skirt down around it!)

When the skirt is down and the mat and the pad are flat, you are now faced with the task of getting the skirt down with a medium/even tension all the way round the cushion. Uneven, too tight, or too loose, will cause it to crease! Turn the edges over the bottom of the spring base and fasten with original log rings. A more practical option here might be the use of seat clips, though some restorers elect to stitch the bottom of the skirt in place. Finally, you need to lay a piece of hessian across the bottom of the springs, and up to the edges of the spring-base, and glue it to the outside edges.

Much more comfortable than the original cushions, and much more practical from a home re-covering point of view, are the modern substitute cushions made from wood and foam. These can be bought as part of a slightly different cushion re-covering kit which, again, includes a pair of covers in your choice of colour and material, but also a pair of plywood bottoms and a pair of seat foams.

The wood and foams are so simple that you could contemplate making them yourself, but, frankly, for something as important as the seat bases, I would suggest you at least buy the foam cushions from an experienced TR specialist like TR Bitz. You are then sure that you have the correct grade and thickness of foam, and that they will fit your covers since it has been cut to the correct shape. This assembly is much more manageable and you should have little trouble sitting the foam on top of the wooden bottom, fitting the (inside-out) seat cover over the foam cushion, turning the assembly over and pulling the skirt down all the way round. It's easiest, quickest and best to staple the edge of the skirt to the underside of the wooden bottom and cut any surplus off with a sharp blade.

Re-covering the bottom of each seat frame is pretty straightforward, in that you just need to apply a vinyl cover to the metalwork. Re-covering the two types of seat - rigid and folding - is pretty much the same, except that the latter has an extra strip of vinyl across the rear of the seat from hinge to hinge. The bottom lip of the frame of each seat requires that a strip of vinyl trim is contact glued right round the outside face of the seat. With the rigid seat, I would situate the join on the side of the seat nearest the prop tunnel. The folding seat, on the other hand, requires that the start and finish points are, of course, the two hinges. With the ring of vinyl stuck securely in place round the outside of the base, and standing proud of the top of the base, turn it over the top lip and stick it right round the inside of base lip in one go.

Replacing the original wooden 'tacking-strips' is next. These three plywood strips need to be riveted to the seats. Two tacking-strips are required for the rigid seat, one riveted to the bottom of the seat frame where the backrest and base pressings join, while second one is riveted under the rear of the rigid seat's base. The folding seat tacking-strip needs to be riveted to the bottom inside edge of the folding backrest. These strips, which you can either buy or make yourself, get their name from the fact that the backrest covers were secured to them by tacks - hence 'tacking strips'.

Since the backrest cover is just a bag, albeit a slightly sophisticated one, you might be tempted to think that we have completed the most difficult parts of the job. This would be a mistake! In due course we will need to focus on a slight but important difference in the final stages of finishing-off the rigid and folding backrests. However, the first steps are identical, regardless of which seat you have chosen to start with.

The backrest padding is basically horsehair. This needs to be stuck to the back of the seat using contact adhesive, and positioned so that there is about 2in (50mm) of padding standing proud of the curved top of the backrest all the way round. Once your contact adhesive has flashed-off, you need to turn the 2in 'excess' right over the rear of the backrest and securely contact glue it to the seat back.

The backrest cover is best pulled over the backrest with the seat base flat on the bench, and with the front edge in your belt buckle. Obviously, both front and back of the cover have to be pulled over the backrest simultaneously. You'll probably need a helper towards the end of the process, for it is a three-handed job! Taking the rigid seat first, pull the back of the cover down reasonably taut, fold the bottom of the cover under the bottom/rear tacking-strip, and, while there is still some tension on the cover, staple the bottom of the cover to the tacking strip so that, once fitted, the staples will be looking at the floor of the car. You can, of course, use tacks for originality, but good luck!

Next, turn your attention to fixing the front of the rigid backrest cover. This is, of course, stapled to the tacking-strip previously secured to the bottom front of the backrest.

The folding backrest is, in fact, the easier to re-cover, as there is only the one tacking-strip to worry about. Secure the back of the cover first, by folding it under the backrest and stapling it to the top half of the tacking-strip. Now, pull the front of the cover down and staple that across the bottom half of the tacking-strip. All that needs to be done is to trim the excess vinyl (or leather, of course) off the bottom of the cover with a sharp blade - whereupon its time to try them in the car.

RE-COVERING TUBULAR FRAMED SEATS (LATE TR4 AND TR4A)

The nature of the construction of these

seats, and the materials used in them, means that restoration at home is pretty straightforward (using pre-manufactured covers, of course). The TR4 and '4A seats covered by this section are generally very similar, though they do differ slightly in detail (mainly the shapes of the foam mouldings). Both use a rubber diaphragm stretched across the base of the frame to furnish the seat's base support, while half-a-dozen webbings hook across the seat back (often called a squab), to provide support. The accompanying photographs tend to show the later seat, but apply equally to the earlier version.

At the same time as you buy your new seat covers, you may as well order a car set of underseat hessian, and diaphragms for the bases, for it's rare that the originals are re-usable.

It's likely that other parts will be needed; you will get some idea from the appearance of your seats before you start. If your seat foam mouldings have obviously collapsed then you are as well ordering a set of foam mouldings at the same time. Start your restoration by stripping one seat only, keeping the other as a reference until you are completely satisfied with the first seat rebuild.

Start by taking a look at the flat round metal retaining clips around the base and rear frames. These need to be removed, probably revealing the base foam for the first time in many years.

Before you actually spring the clips, please take five minutes to note which clip goes where, and make every effort to remove the clips with minimal damage. The bottom of the back cover should hang down, but leave the back cover in place for a few seconds. The base foam moulding could already be crumbling to dust, or may start to do so as you remove the base cover and foam from the frame. In a way, it's better if they are disintegrating, as it takes all the decision-making out of the next step - you obviously need to buy new foams! If they look reasonable, you have that difficult choice of whether to spend money on replacements or whether to re-use what you have. Foams do, eventually, disintegrate, so it's a short-term solution to re-use the old ones. One compromise is to use a new piece of flat foam for the main seat bases, and pad-out any slightly flat foam mouldings with an additional layer of new foam.

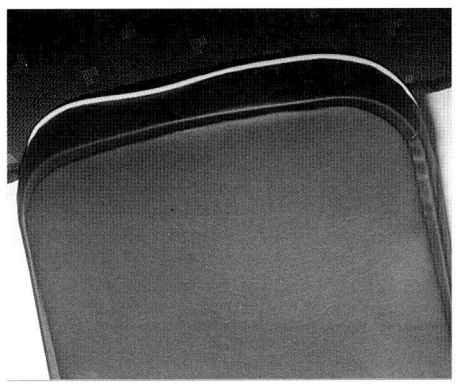

16-30. The rear of the TR4 and TR4A seat has this separate panel which provides some firmness to the rear of the seat, and also makes the rear seat cover easier to position - at least easier than the one-piece cover design used by subsequent TRs! The back panel does, however, need to be removed in a specific way if damage is to be avoided. The routine is described in the main text.

This would be a low-cost compromise that would extend the life of your existing foam mouldings. Generally, though, I would recommend you buy replacement foam mouldings.

The seat back's rear panel (photograph 16-30) can be damaged if you are unaware of how it's clipped in place. You will find it clips to the seat frame with hidden clips, rather like a door trim panel is fixed to the door. It's important that you start at the bottom, and use a broad flat lever to prise the panel off its frame. There are two clips each side. Pull the panel vertically downwards (towards what would be the floor of the car when the seat's in its normal position). This will disengage the top of the panel from two slide clips. The rear board should come off in one piece.

The clips holding the seat back cover will be revealed and should be unclipped carefully, in order to cause the minimum of damage. It doesn't really matter if the cover itself disintegrates, although it may be prudent to only actually bin the discarded parts, including the cover, when the whole job is finished.

The rear frame will now be revealed, along with the foam moulding and the six cross webbings that provide most of the rear 'cushion' feeling. It's rare for the webbings to be beyond further use, but if yours are perished, get replacements. The repair kit comes as a

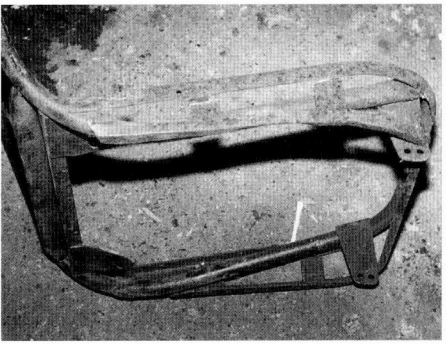

16-31. Once the seat is stripped down to the frame, carry out such repairs as are required, then clean the frame and repaint it.

roll of webbing, together with all requisite fastenings.

You obviously need to get your frame into good shape before too much else can happen. Photograph 16-31 shows a not untypical frame that requires much preparation before restoration can begin. Light shot-blasting and welding are not infrequent preparatory steps, but painting will be inevitable and you need to allow the paint time to harden thoroughly.

Re-assembly starts with the seat base, and replacing the diaphragm in particular (photograph 16-32). Use a loop of string to stretch each of the wire hooks over the frame to secure the new diaphragm to the base. Lightly spray-glue the new hessian to the diaphragm and, if your kit includes it (not all do), fit the thin sheet of foam around the front and sides of the lower part of the frame. This 'skirting' (shown in photograph 16-33), provides some additional cushioning between the metal frame and the cover.

I imagine most covers fitted at home will be made from vinyl, since most restorers investing in leather covers will have the seats professionally re-covered.

Spray-glue a new, flat piece of 0.5in (12mm) firm foam atop the hessian as your base cushion. Those working on TR4A seat cushions will have noted that the sunken seat base shape is actually achieved by an additional 'U'-shaped foam moulding, which now needs to be repositioned to the front, and both sides of the base cushion, with spray glue, as shown in picture 16-34. Allow the glue time to 'flash-off'. If you are following the 'compromise' route of supplementing

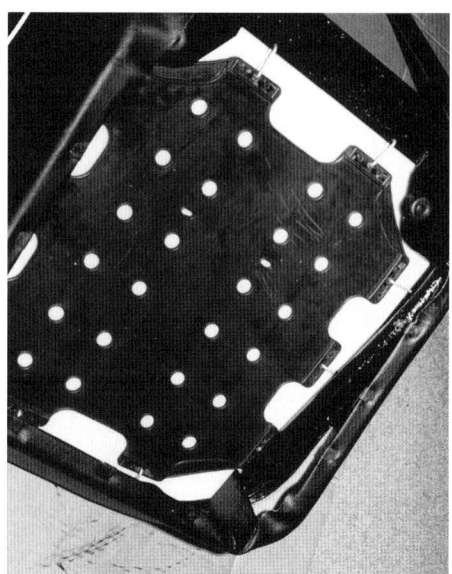

16-32. It is usual, but not mandatory, to start re-assembly with the base, in which case the first step is to fit a new base diaphragm. The technique is described in the main text. This picture also affords a view of the hessian that goes atop the diaphragm.

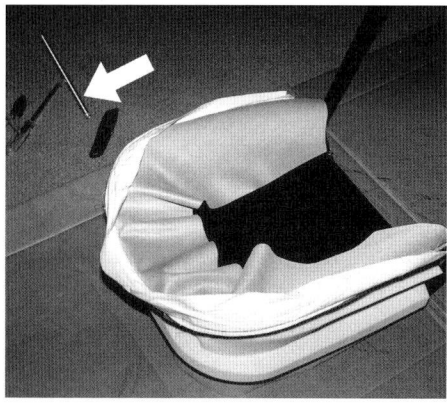

16-33. This picture shows the thin foam being placed in position prior to gluing to the seat frame. Although slightly out of sequence, this picture also shows (top-left and arrowed) the long silver spring that will be fed through a sleeve sewn into the bottom/back of the new base cover. It clips into holes in the base frame and thus provides for some 'give' in the seat bottom when in use.

the original foam with additional thin outer foam, this is the time to apply, with spray glue, the extra layer of, probably, 0.25in (5 or 6mm) foam sheet.

Now to the exciting part. Apply spray glue around the edge of the frame, and offer the cushion cover to the base. This is best achieved by slipping the rear of the base cover over

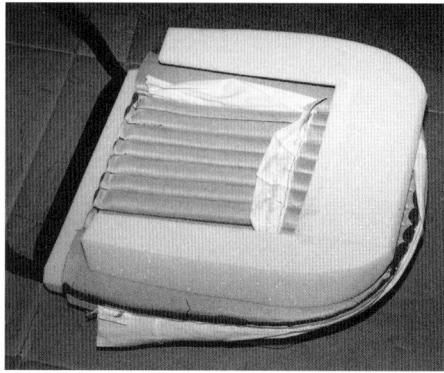

16-34. We have the 0.5in (12mm) flat seat base foam in place and are weighing-up gluing the moulded base cushion to the base foam. From the shape of the base moulding this must be a TR4A seat.

the rear cross spring, fitting the spring to the bottom of the squab, and, by pulling/rolling the front of the cover over the front of the frame before tackling each side. Spend a few minutes pulling and smoothing before taking the penultimate step of applying the retaining clips to the base frame. Finally, trim the excess material off the base and, with the bottom part of the seat looking something like picture 16-35, move on to rebuilding the rear of the seat.

If you are re-using the original lengths of webbing, then re-assembly will just be a matter of re-hooking each end in place. If starting afresh, however, you will need to make them up. Remember, the webbing must be taut when in place, and only after the first one is proven should you press on making up the remaining five pieces. You may find it helpful to lightly glue the rear foam moulding to the webbing (photograph 16-36) and let that set before fitting the seat back cover.

The cover is held in place by those clips we noted right at the beginning of the strip-down. After re-covering, the seat back panel requires you align two clips at the top in the frame, and four clips to the rear board, after which the penultimate step is obvious and easy. We are now up to picture 16-37 so, finally, you need to clip the flap (at the bottom of the new rear panel's cover) to the base frame and under the two rubber 'feet'. Trim off any surplus material at the bottom, and you now have, hopefully, a seat looking very similar to that shown in picture 16-38.

16-35. The base cover is on but we can see that the final clips around the bottom of the frame have yet to be affixed. The cross spring referred to under picture 16-33 can be seen, although I do not think the retaining clips have yet been put in place.

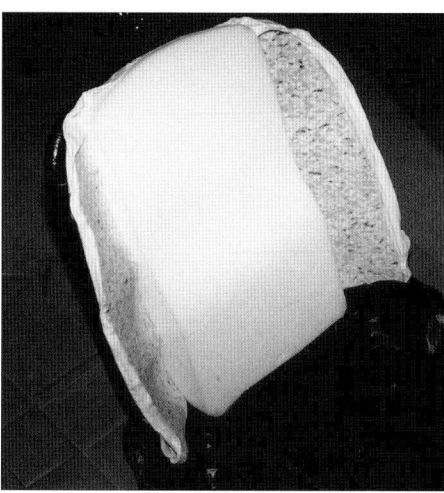

16-36. The first assembly operation on the back of the seat is to replace the webbing. A light spray of glue over a few of the cross webbings may help, but next up you need to get the rear foam moulding in place. The glue only holds the moulding in place while you affix the rear cover and has no subsequent purpose.

THE REAR SEATS

The rear seats are very simple affairs (basically just a cushion on a plywood base). Because of this simplicity, they are very easy to re-cover using pre-made covers.

What's not so simple, however, is to describe the variations that were employed. A number of differences exist between the rear seats of the '4 and the

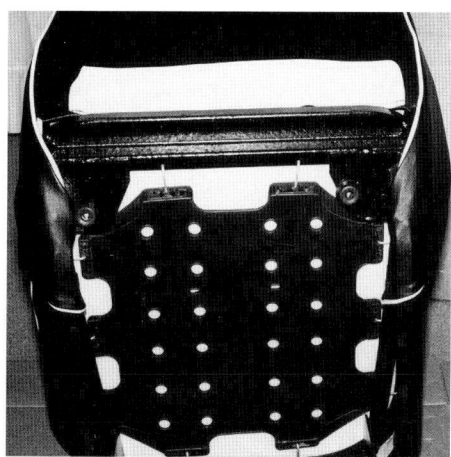

16-37. The seat back cover is not too difficult to fit, since it only needs to be pulled from the front over the sides and top of the seat back. There are numerous clips to position that secure the back cover to the frame. Your next step is to reverse the 'removal' instructions in the main text, and clip the back panel in place, as shown here. This seat is nearly finished but the rear of the seat back has yet to be tucked under the frame and clipped in place. It won't take a moment!

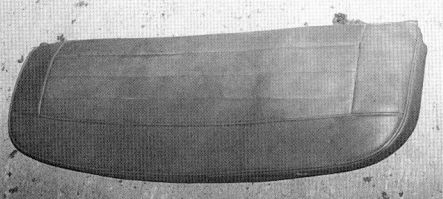

16-39. The earliest TR4 rear seat base, identified by its horizontal pattern, while ...

16-40. ... this photograph shows the plywood underside, and illustrates how one could tack a new cover to the base without too much difficulty.

16-41. The rear seat of the TR4 doubles as a hood frame cover - and makes a very attractive job of it too. This picture is included to illustrate the dividing point (arrowed) where the back and sides can be separated and folded back to reveal the hood frame. The photograph also serves to show how the TR4's rear 'chrome moulding' covers the outer edges of the rear seat trims, and allows them to fold back/sideways.

'4A, and these are compounded by the existence of the 'Surrey' top. However, let's start by looking at the soft top cars.

On the TR4 soft tops, the side and back of the rear seat are probably more accurately described as padded hood frame covers. In that context they are very attractive, although, as I have discussed elsewhere, they do add to the time it takes to erect the hood! The upholstered seat base is simple enough, as can be seen in photograph 16-39,

16-38. Done it! Now for seat number two!

and, of course, can be lifted out as required.

The seat back and sides, shown in photograph 16-41, double up as hood frame stowage. They offer minimal comfort as seats, of course, but are unusual in that they have extra material along their tops which is fastened beneath the 'U'-shaped hood-fastening moulding shown in photograph 16-42. This extra material allows the rear and sides of the seat to be folded back/outwards to reveal the hood frame.

The TR4A rear seat comprises only the upholstered seat base, and is easily re-covered. By the introduction of the TR4A, the hood, hood frame and stowage had been redesigned, so the seat back and the extra material was not required, and was never fitted. Instead, an un-piped tank-board, with a vertical pleat pattern, served to hide the fuel tank. This can be purchased separately, or as part of a trim-kit.

The need for the fold-back rear and sides of the rear seat had disappeared, as did the extra material and even the 'U'-shaped hood-fastening moulding, which made re-trimming the later vehicles even easier.

As for the 'Surrey' top models, the TR4, when fitted with a Surrey top, dispensed with the need for folding-back seat back/sides and, consequently, a TR4A-like tank board with vertical

16-42. This shot provides a closer look at the three piece hood fastener moulding, which is held in place by the 'lift-the-dot' hood fastenings. The arrowed peg (along with its opposite number), is a shade longer than the other 13 pegs, so as to accommodate the TR4 hood webbings which we will explore in detail in the next chapter.

'panels', or bars, is fitted. Since this is already the rear seat back arrangement for the TR4A, the Surrey top makes no difference. The rear panels can be purchased new, and their fitting has already been discussed under the section on internal trim panels.

Chapter 17
Hood/soft top

THE DIFFERENCES

The TR4's hood frame and hood are quite different to the TR4A arrangement. It's not surprising, therefore, that the fastenings to secure each hood are different. Most can be seen in the preceding chapter (photographs 16-1 and 16-2).

With the TR4 hood relying heavily on 'lift-the-dot' fastenings, it seemed important to start this chapter off with a reference to, and a picture of, the almost indispensable punch required to fit the female part of this fastening.

Much more fundamental, however, are the operational and fitting differences between these hoods. The TR4 hood comes completely off its frame for stowage and, consequently, can be stored anywhere that is convenient. Most owners choose the boot. Its relatively small frame folds down out of sight in front of the rear deck (photograph 17-2), but behind the rear seat cushion (photograph 17-3). Quite a neat arrangement, although it takes time to remove and replace the rear seat back and sides, to fix the front of the hood to the windscreen frame (more shortly), and to secure the seemingly endless number of fastenings around the hood. Consequently, if you

 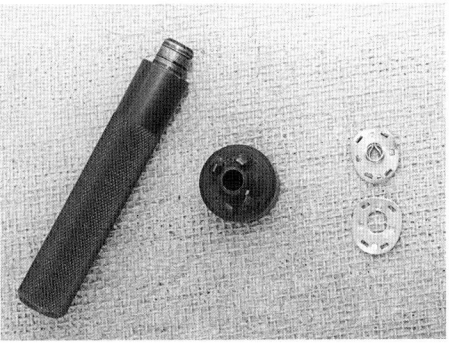

17-1-1 and 17-1-2 (right). There will be numerous references to the female lift-the-dot fasteners throughout this chapter. There are 15 each on the TR4 hood and tonneau, and seven across the rear of a TR4A hood cover. Since there are such a large a number to fit (particularly if you are also contemplating a tonneau) it seemed a good idea to help you with the task. Photograph 17-1-1 shows you how the fastener gets its name (the dot is arrowed), while 17-1-2 not only shows the same fastener in its constituent halves, but also an aid to fitting each. The tool is very useful for several reasons. Clearly it not only punches five holes/slots simultaneously, it correctly positions them too. Furthermore, note that the four slots are not symmetrical but are positioned in harmony with the offset design of the female lift-the-dot, which, in turn, is designed to be lifted off its pegs from one direction only. Not a lot of people know that! You should fix your lift-the-dots as shown in this picture with the writing (and narrow slots) towards the direction you expect to be removing the hood - if you wish the lift-the-dots to separate from their peg easily. The 'bar' on the left of the shot is, in effect, a handle that pushes into the rear of the tool.

and your TR4 get caught in a sudden storm with the hood down, you are definitely going to get wet!

Probably in an effort to reduce the time it takes to erect the hood, Triumph introduced a change for the TR4A. The later car's hood and frame are married

into one inseparable assembly, which folds back and is stored in front of the rear deck (photograph 17-4), usually with a hood cover over the top, as shown in photograph 17-5.

There are no rear seat cushions supplied with a TR4A. Even the method

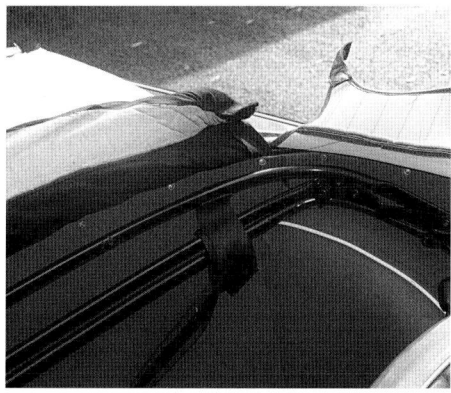

17-2.

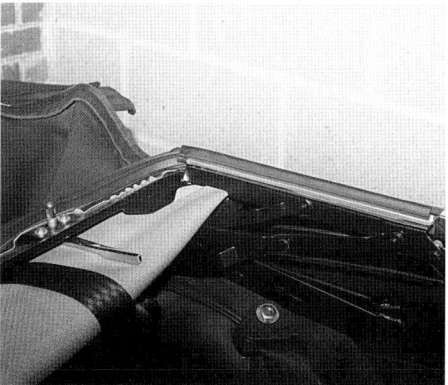

17-4.

17-6.

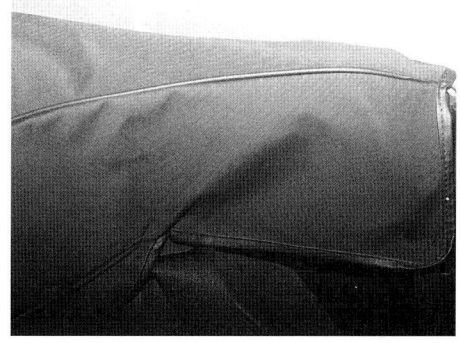

17-2 and 17-3 (above). The TR4 hood frame is smaller, lighter and much less cumbersome than later TR frames. So much so, in fact, that it can be stored behind the rear seat back, as shown in the second picture. The extra time it takes to erect a TR4 hood partly arises from the need to roll the three rear seat trims (shown in the first photograph) out of the way, then to replace them once the hood frame has been erected. You may be able to see in the second picture that the peg just in front of the boot hinge is a fraction taller than those either side of it. This is for securing the rear hood webbing.

17-4 and 17-5 (above). Comparative pictures of the post-TR4 hood frame/hood assembly. Picture 17-4 shows the hood frame without the hood cover, whilst 17-5 shows the hood cover in place. These shots are actually of a TR6, but, nevertheless, illustrate the differences in hood style and stowage of the later cars, compared to the TR4 shown in photographs 17-2 and 17-3.

17-6 and 17-7 (above). The first picture shows the earlier TR4 'lip' that runs right across the top of the windscreen to provide for the hood's front fastening. You can see the male press-stud that secures the end of the hood. The second shot shows the same location of the later car, and the now curtailed 'screen capping'.

used to secure the front of each hood to the top of the windscreen is different, and deserves an explanation. The '4's hood hooks over the slight forward extension to the capping on top of the windscreen, as shown in picture 17-6. The '4A has, I think, the better fastening arrangement, for there is no forward extension to the windscreen, as picture 17-7 shows. Instead, an extra front (or header, as it is known) rail is built into the hood frame and this is pulled down securely onto the top of the windscreen by two hood catch assemblies of the type shown in photograph 17-8. You will note, from photograph 17-9, that the TR4 frame consists of three

crossbars and a very simple single upright. Picture 17-10 shows the header rail, side supports and clamps used on the TR4A frame.

As I mentioned earlier, the two hoods have quite different erection arrangements. The 4A hood is definitely the simpler and quicker to put up. With the hood cover removed you basically pull the hood and frame over the cockpit, secure the front clamps and 'pop' three stud fasteners each side at the rear. Access to the TR4 frame, on the other hand, requires the removal of the rear seats before it can be pulled over the cockpit. Both rear webbings then have to be secured to the rear rail, as per photograph 17-11.

Photograph 17-12 shows the next step, with the hood secured under the front lip/extension atop the windscreen, and both end press studs pushed into

place. Round to the back, and we then need to clip the 15 lift-the-dot fastenings shown in photograph 17-13 (as well as a few 'snap' fastenings inside the car), before tensioning the hood via the two levers shown in picture 17-14. The end result, pictured in 17-15, is very pretty - although the '4's hood does take time to secure, and there can be concerns that the front of the hood (where it hooks over the windscreen extension), is not as foolproof as the later frame/hood fixing arrangement.

REBUILDING THE HOOD FRAMES

Apart from helping you to identify each type of hood frame, and respective

17-8. An important improvement in the TR4A hood was the front clamping arrangement - which was both quick and secure. This shot shows the header rail with the clamping lever part of the arrangement engaged in the windscreen 'half'. The part that would normally screw to the windscreen is at the bottom of the picture (and has no mounting screws).

17-9.

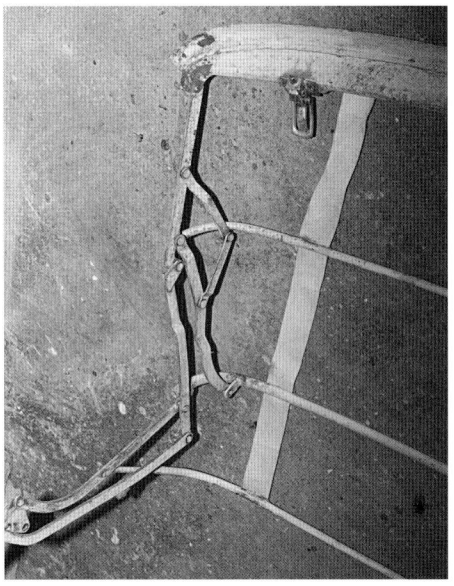

17-9 and 17-10 (above). The first shot shows a TR4 hood frame that could hardly be simpler, consisting of little more than three crossbars. It has no front attachment to the windscreen. The second picture shows a TR4A frame, with the front 'header rail' (that clamps to the 'screen) clearly in evidence. Despite the additional complexity of the later frame, it's easier and quicker to put up, and has a more secure clamping arrangement. The rear of the '4A's webbing has clearly come adrift, though, so it should be quickly replaced before the reference of the second web is lost.

17-11. There are 15 lift-the-dot fastenings around the rear of a TR4 hood - another contributory factor to the time it takes to put it up. This photograph shows the male 'pegs', and the way the frame webbings attach at the rear and hold the frame in place, ready to accept the hood. The two pegs that carry the webbings and the hood need to be longer than the rest of the rear hood securing pegs.

attributes, you will have realised that you must have the right hood frame for your car. Note, too, that neither type is readily available. Believe it or not, some owners lose the hood and hood frame. Typically, the assembly gets put in the garage or loft, maybe to fit a hard top, or perhaps because the climate makes a hood superfluous. In due course the car is sold, but without the hood frame that the owner has not seen for years! So, for whatever reason, hood frames are in short supply, so make sure that your prospective purchase has a (complete) frame, if not a hood.

You should also bear in mind that it's not unknown for a frame to be bent. This can be very difficult to rectify.

Whether you are replacing the hood as part of an upgrade or repair, or carrying out a full-car restoration, the decision to replace the hood should be accompanied by allowing sufficient time and cash to check and improve the hood frame too. The ideal solution is to go for a reconditioned/exchange hood frame from one of our premier TR restorers. The exchange frame will come

back with any bent or mis-shaped sections corrected, the frame beautifully and durably refinished (powder-coated if you wish) and with the correct length webbing straps riveted in place. The cost will be about £125, which may stretch the budget on top of the cost of a new hood, so let's look at the cheaper DIY alternative.

The first, but most important, step is to check frame straightness. This must be done with the frame erected, on the car, and is easier to do if you can borrow a frame to erect alongside for comparison. Although it will be hard to think this far ahead, it makes sense to fit and correct the hood frame before the body is painted. I emphasise the importance of correcting the frame on the car, since more frames are distorted off the car than on. The frame loses its two vital reference points when the rear mounting plates are unbolted from the 'B' posts, so, if your frame is stiff or damaged, correct it in place on the car.

Assuming you are, like most restorers, fitting the frame to the car after trimming, proceed cautiously. The holes

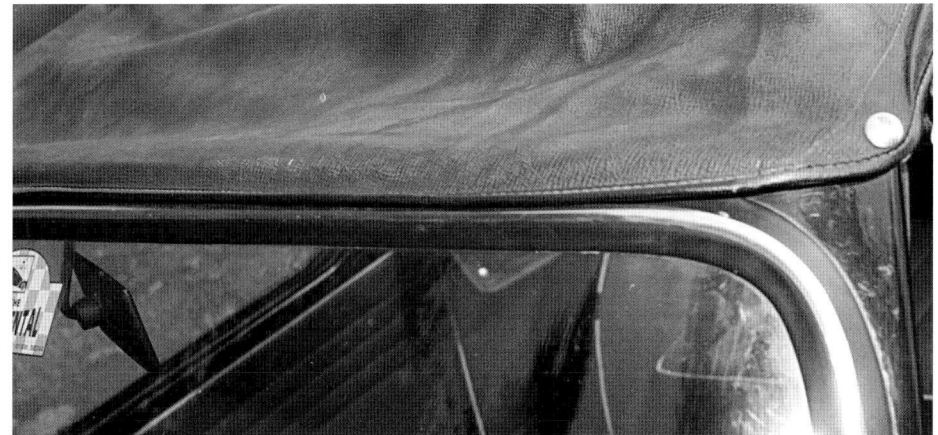

17-12. The front of the TR4 hood clips under a protrusion at the front of the windscreen. Here, the hood is securely in place under the protrusion, but, you will note the front edge of the hood does still stick out. Occasionally, this leads to the hood becoming detached from the 'screen when the wind gets underneath its leading edge. One of the press-stud fastenings (there is one at each end of the front of the hood) is well in evidence. The hood appears very 'baggy' though, due to the fact that it has not been tensioned-up as described in the main text.

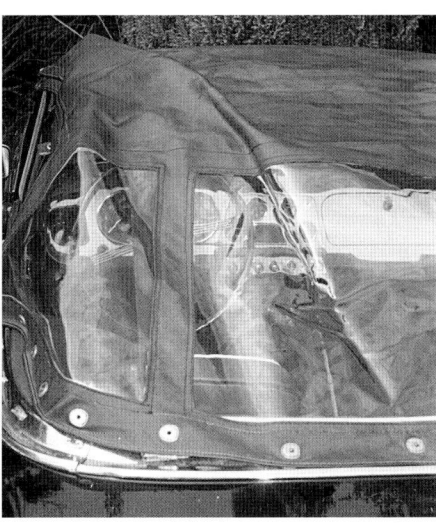

17-13. We have this TR4 hood secured at the front and, by the look of this picture, we are a little over halfway round the back lift-the-dot fastenings.

17-14. With the back lift-the-dots complete, it's time to apply the tension to the hood via a lever on each 'B' post.

17-15. Quickly inside the TR4 to deal with the interior 'poppers', and then we can stand back and admire a complete TR4 hood. Although not the main purpose of the shot, but did you notice the door handles/locks that are unique to the TR4 and '4A. Later TRs have the locks fitted a couple of inches below the door-handle.

for the countersunk frame mounting screws make it seem obvious where the frame mounting bolts go. However, take a thin pointed tool of some sort (a heavy-duty needle would be good), and poke through the vinyl on the quarter panels until you can locate and align the holes in the 'B' posts. There are two

(each side) on the TR4, and three each side on TR4As. Open up the vinyl with an awl, or mark each with your chinagraph/crayon, and cut a small clearance hole in the vinyl for each screw.

The first job is to (gently, probably with a little heat) un-seize any stiff joints. If a joint is seized, don't force it. You could, of course, apply lots of

penetrating oil, twice per day if possible, for several days. The joints usually become unstuck eventually, but a forced frame distorts very easily and is very difficult to completely rectify. If yours already has some bent sections you need to straighten them, and generally ensure that the frame sits square and folds easily. Next I would suggest you rub the frame down; I found this best achieved with the frame securely tied to a washing-line.

You will probably want/need to replace the frame webbings. You can remove the two original webbings, paint the frame, and then fit new webbings, but, I would suggest you replace the webbings before painting, and do so one strip at a time (photographs 17-9 and 17-10). Each webbing needs to duplicate the original and to tie together the header rail (in the case of the TR4A), the three frame hoops and the rear-retaining bar.

In photograph 17-11, we saw that the rear of each TR4 webbing is retained by a lift-the-dot peg, so I suggest your first step should be to secure the end of the webbing in a new end clamp and crimp it tight.

With a TR4A, the first step should be to sew or rivet a loop at what will be the rear of the first piece of webbing. A short rod through the loop beneath the rear bar retains the tails of each piece of webbing, as illustrated by photographs 17-16 and 17-17.

The idea behind replacing only one web at a time is, of course, that the distance between each bar is retained. The webbing should be pop-riveted to each of bar of the frame (photograph 17-18), and, in the case of the '4A, to the header rail. This is probably best achieved with the frame (and the rear bar) temporarily re-attached to the car. This not only holds the frame securely, but also enables you to double-check that the webbings are even and taut when the frame is erected.

As a precaution, and in order to avoid chaffing the hood, carefully check that all plates, washers and rivets (indeed all edges) have no sharp edges. Hammer any flat - again best done with the frame on the car. Although not standard practice, you can glue a small piece of webbing over the top of any really troublesome protrusions. The benefit is that the hood is less likely to chaff but be aware that this may cause a bump in the line of the hood. Once satisfied with the frame and webbings, remove the assembly from the car and put it back on the washing line for painting.

THE HOODS

The following fitting guidelines apply to whichever material you have selected

17-16. This picture shows another small but important detail in how the rear of the TR4A frame webbing is attached to the rear retaining bar. This picture shows the underside of the rear retaining bar. With the hood frame in place the loop at the end of the webbing passes through a slot in the hood flap. One of the holes for the male lift-the-dot pegs is visible here, as is the end mounting hole (one of five) in the rear bar. Another relevant detail is the rivet securing the webbing to the nearest hood bar.

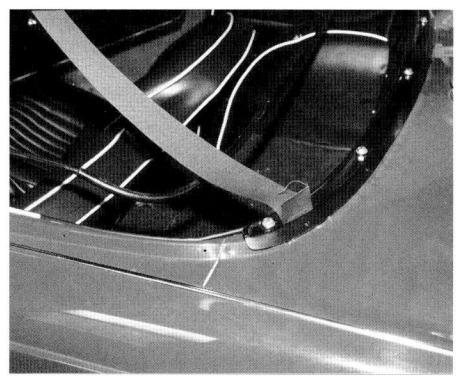

17-17. The TR4A rear bar and webbing correctly test mounted to the rear deck. You can just see the end peg hole in the rear bar awaiting the fitting of the lift-the-dots (but only after the rear bar has been removed from the car).

for your hood. There are two types of material commonly used for TR hoods. Vinyl or PVC hoods, which will top the vast majority of TRs, do sterling service and are probably the easiest to fit. They are easy to clean, light weight and less bulky, but they do tear easily and are prone to cracking in cold conditions. There are some lovely hoods made from what is called 'mohair' material. They do attract dirt, however, and need additional cleaning and the attention detailed later. They are also stronger and flexible in all conditions, but heavier and bulkier than vinyl hoods.

Whichever material you choose, it is advisable (especially in cold weather),

17-18. The webbing runs down the full length of this TR4A frame. The rear of the webbing, where it attaches to the rear rail, is not in shot but can be seen in pictures 17-16 and 17-17. Note the way the webbing is riveted to the cross bars.

to fit the hood in a warm environment. In summer you can lay the hood out in the sun for half-an-hour, but in winter it's important that you really warm the garage with a space heater for a couple of hours before proceeding with the fitting. Avoid using direct heat on the hood, though, as too much can easily mark or burn it.

Fitting the hood effectively secures the top of the windscreen/windshield. This is important, since it is the last chance you will have to ensure good alignment between window (drop) glass and the 'screen frame. Therefore, check that your windows wind up and down easily, yet achieve a full-length seal against door and 'screen seals, *etc*. Once you fit the hood, you are stuck with what you have, unless you are prepared to buy yet another new hood, that is!

Because the TR4 hood separates from the frame during use, you may think that fitting a TR4 hood to its frame will be easy. Wrong, although it could be said that it's easier to fit a TR4 hood than a TR4A! Nevertheless, the TR4 has a lot of fastenings to correctly position and, although you can and should purchase the basic hood pre-made, you should be aware that, like the later cars, the TR4s were all very individual, so you must buy the hood without fastenings and complete the fitting yourself. In fact, never ever be tempted into buying a TR hood (or *tonneau*, for that matter) with its fixing studs or holes pre-positioned ... they will be wrong! That's not to say that the hood manufacturer will have been careless, for I have no doubt that the hood fitted his pattern very well. It's just that every TR is different, and you cannot predetermine where holes or studs are going to go.

FITTING THE TR4'S FRAME AND HOOD

Start your preparations by marking out the 15 rear lift-the-dot pegs and fixing them to the deck, making sure the central peg is absolutely central to the rear deck, and that the two outside pegs of the central five are the long variety (to accommodate the webbings). Measure and mark the centre-point of the windscreen top and rivet a pair of male press-stud bases to the 'screen frame. The male press-stud base can be seen in photograph 16-1 (item 1C) and is shown riveted in place in photograph 17-6. Fully erect and tension the frame and, as a final preparatory step, find the front and rear centres of the hood by turning it inside out and folding it in half and then marking the inside centres (now outside), with a chinagraph or soft removable crayon.

Reverse the hood again, and carefully align the front centre marks from inside the car. Pull the hood under its front securing rail, checking that the hood front is even both sides, and fix a press-stud at one end. I will explain how in a moment. Pull the hood tight across the front and fix the other front press-stud. You can see the finished effect in photograph 17-12.

To fix the press-studs you will need to carefully make a small hole in the correct spot for the button (item 1A in photograph 16-1) to pass through. On the inside of the hood the female half of the press-stud (item 1B) needs to be positioned. The button is secured by spreading the inside of its hollowed brass end over the internal 'female' half

(you will need a small 'flaring' tool and dolly for this). You can buy the necessary tools from TR Bitz, or you may elect to make or borrow them. If you decide to make the tools, you need to have two parts turned. Firstly, a support block of steel or brass machined to accept the outside head of the button. The inside punch actually flares the brass button outwards over the socket, so the punch will need to start with a (blunt) point, and then taper progressively outwards. You might get away with a centre-punch to start the flaring, and follow that up with a piece of 0.25in (6mm) diameter bar to tap the opened end of the brass press-stud flat.

With the front secure, take the tension off the frame and, from inside the car, align the rear centre point of the hood with the appropriate lift-the-dot peg. Make sure the bottom of the hood is positioned correctly on the rear mouldings, as shown in photograph 17-13. Pull the hood backward until the bottom alignment is correct. Mark the position of the hole that will be required for the central peg. Many professionals make such a mark by chalking the top of the peg and pushing the hood material onto it, leaving a chalk dot on the hood. You could use typewriter correction fluid. A good idea is to make a hole in the hood large enough for the lift-the-dot peg to fit through, as this will then hold the hood in the correct place while you move on to establishing the position of the next fastener hole. Get a helper to pull the hood material reasonably tight before you mark and make the next hole. Then repeat this procedure with the next peg on the other side of the rear deck, alternating until all the five central peg positions have been marked. To fit the five central lift-the-dot female fasteners, you are best removing the hood to your bench.

For the cost involved it really is worth purchasing a special punch tool (photograph 17-1) to make both the main hole (which needs to afford unhindered clearance for each peg), and to correctly position the four slots - simultaneously. You still need to get the position of the main hole correct, but this is made easier by the tool allowing you to align the centre of the tool with your mark or hole in the material. However, it is also important that you get the orientation of the tool's slots correct too, so here are a few, hopefully

helpful, thoughts on that subject. Lift-the-dots only separate from their pegs smoothly from one direction - in fact you literally lift the dot on the fastening to achieve a smooth separation. Consequently, you need to orientate the slot punches in the tool so that the narrow pair are oriented towards where you want the dot positioned.

As I said, the actual punching must be done with the hood off the car, for you will appreciate that the punching tool needs to be hammered down onto the hood with a solid backing behind the hood in order to persuade the punch to cut through it. A hefty piece of hardwood is the best backing for this. Although I think it ill advised, you could use an awl/bradawl to carefully pierce the holes in the hood so that the female pins can pass through the hood material - remembering to get the narrow pair of pins in the correct orientation.

Once you have made the main hole and four slots, you must now fix the female lift-the-dots to the hood. Push the pins in the outer half of the female fastening through the hood and locate the inner or back plate over the pins. Bend all four pins inwards, a small hammer is best to achieve a tight clinch, and complete the operation on all five fastenings. Refit the hood to the front of the car and push the five central female lift-the-dots over their pegs. Try the frame for tension, but don't be surprised if it's a struggle, even at this early stage. If it goes up easily you've got something wrong!

Release the frame tension and start on one block of five lift-the-dots on, say, the right side of the car. Don't forget to work outwards and forwards, and to pull the material taut between each peg before you mark the position of the next one. When you have completed one side, repeat the process on the other side. You can take the hood back to the bench and attach the two lots of five female halves in one go if you wish, although, you might prefer to do this in stages.

Finally you need to move to the inside of the car and fit a popper to the elasticated side straps, one each side above the 'B' posts. The straps are best kept as taut as you can in order to hold the hood material as tight to the frame as possible, thus guarding against its tendency to 'balloon' at speed. Don't be alarmed if it takes time and lots of hard work to get the frame up initially. All materials stretch, particularly Vinyl, so, if you fit the hood too loosely to start with, it will stretch and become baggy later.

FITTING THE TR4A HOOD

This time you should start from the back of the hood/frame. Drill the lower-half of your rear retaining bar (photograph 17-16) for seven lift-the-dot pegs, starting with the central hole. If the bar is pre-drilled, check that the centre peg hole is indeed central to the bar. Check that the rear deck's five 'riv-nuts' are in place, that they are secure, and that the five mounting holes in the rear bar are properly disposed about the centre. If in any doubt, do an alignment check with the five holes along the front edge of your rear deck. It's worth mentioning that TR hoods have been fitted with the rear bar in place on the rear deck and, in error, the peg holes have been drilled through the rear deck. For the record, the pegs are fixed to the rear bar, and the rear bar is fitted to the car only after the rear of the hood has been secured to it. That's got that potential mistake out of the way!

Moving forward, the next few steps really need an assistant, initially to help swing and screw the frame into place. Commence the hood fitting by finding the exact centre points of the rear and front edges of your new hood. This is best carried out off the car. While you can find the centre using a tape-measure, the easiest and, frankly, the surest way is to fold the hood in half inside-out. Take the two rear corners of the hood that will shortly sit above your 'B' posts, and fold them together, while at the same time folding the two 'A' post tops together. Now, clearly mark the centre-points on the inside of the hood (currently on the outside), with a 1in (25mm) line at the rear and a 2in line at the front. Use a chinagraph, chalk or a soft crayon that can be rubbed off later. Fold the hood the correct way out and, from the inside of the hood, push the rear retaining bar down into the hood's rear flap/corner. Carefully align the centre peg hole in the bar with the centre line you marked on the hood and, if there is any doubt in your mind as to the assembly sequence, take a look at drawing D17-1.

Check carefully that the centre hole is correctly positioned, that the rear bar

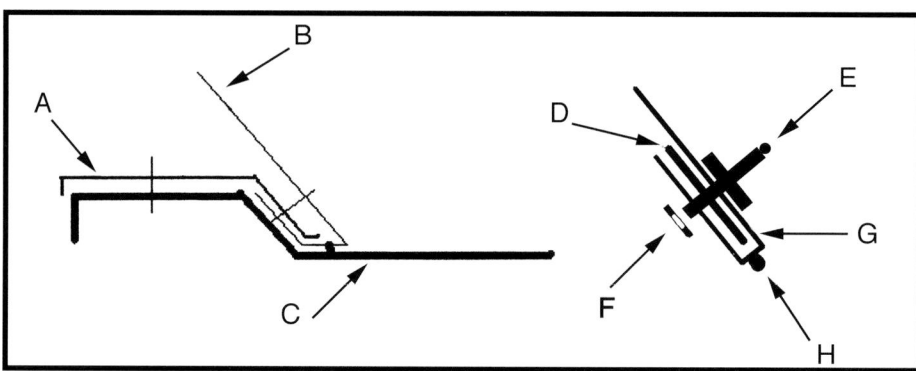

D17-1. Schematic assembly sequence for riveting the hood to the rear retaining bar, with an outline view on the left, and a more detailed view on the right. A. Rear retaining bar. B. Hood. C. Rear deck. D. Rear retaining bar. E. Lift the dot peg. F. Peg internal fastening. G. Hood material. H. Hood binding.

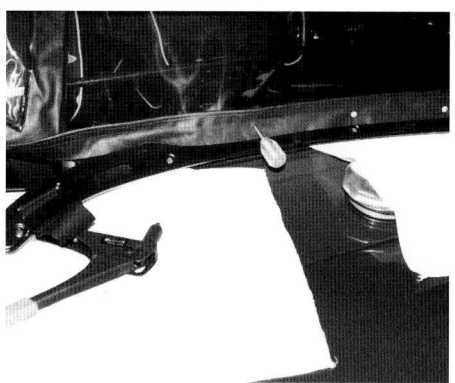

17-19. Finding the position of the third peg in the rear bar to hood sequence from inside the '4A's hood. The first peg fitted was dead centre (in front of the filler cap), and the second was the first one to the right side. Now it's the left side's turn, before alternating back to the next peg on the right side. You are seeing the tails of the pegs in this shot, with the main part of the peg hidden from view on the other side of the hood. The completion of all seven pegs will roll the rear bar forwards some 180 degrees.

17-20. This shot of a completed hood will enable you to see what the pegs look like in situ when the rear bar has been turned through the 180 degrees and bolted in place on the rear deck.

is indeed pushed tight into the hood flap, and that the turned-up edge of the hood is tight up against the rear bar. From the inside of the hood pass an awl or similar through the inside edge of the hood (as illustrated in photograph 17-19), the centre hole in the bar and out through the back edge of the hood. Secure this position by pushing a lift-the-dot peg through hood, the central hole in the bar and the inner hood flap. Place a special fastener on the inside of the peg and peen the base of the peg so that the hood, bar and inside flap are held tightly together. A centre-punch is usually sufficient for the peening, but you will need to hold a drilled weight

tight to the outside of the hood over each peg.

This could be the moment to place the hood over the frame on the car (in which case, do use a dustsheet to protect the rear deck and boot paintwork) or you might choose to complete the rear bar to hood peg-peening off the car. In either event, there are three further pegs either side of the central one. Each of the remaining six will have to be positioned and peened through the hood to the rear bar.

It's absolutely vital that these are fitted one at a time, that you stretch the hood material outwards before pushing your awl through the next hole, that you work from the centre outwards, and that you progress each hole/peg/peen on alternate sides of the bar. If you concentrate, as too many have, on one side of the rear bar and work straight across, you will probably end up with an off-centre, unbalanced looking hood.

You should also make sure that you pull each section of hood between the pegs as tight as you can to avoid wrinkles in the rear window, and an ill-fitting hood generally.

Now you do have to throw the hood over the frame for we need to slip the tail loops of both webbings through the rear bar and the slots in the hood. Using something like welding wire, secure them to what will be the underside of the rear-retaining bar. To secure the rear bar to the car, use a large washer on the top of the bar and, starting with locating bolts through holes two and four, secure all five rear bar retaining bolts, thus completing the first stage of attaching the hood to the rear of the car. The end result of this stage should look something like picture 17-20.

Many hoods have two rows of three 'poppers' in the roof of the hood; undo them, position the frame rails through them and re-fasten the poppers.

It is now time to deal with the three press-studs each side, located below the quarter windows. This time, the male press-stud base (item 1C in photograph 16-1) is located directly on the rear deck and, if they are not already in place, this is the moment to attach all six (three per side). If you have fitted new rear deck extensions, there will be no existing holes to rivet the press-stud bases to, and six holes will have to be drilled.

Bearing in mind that the body will be painted at this point, I suggest you start by applying a couple of layers of masking tape to both rear deck side extensions, to guard against scratching the paintwork. The first deck hole to drill is that nearest the door, although it will actually be the last one you will use. However, you need to position the chrome 'B' post finisher on top of the furflex door seal, and use the finisher's hole as your first rear deck 'spot'. This will give you the height of all three holes that side of the car.

Now go to the other/rear end of the side extensions and spot your second hole 0.5in (12mm) in front of the main deck panel joint with the forward extensions. The third and final hole this side of the car comes as near to the middle of holes one and two as you can get it. Drill your six holes, remove the masking tape and rivet the press-stud bases in place, as illustrated by photograph 17-21. Our next task is to

fix six press-stud buttons to the outside of the hood and six press-stud sockets to the inside of the hood so that they correspond to the bases fixed to the rear deck. Since the hood is now securely centralised, there's no harm in concentrating on the three press-studs on one side of the car at a time - provided you work away from the central group of seven, forward towards the 'B' posts. Complete each button/socket and secure the hood with it before you stretch the material taut and move on to the next. Never try to do all three in one go.

These six buttons require a small 'flaring' tool to spread the inside of the hollowed brass end to the button, and you may need to make, borrow or buy one. If you decide to make a tool, you need to turn two parts. Firstly, a support block of steel or brass machined to accept the outside head of the button. The inside punch actually flares the brass button outwards over the socket, so the punch will need to start with a (blunt) point and taper progressively outwards. You might get away with a centre-punch to start the flaring, and follow that up with a piece of 0.25in (6mm) diameter bar to tap the opened end of the brass press-stud flat.

Moving forward, position the frame header rail on the top of the windscreen/windshield frame; it should just rest in place and not be secured. Again ensure that the centre of the header rail and the centre of the front of the hood are clearly marked and exactly aligned. Clamp the header rail to the 'screen frame using the hood catches and, using a (strong) partner, stretch the hood forward as far as it will go. Mark a chalk line along the front edge of the hood where it leaves the front of the header rail and check that the two lines on your hood resemble those in photograph 17-22. Release the catches and, using spray glue, apply adhesive to the top of the header rail. If it's a vinyl hood you are fitting, pull the hood a further $1/2$in (12mm) forward over the header rail and, working from the centre towards the outside of the hood, stick the hood to the top of the header rail - ensuring a smooth appearance. Using the catches, try clamping the hood/header rail to the windscreen frame. If the hood seems too tight (bearing in mind that all materials, and vinyl in particular, will stretch a little, and that an overly loose

17-21. Here, the rear bar has been bolted in place (you can just see the end screw), and the three male press-stud bases have been riveted along this side's deck extension pieces. The third/front stud is out of shot but is attached to the rear of the door seal end cap. The join (arrowed) between rear deck and the extension piece is a reference point in that the rear press-stud is positioned about $1/2$in in front of the join.

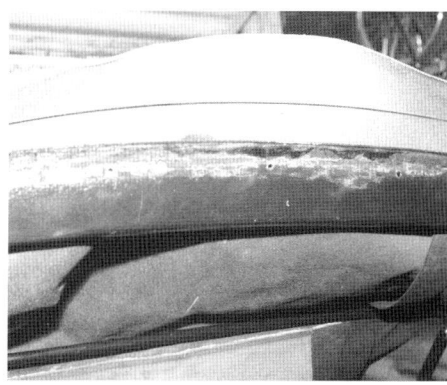

17-22. Note the central chalk mark and the frontal arc showing where the '4A hood should be glued and fixed to the header rail. Being a vinyl hood, this material will probably benefit from being pulled a further $1/2$in forward still, before being stuck to the header rail!

hood flaps about in use) peel the hood off the header rail and reposition it slightly. Try the clamping again, if too loose peel off and reposition, remembering that you have about 10 minutes before this sprayed adhesive sets.

Before you get to this point, you need to comfortable with the position and tightness of the hood. Release the frame catches, fold the front of the hood under the header rail and fix the underside with some really strong contact adhesive (so that it looks like photograph 17-23). Rivet the (three) top channels to the underside of the header rail and cut off any surplus material from the inside with a nice sharp blade, as shown in photograph 17-24. Push the header rail seal into its channels with a broad blunt screwdriver.

It is generally thought to be advantageous to leave the hood (be it TR4 or '4A) erected for a couple of weeks to aid the stretching process, and it helps if you can allow the car/hood to stand in the sun for as much time as possible during this period.

HOOD MAINTENANCE

We'll take a look at some hood maintenance details in a moment, but first, on the basis that prevention is better than cure, let's discuss a couple of details that will help reduce hood maintenance to a minimum.

The way you fold your hood is a case in point; you will prolong the life of the windows if you fold the hood with as few sharp creases across them as possible. You will put less strain on the hood material if you remember, in the case of a TR4, to faithfully take the tension off the frame before attacking the lift-the-dots and, as far as possible, don't fold the rear window tightly. In the case of a TR4A, the tension is removed by releasing the two hood catches. However, please remember not to try folding the '4A's frame back until you have also un-popped the (three per side) fastenings from beneath the quarter windows. Failure to undo these could result in a torn hood.

As you fold the TR4A hood frame back from the windscreen, be sure to pull the top of the rear window out backwards until the hood frame is fully folded and the rear window and most of the hood lays flat along the rear-deck/boot/trunk, with the two quarter windows sticking-out sideways. You will prevent window chaffing by placing a pair of old towels each side of the rear window. Fold the two-quarter windows towards the middle of the hood, without creasing the quarter windows, and, finally, fold the very tail of the hood forward into the rear of the cockpit, making sure you don't crease the rear window. Fit the tonneau or hood cover.

There is little you can do to repair a worn, torn or cut hood. If, however, your hood is not quite that bad, I trust some of the following tips will help you

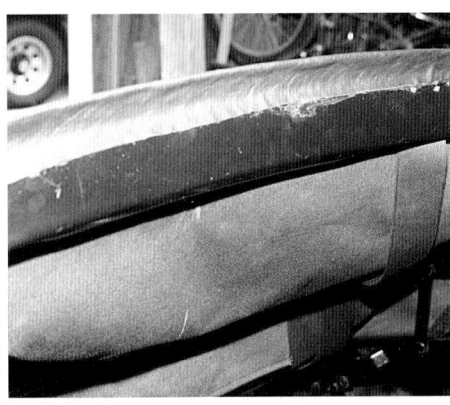

17-23. The hood is correctly positioned on top of the header rail, and fixed with spray glue. The next step is to apply stronger contact adhesive to the rest of the front hood material, and to wrap it over the header rail.

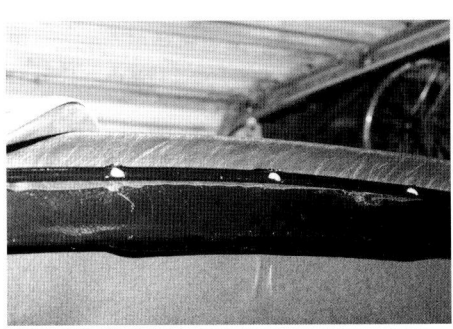

17-24. The final step is to rivet three lengths of channel to the '4A's header rail and, as depicted here, press the header rail soft rubber seal into the channels. If there is any significant excess hood material, cut it off with a Stanley knife.

with 'rag top' maintenance.

I am disappointed to report that hoods made from mohair material attract dirt, even with everyday driving. I have owned cars with vinyl and mohair hoods, but, in future, will stick to vinyl. The colour coordinated mohair certainly looked magnificent when first fitted, but very quickly got very grimy in today's traffic conditions, and needed an application of a specialist shampoo. (I can speak very highly of Renovo's products in this respect). The vinyl hood has gone four times the mileage and time and still requires nothing more than the occasional soapy water wash and rinse, so has proved the more practical material by far.

A garage once put an oily component on the mohair hood of my car, which left a dark stain the size of a

dinner plate, outside and inside, which I thought initially had totally ruined the £300 hood. Not so, you will be delighted to hear, for the problem was rectified after several applications of carb and choke cleaner! The product is made by Auto Chemicals, which was very helpful when I explained that I was ideally seeking something that was virtually 100% carbon tetrachloride to act as an *in-situ* dry cleaning agent. The carb cleaner is mostly toluene but worked in the same way as carbon-tet. I had to rub the surfaces with clean towels to absorb as much of the dirty oil as possible after each application, and I would not recommend this treatment in anything other than a crisis. However, you can imagine what a relief it was to find a solution.

I mentioned earlier that prevention is better than cure, and suggested you protect your (folded) rear window with a couple of towels. However, if your rear window is already cloudy, microscopically scratched, or just covered in film, then I would recommend another Renovo product - this time the Plastic Window Polish. If your rear window has been folded repeatedly, it will either be opaque, cracked, or so distorted as to make rearward vision very difficult. Naturally this condition won't be helped by polishing and may get you thinking about a completely new hood.

Certainly, if you are at the viewing stage of a prospective purchase, this is the prudent attitude. However, when you have the car home do take a close look at the rest of the hood first, for, if it's in reasonable shape, you could at least postpone the purchase of a completely new hood for a while by having a new rear window fitted. This work can be undertaken in the UK by Perfect Rear Vision (020 8777 6764) for about half the cost of what you would have to pay for a new vinyl hood. The work can be completed within 24 hours, and you will be saved the task of fitting a new hood.

A couple of final tips. A candle lightly rubbed over the tonneau zip a couple of times each year should ensure they always operate smoothly. A faded canvas, double duck or mohair hood can be re-coloured to black, dark blue or brown, and can be re-proofed. Renovo can again offer the appropriate products.

Chapter 18

Lefthand drive to righthand drive conversion

PREDOMINANCE OF LHD CARS

The majority of Triumph TR production went to the USA, initially to help the UK's balance of payments, but, latterly, to supply the apparently ever-growing demand for UK sportscars. Sadly, this trend has not continued and the current reversal and repatriation of Triumph TRs is partly explained by the better weather conditions that prevail in large areas of the United States of America, particularly, of course, in California.

The sheer number of cars sold in the USA is, of course, another factor in the current west-east flow of classic cars. Although not all lefthand drive TRs went to the USA, the vast majority did, as the table shows.

So, not only did America have the lion's share of production but, by virtue of better weather conditions, were able to preserve more examples. In fact, it's quite extraordinary to see what detail has been preserved in a 25 or 30 year old car that has been repatriated from a hot/dry climate such as Southern California's. The fastenings still undo with the minimum of effort, leaving the plating still in evidence while, more importantly, the chassis and panels can be totally free of rust, to the point that

UK restorers have to see an ex US 'dry state' car to believe it.

Take care, however, when offered such a car, for it's all too easy to presume that a state is dryer than it really is. Arizona is a case in point: parts of Arizona are unquestionably very dry indeed, but over half of Arizona is 6000 feet above sea level, with snow still in evidence in late March. Furthermore, it's not unknown for a car that has spent most of its life in a less ideal climate to be shipped to, say, California and sold

as an ex-Californian car. So examine all dry state cars initially with a jaundiced eye; it should quickly become evident whether you are looking at a dry state car, or one that has, let's say, moved about a bit! You will also need to check out the mechanical condition, and weigh up what's involved in converting it to righthand drive.

PREPARATION/STRIPPING

Disconnect the battery and remove the

Model	Total made	Number exported	LHD Sales
TR2	8636	5182	2332
TR3	13,377	10,032	6019
TR3A	58,309	52,478	41,982
TR3B	3334	3334	3334
TR4	40,253	36,803	31,285
TR4A	28,465	22,826	19,400
TR5	2947	1171	995
TR250	8484	8484	8484
TR6PI	13,912	5542	5347*
TR6	77,938	77,938	77,938
TR7/8	11,4463	88,007	74,800

* Includes 3577 shipped CKD for assembly in Belgium

Production figures.

lefthand drive steering column, dashboard, instruments, metal dash back, steering rack, and carburettors and linkages. You can leave the exhaust manifold *in situ*. As surprising as it sounds, it's best to take the heater out to allow unrestricted access to the area where the new righthand drive bottom steering column bracket will go. You will also need to remove the righthand seat, and, if you plan to weld closed the original LHD holes, it's probably best to remove the left side seat too.

It's wise to remove any trim/carpets from the vulnerable areas and, if a new righthand drive electrical harness is your choice, then I would remove the lefthand drive front harness at this point too.

So, let's get down to what's involved in converting the car to drive on the proper (just kidding, no letters please!) side of the road!

THE STEERING

The steering rack is probably the first item most lefthand drive to righthand drive converters think about. With the TR4, however, there is a minor complication which you may remember we discussed in chapter 11. At car number CT20063 the vertical-eared brackets that mounted the steering rack were dramatically improved by using a horizontally-mounted chassis plate. The rack also changed length during the TR4 production run, and the earlier solid aluminium rack clamps were replaced by rubber bushed ones held captive by a U-shaped clamp. Whichever TR4/4A you have to changeover, procuring a righthand drive rack is unavoidable, but at least you are spared these complications. However, if you have a TR4, take care to acquire the correct steering rack for your particular car. Obviously, any of our premier TR specialists can help. This could also be an opportunity for you to fit the type of rack, mounting brackets and clamping you prefer.

We went into the different chassis mounting brackets and their respective advantages in Chapter 11. The TR's 'U'-bolt mounts are the same for RHD or LHD and can be re-used, but you are advised to fit new rubber cushions if you elect to stay with the later 'softer' type. Solid aluminium rack mounting blocks are available as an upgrade which

replaces the U-bolts and the rubbers - and this secures the rack far more rigidly than the original design, but transmits more road noise and vibration.

If you spread your U-bolts/rubber bushes with a suitable tool, or use a weld clamp to pull each end of the rack hard into its rubber cushion before tightening them, you are probably going to get the optimum mountings for a roadgoing car. However, with an early TR4, the question arises as to whether you should take this opportunity to not only switch the car to RHD, but to also bring the steering up to the standard of the later TR4s. The question of originality does not come into the issue, as your car will be non-original (in RHD configuration) anyway.

The availability of TR4 and 4A racks in RHD seems satisfactory at the time of writing, but I think it may be prudent to summarise the three racks involved in the cars we are studying:

For early cars with 1023mm long racks and an alloy clamp - use RHD rack number 305648.

For cars with a 1023mm long rack (and rubber bush mountings) - use RHD rack 305930.

For late cars with a 1003mm (*i.e.* shorter track rods) rubber-mounted rack - use part number 306829.

Incidentally, the last of these racks was used right through to the end of the TR6s.

TR4s with the earliest rack/mounting would be best altered to use rack 305930, since the later mounting is regarded as much better, with a far superior feel, even with the rubber bushes. If you seek even more direct steering, then the rack mounting can be changed to aluminium clamps - available from Revington TR.

Steering racks from a variety of other Triumph cars look the same externally as the TR racks, but, unfortunately, the ratios are different.

When finalising the fitting of your righthand drive rack, do be careful to ensure a good earth/ground is looped from the new rack to the chassis. If you have pre-installed, or plan to later install a righthand drive electrical harness, you will find that a suitable earth/ground wire (lengthy black wire with a ring terminal) is pre-supplied. If you are using a lefthand drive harness, then a little ingenuity or an earth/ground extension may be required to ensure your horns

18-1. The new steering column hole has been formed, and a righthand lower steering column support has been securely welded to the corner of the plenum box. Take this opportunity to make any repairs necessary to the plenum chamber. A water test via the air inlet (just in front of the windscreen) is worthwhile.

eventually work. To get the horns functioning you must earth the rack and, incidentally, loop an earth lead across the rubber doughnut top joint in the steering column.

Regardless of the car you are converting, you will need to purchase a support bracket to secure the steering column lower clamp to the bulkhead/firewall. The lower steering column mounting is a platform formed by a bracket welded to the inside of the bulkhead/firewall/plenum chamber, between the engine and passenger compartments. The new bracket can be seen welded in place in photograph 18-1. However, before you start welding brackets in place, first use a 2.25in (55-57mm) hole saw to cut your new steering column bulkhead hole (located some 1in (25mm) from the corner of the bulkhead top panel). You can mirror image the LH hole dimensions to get it absolutely correct.

The bracket that goes just in front of the new hole is handed, so the LHD bracket is not suitable for RHD conversions, but it is available as a separate unit (part number 815834SB), from Revington TR and, I expect, from most of our TR specialists. The original bracket was a single piece pressing, but it's quite practical to manufacture a two piece righthand drive bracket using your original bracket for the dimensions. The advantage of making your own two piece bracket is that you can, and, if yours is a non-concours car, should, enhance the thickness of the material. I

18-2. Here is the pedal, steering and bodywork challenge. The upper steering column obviously exits the bulkhead/firewall and a grommet fills the void between column outer and bulkhead hole. It is, therefore, important that the hole you trepan (or hole saw) in the bulkhead must be of the correct size for the grommet's outer diameter. The pedal box and master cylinders transfer across to the right side of the car without too many complications, leaving some now superfluous holes to close. However, you should not close the bonnet release cable hole (arrowed)!

18-4. The alterations 'under' the dashboard involve removing the left side lower steering column support that is welded to the inside of the plenum chamber and filling the hole in the bulkhead/firewall where the column went through. Here they are gone! Needless to say, on the right side of the car you need to fit the different RHD lower steering bracket shown in photograph 18-1, and cut the new steering column hole as described in the main text.

emphasising the importance of cleaning up the bulkhead beforehand, and of ensuring the highest quality plug welds!

I suggest you replace the two internal steering column bushes before

18-3. Again the procedure involves closing most of the holes on the left side of the footwell. You will also need to leave one hole for the bonnet/hood release cable. The main LHD holes have been beautifully closed and this converter has added extra holes for either a wash bottle cradle mounting or a brake servo.

used 0.125in (3mm) thick mild steel plate to make my 'bridge' support for the steering column. The original bracket was spot-welded to the bulkhead, but it's more practical to plug weld your replacement. It's hardly necessary, but in view of the importance of the component, it's worth

18-5. This is the sort of brake and clutch master cylinder mounting arrangement you should be aiming for if you are converting to RHD. The master cylinder mounting bracket is the standard used on all UK RHD TR4 and '4A cars, although the brake light mounting bracket (arrowed) was added at TR4 number CT 26929 along with its 'mechanical' brake light switch. Prior to this, there was no bracket welded to the master cylinder mounting and the brake light switch was hydraulically actuated.

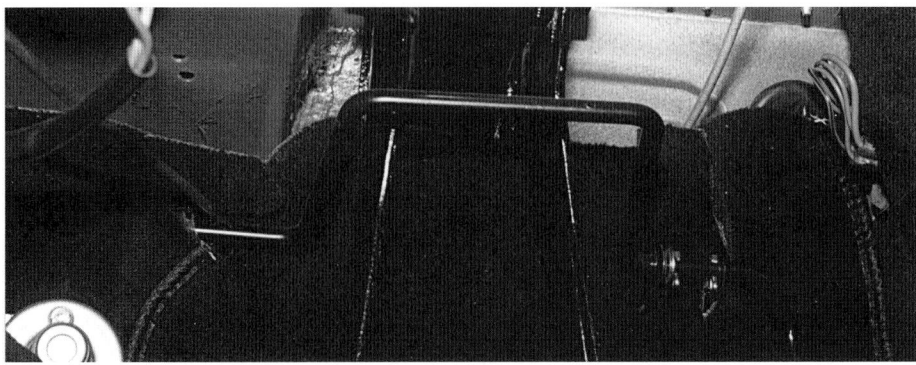

18-6. This should give you an idea as to the clutch/brake pedal pivot shaft cover and mounting arrangements.

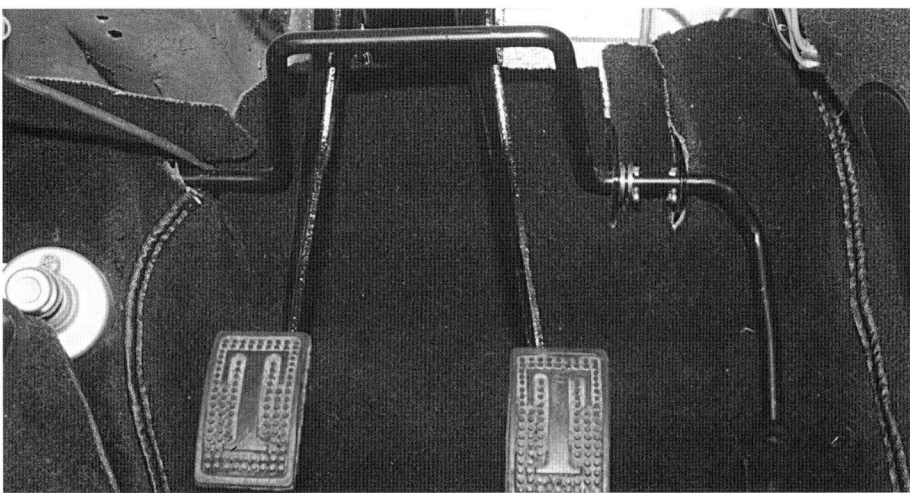

18-7.

18-7 and 18-8 (above). RHD pedal arrangement - with the more complex throttle pedal clearly visible from inside the car and from the engine compartment. You can just see the right throttle pedal mounting bracket poking through the carpet in the first shot. As described in the main text the clutch and brake pedals will require resetting, and their mounting brackets fixing to the bulkhead/firewall.

you reassemble your column to the car. There's a neat trick that makes this otherwise difficult job much easier. Furthermore, it really is too easy to ruin your steering column if you try to remove the old bushes. Instead, use a blade to cut off the original rubber locating 'pips' as near flush with inside of the column as you can. Now, push the new bushes in from, respectively, the top and bottom, simultaneously pushing the old bushes further into the column.

You also need to attend to the steering column rubber 'doughnut' flexible joint. There are two types, an 'early' and a 'late' type, and, in the interest of safety, it's best to replace these as a matter of course, along with the thin/braided earth/ground straps which are important to the subsequent operation of the horn.

SWITCHING THE PEDALS

After stripping the LHD pedal arrangement, shown in photograph 18-2, and the associated parts from the car, the first action you need to take is to carefully close the original holes.

TR bodyshells of this era were not 'handed', so there should be no 'surplus' holes when the car is converted. You will have to weld closing metalwork into the LHD steering and pedal bracket holes, and pictures 18-3 and 18-4 show the end result, and then open the equivalent slots and holes in your right bulkhead top.

Use your top pedal box as a pattern, noting that there is no need to buy a new pedal box, just remove and strip the lefthand drive pair (top and inner) completely - noting the position of various spacers and washers - so you can reset the brake and clutch pedals. The relocated top box is shown in photograph 18-5, and the inner one in picture 18-6.

You can buy new brake and clutch pedals if you wish, but both can be reset the opposite way using a sturdy vice and some muscle. Before you start 'adjusting' them, it might be an idea to make a card template of each which you can then reverse to help you with the respective angles in RHD format. Your brake and clutch 'target' arrangement is shown in picture 18-7, as is the RHD throttle pedal fixing.

The throttle pedal (part number 209411) and one mounting bracket

18-9. A TR4/4A throttle mechanism, showing where and how the (arrowed) the cross shaft is cranked up to control the front carburettor.

(part number 131253) have to be replaced, and, for what the set costs, you are as well to buy new. Re-use the lever arm and inner plate/bush pivot, though, shown in picture 18-8. For completeness, I also illustrate the throttle linkage to the (front) carburettor in photograph 18-9.

HYDRAULICS

Clearly, if you feel the condition of the pipework warrants replacing the whole car's brake pipe system, you need to buy a righthand drive brake pipe kit. I would suggest using copper, since it's both easier to work with and offers longevity at very little extra cost. If your pipework is in excellent condition, then all you need to do is buy the RHD pipe that feeds away from the brake master cylinder.

In most cases, the clutch hydraulics can be dealt with by purchasing the RHD 'top' pipe.

WIPERS

The LHD wiper arms, with their different crank angle, will not park as RHD arms are intended to. You could leave this detail for the moment, but sooner or later you will need to fit RHD wiper arms onto the existing wiper spindles, and change the parking

position of the wiper motor. You will hardly need me to detail the first operation but a few words about the second task may be helpful. The operation is outlined in the repair manual but all you basically need to do is rotate the top, shown in photograph 18-2, by 180 degrees.

ELECTRICS, DASHBOARD AND INSTRUMENTS

Electrics

The electrical harness on your car will probably be in the order of 35 years old, so, for the cost involved and mindful of its effect on the ongoing reliability of your car, I would recommend you purchase a new RHD electrical harness.

The TR4 lighting switch is mounted on the fascia/dashboard, and is, of course, transferable to your RHD dash. The TR4A switch, on the other hand (pun intended!), is handed, and you will need to fit a new one.

Be aware that almost all the lights will need your attention in some way. In the majority of cases it will be a change of lens that is required, but you will need to change the whole headlamp bulb/sealed units to the opposite dip pattern to be legal on UK roads. This is your opportunity to upgrade them, too. If you are not sure what coloured lenses go where in the UK, just ask your preferred

TR specialist for a UK lens set for your particular car. Alternatively, take a notebook to your next Triumph meeting or ask the local group to help you out. Speaking of headlights, I'm sure it will not have escaped your notice that the headlamp foot/dip switch will work much more effectively if it's transposed to the driver's side of the car. No mounting bracket is required.

Dashboards and fascias

With the TR4A, Triumph used a wooden fascia over the metal dash back which allows converters to 'cut and shut' the original LHD metal dash back. There's no wooden fascia on the vast majority of TR4s, so that route provides no solution. Thankfully, few TRs of any vintage are being broken these days, which is probably why so few secondhand RHD metal dash panels are available. Having said that, however, secondhand RHD ones do pop up from time to time for both TR4 and 4A cars, and the usual TR events are worth visiting just to search the secondhand parts stalls. The annual 'International' meeting held by the TR Register is particularly good for sourcing secondhand parts, but get to any event you can.

If you cannot find what you need, Revington TR can supply new replica RHD metal dash panels for both the TR4 and TR4A.

You will also need a pair of RHD crash pads. In my experience, those that have enjoyed hours of sunshine will need to be replaced anyway, and they are available new, as is the cubby box. However, since the latter is not handed (in spite of different part numbers) you should re-use the original.

Instrumentation

Most instruments transfer across without difficulty, although you will need to buy new drive cables for the speedo and tachometer. You should also get the speedo recalibrated if you plan to change the differential's ratio. If your car comes with metric calibrated instruments (speedo and oil pressure gauge) you will probably need to purchase exchange/reconditioned units, which are available.

Chapter 19
Conclusions

The TR models that this book covers were built to be used, and you should - must - use them. Part of the pleasure of ownership for a good many enthusiasts is 'tinkering' with their toy. However, whilst many readers will enjoy the tinkering just as much as the driving, it should be done at an appropriate time.

I really enjoy the planned repair or overhaul of some particular part (even the whole) of the car - in my garage. But no-one dislikes a roadside investigation, repair or breakdown more than I do. I have gone to great lengths to establish the problems that TRs have, and how to guard against them during your refurbishment, in an effort to maximise 'on-the-road' reliability. Triumph initially built very solid, dependable sportscars but, from the introduction of the TR4A, the IRS cars became less rugged. Still highly desirable, of course (remember, I have a TR6), but the passage of time has revealed more retrospective chassis strengthening than was required by all the pre-IRS cars combined. You now know not only the weaknesses, but also the corrective and preventative measures.

A final cautionary thought. We all want the best - the best looking car, the fastest, the quickest off the line, the most outstanding specification, *etc*. It's only human nature. So, I implore would-be restorers to consider carefully what they can afford and to prepare their specification, budget and a game plan that is comfortably within their financial limitations. Allow for the apparently inescapable fact that, however carefully you think the project through, it will still end up costing more than you expect - perhaps as much as 20 per cent more. Accept that some specifications or cars are just outside of your budget.

One method to achieving the car of your dreams is to tackle it in stages. Obviously, the bodyshell and the integrity of the chassis and brakes must be the first consideration, but you could then pause and run with your original engine and gearbox, or a somewhat tired suspension for, say, a year or so before starting on the second phase. Top-notch suspension improvements might be the focus of phase two, possibly fitted during your car's winter lay-up, followed by a further period of financial recovery. Finally, maybe a further year or so later, it's time to put in that fast road engine and/or overdrive on the gearbox. You could even re-trim the car a year later still.

Think your own project through; please don't become one of the all-too-frequent 'Abandoned Project' advertisements. It really is very easy to overstretch resources and enthusiasm as expectations and component costs rise, and the project takes longer than expected.

Enjoy the camaraderie of the TR fraternity; not impossible with your car off the road but much more practical with your car on the road, even if it is a 'rolling project'. No-one will think any the less of you or your car if you turn up with a roadworthy but obviously unfinished project. The relevant TR club will help you enjoy the car, generate some great friendships and solve some technical difficulties, too. The premier TR club in the UK is the TR Register, whilst Stateside there is the VTR (Vintage Triumph Register).

So, do have fun on and off the road, and show off your TR as often as you possibly can.

Appendix 1
Clubs, suppliers and specialists

CLUBS

TR Register,
1B Hawksworth,
Southmead Industrial Park,
Didcot,
Oxon OX11 7HR,
England.
Tel: 01235 818866
E-mail: tr.register@onyxnet.co.uk

Vintage Triumph Register,
15218 West Warren Avenue,
Dearborn, MI 48126,
USA.
Web: http://www.vtr.org
E-mail: vtr-www@www.vtr.org

UK SPECIALIST TR RESTORERS, REPAIRERS, DEALERS AND SPARES SUPPLIERS

Faversham Restorations,
Unit 20 Upper Brents Shipyard,
Faversham ME13 7DZ,
England.
Tel: 01795 590263

Revington TR,
Home Farm,
Middlezoy,
Somerset TA7 0PD,
England.
Tel: 01823 698437
E-mail: neil@revington.com

TR Bitz,
Lyncastle Way,
Barley Castle Trading Estate,
Appleton Thorn,
Warrington,
Cheshire WA4 4ST,
England.
Tel: 01925 861861
E-mail: triumph@trbitz.u-net.com

TR Workshop,
Unit 4 Bankside,
Love Lane,
Cirencester
Glos GL7 1YG,
England.
Tel: 01285 659900
E-mail:
alanmike@trworkshop.demon.co.uk

TR Enterprises,
Dale Lane,
Blidworth,
Mansfield,
Nottinghamshire NG21 0SA,
England.
Tel: 01623 793807

E-mail: stevehall@trenterprises.com

TRGB Ltd,
Unit 1 Sycamore Farm Industrial Estate,
Long Drove,
Somersham,
Huntingdon,
Cambs PE17 3HJ,
England.
Tel: 01487 842168
Web: www.trgb.co.uk

Overdrive repair specialists

Overdrive Repair Services,
Units C3/4 Ellisons Road,
Norwood Industrial Estate,
Killamarsh,
Sheffield,
Yorks S21 2JG,
England.
Tel: 0114 2482632
Web: www.overdrive-repairs.co.uk/
products

Overdrive Spares,
Unit A2 Wolston Business Park,
Main Street,
Wolston,
Nr Coventry,
West Mid CV8 3FU,
England.
Tel: 02476 543686

E-mail: odspares@aol.com

Gearbox rebuilding
First Gear,
3 Church View,
Beckingham,
Doncaster,
South Yorks DN10 4PD,
England.
Tel: 01427 848101

Chassis repair and manufacture
CTM Engineering,
Unit 3A, Bury Farm,
Curbridge,
Nr Botley,
Hants SO30 2HB,
England.
Tel: 01489 782054
E-mail: colin@ctmeng.freeserve.co.uk

Paint manufacturers/ specialists
Bondaglass-Voss Ltd,
158, Ravenscroft Rd,
Beckenham,
Kent BR3 4TW,
England.
Tel: 020 8778 0071
(rust preventative primer paint)

International Coatings,
24-30, Canute Road,
Southampton,
Hants SO14 3PB,
England.

Witham Oil and Paint Ltd,
Stanley Rd,
Oulton Broad,
Lowestoft,
Suffolk NR33 9ND,
England.
Tel: 01502 563434
(rust preventative primer paint)

Hood renovation products
Renovo International,
PO Box 404,

Haywards Heath,
West Sussex RH17 5YN,
England.
Tel: 01444 443277
E-mail: renovo@dial.pipex.com

Chrome restoration
Central Engineering Services,
Unit 1 Riverside Industrial Estate,
West Hythe,
Kent CT21 4NT,
England.
Tel: 01303 268969
Web: www.c-e-s.demon.co.uk

Electrical
TR250/6 Maintenance Handbook
Written by Dan Masters and available
from DMP, PO Box 6430, Maryville, TN
37802-6430, USA. Cost: $30 surface;
$36 air mail.
Web: http://members.aol.com/danmas6/

Bonnet release mechanisms
Prestige Developments & Injection,
77 Box Lane,
Wrexham,
Clwyd LL12 8DA,
England.
Tel: 01978 263449
Web: www.prestigeinjection.fsnet.co.uk
(bonnet release mechanisms)

Cylinder head refurbishment/ unleaded compatibility
Bailey & Liddle,
Unit 16, Upper Brents Estate,
Faversham,
Kent ME13 7DZ,
England.
Tel: 01795 535068
*(Engine reconditioner and unleaded
cylinder head conversions)*

BODY REPAIR TOOLS AND EQUIPMENT

Frost Auto Restoration Techniques,
Crawford Street,
Rochdale,

Lancashire, OL16 5NU,
England.
Tel: 01706 658619
*(Clamps, cutters, tools and equipment
for auto body repairs)*

TR4 Steering Improvements
Protek Engineering,
Unit 13 Bushells Business Estate
Wallingford
Oxon,
England.
Tel: 01491 832372

US SPARES SUPPLIERS

Moss Motors,
PO Box 847,
440 Rutherford Street,
Goleta, CA 93116,
USA.
Tel: (800)667-7872
Web: http://www.mossmotors.com/

The Roadster Factory,
PO Box 332,
Killen Road,
Armagh, PA 15920,
USA.
Tel: (800) 678-8764
Web: http://www.the-roadster-
factory.com

Victoria British Ltd,
Box 14991,
Lenexa, KS 66285-4991,
USA.
Tel: (800)255-0088
Web: http://www.longmotor.com/

Paint manufacturers/ specialists
Interlux,
2270 Morris Ave,
Union, NJ 07083,
USA.
(Marine industry paint suppliers)
Multi-language website:
www.yachtpaint.com

Appendix 2
Welding, tools and techniques

WELDING

Your restoration plan will almost certainly necessitate some welding, as even the most restored car will require some attention sooner or later.

A relatively simple job - like left- to righthand drive conversion - will involve a small amount of welding almost as soon as you have the car in your garage, and a full body-off restoration will give you lots of welding practice! The prospect of welding can be daunting, especially if you don't own a welder, but don't be put off; and ladies, that includes you (ladies made up 25 per cent of my welding course). Your restoration plan, budget and timescale should allow for the purchase of a welder of one size or another, and possibly some tuition on how to use it. Mind you, preparation for welding is dirty, noisy and unsociable; give some thought to whether your family and neighbours will put up with the cutting, chiselling and grinding involved in removing all of the old rusty material before the quieter/cleaner/constructive work begins!

THE ALTERNATIVE METHODS

Although it is unlikely that your first task will involve welding, it is something you must prepare for, and buy not only the obvious welding equipment, but some important ancillary items, too. Without some form of welding facility you won't complete a body restoration at home, so let's look at two most relevant forms of welding: gas and MIG. You may see references to stick and/or TIG welding, both of which have their advantages, but we will gloss over these techniques simply because they are less suited to DIY bodywork repair.

The first principal to explore is the advantages and disadvantages of heat and distortion. I certainly do not want distortion, I hear you cry, which is true, but you may want to shrink an area of steel, which can be accomplished by (gas) heating the area you wish to shrink and then allowing it to cool. As it cools, it shrinks beyond the starting point. However, in general, heat generates distortion and, in the vast majority of cases, this is not welcome.

So, the welding technique that generates the least heat is the preferred method for most home bodywork restorations. MIG welding is the almost universally preferred welding method for home panel repair. Let's explore MIG welding and the variations that are available first, starting with a brief overview of what MIG welding is.

MIG stands for Metal Inert Gas. A MIG set consists of the welding set itself, an umbilical cord and a hand-held 'torch', which has a trigger set in the handle. The trigger, when squeezed on, activates three things: a welding current is switched on, welding or filler wire starts to feed forward from the welding set, and the inert gas starts to flow through the umbilical cord and out through the torch. The wire speed, or amount of wire fed through the touch is variable, as is the welding current. Very broadly speaking, the thicker the material you wish to weld, the faster the wire speed and higher the amperage settings required.

The main advantage of MIG welding is that it does generate less heat than gas in the panel(s) you are welding, but it has a downside, too. The filler wire has to be reasonably hard to withstand the feed mechanism without kinking; consequently, a weld applied by MIG is hard and has to be ground flat. A MIG weld cannot be dressed by hammer and dolly without splitting, whilst a gas weld is generally softer and more malleable.

If you plan to mostly plug or seam weld (as would be required to, say, fit a new floor or bulkhead), then MIG welding would be your first choice. If, however, you are carrying out a concours restoration and want an invisible wing repair, then butt welding by gas would be the preferred method. It will be much easier to plenish the weld flat and, with a very light grind, it would be virtually invisible with just a coat of zinc primer.

Please don't think that it's impossible to butt weld with MIG. To do so you'll need a 1mm gap between the two panels (that might come as a surprise). However, it is easier, quicker and just as aesthetically acceptable to most restorations to joggle the new panel and plug weld or even seam weld down the edge of the overlap. A short spell with an angle grinder is all that is subsequently required to form an equally almost invisible repair from the outside of the car.

You can, of course, have the best of both worlds by tackling the tub of the car with a MIG welder, and subcontracting the gas welding repairs to your detachable panels, such as wings, etc. However, for the majority of home restorers aiming for a high quality usable restoration, MIG welding will be the choice right throughout the car. Plug welding is a very frequent restoration requirement, and MIG is infinitely superior for plug welds. MIG and gas are equally effective on thicker chassis welding, but most of us are only able to buy one piece of kit, so I would opt for MIG. A MIG set is easier to buy and store than a gas set, in any case. With gas equipment there are two large gas bottles to worry about. Of course, you will have a similar problem with MIG, unless you go for one of the much advertised 'No Gas' MIG welding sets.

Most manufacturers of MIG sets designed for domestic use offer 'No gas' models, usually at the bottom end of the range. As the title implies, they are designed for use without the shield of inert gas the more professional MIG set employs. The 'No Gas' sets actually generate a local inert gas shield at the weld point, via a flux core that is incorporated into the centre of a no gas welding wire. If you have a no gas set you must use no gas wire, but you will not want to use no gas cored wire when you have a gas shielded set.

Why choose a gas shield set when you can avoid the problems and costs associated with a large gas bottle by using a no gas set and wire? Good

---

Mild steel MIG wire ('No gas' wire has fluxed core)

0.45kg of 'no gas' wire 0.9mm diameter	£8
0.8kg of 'gas' wire 0.8mm diameter	£4
4.5kg of 'no-gas' wire 0.9mm diameter	£50
5.0kg of 'gas' wire 0.8mm diameter	£12

Gas cylinders

Gas	Approx. bottle capacity	Bottle monthly rental	Gas charge
Oxygen	10 cu. metres	£5	£15
Acetylene	6 cu. metres	£6.00	£35
CO2/argon mix	12 cu. metres	£5	£30
Disposable canister of CO2/Argon	about 30 minutes of gas usage	NIL	£8

US prices
The flux core (no-gas) wire is sold in 2lb and 10lb spools. Wire sizes typically vary in inches as 0.030, 0.032, 0.035 and 0.045 although with enough persistence one can find other sizes. A 2lb (.9kg) spool of 0.035 (about 0.9mm) will cost approximately $17. A 10lb (4.5kg) spool of the same wire will cost about $60. Regular MIG wire comes in the same wire sizes as the flux core wire. A 2lb (.9kg) spool of 0.035 (about 0.9mm) will cost approximately $9. An 11lb (5kg) spool of the same wire will cost about $34.

Gas cylinders
These can be purchased outright or leased on an annual basis. The most recent lease rate quoted was $60 per year, regardless of bottle size. Information below is for the refill. Bottle sizes come in 40, 60, 80, and 390 cu. feet. (390 is a little larger than the 10 cu. meter bottle you refer to). The 60 cu. feet size is about right for most home hobbyist needs.

A refill of CO2/argon mix for the 60 cu. feet bottle will cost about $35. A refill of the 390 cu. feet bottle will cost $85. Costs of other sizes vary accordingly with bottle capacity.

Acetylene comes in a 150 cu. feet bottles and costs $40 per refill.

MIG welding consumables – price comparison.

---

question. Firstly, note that no gas cored wire is more expensive than the more usual plain MIG wire. Secondly, I have seen experienced MIG welders lay down some excellent welding using a no gas set, and have even declared the set to be first-class. However, I must confess that I found it much more difficult to weld with a no gas MIG set, although my gas shielded MIG welding is quite acceptable. Furthermore, I do not believe anyone would argue with the fact that no gas sets generate much more by way of spatter, slag and smoke. My advice would be to buy a conventional gas shielded MIG set. Get round the gas bottle problem by hiring a large bottle for your main welding stint (say, for 3 months) and using small disposable canisters for smaller,

intermittent welding that comes up from time to time. The table should help you to decide.

Which gas you use is very important and, for MIG welding, always use carbon dioxide with 5 per cent argon – called Argoshield. This makes for maximum ease of welding. When ordering the large rented gas bottles, expect to pay for the gas when ordering your cylinder(s), along with a cylinder deposit equivalent to at least 3 months' rental and a delivery charge (about £15). Many suppliers do not charge for collecting the empty cylinder(s).

WELDING EQUIPMENT

When setting out on your restoration, decide whether or not you want to buy all of the equipment that will be required. For the cost of a welding set, extra gear and possibly some training, you might be better off paying a specialised/professional restorer to do most of the welding, or buying an ex-Californian shell/part-shell that should need very little welding. If you buy an ex-Californian shell it may be practical to hire a welding set for a week, or buy the smallest size of welding set and very minimum of ancillary gear.

Only you can decide but it may help if we spend a short while deciding what equipment you might have to budget for. The size (or capacity) of the welding set you buy is very important. A very small capacity set - say, 90 amps - may be a false economy for a full restoration, although perfectly suited for small jobs. In my judgement the best value for money - particularly if a full restoration is planned - is offered by a 150 amp capacity set, available from selected retailers for under £200. Choose one with a non-live torch; in other words, the torch will not transmit current until you pull the trigger. You should get various valves and gas pipes included for this sum, but not a gas bottle.

ADDITIONAL EQUIPMENT

Allow a minimum of £300 for tools and equipment specifically for the sheet metal work involved in a full restoration. Assume at least the following additional equipment:
- A substantial electric drill. Choose one with the highest torque at low rpm that you can find. It might be prudent to pay the extra for an industrial standard drill to get the torque and robustness you will need, so assume at least £75.
- Angle grinder at £50
- Face mask/goggles for protection when grinding at £15
- Pneumatic nibbler at £45 or pneumatic 3 inch cut-off saw at £25
- Hand edge setter (or joggler) combined with hole punch at £30 or Sealey pneumatic version at £50
- Combination welding head shield with flip-down front at £15
- A small selection of cold chisels and bolsters - say £15
- Best quality tin snips - about £20
- Any angle magnet clamps at £12 each x say 3 = £36
- Locking welding clamps about £5

each x 4 = £20
- 4 to 6 'Intergrip' butt welding clamps.
- Gloves - cut-resistant for handling very sharp sheet metal.
- You will need to separate numerous spot welds, and zip-cutters are okay for this although I get on better with a sharp 10mm drill reground to give a flatter than usual (say, about 130 degree) point.

Most welding and metalworking tools can be purchased from Frost Auto Restorations.

It will not have escaped your notice that the above pneumatic equipment will require a compressor. Whilst not something you need to buy - although it is possible to - you may need to have some way of rolling over the body tub to make it more accessible for underside welding. A pair of triangular angle iron frames clamped front and back of the shell is the usual method. If you need to completely roll the shell, ensure the pivot is sufficiently far off the ground to allow the full width of the shell to pivot through 180 degrees.

SAFETY

This is largely a question of common sense. In the garage, do not smoke when welding or around flammable gases. Do not have heaters near to compressed gas bottles. Chain gas bottles to a wall when not in use. Always, absolutely always, wear a good welding mask with the dark eye shield in place. Always wear thick welding gloves and protective overalls when welding, and thick leather or the latest no-cut gloves whenever handling rusted and new sheet metal. Never grind without proper eye protection. Remove the fuel tank from the car, drain or blow through fuel lines, and disconnect the alternator before welding.

LEARNING TO WELD

Although you will benefit from some expert tuition, which we will discuss in a short while, the following are a few of the absolute basics for seam (or continuous) MIG welding for you to experiment with first.

Hold the body of the touch about 5-10mm from the workpiece, but angled slightly (about 30 degrees) so you can see the end of the filler wire touching the

workpiece/arc. If you are righthanded lean the top of the torch away from you while you move the arc towards your left side (called pushing the torch) for best penetration. Here are the main problems you will probably experience -
1 If your wire 'bounces' off the work, pushing the torch away from the workpiece, then, almost certainly, the wire feed is too fast. Rectify by turning down wire speed; a slightly higher amperage may also help.
2 Opposite to the above problem is if the torch virtually touches the workpiece. Speed up the wire feed.
3 Frequent holes burnt in the workpiece suggest too high an amperage, rectified by turning the amps down a little.
4 Welding is all about joining molten metal from both panels. A good strong weld is therefore only possible if the amperage is high enough to fully penetrate both panels. Full penetration (melting) is achieved when a bubble appears along the line of the weld on the lower panel. This is often difficult to see working on a full panel on the car, so do try numerous 'off the job' test pieces until confident you are getting proper penetration. A discolouration of the lower panel is not sufficient and, in this event, a higher amperage setting is almost certainly called for.

You can undoubtedly learn to weld from a specialised tuition book and lots of off-the-job practise. However, remembering the safety aspect, some expert guidance is very worthwhile. The obvious way to get this in the UK is via evening classes at your local Technical College. Most run Motor Vehicle Technician courses, and one year's classes (about 30 two-hour sessions) will get you to an adequate and safe welding standard. I cannot speak for all Colleges but my experience is that, in addition to learning to weld, you will be able to take smaller panels (wings, doors, boot lid and bonnet) into college and work on them under expert guidance. Furthermore, if you need to make up, say, a couple of curved false lips to weld to your tub's inner wings, then the requisite joggle or rolling equipment will be available at college, and all you will need pay for is the material you use. In the USA, via the American Welding Society (phone 800-443-9353) you can get in touch with your local chapter, which will have knowledge of local learning opportunities. Alternately, contact your local Community College or High School, either or both of which will quite likely know of, perhaps even run, evening vocational classes.

You can buy a full sheet of mild steel from your local steel stockist, but if you attend college you will be able to buy the steel in small, manageable pieces, guillotined to the precise size you need, when you need it. Most steel stockists are listed in the telephone directory and will be pleased to deliver one 2x1 cold reduced mild steel sheet to your home on a next-day basis. The gauge you should ask for is, in today's parlance, 1.2mm, which anyone of my vintage will know as 18swg or 0.048in. Cost will be around £30, including delivery. By the way, if you need the 2x1 bit translating too, it means roughly 6 feet x 3 feet.

In the next section we will look at the basics of forming steel panels from scratch, and, of course, adjusting pre-made panels to fit your car. It's unlikely you'll have both gas and MIG equipment at home, nor are you likely to have a wheel or rollers, which are indispensable for even minor tweaking of a pre-made but slightly errant new panel. Your local Technical College will have all of this equipment and will help you use it. You can always take the old panel, or maybe a template, with you. The cost of a year's evening classes is about the same as a MIG set - £200. Go for it; you can't afford not to!

TYPES OF WELDS

You will come across the following terms as the body restoration progresses. Tack welding usually precedes all of the following and involves a series of 1mm long 'tacks'. These can be easily broken to allow repositioning of the panel, but are sufficient to hold the panel in place while measurements and/or other checks are done, or even additional panels put in place.

SEAM/STITCH WELDING

Seam or continuous welding will be required very frequently, and is usually best done in 30mm long stitches, with a gap then a second stitch then another gap. Eventually, you go back over all the gaps and fill them in. This technique minimises distortion.

Butt welding - As the name implies, this is a weld that joins two flush-fitting panels. A typical application would be joining the front half of a curved wing/ fender to the rear half, or letting-in a repair section. A small (1mm) gap between abutting sections helps the welding. After tacking, you will effectively seam welding the join.

Plug welds are perfectly acceptable and often used as a substitute for spot welding, but are best positioned closer together (more frequently) than the original spot welds. They must be carried out in such a manner as to achieve first-class penetration of the lower steel sheet. It's too easy to weld closed the hole you have made without properly penetrating the lower sheet. Consequently, what seems to be a good weld has no strength at all. Start with a good-sized hole in the top sheet, about $1/4$in (6mm) diameter. This is slightly bigger than most factory spot welds, but gives you a sporting chance. Prepare the lower sheet by linishing it with a paper disc on an angle grinder. Start the welding in the centre of each hole by melting the lower material and spiralling outwards to puddle the hole, including the periphery of the top material layer. Do lots of trials on scrap material to ensure you are putting the maximum amps into the welds and that penetration is right through to the lower material. You will see a molten 'bubble' or spot on the lower material if you have got it right. A circular discolouration is NOT sufficient. Your life may depend on having good welds so take a hammer to some of your test pieces and see if they really have 'stuck'. It depends on the application, but most plug welding is carried out with the 'spots' pitched about $3/4$in to 1in (20 to 25mm) apart. You can minimise distortion of plug welded materials by plugging only every 5th hole initially. Then go back and plug the 'middle' hole in each block of 5, again welding, in effect, every 5th hole. Now there will be a strong temptation to fill in all the remaining plug holes in one run, and in some circumstances this will be quite satisfactory (say, when there is a lipped flange within the joint). However, the safest approach is to go down the length of the seam repeatedly, again welding every 5th spot on each run. Finish with a paper linishing disc on an angle grinder.

'V'-notch welding - Not widely practised but does have advantages in certain circumstances. It can really only be used when two pieces of metal are to be joined at an angle of between 45 and 90 degrees. You can, of course, seam weld the join, but strength is added to the structure if you fold a lip of, say, 12mm to the edge of the joining piece, Your first inclination would probably be to seam weld or plug weld the panels together. However, you can snip a series of 'V'-shaped notches from the 12mm flange and then seam weld down the edge of each V. You will spread the stresses further by this method and put more weld length into the joint than via a straight seam weld run.

BASIC METAL FORMING AND ADJUSTMENT

Assuming you are planning to repair an existing rusted panel, the first step is to establish the area to replace. There is an understandable initial temptation to replace only the most severely rusted part of the panel to minimise the size of the replacement, but you must plan to completely remove all of the old rusted metal, whilst bearing in mind what repair panels you have available. You do not have to use a full repair panel, but it's absolutely pointless choosing a repair panel that leaves rusted material in the original panel. If the largest repair panel available is insufficient to allow you to remove all of the damaged area from the old panel, consider either a full replacement panel or whether you should make your own repair section. Earlier TR replacement panels are not a wonderful fit so, with the exception of TR6 panels, you're probably better off repairing the original panel if this is feasible. There's always the good old standby of secondhand replacement panels, and wings in particular, from an ex-Californian car. The trouble is, ex-Californian cars are getting harder and harder to find, and those panels that are available are less and less suitable. In the not-too-distant future, the superb hot climate body (and chassis) parts we have been used to in recent years may be exhausted. You may still be better off repairing the bottom 4 inches (100mm) of a disappointing ex-Californian panel than, say, 20 inches (500mm) on original panels. Either way, a repair is a repair, which brings me to conclude that a few words of basic advice on fitting, even making, a replacement panel, are possibly appropriate.

Basically, panels have either a single curvature or double curvature, and although it may look daunting, remember that steel is inexpensive, and if you have to make a replacement several times, so what? The first thing to do is make a couple of cardboard templates of the original panel profile. Most single curvature panels, like, say, a wing or a door, curve from top to bottom, and this is the section, plane or curvature your first template should record. The second template is, in effect, the shape of the panel as you view it from the side of the car. It's a good idea to mark the original panel with a couple of blobs of paint, nail varnish or typing correction fluid to record where your first or curvature template has been prepared, obviously ensuring that you don't subsequently cut away your template positioning points. Paper really is not suitable for making templates and I would suggest a roll of pattern maker's card. This is usually green, about 0.5mm thick and will have the rigidity you need.

Do not be tempted to sand or shotblast the old panel before the repair is complete. You will more than likely have insufficient metal left to act as a pattern of the area that needs replacing, and could even distort the area you plan to keep. We might give the edges a light blast later, but only after we have completed our repair and satisfactorily offered up the repaired panel to the car. Purely from a economic point of view, you don't want to be taking one panel at a time to the blaster for even a light edge-only treatment, so it's best to complete all the panel repairs and if there is any light surface (and it should only be light surface) corrosion, have the lot lightly, gently and ever-so-carefully blasted around the edges and zinc primed straight away (within the hour is best if possible). By this route, if a repaired panel does gather a little surface rust from fingerprints or atmospheric dampness, there's no real need to panic. That said, obviously, repaired panels are best kept as dry and as rust-free as possible. If you think it might be 12 months before your collection of repaired panels are ready, a light spray of oil, a wipe with an oily rag, a coat of lanolin or even a coat of zinc primer, is a good idea. The oil or lanolin can be largely removed with thinners

just before blasting, and the primer will last little more than a second under even the lightest blasting.

Returning to actually fitting a single curvature repair panel to the original, you'll appreciate that a pre-formed repaired panel does much of the hard work for you, but I hope that the following will be of help if you are forced by cost or availability into making a repair section yourself. Whatever you do, if using a pre-formed repaired panel remember to allow at least $1/2$in (13mm) overlap between the repair panel and original. The first step for your homemade repair panel is to cut a blank piece of steel sheet that is initially at least 1inch larger in each direction than you think you will need. Do not try and be too accurate at first. Mark out the edge you plan to marry to the original panel, remembering that you will need a shade over $1/2$in (13mm) of extra material above the join line for a joggled, overlapped, plug welded joint. Your next step is to form the basic single curvature. Slowly is the operative word here, but frequently checking progress with your curvature template, bend the blank panel over your knee or a (usually large diameter) tube until it conforms to the first template. If you attend college you should have access to a set of rollers, and these will do a wonderful job. If you make a mess of the bend, get a fresh piece of steel sheet and start again, but don't throw away your first effort, it could still be a very useful trial piece for subsequent steps.

Next turn your attention to the joint between the original panel and your repair panel; this is point of no return when you need to cut the original panel at your joint line, which should be absolutely straight.

We now have a choice about the order in which to complete the next two steps: joggle first or form the plug weld holes first. I will proceed on the basis of holes first and explain why a little later. Punch or drill a series of holes across the edge of the repair panel where it will overlap the original panel. These holes will eventually be used to plug weld the new repair panel (from the rear) to the original panel. The holes should be at $3/4$in to 1in (20–25mm) intervals and be about $1/4$in (6mm) in diameter. It is far better to have too large a plug weld hole than too small, so if you are not very experienced at plug welding, go to 7mm

diameter with your test pieces. You can even consider 8mm diameter holes if you not absolutely certain of getting a weld that fully penetrates the lower (original in this case) panel. The centre of each hole should be $1/4$in (say 7mm) in from the edge of the repair panel. Drilling is a perfectly good way of making these holes, but you must ensure that you support your new curved repair section with a piece of wood behind the drill line before you start drilling the holes. Nor must you distort the lip too much, so use a sharp drill.

There is, however, a better way to form these holes. A Sealey hand-held pneumatic punch does the job far quicker than drilling, and with no chance of distortion. It is my recommendation that you buy or hire one of these admirable tools. The Sealey also has the invaluable advantage of also enabling you to put the 1mm joggle along the overlapping edge of your repair panel (be it pre-punched or handmade). This is where the 'joggle first or hole first' question comes in. With the Sealey equipment you can put the holes in, then run along the overlapping edge and in $1/2$in (12mm) 'bits', with no more effort than a squeeze of the Sealey's trigger, can effect the joggle or step in the overlap joint. This is important as it will subsequently minimise the amount of filler needed to make the repair joint invisible. Sealey equipment is available in most Technical College vehicle repair workshops.

If you don't have access to a Sealey punch/joggler, you need to joggle the $1/2$in overlap joint on a folder. Even then it's not easy to achieve the joggle since it consists of two 90 degree bends virtually on top of each other. You can use a set of joggling rollers, or choose to ignore the joggle/overlap joint and go for a straightforward overlapped joint. In this case I would put the holes in after achieving the joggle/overlap.

So, we have a curved repair panel with the top $1/2$in joggled and holed to provide for an overlapped plug welded joint. Now we get to the point when some of the surplus metal needs to be trimmed off.

Your second template comes into its own for the first time. Lay it on your repair panel, lining up the top cut or joint line and (soft) pencil round the edge of the template. It's best not to use 'tin snips' or 'Gilbows' as both are hand-held trimmers that cut by a scissor-like action which will distort the metal somewhat. Use a powered nibbler to cut all but a $^1/_2$in (12mm) lip allowance down one side of your repair section. The basic thing you must remember before starting to form a lip on any curved, even slightly curved, panel is that it will try and straighten the panel curvature unless you take precautions. This paragraph is intended to help and we will cover initially an outside lip that is relatively unusual in external panels like wings, but could be required as part of an inner wing or bulkhead repair panel.

The outside lipped single curvature panels need the lip to be progressively stretched as the (90 degree) lip is turned out. As with all metal working, slow and progressive progress brings the best results. Tap the 1/2in lip over the end of a (flat) steel mandrel or steel dressing dolly. For slight single plane curves, the mandrel/dolly can be 1in (25mm) wide, but as panel curvature increases you will need to reduce the width of your mandrel and also the size of the 'bite' you take. Go right down the length of the panel lip and turn the lip out by 20/25 degrees. Check panel curvature with your first template and tap the outside edge of the lip (to stretch it) until the curvature again coincides with the curvature (first) template. Repeat this slow but sure approach, reaching the lip's 90 degree angle only after about 4 runs down the whole of the flange length. Never turn one end out completely and then tackle the other end.

There's a very useful shrinking and stretching tool that would be invaluable for the above and also in the following circumstances. Called a shrinker/stretcher, it costs about £200, but will enable you to fabricate repair panels for numerous situations. It can be bolted to your workbench or gripped in your vice and is available from Frost Auto Restorations.

Turning a $^1/_2$in flange inwards requires the same approach as described in the foregoing, except that you will have a surplus of material in the flange to cope with, so the last thing you want is to stretch the flange. The technique, in this case, is to deliberately wrinkle the inside lip as you turn it in. A pair of pliers and a sort of twisting

motion will create a series of ripples or puckers. Where the repair panel has only gentle radiuses you could shrink the lip by oxyacetylene heating it to red heat in the knowledge that it will shrink on cooling without further dressing.

As the severity of your main panel radius increases, so too will lip wrinkling. In fact, you may have to resort to snipping out a shallow V from the lip to compensate for a very tight main panel radius that can occur at the very bottom of, say, a wing. In these cases you will need to oxyacetylene weld the V back together and then plenish flat the resultant weld. Where lip wrinkling is considerable, but not so great that you have had to resort to V snipping, you will need the help of oxyacetylene to heat the lip to cherry-red. You then need to plenish the wrinkles, actually thickening the lip material in the process – so do not overdo the hammer/dolly plenishing or you will stretch the lip material!

If you seek reassurance, just take a look at any pressed repair panels you have to hand. You will note a crinkled lip at, say, the bottom of a wing pressing where the internally formed lip has 'bunched-up' the surplus material. That is how a pressed component handles the surplus material. However, when you are hand-forming a panel, the 'support' of a press die is not there to make the metal flow in the same way' so we have to adjust the compensation - and that is what edge wrinkling and occasional snipped cuts will do.

Two other areas will require you to cut into the lip; firstly at each corner of your panel and, secondly, at any 'swage' you need to introduce into a panel. A swage is basically a large joggle, which is mostly introduced horizontally into wing or door panels for aesthetic reasons, presenting you with something of a challenge, but swages (small swages, anyway) are not without advantages, too. Dealing with possible advantages first, when joining a single curvature panel down its flat plane or length, it's all too easy to generate an unintentional curve in what was the flat plane of the panel. This occurs due to heating and cooling when welding and can look like a gentle ripple or wave when viewed end-on (say, from the front edge of a door, looking backwards down its length). A swage increases the resistance of the door to ripple if your

repair section or panel is married to the original panel in close proximity to the swage. Indeed, if you look at some pre-made repair panels, they will often be pressed so as to come to a swage line in the original panel, and may have a lip pressed into the repair panel at that point. Many amateur body repairers do not appreciate that the lip on the repair panel is there to strengthen the repair panel, and, if left in place, will dramatically reduce rippling of the finished assembly. Sadly, these lips are often removed at home and their objective nullified.

Reverting back to the original swage line, any repair joint made immediately adjacent to a swage line is also less visible. So the area adjacent to a swage line is actually a good spot to consider for your cut line of a repair panel. Not that you should cut away large areas of good, un-corroded metal just to make your joint adjacent to a swage line some 10-15 inches (250/375mm) further up the panel!

There are bound to be occasions when it is necessary to make a repair panel incorporating a swage line, so we'd better spend a moment explaining how this can be done. Firstly, carefully measure the height and depth of the swage, and even cut a small cross-section template to allow you to check your efforts to replicate it. Secondly, form a swage in your blank panel before introducing the single curvature and, thirdly, you MUST snip the turn-in or turn-out panel lips at the top and bottom of the swage before you start turning the lip. Forming a swage is not difficult, but forming a specifically dimensioned swage will take a few attempts. Get it right on some off-cuts before you approach the repair panel blank.

At college you should have a folder available to make the job easier. At home, you'll need a little more ingenuity. To form the swage, first find a piece of bar or tube as long or a shade longer than the length of your swage. On a repair panel this may be too daunting, but if you were tackling a door, the bar would need to be at least the width of it. Not only must the length be adequate, but the diameter must also be correct – which is where that small section of original swage again comes into its own, for the tube you have in mind needs to nestle comfortably in the radius of the original swage. Now we are set to go, and start by clamping the flat repair panel blank onto the workbench under a stout piece of angle iron. A couple of large 'G' clamps will usually do the job. Now place the sectioned piece of correctly radiused bar or tube on top of the blank, and up against the clamped stop, and bend the blank up by the prescribed angle (rarely 90 degrees; often not even 45 degrees). When the front is correctly in place, unclamp the stop, turn the blank over, re-clamp it in the correct place and make the same degree of upward bend. Get your sample section and check right along the length of the repair panel that the swage is properly formed.

It will be obvious that the longer the swage the more difficult it is to get the full definition along the full length of both bends. You are unlikely to achieve the definition you need on anything but the shortest sections without dressing the central areas of each bend during each

bending operation. This is best achieved by a polished square section of steel, but a square section of brass or hardwood will also do a pretty good job. I rarely use anything but wood, but whatever your choice the idea is to place the length of steel, brass or wood against the panel material and strike it fairly hard with a club hammer to ensure that the definition of the radiused bar is translated into the blank. If you use a rough-faced piece of hard material such a steel, you will reproduce the imperfections in the face of your component blank. Not so important when you are bashing the unseen side of the repair panel, but not a good idea when it comes to dressing the outside of, say, a door panel.

Throughout all of the above I have glossed over the vital 'preparation' that is essential to good welding. You must clean each of the mating surfaces until they look like new. All old welds must

be ground off to allow panels to come together without gaps, and you must also remove all contaminates like paint, oil and grease. This preparation will take much longer than the actual welding, but is of the utmost importance.

Finally, remember that it is unwise to fully weld a series of panels until you are absolutely sure they not only correctly interface with each other, but that the fit of related panels and parts (such as boot/trunk lids, doors, bonnets, lights, etc.) are to your complete satisfaction. So, start by positioning each panel with self-tapping screws, pop-rivets and/or weld clamps. As your confidence grows, do some tack-welding of the whole assembly but continue to offer-up the mating panels and parts. Only when you are absolutely sure all is well should you start fully welding the assembly, removing the temporary fixings and filling the resultant holes right at the end of, say, that side of the car.

ALSO FROM VELOCE PUBLISHING:

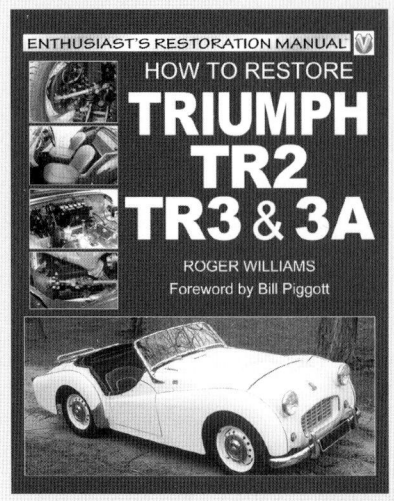
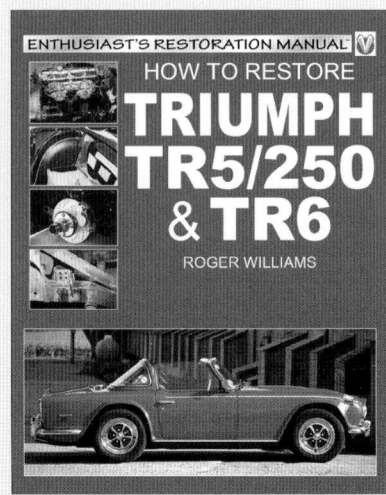

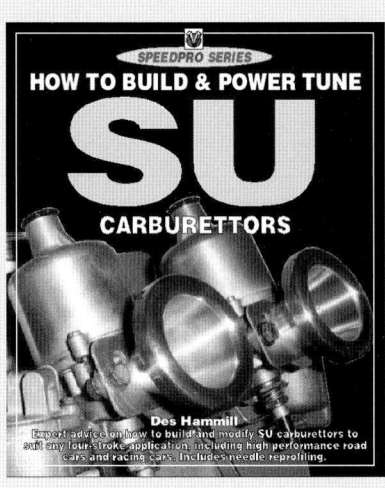

Index